Number Lesson #1 : Prime Factors

Class Ex. #1

a) 15   1, 3, 5, 15

b) 24   1, 2, 3, 4, 6, 8, 12, 24

Class Ex. #2

a) 1, 3   b) 1, 2, 5, 10   c) 1   d) 1, 7   e) 1, 2, 3, 6, 9, 18

two   four   one   two   six

Prime and Composite Numbers

Complete the list of the first ten prime numbers;

2, 3, 5, 7 , 11 , 13 , 17 , 19 , 23 , 29 , ...

2   Number Lesson #1: Prime Factors

Class Ex. #3

a) Composite   b) prime   c) composite   d) prime   e) prime

Class Ex. #4

a) State the factors of 12.
   1, 2, 3, 4, 6, 12

b) State the prime factors of 12.
   2, 3

c) Express 12 as a product of prime factors.
   $2 \times 2 \times 3$

Prime Factorization

division table

2	48
2	24
2	12
2	6
3	3
	1

tree diagram

$48 = 2 \times 2 \times 2 \times 2 \times 3$ or $2^4 \times 3$

Publisher: Absolute Value Publications

Authors: Alan Appleby, Greg Ranieri

Copyright © 2010.
All rights reserved.

Printed in Canada.

ISBN 978-0-9780872-6-5

For information contact:
Absolute Value Publications Inc.
P.O. Box 71096
8060 Silver Springs Blvd. N.W.
Calgary, Alberta
T3B 5K2

Eus: (403) 313-1442
Fax: (403) 313-2042

e-mail: workbooks@absolutevaluepublications.com
web site: www.absolutevaluepublications.com

10. a) 390

10, 39; 2, 5; 3, 13

$2 \times 3 \times 5 \times 13$

b) 546

2, 273; 3, 91; 7, 13

$2 \times 3 \times 7 \times 13$

c) 3 705

5, 741; 3, 247; 13, 19

$3 \times 5 \times 13 \times 19$

d) 6 762

6, 1127; 2, 3; 7, 161; 7, 23

$2 \times 3 \times 7 \times 7 \times 23$
or $2 \times 3 \times 7^2 \times 23$

11. a) 189

9, 21; 3, 3; 3, 7

$3 \times 3 \times 3 \times 7$
or $3^3 \times 7$

b) 685

5, 137

5×137

c) 4 235

5, 847; 7, 121; 11, 11

$5 \times 7 \times 11 \times 11$
or $5 \times 7 \times 11^2$

d) 7 980

10, 798; 2, 5; 2, 399; 3, 133; 7, 19

$2 \times 2 \times 3 \times 5 \times 7 \times 19$
or $2^2 \times 3 \times 5 \times 7 \times 19$

1925?
5, 385; 5, 77; 7, 11
$5 \times 7 \times 11^2$

2 592?
8, 324; 4, 2; 9, 36; 2, 2, 3, 3; 6, 6; 2, 3, 2, 3

12.
A. 5
B. 7
C. 11
D. (13)

13.
A. 4
B. 3
C. (2)
D. 1

2, 3 and 9 are factors
but only 2 and 3 are prime factors.

9 and 13 are not prime factors.

Class Ex. #5

```
2 | 2772
2 | 1386
3 |  693
3 |  231
7 |   77
11|   11
  |    1
```

$2 \times 2 \times 3 \times 3 \times 7 \times 11$
or $2^2 \times 3^2 \times 7 \times 11$

Class Ex. #6

33250
10, 3325; 5, 665; 5, 133; 7, 19; 2, 5

$2 \times 5 \times 5 \times 5 \times 7 \times 19$
or
$2 \times 5^3 \times 7 \times 19$

Assignment

1.a) 1, 3, 7, 21 **b)** 1, 2, 11, 22 **c)** 1, 5, 25 **d)** 1, 2, 3, 4, 6, 9, 12, 18, 36

2. a) 8 1, 2, 4, 8 four **b)** 11 1, 11 two **c)** 17 1, 17 two **d)** 33 1, 3, 11, 33 four **e)** 45 1, 3, 5, 9, 15, 45 six

3. a) 11, 17 **b)** 8, 33, 45

4.a) composite **b)** prime **c)** prime **d)** composite **e)** prime **f)** composite **g)** composite **h)** composite

5. 3 and 5, 11 and 13, 17 and 19, 29 and 31, 41 and 43, 59 and 61, 71 and 73.

6.a) 1, 2, 4, 5, 10, 20 **b)** 2, 5 **c)** $2 \times 2 \times 5$ **7. a)** 3, 5 **b)** 2, 3 **c)** 3, 5 **d)** 2, 3, 11

8. 0 is defined to have no factors and 1 has only one factor. Since a prime number has exactly two factors there cannot be any prime numbers which are factors of 0 or 1.

9. a)
```
2 | 140
2 |  70
5 |  35
7 |   7
  |   1
```
$2 \times 2 \times 5 \times 7$
or $2^2 \times 5 \times 7$

b)
```
2 | 330
3 | 165
5 |  55
11|  11
  |   1
```
$2 \times 3 \times 5 \times 11$

c)
```
3 | 1911
7 |  637
7 |   91
13|   13
  |    1
```
$3 \times 7 \times 7 \times 13$
or $3 \times 7^2 \times 13$

d)
```
5 | 1925
5 |  385
7 |   77
11|   11
  |    1
```
$5 \times 5 \times 7 \times 11$
or $5^2 \times 7 \times 11$

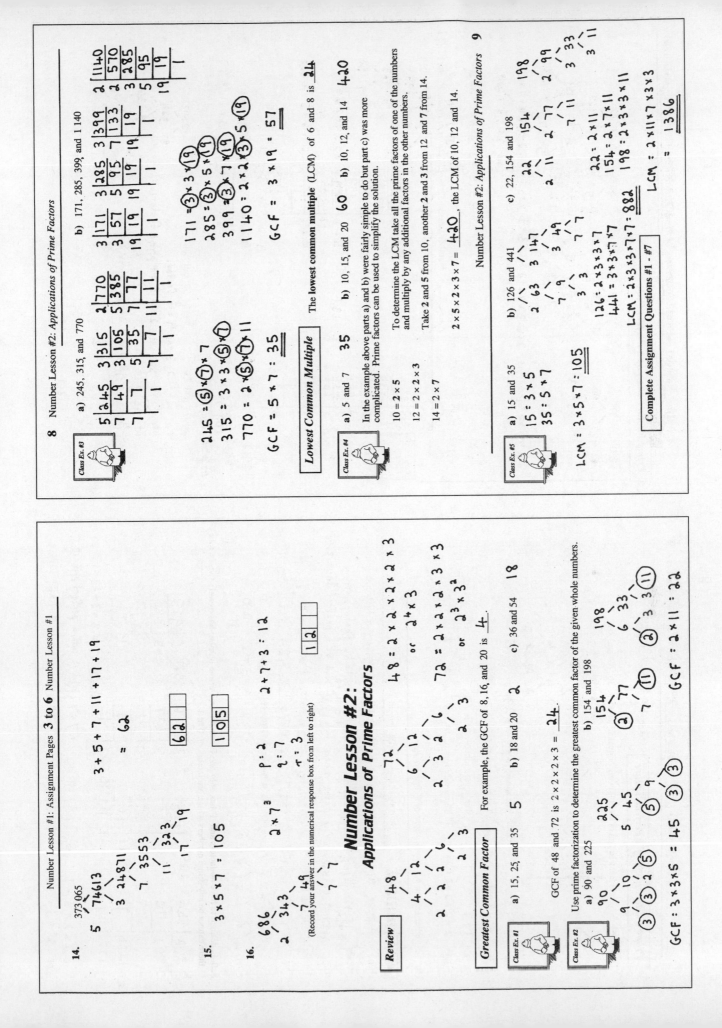

Number Lesson #1: Assignment Pages 3 to 6 Number Lesson #1

14. $3 + 5 + 7 + 11 + 17 + 19$
$= 62$

373 065
$5\overline{)74613}$ ...

15. $3 \times 5 \times 7 = 105$

16. 2×7^3

(Record your answer in the numerical response box from left to right)

Number Lesson #2:
Applications of Prime Factors

$48 = 2 \times 2 \times 2 \times 2 \times 3$ or $2^4 \times 3$

$72 = 2 \times 2 \times 2 \times 3 \times 3$ or $2^3 \times 3^2$

Review For example, the GCF of 8, 16, and 20 is 4.

Greatest Common Factor

Class Ex. #1 a) 15, 25, and 35   5   b) 18 and 20   2   c) 36 and 54   18

GCF of 48 and 72 is $2 \times 2 \times 2 \times 3 = 24$.

Use prime factorization to determine the greatest common factor of the given whole numbers.

Class Ex. #2 a) 90 and 225
GCF: $3 \times 3 \times 5 = 45$

b) 154 and 198
GCF: $2 \times 11 = 22$

---

8 Number Lesson #2: Applications of Prime Factors

Class Ex. #3 a) 245, 315, and 770   b) 171, 285, 399, and 1 140

$245 = 5 \times 7 \times 7$
$315 = 3 \times 3 \times 5 \times 7$
$770 = 2 \times 5 \times 7 \times 11$
GCF $= 5 \times 7 = 35$

$171 = 3 \times 3 \times 19$
$285 = 3 \times 5 \times 19$
$399 = 3 \times 7 \times 19$
$1140 = 2 \times 2 \times 3 \times 5 \times 19$
GCF $= 3 \times 19 = 57$

Lowest Common Multiple The lowest common multiple (LCM) of 6 and 8 is 24

Class Ex. #4 a) 5 and 7   35   b) 10, 15, and 20   60   b) 10, 12, and 14   420

In the example above parts a) and b) were fairly simple to do but part c) was more complicated. Prime factors can be used to simplify the solution.

$10 = 2 \times 5$
$12 = 2 \times 2 \times 3$
$14 = 2 \times 7$

To determine the LCM take all the prime factors of one of the numbers and multiply by any additional factors in the other numbers.

Take 2 and 5 from 10, another 2 and 3 from 12 and 7 from 14.

$2 \times 5 \times 2 \times 3 \times 7 = 420$, the LCM of 10, 12 and 14.

Number Lesson #2: Applications of Prime Factors 9

Class Ex. #5 a) 15 and 35   b) 126 and 441   c) 22, 154 and 198

a) 15 and 35
$15 = 3 \times 5$
$35 = 5 \times 7$
LCM $= 3 \times 5 \times 7 = 105$

b) 126 and 441
$126 = 2 \times 3 \times 3 \times 7$
$441 = 3 \times 3 \times 7 \times 7$
LCM $= 2 \times 3 \times 3 \times 7 \times 7 = 882$

c) 22, 154 and 198
$22 = 2 \times 11$
$154 = 2 \times 7 \times 11$
$198 = 2 \times 3 \times 3 \times 11$
LCM $= 2 \times 11 \times 7 \times 3 \times 3 = 1386$

Complete Assignment Questions #1 - #7

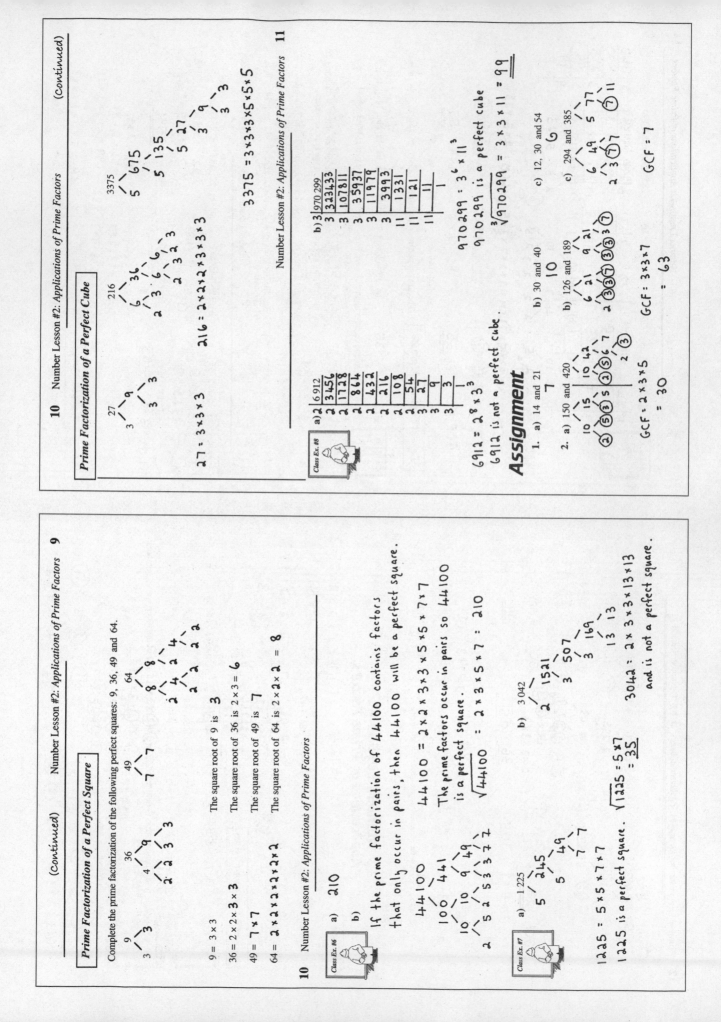

Prime Factorization of a Perfect Square

Complete the prime factorization of the following perfect squares: 9, 36, 49 and 64.

$9 = 3 \times 3$ The square root of 9 is **3**

$36 = 2 \times 2 \times 3 \times 3$ The square root of 36 is $2 \times 3 =$ **6**

$49 = 7 \times 7$ The square root of 49 is **7**

$64 = 2 \times 2 \times 2 \times 2 \times 2 \times 2$ The square root of 64 is $2 \times 2 \times 2 =$ **8**

Class Ex. #6

a) **210**

b) If the prime factorization of 44100 contains factors that only occur in pairs, then 44100 will be a perfect square.

$44100 = 2 \times 2 \times 3 \times 3 \times 5 \times 5 \times 7 \times 7$

The prime factors occur in pairs so 44100 is a perfect square.

$\sqrt{44100} = 2 \times 3 \times 5 \times 7 = 210$

Class Ex. #7

a) 1 225

$1225 = 5 \times 5 \times 7 \times 7$

1225 is a perfect square. $\sqrt{1225} = 5 \times 7 = \underline{35}$

b) 3 042

$3042 = 2 \times 3 \times 3 \times 13 \times 13$

and is not a perfect square.

Prime Factorization of a Perfect Cube

$27 = 3 \times 3 \times 3$

$216 = 2 \times 2 \times 2 \times 3 \times 3 \times 3$

$3375 = 3 \times 3 \times 3 \times 5 \times 5 \times 5$

Class Ex. #8

a)

2	6 912
2	3 456
2	1 728
2	864
2	432
2	216
2	108
2	54
3	27
3	9
3	3
	1

$6912 = 2^8 \times 3^3$

6912 is not a perfect cube.

b)

3	970 299
3	323 433
3	107 811
3	35 937
3	11 979
3	3 993
11	1 331
11	121
11	11
	1

$970299 = 3^6 \times 11^3$

970299 is a perfect cube.

$\sqrt[3]{970299} = 3 \times 3 \times 11 = \underline{\underline{99}}$

Assignment

1. a) 14 and 21   **7**
    b) 30 and 40   **10**
    c) 12, 30 and 54   **6**

2. a) 150 and 420
    GCF: $2 \times 3 \times 5$
    $= 30$

    b) 126 and 189
    GCF: $3 \times 3 \times 7$
    $= 63$

    c) 294 and 385
    GCF $= 7$

3.

a) 483 and 575

GCF = 23

b) 180 and 504

GCF = 2×2×3×3 = 36

c) 1 700 and 1 938

GCF = 2×17 = 34

d) 663 and 910

GCF = 13

e) 84 and 231

GCF = 3×7 = 21

f) 525 and 850

GCF = 5×5 = 25

4.

a) 66, 495, and 2 541

66 = 2×3×11
495 = 3×3×5×11
2541 = 3×7×11×11
GCF = 3×11 = 33

b) 128, 984, 1 496, and 3 080

128 = 2×2×2×2×2×2×2
984 = 2×2×2×3×41
1496 = 2×2×2×11×17
3080 = 2×2×2×5×7×11
GCF = 2×2×2 = 8

5.

a) 4 and 6   b) 3 and 9   c) 9 and 15   d) 40, 60, and 100

12   9   45   600

6.

a) 14 and 30

LCM = 2×7×3×5 = 210

b) 28 and 60

LCM = 2×2×7×3×5 = 420

c) 10 and 115

LCM = 2×5×23 = 230

d) 18 and 63

LCM = 2×3×3×7 = 126

e) 55 and 143

LCM = 5×11×13 = 715

f) 72 and 252

LCM = 2×2×2×3×3×7 = 504

g) 125 and 175

LCM = 5×5×5×7 = 875

h) 39 and 52

LCM = 3×13×2×2 = 156

i) 58 and 124

LCM = 2×29×2×31 = 3596

7.

a) 6, 10 and 42

$6 = 2 \times 3$
$10 = 2 \times 5$
$42 = 2 \times 3 \times 7$

LCM: $2 \times 3 \times 5 \times 7$
= **210**

b) 12, 30 and 105

$12 = 2 \times 2 \times 3$
$30 = 2 \times 3 \times 5$
$105 = 3 \times 5 \times 7$

LCM: $2 \times 2 \times 3 \times 5 \times 7$
= **420**

c) 3, 5, 7 and 13

LCM = $3 \times 5 \times 7 \times 13$
= **1365**

d) 3, 14, 70, and 150

$3 = 3$
$14 = 2 \times 7$
$70 = 2 \times 5 \times 7$
$150 = 2 \times 3 \times 5 \times 5$

LCM = $3 \times 2 \times 7 \times 5 \times 5$
= **1050**

8.

a) 216

$216 = 2 \times 2 \times 2 \times 3 \times 3 \times 3$

216 is not a perfect square.

b) 11025

$11025 = 3 \times 3 \times 5 \times 5 \times 7 \times 7$

11025 is a perfect square.

square root = $3 \times 5 \times 7$ = 105

c) 882

$882 = 2 \times 3 \times 3 \times 7 \times 7$

882 is not a perfect square.

d) 1225

$1225 = 5 \times 5 \times 7 \times 7$

1225 is a perfect square.

square root = 5×7 = 35

---

9. Consider the number 74 088.

a) Use a calculator to find the cube root of 74 088.   **42**

b) Explain how we can use the prime factorization of 74 088 to show that 74 088 is a perfect cube. Verify your calculator answer by this method.

If the prime factorization of 74088 has factors which each appear three times, then 74088 is a perfect cube.

$74088 = 2 \times 2 \times 2 \times 3 \times 3 \times 3 \times 7 \times 7 \times 7$

Cube root = $2 \times 3 \times 7$

= **42**

2	74088
2	37044
2	18522
3	9261
3	3087
3	1029
7	343
7	49
7	7
	1

10. In each case use prime factorization to determine whether the number is a perfect cube. Verify your answer by using a calculator to determine the cube root.

a)

2	216
2	108
2	54
3	27
3	9
3	3
	1

216 is a perfect cube

cube root = 2×3 = 6

b)

3	11025
3	3675
5	1225
5	245
7	49
7	7
	1

11025 is not a perfect cube

c)

3	27783
3	9261
3	3087
3	1029
7	343
7	49
7	7
	1

27783 is not a perfect cube

d)

3	421875
3	140625
5	46875
5	15625
5	3125
5	625
5	125
5	25
5	5
	1

421875 is a perfect cube

Cube root = $3 \times 5 \times 5$ = **75**

11. Explain how you could use prime factorization to determine if a particular whole number is both a perfect square and a perfect cube.

If the prime factorization of the number has factors which each appear six times, then the number will be both a perfect square and a perfect cube.

12. The greatest common factor of 399 and 462 is

A.   3
B.   7
C.   19
D.   21   (circled)

$399 = 3 \times 7 \times 19$
$462 = 2 \times 3 \times 7 \times 11$

GCF: 3×7
= 21

13.
A. x and y must be even numbers. ✓
B. The product xy must be divisible by 100. ✓
C. x and y are both divisible by 5. ✓
D. Neither x nor y can be a prime number.
Answer (E) if none of the statements is false.

$x = 10a$ $y = 10b$

$xy = 100ab$

14. The lowest common multiple of 35, 231, and 275 is _____
(Record your answer in the numerical response box from left to right)

```
35      231      275
5  7    3  7 11   5  5  11
```
$35 = 5 \times 7$
$231 = 3 \times 7 \times 11$
$275 = 5 \times 5 \times 11$
$LCM = 5 \times 7 \times 3 \times 11 \times 5 = 5775$

[5][7][7][5]

15. (Record your answer in the numerical response box from left to right)

Find the LCM of 8 and 18.
$8 = 2 \times 2 \times 2$ $18 = 2 \times 3 \times 3$
$LCM = 2 \times 2 \times 2 \times 3 \times 3 = 72$

Page 72 and every 72nd page thereafter.

$\dfrac{950}{72} = 13.1...$

[1][3]

Number Lesson #3:
Rational and Irrational Numbers

Review

a) The decimal representing $\dfrac{28}{11}$ has a (repeating non-repeating) pattern and (terminates does not terminate). 2.545454...

b) The decimal representing $\dfrac{28}{8}$ has a (repeating non-repeating) pattern and (terminates does not terminate). 3.5

c) The decimal representing $\sqrt{2}$ has a (repeating non-repeating) pattern and (terminates does not terminate). 1.4142135...

Class Ex. #1
a) $\dfrac{1}{8}$ non-repeating terminating
b) $\dfrac{2}{11}$ repeating non-terminating
c) $\dfrac{9}{7}$ repeating non-terminating
d) 0.94 repeating non-terminating
e) $\sqrt{8}$ non-repeating non-terminating
f) $\sqrt{0.16}$ non-repeating terminating

Class Ex. #2
a) 1.493 rational terminating $\dfrac{1493}{1000}$
b) $\sqrt{5}$ irrational non-repeating and non terminating
c) 2.347 347 347 347... rational repeating $\dfrac{2345}{999}$
d) $-\sqrt{81}$ -9 rational terminating
e) $\sqrt{4.41}$ $\dfrac{21}{10}$ rational terminating
f) $-8.1122111222111...$ irrational non-repeating and non-terminating

Class Ex. #3

```
<---|----|----|----|----|----|----|----|----|----|----|--->
    0    1    2    3    4    5    6    7    8    9    10
            e        b a              d   c
```

a) $\sqrt{14}$ 3.741...   3.741...
b) π 3.141...   3.141...
c) $\sqrt{80}$ 8.944...   8.944...
d) $2\sqrt{15}$ 7.745...   7.745...
e) $\sqrt{0.1}$ 0.316...   0.316...

Class Ex. #4
a) $0.\overline{36}$ = .36363636363636363   ▸Frac   4/11
= 0.363636...

a) $\dfrac{4}{11}$
b) 3.9̄5̄ $\dfrac{178}{45}$

Class Ex. #5
Step 5. $1000x = 2051.5\overline{1}$
$\dfrac{10x = 20.5\overline{1}}{}$
subtract $990x = 2031$
$x = \dfrac{2031}{990} = \dfrac{677}{330}$

a) $0.\overline{36}$ Let $x = 0.\overline{36}$
= 0.363636...
$100x = 36.3\overline{6}$
$x = 0.3\overline{6}$
subtract: $99x = 36$
$x = \dfrac{36}{99} = \dfrac{4}{11}$
$0.3\overline{6} = \dfrac{4}{11}$

b) $3.9\overline{5}$ Let $x = 3.9\overline{5}$
= 3.9555...
$100x = 395.\overline{5}$
$10x = 39.\overline{5}$
subtract: $90x = 356$
$x = \dfrac{356}{90} = \dfrac{178}{45}$
$3.9\overline{5} = \dfrac{178}{45}$

Assignment

1. a) non-repeating, non-terminating   b) repeating, non-terminating   c) repeating, non-terminating
   d) repeating, non-terminating   e) non-repeating, non-terminating   f) non-repeating, terminating
   g) non-repeating, terminating   h) non-repeating, non-terminating

2. a) true   b) false   c) false   d) true   e) false   f) true

3. a) rational since it is a terminating decimal   b) rational since it is a repeating decimal
   c) rational since it is a terminating decimal
   d) irrational since it is a non-repeating and non-terminating decimal

4. (number line showing $\sqrt{0.2}$, $\sqrt{\pi}$, $\sqrt{10}$, $\sqrt{60}$, $2\sqrt{30}$, $3\sqrt{20}$)
   0 1 2 3 4 5 6 7 8 9 10 11 12 13 14 15

21

5. a) rational, $\frac{4}{5}$ b) rational, $\frac{1}{3}$ c) rational, $\frac{2}{25}$ d) irrational   e) rational, $\frac{111}{200}$
   f) rational, $-\frac{5}{4}$ g) rational, $\frac{1366}{333}$ h) irrational   i) rational, $\frac{3}{4}$

6. a) $\frac{2}{3}$ b) $\frac{7}{33}$ c) $\frac{49}{45}$ d) $\frac{41}{333}$ e) $-\frac{16073}{4950}$

7. a) $0.\overline{2}$

Let $x = 0.\overline{2} = 0.2222...$
$10x = 2.\overline{2}$
$x = 0.\overline{2}$
Subtract $9x = 2$
$x = \frac{2}{9}$
$0.\overline{2} = \frac{2}{9}$

b) $0.\overline{61}$

Let $x = 0.\overline{61} = 0.6161...$
$100x = 61.\overline{61}$
$x = 0.\overline{61}$
subt. $99x = 61$
$x = \frac{61}{99}$
$0.\overline{61} = \frac{61}{99}$

c) $0.9\overline{8}$

Let $x = 0.9\overline{8} = 0.9888...$
$100x = 98.\overline{8}$
$10x = 9.\overline{8}$
subt. $90x = 89$
$x = \frac{89}{90}$
$0.9\overline{8} = \frac{89}{90}$

8. a) $2.00\overline{5}$

Let $x = 2.00\overline{5}$
$= 2.005050505...$
$1000x = 2005.0\overline{5}$
$10x = 20.0\overline{5}$
subt. $990x = 1985$
$x = \frac{1985}{990} = \frac{397}{198}$
$2.00\overline{5} = \frac{397}{198}$

b) $-1.\overline{234}$

Let $x = -1.\overline{234}$
$= -1.234234...$
$1000x = -1234.\overline{234}$
$x = -1.\overline{234}$
subt. $999x = -1233$
$x = \frac{-1233}{999} = \frac{-137}{111}$
$-1.\overline{234} = \frac{-137}{111}$

c) $4.4\overline{73}$

Let $x = 4.4\overline{73}$
$= 4.47333...$
$1000x = 4473.\overline{3}$
$100x = 447.\overline{3}$
subt. $900x = 4026$
$x = \frac{4026}{900} = \frac{671}{150}$
$4.4\overline{73} = \frac{671}{150}$

---

9. $\frac{4}{9}$ is (C.) non-terminating and repeating
   $0.4444....$

10. A. $\sqrt{169}$ (B.) $\sqrt{0.025}$ C. $\frac{5}{6}$ D. 3.14
        13               $0.1581...$

11. (D.) 10

12. $\frac{236}{495}$ $a = 236$
    $b = 495$ $b - a = 495 - 236$
    $= 259$ [259]

Number Lesson #4:
Number Systems

The Real Number System

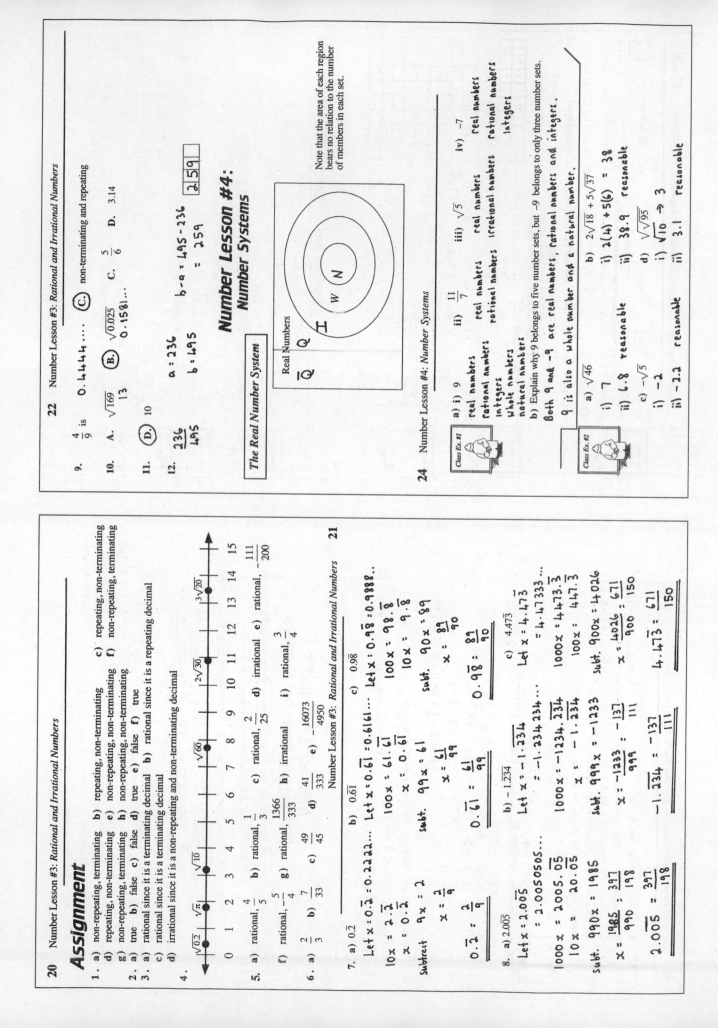

Note that the area of each region bears no relation to the number of members in each set.

---

24 Number Lesson #4: Number Systems

Class Ex. #1

a) i) 9   ii) $\frac{11}{7}$ iii) $\sqrt{5}$ iv) -7

i) real numbers, rational numbers, integers, whole numbers, natural numbers
ii) real numbers, rational numbers
iii) real numbers, irrational numbers
iv) real numbers, rational numbers, integers

b) Explain why 9 belongs to five number sets, but -9 belongs to only three number sets.
Both 9 and -9 are real numbers, rational numbers and integers.
9 is also a whole number and a natural number.

Class Ex. #2

a) $\sqrt{46}$
i) 7
ii) 6.8   reasonable

b) $2\sqrt{18} + 5\sqrt{37}$
i) $2(4) + 5(6) = 38$
ii) 38.9   reasonable

c) $-\sqrt{5}$
i) -2
ii) -2.2 reasonable

d) $\sqrt{95}$
i) $\sqrt{10} \to 3$
ii) 3.1   reasonable

Assignment

1.

	N	W	I	Q	$\overline{Q}$	$\Re$
$\frac{1}{8}$				✓		✓
123.983				✓		✓
−2			✓	✓		✓
7.5̄3̄4̄				✓		✓
9.5				✓		✓
$\sqrt{75}$					✓	✓
−3.159₁₁₃				✓		✓
−π					✓	✓
$-\sqrt{49}$			✓	✓		✓
0.000005				✓		✓
2.232425...					✓	✓
$\sqrt[3]{0.016}$					✓	✓

2. a) real numbers, rational numbers, integers
b) real numbers, rational numbers, integers, whole numbers, natural numbers
c) real numbers, rational numbers
d) real numbers, rational numbers
e) real numbers, rational numbers, integers, whole numbers
f) real numbers, irrational numbers
g) real numbers, irrational numbers
h) real numbers, irrational numbers

3. −7 is a real number, rational number and integer whereas $-\frac{7}{2}$ is a real number and a rational number but not an integer.

4.

5. a) −3   **b)** $\frac{4}{5}$ **c)** $\sqrt{3}$ **d)** 0

6. a) sometimes   **b)** sometimes   **c)** always
d) always   **e)** never   **f)** never

7. a) true   **b)** true   **c)** true
e) true   **f)** false   **g)** false

8. a) true   **b)** true

9. a) $\sqrt{8} + \sqrt{17}$ is approximately $3 + 4 = 7$
   $\sqrt{8} \to 3$
   $\sqrt{17} \to 4$ so $\sqrt{25} = 5$ $\sqrt{8} + \sqrt{17} \neq \sqrt{25}$

   b) $\sqrt{2} + \sqrt{3} + \sqrt{4}$ is approximately $1 + 2 + 2 = 5$
   $\sqrt{2} \to 1$
   $\sqrt{3} \to 2$ so $\sqrt{2} + \sqrt{3} + \sqrt{4} \neq \sqrt{9}$
   $\sqrt{4} = 2$ $\sqrt{9} = 3$

10. a) false   **b)** false   **c)** true   **d)** true

Class Ex. #3

a) $\sqrt{6\,210}$ **b)** $\sqrt{82\,147.3}$ **c)** $\sqrt{0.002\,43}$ **d)** $\sqrt{0.024\,3}$

$\sqrt{62\,10}$ $\sqrt{8\,21\,47.3}$ $\sqrt{0.00\,24\,3}$ $\sqrt{0.02\,43}$
$= 80$ $= 300$ $= 0.05$ $= 0.1$

a) $\sqrt[3]{11}$ **b)** $\sqrt[3]{120}$
i) 2   i) 5
ii) 2.2 reasonable   ii) 4.9 reasonable

c) $4\sqrt{70} - 4\sqrt[3]{70}$
i) $4(8) - 4(4) = 16$
ii) 17.0 reasonable

26 Number Lesson #4: *Number Systems*

Extension - Absolute Value

Class Ex. #5

a) $|-7| + |7|$ **b)** $|1 - 5|$ **c)** $-|-\sqrt{81}|$
$7 + 7$ $|-4|$ $-|-9|$
$= 14$ $= 4$ $= -9$

Class Ex. #6

In each case state the absolute value inequality represented by the graph.

a)
$|a| \leq 3$

b)
$|a| > 4$

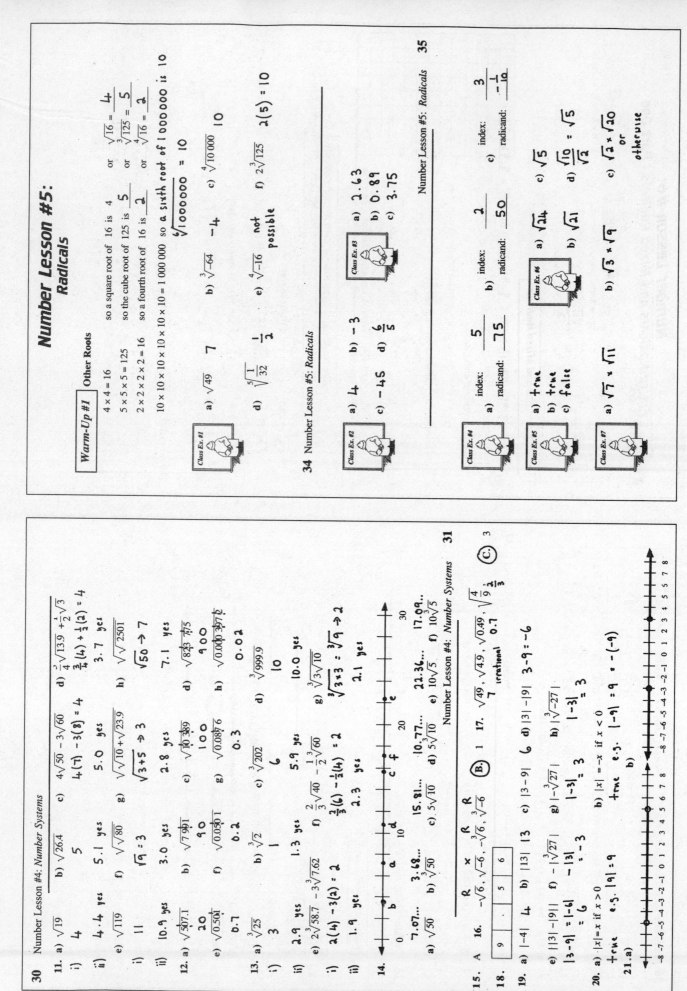

Number Lesson #5: Radicals

Number Lesson #5:
Radicals

Warm-Up #1 Other Roots

$4 \times 4 = 16$ so a square root of 16 is 4 or $\sqrt{16} = 4$

$5 \times 5 \times 5 = 125$ so the cube root of 125 is 5 or $\sqrt[3]{125} = 5$

$2 \times 2 \times 2 \times 2 = 16$ so a fourth root of 16 is 2 or $\sqrt[4]{16} = 2$

$10 \times 10 \times 10 \times 10 \times 10 = 1\,000\,000$ so a sixth root of 1 000 000 is 10

$\sqrt[6]{1000000} = 10$

Class Ex. #1

a) $\sqrt{49}$ 7

b) $\sqrt[3]{-64}$ -4

c) $\sqrt[4]{10\,000}$ 10

d) $\sqrt[5]{\dfrac{1}{32}}$ $-\dfrac{1}{2}$

e) $\sqrt[4]{-16}$ not possible

f) $2\sqrt[3]{125}$ $2(5) = 10$

34 Number Lesson #5: Radicals

Class Ex. #2

a) 4   b) -3

c) -45 d) $\dfrac{6}{5}$

Class Ex. #3

a) 2.63

b) 0.89

c) 3.75

35 Number Lesson #5: Radicals

Class Ex. #4

a) index: 5 radicand: 75

b) index: 2 radicand: 50

c) index: 3 radicand: $-\dfrac{1}{10}$

Class Ex. #5

a) true

b) true

c) false

Class Ex. #6

a) $\sqrt{24}$

b) $\sqrt{21}$

c) $\sqrt{5}$

d) $\dfrac{\sqrt{10}}{\sqrt{2}} = \sqrt{5}$

Class Ex. #7

a) $\sqrt{7} \times \sqrt{11}$

b) $\sqrt{3} \times \sqrt{9}$

c) $\sqrt{2} \times \sqrt{20}$ or otherwise

---

30 Number Lesson #4: Number Systems

11. a) $\sqrt{19}$ i) 4   ii) 4.4 yes

b) $\sqrt{26.4}$ 5   5.1 yes

c) $4\sqrt{50} - 3\sqrt{60}$ $4(7) - 3(8) = 4$ 5.0 yes

d) $\dfrac{3}{4}\sqrt{13.9} + \dfrac{1}{2}\sqrt{3}$ $\dfrac{3}{4}(4) + \dfrac{1}{2}(2) = 4$ 3.7 yes

e) $\sqrt{119}$ 11 $\sqrt{9} = 3$

f) $\sqrt{80}$ $\sqrt{10 + \sqrt{23.9}}$ $\sqrt{3 + 5} \to 3$

g) $\sqrt{10 + \sqrt{23.9}}$

h) $\sqrt{\sqrt{2501}}$ $\sqrt{50} \to 7$

i) 10.9 yes   3.0 yes   2.8 yes   7.1 yes

12. a) $\sqrt{507.1}$ 20

b) $\sqrt{79.91}$ 90

c) $\sqrt{10.389}$ 100

d) $\sqrt{823.75}$ 900

e) $\sqrt{0.501}$ 0.7

f) $\sqrt{0.0501}$ 0.2

g) $\sqrt{0.0876}$ 0.3

h) $\sqrt{0.000397.2}$ 0.02

i) 2.9 yes   1.3 yes   5.9 yes   10.0 yes

13. a) $\sqrt[3]{25}$ 3

b) $\sqrt[3]{2}$ 1

c) $\sqrt[3]{202}$ 6

d) $\sqrt[3]{999.9}$ 10

e) $2\sqrt[3]{58.7} - 3\sqrt[3]{7.62}$ $2(4) - 3(2) = 2$

f) $\dfrac{2}{3}\sqrt[3]{40} - \dfrac{1}{2}\sqrt[3]{60}$ $\dfrac{2}{3}(6) - \dfrac{1}{2}(4) = 2$

g) $\sqrt[3]{3\sqrt{10}}$

i) 1.9 yes   2.3 yes $\sqrt[3]{3 \times 3} = \sqrt[3]{9} \to 2$

ii)   2.1 yes

14.

$\begin{array}{l} 0 \quad b \quad a \quad d \quad c \quad f \quad e \\ 0 \quad\quad 10 \quad\quad 20 \quad\quad 30 \end{array}$

7.07...   3.68...   15.81...   10.77...   21.36...   17.09...

a) $\sqrt{50}$ b) $\sqrt[3]{50}$ c) $5\sqrt{10}$ d) $5\sqrt[3]{10}$ e) $10\sqrt{5}$ f) $10\sqrt[3]{5}$

31 Number Lesson #4: Number Systems

15. A

16.

R	x	R	R
$-\sqrt{6}$	$\sqrt{-6}$	$-\sqrt{6}$	$\sqrt[3]{-6}$
9	.	5	6

17. $\sqrt{49}, \sqrt{4.9}, \sqrt{0.49}, \sqrt{\dfrac{4}{9}}, \sqrt{\dfrac{2}{3}}$ C. 3

$\quad$ 7   irrational   0.7

18. 1

19. a) $|-4|$ 4

b) $|13|$ 13

c) $|3 - 9|$ 6

d) $|3| - |9|$ $3 - 9 = -6$

e) $||3| - |9||$ $|3 - 9| = |-6|$ $= 6$

f) $-|\sqrt[3]{27}|$ $-|3| = -3$

g) $|\sqrt[3]{-27}|$ $|-3| = 3$

h) $|\sqrt[3]{-27}|$ $|-3| = 3$

20. a) $|x| = x$ if $x > 0$ true

b) $|x| = -x$ if $x < 0$ true

e. 5. $|9| = 9$

e. 3. $|-9| = 9$ $= -(-9)$

21. a)

$\begin{array}{c} -8\,-7\,-6\,-5\,-4\,-3\,-2\,-1\,0\,1\,2\,3\,4\,5\,6\,7\,8 \end{array}$

b)

$\begin{array}{c} -8\,-7\,-6\,-5\,-4\,-3\,-2\,-1\,0\,1\,2\,3\,4\,5\,5\,7\,8 \end{array}$

Class Ex. #1

a) $\sqrt{24} = \sqrt{4 \times 6} = \sqrt{4} \times \sqrt{6}$
$= 2\sqrt{6}$

b) $\sqrt{18} = \sqrt{9 \times 2} = \sqrt{9} \times \sqrt{2} = 3\sqrt{2}$

c) $\sqrt{\dfrac{11}{4}} = \dfrac{\sqrt{11}}{\sqrt{4}} = \dfrac{\sqrt{11}}{2}$

Entire Radicals and Mixed Radicals

i) $\sqrt{80} = 8.94427$ ii) $2\sqrt{20} = 8.94427$ iii) $4\sqrt{5} = 8.94427$

What do you notice about the answers?   __Same__

Complete the following to explain why the three radicals are equivalent.

$\sqrt{80} = \sqrt{4 \times 20} = \sqrt{4} \times \sqrt{20} = 2\sqrt{20}$

$\sqrt{80} = \sqrt{16 \times 5} = \sqrt{16} \times \sqrt{5} = 4\sqrt{5}$

40   Number Lesson #6: *Entire Radicals and Mixed Radicals- Part One*

Converting Entire Radicals *(with an index of 2)* to Mixed Radicals

Complete the following to convert $\sqrt{108}$ to a mixed radical.

Entire Radical $\Rightarrow$ Mixed Radical

$\sqrt{108} = \sqrt{36 \times 3}$
$= \sqrt{36} \times \sqrt{3}$
$= 6 \times \sqrt{3}$
$\sqrt{108} = 6\sqrt{3}$

Class Ex. #2

a) $\sqrt{50}$
$= \sqrt{25 \times 2}$
$= \sqrt{25} \times \sqrt{2}$
$= 5\sqrt{2}$

b) $\sqrt{45}$
$= \sqrt{9 \times 5}$
$= \sqrt{9} \times \sqrt{5}$
$= 3\sqrt{5}$

c) $\sqrt{320}$
$= \sqrt{64 \times 5}$
$= \sqrt{64} \times \sqrt{5}$
$= 8\sqrt{5}$

---

1. a) 9   b) 3   c) 15   d) 10   e) $\dfrac{4}{5}$ f) $\dfrac{1}{2}$ g) 1   h) −1   i) not possible
   j) −1   k) −35   l) not possible   m) 36   n) 1   o) 1   p) $-\dfrac{2}{3}$

2. a) true   b) false   c) true
3. a) 8   b) −3   c) −7   d) −9   e) −9   f) −2   g) 2   h) not possible   i) 1
4. a) 3.16   b) 1.52   c) 3.01   5. a) −1.9   b) −18.0   c) −2.2

Number Lesson #5: *Radicals*   **37**

6. a) index 3, radicand 42   b) index 4, radicand 36   c) index 2, radicand 17

7. The index 4 refers to the number of times the value of the $\sqrt[4]{36}$ must be multiplied by itself to give a product of 36.

8. a) true   b) false   c) true   d) false   e) false   f) true   g) true   h) false
9. a) $\sqrt{35}$ b) $\sqrt{28}$ c) $\sqrt{24}$ d) $\sqrt{66}$ e) $\sqrt{2}$ f) $\sqrt{5}$ g) $\sqrt{30}$ h) $\sqrt{3}$
10. a) $\sqrt{5}\sqrt{7}$ b) $\sqrt{3}\sqrt{11}$ c) $\sqrt{5}\sqrt{13}$ d) $\sqrt{7}\sqrt{7}$

11. Consider the following statements.

   I.   The cube roots of −27 are ±3.   F
   II. The fourth roots of 81 are ±3.   T
   III. $\sqrt[3]{1000} = \sqrt[3]{-1000}$ T
        $-10 \ne -10$
        -10
   IV. $-\sqrt[4]{16} = \sqrt[4]{-16}$ F
        -2 not possible

   Which of the statements above are true?

   (A) II and III only

11. A   12. D   13. | 0 | . | 9 | 5 |

Class Ex. #3

a) $2\sqrt{192}$

b) $\frac{3}{4}\sqrt{160}$

$= 2(\sqrt{64}\cdot\sqrt{3})$

$= \frac{3}{4}(\sqrt{16}\cdot\sqrt{10})$

$= 2(8\sqrt{3})$

$= \frac{3}{4}(4\sqrt{10})$

$= 16\sqrt{3}$

$= 3\sqrt{10}$

c) $\sqrt{\frac{7}{9}}$

$= \frac{\sqrt{7}}{\sqrt{9}}$

$= \frac{\sqrt{7}}{3}$ or $\frac{1}{3}\sqrt{7}$

Converting Mixed Radicals (with an index of 2) to Entire Radicals

Complete the following to convert $3\sqrt{14}$ to an entire radical.

$$\text{Mixed Radical} \Rightarrow \begin{array}{c}\text{Entire Radical}\\ 3\sqrt{14} = \sqrt{9}\times\sqrt{14}\end{array}$$

$$= \sqrt{9\times 14}$$

$$3\sqrt{14} = \sqrt{126}$$

Class Ex. #4

a) $2\sqrt{5}$

$= \sqrt{4}\cdot\sqrt{5}$

$= \sqrt{4\times 5}$

$= \sqrt{20}$

b) $4\sqrt{7}$

$= \sqrt{16}\cdot\sqrt{7}$

$= \sqrt{16\times 7}$

$= \sqrt{112}$

c) $10\sqrt{6}$

$= \sqrt{100}\cdot\sqrt{6}$

$= \sqrt{100\times 6}$

$= \sqrt{600}$

Class Ex. #5

a) $\frac{3}{2}\sqrt{8}$

$= \sqrt{\frac{9}{4}}\cdot\sqrt{8}$

$= \sqrt{\frac{9}{4}\times 8}$

$= \sqrt{18}$

b) $0.4\sqrt{50}$

$= \sqrt{0.16}\cdot\sqrt{50}$

$= \sqrt{0.16\times 50}$

$= \sqrt{8}$

c) $-5\sqrt{7}$

$= -\sqrt{25}\cdot\sqrt{7}$

$= -\sqrt{25\times 7}$

$= -\sqrt{175}$

Class Ex. #6

i) $3\sqrt{5}$

$= \sqrt{9}\cdot\sqrt{5}$

$= \sqrt{45}$

ii) $5\sqrt{3}$

$= \sqrt{25}\cdot\sqrt{3}$

$= \sqrt{75}$

iii) $\sqrt{15}$

iv) $2\sqrt{8}$

$= \sqrt{4}\cdot\sqrt{8}$

$= \sqrt{32}$

v) $8\sqrt{2}$

$= \sqrt{64}\cdot\sqrt{2}$

$= \sqrt{128}$

order is $8\sqrt{2}, 5\sqrt{3}, 3\sqrt{5}, 2\sqrt{8}, \sqrt{15}$

Class Ex. #7

In $\triangle ADC$

$AD^2 = 12^2 - 8^2$

$AD^2 = 80$

$AD = \sqrt{80}$

In $\triangle ABD$

$AB^2 = 6^2 + (\sqrt{80})^2$

$AB^2 = 36 + 80 = 116$

$AB = \sqrt{116} = \sqrt{4}\cdot\sqrt{29}$

a) $AB = 2\sqrt{29}$ b) $AB = 10.77$ (nearest hundredth)

(triangle with A, B, C, D; sides 12, 6, D, 8)

Assignment

1. a) entire   b) mixed   c) entire   d) mixed

2. a) $\sqrt{8}$ b) $\sqrt{20}$ c) $\sqrt{75}$ d) $\sqrt{98}$

a) $= \sqrt{4}\cdot\sqrt{2}$ b) $= \sqrt{4}\cdot\sqrt{5}$ c) $= \sqrt{25}\cdot\sqrt{3}$ d) $= \sqrt{49}\cdot\sqrt{2}$

$= 2\sqrt{2}$ $= 2\sqrt{5}$ $= 5\sqrt{3}$ $= 7\sqrt{2}$

e) $3\sqrt{32}$ f) $-5\sqrt{45}$ g) $2\sqrt{54}$ h) $-4\sqrt{48}$

$= 3(\sqrt{16}\cdot\sqrt{2})$ $= -5(\sqrt{9}\cdot\sqrt{5})$ $= 2(\sqrt{9}\cdot\sqrt{6})$ $= -4(\sqrt{16}\cdot\sqrt{3})$

$= 3(4\sqrt{2})$ $= -5(3\sqrt{5})$ $= 2(3\sqrt{6})$ $= -4(4\sqrt{3})$

$= 12\sqrt{2}$ $= -15\sqrt{5}$ $= 6\sqrt{6}$ $= -16\sqrt{3}$

3. a) $= \sqrt{16}\cdot\sqrt{6}$ b) $\sqrt{121}\cdot\sqrt{2}$ c) $-\frac{2}{3}(\sqrt{36}\cdot\sqrt{5})$ d) $\frac{1}{8}(\sqrt{64}\cdot\sqrt{5})$

$= 4\sqrt{6}$ $= 11\sqrt{2}$ $= -\frac{2}{3}(6\sqrt{5})$ $= \frac{1}{8}(8\sqrt{5})$

$= -4\sqrt{5}$ $= \sqrt{5}$

e) $\sqrt{49}\cdot\sqrt{5}$ f) $4\sqrt{169}\cdot\sqrt{2}$ g) $\sqrt{625}\cdot\sqrt{2}$ h) not possible

$= 7\sqrt{5}$ $= 4(13\sqrt{2})$ $= 25\sqrt{2}$ 66 does not have a factor which is a perfect square.

$= 52\sqrt{2}$

i) $= -\frac{5}{6}(\sqrt{16}\cdot\sqrt{19})$ j) $\sqrt{196}\cdot\sqrt{5}$ k) $4\cdot\sqrt{16}\cdot\sqrt{11}$ l) $-3(\sqrt{144}\cdot\sqrt{2})$

$= -\frac{5}{6}(4\sqrt{19})$ $= 14\sqrt{5}$ $= 4(4\sqrt{11})$ $= -3(12\sqrt{2})$

$= -\frac{10}{3}\sqrt{19}$ $= 16\sqrt{11}$ $= -36\sqrt{2}$

m) $2(\sqrt{9}\cdot\sqrt{4})$ n) $\sqrt{4}\cdot\sqrt{91}$ o) $= \frac{2}{5}(\sqrt{225}\cdot\sqrt{2})$ p) not possible

$= 2(3\sqrt{4})$ $= 2\sqrt{91}$ $= \frac{2}{5}(15\sqrt{2})$ 341 does not have a factor which is a perfect square

$= 6\sqrt{4}$ $= 6\sqrt{2}$

4. a) $= \frac{\sqrt{2}}{\sqrt{9}}$ b) $= \frac{\sqrt{5}}{\sqrt{4}}$ c) $\frac{\sqrt{18}}{\sqrt{25}} = \frac{\sqrt{9}\cdot\sqrt{2}}{5}$ d) $= 7\sqrt{\frac{20}{49}}$

$= \frac{\sqrt{2}}{3}$ or $\frac{1}{3}\sqrt{2}$ $= \frac{\sqrt{5}}{2}$ or $\frac{1}{2}\sqrt{5}$ $= \frac{3\sqrt{2}}{5}$ or $\frac{3}{5}\sqrt{2}$ $= 7\left(\frac{\sqrt{20}}{\sqrt{49}}\right) = 7\left(\frac{\sqrt{4}\cdot\sqrt{5}}{7}\right) = 7\left(\frac{2\sqrt{5}}{7}\right)$

$= 2\sqrt{5}$

5. Convert the following to entire radical form.

a) $2\sqrt{6}$
= $\sqrt{4}\sqrt{6}$
= $\sqrt{24}$

b) $3\sqrt{7}$
= $\sqrt{9}\sqrt{7}$
= $\sqrt{63}$

c) $5\sqrt{15}$
= $\sqrt{25}\sqrt{15}$
= $\sqrt{375}$

d) $12\sqrt{2}$
= $\sqrt{144}\sqrt{2}$
= $\sqrt{288}$

e) $3\sqrt{25}$
= $\sqrt{9}\sqrt{25}$
= $\sqrt{225}$

f) $-8\sqrt{3}$
= $-\sqrt{64}\sqrt{3}$
= $-\sqrt{192}$

g) $9\sqrt{10}$
= $\sqrt{81}\sqrt{10}$
= $\sqrt{810}$

h) $-4\sqrt{5}$
= $-\sqrt{16}\sqrt{5}$
= $-\sqrt{80}$

6. Convert the following to entire radical form.

a) $\frac{1}{3}\sqrt{27}$
= $\sqrt{\frac{1}{9}}\sqrt{27}$
= $\sqrt{3}$

b) 15
= $\sqrt{225}$

c) $\frac{3}{2}\sqrt{8}$
= $\sqrt{\frac{9}{4}}\sqrt{8}$
= $\sqrt{18}$

d) $3^2\sqrt{21}$
= $9\sqrt{21}$
= $\sqrt{81}\sqrt{21}$
= $\sqrt{1701}$

Do not use a calculator to answer question #7 or #8.

7. Given that $\sqrt{6}$ is approximately equal to 2.45, and $\sqrt{60}$ is approximately equal to 7.75, then find the approximate value of

a) $\sqrt{600}$
= $\sqrt{100}\sqrt{6}$
= $10\sqrt{6}$
= 24.5

b) $\sqrt{6000}$
= $\sqrt{100}\sqrt{60}$
= $10\sqrt{60}$
= 77.5

c) $\sqrt{600000}$
= $\sqrt{10000}\sqrt{60}$
= $100\sqrt{60}$
= 775

d) $\sqrt{0.06}$
= $\frac{\sqrt{6}}{\sqrt{100}}$
= $\frac{\sqrt{6}}{10}$
= 0.245

e) $\sqrt{0.6}$
= $\frac{\sqrt{60}}{\sqrt{100}}$
= $\frac{\sqrt{60}}{10}$
= 0.775

f) $\sqrt{24}$
= $\sqrt{4}\sqrt{6}$
= $2\sqrt{6}$
= 2(2.45)
= 4.9

g) $\sqrt{540}$
= $\sqrt{9}\sqrt{60}$
= $3\sqrt{60}$
= 3(7.75)
= 23.25

h) $\sqrt{\frac{6}{25}}$
= $\frac{\sqrt{6}}{\sqrt{25}}$
= $\frac{\sqrt{6}}{5}$
= $\frac{2.45}{5}$
= 0.49

8. Arrange the following radicals in order from greatest to least.

$3\sqrt{7}, \ 5\sqrt{3}, \ \sqrt{60}, \ 2\sqrt{11}, \ \frac{1}{2}\sqrt{200}$

$3\sqrt{7} = \sqrt{9}\sqrt{7} = \sqrt{63}$
$5\sqrt{3} = \sqrt{25}\sqrt{3} = \sqrt{75}$
$\sqrt{60}$
$2\sqrt{11} = \sqrt{4}\sqrt{11} = \sqrt{44}$
$\frac{1}{2}\sqrt{200} = \sqrt{\frac{1}{4}}\sqrt{200} = \sqrt{50}$

order $\sqrt{75}, \sqrt{63}, \sqrt{60}, \sqrt{50}, \sqrt{44}$

order is $5\sqrt{3}, \ 3\sqrt{7}, \ \sqrt{60}, \ \frac{1}{2}\sqrt{200}, \ 2\sqrt{11}$

9. a)

Louis	Asia
$(PQ)^2 = (QR)^2 + (PR)^2$	$(PQ)^2 = (QR)^2 + (PR)^2$
$= 5.83^2 + 6.16^2$	$= (\sqrt{34})^2 + (\sqrt{38})^2$
$= 71.9345$	$= 34 + 38 = 72$
$PQ = \sqrt{71.9345}$	$PQ = \sqrt{72}$
$= 8.48$	$= 8.49$

b) Asia's answer is more precise because she uses exact values rather than rounded values in her calculations.

10. c) $\sqrt{72} = \sqrt{36}\sqrt{2} = 6\sqrt{2}$

i) $\sqrt{336}$ cm

$XY^2 = 19^2 - 5^2 = 336$
$XY = \sqrt{336}$
$= \sqrt{16}\sqrt{21}$
$= 4\sqrt{21}$
$= 18.3303...$

ii) $4\sqrt{21}$ cm

iii) 18.33 cm

11. a) $x^2 = 4^2 + 8^2 = 80$
$x = \sqrt{80}$
$= \sqrt{16}\sqrt{5}$
$x = 4\sqrt{5}$

b) $x^2 = 5^2 + 6^2 = 61$
$x = \sqrt{61}$

c) $a^2 = 6^2 - 4^2 = 20$
$a = \sqrt{20}$

$x^2 = 8^2 - (\sqrt{20})^2$
$x^2 = 64 - 20 = 44$
$x = \sqrt{44}$
$= \sqrt{4}\sqrt{11}$
$x = 2\sqrt{11}$

12. $KL^2 = JL^2 - JK^2$
$= (\sqrt{24})^2 - (\sqrt{6})^2$
$= 24 - 6 = 18$
$KL = \sqrt{18} = \sqrt{9}\sqrt{2}$
$= 3\sqrt{2}$

(B.) $3\sqrt{2}$

13. A. $12\sqrt{2} = \sqrt{144}\sqrt{2} = \sqrt{288}$
B. $\sqrt{288}$
C. $6\sqrt{8} = \sqrt{36}\sqrt{8} = \sqrt{288}$
(D.) $4\sqrt{72} = \sqrt{16}\sqrt{72} = \sqrt{1152}$

14. $h = 698.2 \div 1.8 = 700$ m

$d = \sqrt{13h} = \sqrt{13(700)} = \sqrt{13}\sqrt{700} = \sqrt{13}\sqrt{7}\sqrt{100}$

$= \sqrt{91}\sqrt{100} = 10\sqrt{91}$

$a = 10$
$b = 91$
$a + b = 101$

1	0	1

15. $s = \dfrac{14 + 15 + 25}{2} = 27$

$A = \sqrt{27(27-14)(27-15)(27-25)} = \sqrt{8424}$

$= \sqrt{324}\sqrt{26} = 18\sqrt{26}$

$P = 18$

1	8

---

16. The smaller square has side length 8 cm. The side length of the larger square can be written in simplest form as $p\sqrt{q}$, where $p, q \in N$. The value of pq is _____

(Record your answer in the numerical response box from left to right)

1	6

$x^2 + x^2 = 8^2$
$2x^2 = 64$
$x^2 = 32$

$x = \sqrt{32} = \sqrt{16}\sqrt{2}$
$= 4\sqrt{2}$

side length of larger square
$= 2x = 2(4\sqrt{2}) = 8\sqrt{2}$

$P = 8$
$q = 2$
$pq = 16$

Number Lesson #7:
Entire Radicals and Mixed Radicals - Part Two

Converting Entire Radicals (with an index of 3 or greater) to Mixed Radicals

Complete the following to convert $\sqrt[3]{54}$ to a mixed radical.

$$\text{Entire Radical} \Rightarrow \text{Mixed Radical}$$

$$\sqrt[3]{54} = \sqrt[3]{27 \times 2}$$
$$= \sqrt[3]{27} \times \sqrt[3]{2}$$
$$= 3 \times \sqrt[3]{2}$$
$$\sqrt[3]{54} = 3\sqrt[3]{2}$$

Class Ex. #1 Convert the following radicals to mixed radicals in simplest form.

a) $\sqrt[3]{6000}$
$= \sqrt[3]{1000 \times 6}$
$= \sqrt[3]{1000} \times \sqrt[3]{6}$
$= 10\sqrt[3]{6}$

b) $\sqrt[5]{320}$
$= \sqrt[5]{32 \times 10}$
$= \sqrt[5]{32} \times \sqrt[5]{10}$
$= 2\sqrt[5]{10}$

c) $\sqrt[3]{-16}$
$= \sqrt[3]{-8 \times 2}$
$= \sqrt[3]{-8} \times \sqrt[3]{2}$
$= -2\sqrt[3]{2}$

Converting Mixed Radicals (with an index of 3 or greater) to Entire Radicals

Complete the following to convert $\frac{1}{2}\sqrt[3]{80}$ to an entire radical.

$$\text{Mixed Radical} \Rightarrow \text{Entire Radical}$$

$$\frac{1}{2}\sqrt[3]{80} = \sqrt[3]{\tfrac{1}{8}} \times \sqrt[3]{80}$$
$$= \sqrt[3]{\tfrac{1}{8} \times 80}$$
$$\frac{1}{2}\sqrt[3]{80} = \sqrt[3]{10}$$

Class Ex. #2

a) $2\sqrt[4]{3}$
$= \sqrt[4]{16}\sqrt[4]{3}$
$= \sqrt[4]{48}$

b) $-4\sqrt[3]{7}$
$= -\sqrt[3]{64}\sqrt[3]{7}$
$= -\sqrt[3]{448}$
or $\sqrt[3]{-448}$

c) $\dfrac{2}{5}\sqrt[3]{100}$
$= \sqrt[3]{\dfrac{8}{125}}\sqrt[3]{100}$
$= \sqrt[3]{\dfrac{32}{5}}$

d) $-3\sqrt[4]{2}$
$= -\sqrt[4]{81}\sqrt[4]{2}$
$= -\sqrt[4]{162}$

Extension: Radicals involving Variables

Since $x^3 \times x^3 = x^6$ then $\sqrt{x^6} = \underline{x^3}$. Also, since $x^5 \times x^5 \times x^5 = x^{15}$ then $\sqrt[3]{x^{15}} = \underline{x^5}$.

So $\sqrt{x^4} = \underline{x^2}$. $\sqrt[5]{y^{10}} = \underline{y^2}$. $\sqrt{a^8 b^6} = \underline{a^4 b^3}$. $\sqrt[3]{x^{24}} = \underline{x^8}$. $\sqrt[3]{y^6} = \underline{y^2}$.

Complete the following to convert $\sqrt{x^5}$ to a mixed radical.

Entire Radical $\Rightarrow$ Mixed Radical

$\sqrt{x^5} = \sqrt{x^4 \times x}$
$\qquad = \sqrt{x^4} \times \sqrt{x}$
$\qquad = x^2 \times \sqrt{x}$

$\sqrt{x^5} = x^2\sqrt{x}$

Class Ex. #3

a) $\sqrt{a^7}$
$= \sqrt{a^6}\sqrt{a}$
$= a^3\sqrt{a}$

b) $\sqrt{t^9}$
$= \sqrt{t^8}\sqrt{t}$
$= t^4\sqrt{t}$

c) $\sqrt[3]{x^5}$
$= \sqrt[3]{x^3}\sqrt[3]{x^2}$
$= x\sqrt[3]{x^2}$

d) $\sqrt[3]{x^7}$
$= \sqrt[3]{x^6}\sqrt[3]{x}$
$= x^2\sqrt[3]{x}$

Class Ex. #4

a) $\sqrt{x^6 y^5}$
$= \sqrt{x^6 y^4}\sqrt{y}$
$= x^3 y^2\sqrt{y}$

b) $\sqrt{18x^3}$
$= \sqrt{9x^2}\sqrt{2x}$
$= 3x\sqrt{2x}$

c) $\sqrt{32y^7 z^8}$
$= \sqrt{16y^6 z^8}\sqrt{2y}$
$= 4y^3 z^4\sqrt{2y}$

d) $\sqrt[3]{40x^4 y^9}$
$= \sqrt[3]{8x^3 y^9}\sqrt[3]{5x}$
$= 2xy^3\sqrt[3]{5x}$

Class Ex. #5

a) $2\sqrt{x^3}$
$= \sqrt{4}\sqrt{x^3}$
$= \sqrt{4x^3}$

b) $a^2\sqrt{a}$
$= \sqrt{a^4}\sqrt{a}$
$= \sqrt{a^5}$

c) $x^5\sqrt{xy}$
$= \sqrt{x^{10}}\sqrt{xy}$
$= \sqrt{x^{11}y}$

d) $3xy^3\sqrt[3]{2z^4}$
$= \sqrt[3]{27x^3y^9}\sqrt[3]{2z^4}$
$= \sqrt[3]{54x^3y^9z^4}$

Assignment

1.

a) $\sqrt[3]{48}$
$= \sqrt[3]{8}\sqrt[3]{6}$
$= 2\sqrt[3]{6}$

b) $\sqrt[3]{128}$
$= \sqrt[3]{64}\sqrt[3]{2}$
$= 4\sqrt[3]{2}$

c) $\sqrt[3]{2000}$
$= \sqrt[3]{1000}\sqrt[3]{2}$
$= 10\sqrt[3]{2}$

d) $5\sqrt[3]{-81}$
$= 5\left(\sqrt[3]{-27}\sqrt[3]{3}\right)$
$= 5\left(-3\sqrt[3]{3}\right)$
$= -15\sqrt[3]{3}$

e) $\dfrac{5}{6}\sqrt[3]{108}$
$= \dfrac{5}{6}\left(\sqrt[3]{27}\sqrt[3]{4}\right)$
$= \dfrac{5}{6}\left(3\sqrt[3]{4}\right)$
$= \dfrac{5}{2}\sqrt[3]{4}$

f) $5\sqrt[4]{162}$
$= 5\left(\sqrt[4]{81}\sqrt[4]{2}\right)$
$= 5\left(3\sqrt[4]{2}\right)$
$= 15\sqrt[4]{2}$

g) $\sqrt[5]{-192}$
$= \sqrt[5]{-32}\sqrt[5]{6}$
$= -2\sqrt[5]{6}$

h) $-2\sqrt[3]{625}$
$= -2\left(\sqrt[3]{125}\sqrt[3]{5}\right)$
$= -2\left(5\sqrt[3]{5}\right)$
$= -10\sqrt[3]{5}$

2.

a) $2\sqrt[4]{2}$
$= \sqrt[4]{16}\sqrt[4]{2}$
$= \sqrt[4]{32}$

b) $3\sqrt[3]{4}$
$= \sqrt[3]{27}\sqrt[3]{4}$
$= \sqrt[3]{108}$

c) $-3\sqrt[4]{3}$
$= -\sqrt[4]{81}\sqrt[4]{3}$
$= -\sqrt[4]{243}$

d) $-10\sqrt[3]{5}$
$= -\sqrt[3]{1000}\sqrt[3]{5}$ or $\sqrt[3]{-1000}\sqrt[3]{5}$
$= -\sqrt[3]{5000}$ or $\sqrt[3]{-5000}$

e) $2\sqrt[5]{6}$
$= \sqrt[5]{32}\sqrt[5]{6}$
$= \sqrt[5]{192}$

f) $\dfrac{1}{2}\sqrt[3]{16}$
$= \sqrt[3]{\dfrac{1}{8}}\sqrt[3]{16}$
$= \sqrt[3]{2}$

g) $\dfrac{3}{10}\sqrt[4]{100\,000}$
$= \sqrt[4]{\dfrac{81}{10000}}\sqrt[4]{100\,000}$
$= \sqrt[4]{810}$

h) $-5\sqrt[3]{9}$
$= -\sqrt[3]{125}\sqrt[3]{9}$ or $\sqrt[3]{-125}\sqrt[3]{9}$
$= -\sqrt[3]{1125}$ or $\sqrt[3]{-1125}$

3. Arrange the following radicals in order from least to greatest.

$7\sqrt[6]{1}, \ -3\sqrt[3]{-27}, \ \frac{5}{2}\sqrt[4]{16}, \ 3\sqrt[3]{\sqrt{64}}$ order is $\frac{5}{2}\sqrt[4]{16}, \ 3\sqrt[3]{\sqrt{64}}, \ 7\sqrt[6]{1}, \ -3\sqrt[3]{-27}$

$= 7(1) \quad = -3(-3) \quad = \frac{5}{2}(2) \quad = 3\sqrt[3]{4}$

$= 7 \qquad = 9 \qquad = 5 \qquad = 3(2) = 6$

4. Consider the following radicals $2\sqrt{11}, \ 3\sqrt[3]{3}, \ 4\sqrt{2}, \ 2\sqrt[3]{6}$.

a) **Explain** how to arrange the radicals in order from least to greatest without using a calculator.

Convert the mixed radicals to entire form and compare the radicals.

b) Arrange the radicals in order from least to greatest.

$\sqrt[3]{8}\sqrt[3]{11} \qquad \sqrt[3]{27}\sqrt[3]{3} \qquad \sqrt[4]{64}\sqrt{2} \qquad \sqrt[3]{8}\sqrt[3]{6}$

order is

$= \sqrt[3]{88} \quad = \sqrt[3]{81} \quad = \sqrt{128} \quad = \sqrt[3]{48}$ $\qquad 2\sqrt[3]{6}, \ 3\sqrt[3]{3}, \ 2\sqrt[3]{11}, \ 4\sqrt{2}$

5. $\sqrt[3]{240}$ is equivalent to

A. $2\sqrt[3]{40}$ B. $4\sqrt[3]{15}$ $\qquad \sqrt[3]{8}\sqrt[3]{30}$

C. $2\sqrt[3]{30}$ D. $8\sqrt[3]{30}$ $\qquad = 2\sqrt[3]{30}$

(C is circled)

6. Consider the following two statements:

Statement 1: $-3\sqrt[4]{8} = 3\sqrt[4]{-8}$. Statement 2: $-2\sqrt[3]{7} = 2\sqrt[3]{-7}$

$= -5.0...$ not possible $\qquad = -3.8...$

Which of the following is correct? $\qquad -3.8... = -3.8...$

A. Both statements are true.

B. Both statements are false.

C. Statement 1 is true, and statement 2 is false.

D. Statement 1 is false, and statement 2 is true.

(D is circled)

7. The mixed radical $\frac{1}{12}\sqrt[3]{128}$ can be converted to a mixed radical in simplest form $a\sqrt[3]{b}$.

The value of $a + b$, to the nearest tenth, is _____.

(Record your answer in the numerical response box from left to right)

$\frac{1}{12}\left(\sqrt[3]{64}\sqrt[3]{2}\right) = \frac{1}{12}\left(4\sqrt[3]{2}\right) = \frac{1}{3}\sqrt[3]{2}$

$a = \frac{1}{3} \qquad a+b = \frac{1}{3}+2 = \frac{7}{3} = 2.33...$

$b = 2$

2	.	3

Extension Assignment

8. Express as an entire radical.

a) $6\sqrt{y}$

$= \sqrt{36}\sqrt{y}$

$= \sqrt{36y}$

b) $8\sqrt{c^2}$

$= \sqrt{64}\sqrt{c^2}$

$= \sqrt{64c^2}$

c) $10\sqrt{2yz^3}$

$= \sqrt{100}\sqrt{2yz^3}$

$= \sqrt{200yz^3}$

d) $-3\sqrt[3]{x^2}$

$= -\sqrt[3]{27}\sqrt[3]{x^2}$

$= -\sqrt[3]{27x^2}$ or $\sqrt[3]{-27x^2}$

e) $c\sqrt{c}$

$= \sqrt{c^2}\sqrt{c}$

$= \sqrt{c^3}$

f) $x^2\sqrt{3y^3}$

$= \sqrt{x^4}\sqrt{3y^3}$

$= \sqrt{3x^4y^3}$

g) $11c^2\sqrt{c^2d}$

$= \sqrt{121c^4}\sqrt{c^2d}$

$= \sqrt{121c^6d}$

h) $5a^3b\sqrt{3a^2b}$

$= \sqrt{25a^6b^2}\sqrt{3a^2b}$

$= \sqrt{75a^8b^3}$

i) $4\sqrt{3}\,a^2b$

$= \sqrt{16}\sqrt{3}\sqrt{a^4b^2}$

$= \sqrt{48a^4b^2}$

j) $2p^2q\sqrt[3]{5pq^2}$

$= \sqrt[3]{8p^6q^3}\sqrt[3]{5pq^2}$

$= \sqrt[3]{40p^7q^5}$

k) $7p^8q^9\sqrt{p^2r}$

$= \sqrt{49p^{16}q^{18}}\sqrt{p^2r}$

$= \sqrt{49p^{18}q^{18}r}$

l) $2xy^3\sqrt[4]{9x}$

$= \sqrt[4]{16x^4y^{12}}\sqrt[4]{9x}$

$= \sqrt[4]{144x^5y^{12}}$

9. Express each as a mixed radical in simplest form.

a) $\sqrt{a^5}$

$= \sqrt{a^4}\sqrt{a}$

$= a^2\sqrt{a}$

b) $\sqrt{t^3}$

$= \sqrt{t^2}\sqrt{t}$

$= t\sqrt{t}$

c) $\sqrt[3]{x^4}$

$= \sqrt[3]{x^3}\sqrt[3]{x}$

$= x\sqrt[3]{x}$

d) $\sqrt[3]{x^{11}}$

$= \sqrt[3]{x^9}\sqrt[3]{x^2}$

$= x^3\sqrt[3]{x^2}$

e) $\sqrt[3]{b^8}$

$= \sqrt[3]{b^6}\sqrt[3]{b^2}$

$= b^2\sqrt[3]{b^2}$

f) $\sqrt[4]{x^6}$

$= \sqrt[4]{x^4}\sqrt[4]{x^2}$

$= x\sqrt[4]{x^2}$

10. Express each as a mixed radical in simplest form.

a) $\sqrt{8y^2}$

$= \sqrt{4y^2}\sqrt{2}$

$= 2y\sqrt{2}$

b) $\sqrt{16p^3}$

$= \sqrt{16p^2}\sqrt{p}$

$= 4p\sqrt{p}$

c) $\sqrt{75y^3z^4}$

$= \sqrt{25y^2z^4}\sqrt{3y}$

$= 5yz^2\sqrt{3y}$

d) $\sqrt{300a^9w^7}$

$= \sqrt{100a^8w^6}\sqrt{3aw}$

$= 10a^4w^3\sqrt{3aw}$

e) $5\sqrt{28c^4d^3}$

$= 5\left(\sqrt{4c^4d^2}\sqrt{7d}\right)$

$= 5\left(2c^2d\sqrt{7d}\right)$

$= 10c^2d\sqrt{7d}$

f) $-6\sqrt{29a^4b^8}$

$= -6\left(\sqrt{a^4b^8}\sqrt{29}\right)$

$= -6\left(a^2b^4\sqrt{29}\right)$

$= -6a^2b^4\sqrt{29}$

Numerical Response 2.

$$6699$$
$$3\sqrt{2233} \quad 8265 \quad GCF: 3 \times 29 = 87$$
$$11\sqrt{203} \quad 5\sqrt{1653} \quad 551$$
$$7\sqrt{(29)} \quad 3\sqrt{(29)} \quad 19\sqrt{(29)} \quad 105$$
$$14 \quad 2\sqrt{7} \quad 5\sqrt{21}$$
$$3\sqrt{7}$$

$$\boxed{8\,7}$$

4. A. P is a multiple of 7. ✓
   B. Q is a multiple of 21. ✓
   C. P could be less than 200. ✗
   D. Q could be greater than 2 000.
   $LCM : 2 \times 7 \times 3 \times 5 = 210$
   210 is a factor of both P and Q

5. min. $x = 2 \times 3 \times 2 \times 2 \times 3 = 2^4 \times 3^2$
   d
   $2 \quad 3$
   d
   $3 \quad 3$
   $= 216$ **C.** 6

$$\boxed{2\,1\,6}$$

Numerical Response 3. min. $x = 2 \times 3 \times 2 \times 2 \times 3 \times 3 = 2^3 \times 3^3$
$= 216$

6. **D.** non-terminating and non-repeating

7. I $1.010010010001…$ ✗
   II $\sqrt[3]{\dfrac{8}{27}} = \dfrac{2}{3}$ ✓
   III ✓
   IV $\sqrt{0.04} = \dfrac{1}{5}$ $=0.2 = \dfrac{1}{5}$ ✓
   $\sqrt{0.29}$ $\dfrac{29}{99}$ ✓
   B. II, III and IV only.

8. $\dfrac{17}{11}$ $c = 17$ **A.** 17

9.
P   Q   R   S
0 1 2 3 4 5 6 7 8 9 10

$\sqrt{M}$ is approx. 6 $\sqrt{M} + \sqrt{N}$ is approx. $6 + 2 = 8$
$\sqrt{N}$ is approx. 2   R   **C.** R

10. **A.** $\sqrt{19}$ 11. **A.** 4 and 4 000

Numerical Response 4. $\sqrt[3]{343}\,\sqrt[3]{6} = \sqrt[3]{2058}$

$$\boxed{2\,0\,5\,8}$$

---

54   Number Lesson #7: Entire Radicals and Mixed Radicals– Part Two

10. (continued)
g) $7p^3q^2\sqrt{27p^5q^6}$
$= 7_p^3q^2(\sqrt{9p^4q^6}\sqrt{3p})$
$= 7p^3q^2(3p^2q^3\sqrt{3p})$
$= 21p^5q^5\sqrt{3p}$

h) $\dfrac{2}{3}c\sqrt{81c^3d^{12}}$
$= \dfrac{2}{3}c(\sqrt{81c^2d^{12}}\sqrt{c})$
$= \dfrac{2}{3}c(9cd^6\sqrt{c})$
$= 6c^2d^6\sqrt{c}$

i) $11x^7y^{15}\sqrt{242x^9y^{10}}$
$= 11x^7y^{15}(\sqrt{121x^8y^{10}}\sqrt{2x})$
$= 11x^7y^{15}(11x^4y^5\sqrt{2x})$
$= 121x^{11}y^{20}\sqrt{2x}$

j) $\sqrt[3]{2000x^7}$
$= \sqrt[3]{1000x^6}\sqrt[3]{2x}$
$= 10x^2\sqrt[3]{2x}$

k) $4\sqrt[3]{250b^{13}}$
$= 4(\sqrt[3]{125b^{12}}\sqrt[3]{2b})$
$= 4(5b^4\sqrt[3]{2b})$
$= 20b^4\sqrt[3]{2b}$

l) $\sqrt[4]{32x^9}$
$= \sqrt[4]{16x^8}\sqrt[4]{2x}$
$= 2x^2\sqrt[4]{2x}$

11. $\sqrt{3x}\sqrt{2x}$ is equivalent to
A. $\sqrt{6x}$ B. $\sqrt{36x^2}$ C. $6\sqrt{x}$ **D.** $x\sqrt{6}$
$\sqrt{6x^2} = \sqrt{x^2}\sqrt{6} = x\sqrt{6}$

Number Lesson #8:
Practice Test

Numerical Response 1.
1. 14014?
$7\sqrt{2002}$
$11\sqrt{182}$
$13\sqrt{14}$
$2\sqrt{7}$

2. 3234?
$7\sqrt{462}$
$11\sqrt{42}$
$2\sqrt{21}$
$3\sqrt{7}$
21 is not prime
7 and 11 are prime factors
D. 17   **B.** 2

3. $160797 = 3 \times 7 \times 13 \times 19 \times 31$
$3\sqrt{53599}$
$7\sqrt{7657}$
$13\sqrt{589}$
$19\sqrt{31}$

Sum of prime factors
$= 3 + 7 + 13 + 19 + 31$
$= 73$

$$\boxed{7\,3}$$

3. 33
$3\sqrt{11}$
110
$2\sqrt{55}$
5

$LCM = 3 \times 11 \times 2 \times 5$
$= 2 \times 3 \times 5 \times 11$
$a \; b \; c \; d$
$33 : 3 \times 11$
$110 : 2 \times 5 \times 11$ $c = 5$ **B.** 5

Written Response - 5 marks

1.
- A student selects a card. The number on the card is 7. Explain why this card is valued at 18 points.

  7 is a natural number, a whole number, an integer, and a rational number.

  Points = 4 + 5 + 6 + 3 = 18

- A second student selects a card which has the number -5 on it. How many points are awarded for this card?

  -5 is an integer and a rational number.

  Points = 6 + 3 = 9

- In the game each student is dealt three cards and the student with the most points wins. Which of the following three students wins the game?

  Student A with the following cards $\frac{3}{4}$, $\sqrt{15}$ and 0.   3+10+14 = 27

  Student B with the following cards -3, $\sqrt{\frac{4}{9}}$ and π.   9 + 3 + 10 = 22

  Student C with the following cards $-\sqrt{36}$, $\sqrt{-36}$ and 36.   9+1+18 = 28 C wins

Number :	$\frac{3}{4}$	$\sqrt{15}$	0	-3	$\sqrt{\frac{4}{9}}$	π	$-\sqrt{36}$	$\sqrt{-36}$	36
Sets :	Q	$\bar{Q}$	W,I,Q	I,Q	6+3 =9 Q	$\bar{Q}$	I,Q	non-real	N,W,I,Q
Points :	3	10	5+6+3 =14	6+3 =9	3	10	6+3 =9	1	4+5+6+3 =18

---

12. **Statement 1** : $35 = 7\sqrt{5}$ ✗ $35 \neq 7 \times 5$

    Statement 2 : $\sqrt{28} = 2\sqrt{7}$ ✓ $\sqrt{28} = \sqrt{4}\sqrt{7} = 2\sqrt{7}$

    Statement 3 : $4\sqrt{3} = 48$ ✗ $4\sqrt{3} = \sqrt{16}\sqrt{3} = \sqrt{48}$

    B. 2 only

13. Student I $405\sqrt{10}$: $\sqrt{164025}\sqrt{10} = \sqrt{1640250}$

    Student II $15\sqrt{18}$: $\sqrt{225}\sqrt{18} = \sqrt{4050}$

    Student III $45\sqrt{2}$ = $\sqrt{2025}\sqrt{2} = \sqrt{4050}$

    B. only Students II and III

14. $A = \pi r^2 = 120\pi$

    $r^2 = 120$

    $r = \sqrt{120} = \sqrt{4}\sqrt{30} = 2\sqrt{30}$

    C. $2\sqrt{30}$

Numerical Response 5. $x^3 = 720$

    $x = \sqrt[3]{720} = \sqrt[3]{8}\sqrt[3]{90} = 2\sqrt[3]{90}$

    $a = 2$
    $b = 90$
    $a+b = 92$

9	2

15. Consider the following three equations.

    $4\sqrt[3]{3} = \sqrt[3]{x}$ $5\sqrt{x} = y\sqrt{3}$ $16\sqrt{y} = z\sqrt{10}$

    Which of the statements below is correct?

    A. $x<y<z$ B. $z<x<y$ C. $y<z<x$ **D.** $z<y<x$

    $\sqrt[3]{x} = 4\sqrt[3]{3} = \sqrt[3]{64}\sqrt[3]{3} = \sqrt[3]{192}$

    $x = 192$

    $y\sqrt{3} = 5\sqrt{192}$

    $y = \dfrac{5\sqrt{192}}{\sqrt{3}} = 5\sqrt{64}$
    $= 5(8) = 40$

    $z\sqrt{10} = 16\sqrt{40}$

    $z = \dfrac{16\sqrt{40}}{\sqrt{10}}$
    $= 16\sqrt{4} = 16(2) = 32$

    $x = 192$
    $y = 40$
    $z = 32$

    $z < y < x$

Exponents Lesson #1: Powers with Whole Number Exponents

Class Ex. #1

a) 4^5 　　　 b) $(-3)^6$ 　　　 c) x^y

base : 　　4　　　 　-3　　　 　x

exponent : 　5　　　 　6　　　 　y

62　Exponents Lesson #1: *Powers with Whole Number Exponents*

State the coefficient in each of the following.

Class Ex. #2

a) $8x^2$ 　　8 　　　 b) $-3z^9$ 　　-3 　　　 c) $\dfrac{a^8}{7}$ 　　$\dfrac{1}{7}$

Write each of the following as a repeated multiplication.

Class Ex. #3

a) $3a^4b$
$= 3 \times a \times a \times a \times a \times b$
$= 3 \times a \times a \times a \times a \times b$

b) $3ab^4$
$= 3 \times a \times b \times b \times b \times b$

c) $3(ab)^4 = 3 \times a \times b \times a \times b \times a \times b \times a \times b$
$= 3 \times a \times a \times a \times a \times b \times b \times b \times b$

d) $(3ab)^4 = 3 \times a \times b \times 3 \times a \times b \times 3 \times a \times b \times 3 \times a \times b$
$= 3 \times 3 \times 3 \times 3 \times a \times a \times a \times a \times b \times b \times b \times b$

Evaluating Powers

$10^3 = 10 \times 10 \times 10 = 1000$ 　　$3^4 = 3 \times 3 \times 3 \times 3 = 81$ 　　$(-6)^2 = (-6) \times (-6) = 36$

$-6^2 = -(6 \times 6) = -36$

The Zero Exponent

$10^0 = 1$ 　　$3^0 = 1$

The results above are examples of a general rule when a base is raised to the exponent zero.
Complete: $a^0 =$ __1__ .

Class Ex. #4　Evaluate the following.　a) 6^0 　1 　 b) $(-9)^0$ 　1 　 c) -9^0 　-1 　 d) $2(6^2)^0$ 　$2(1) = 2$

Numerical Bases	Variable Bases	Exponent Laws
		Product Law
$8^3 \times 8^2 = (8 \cdot 8 \cdot 8)(8 \cdot 8)$ $= 8^5$ or 8^{3+2}	$a^3 \times a^2 = (a \cdot a \cdot a)(a \cdot a)$ $= a^5$ or a^{3+2}	$(a^m)(a^n) = a^{m+n}$
		Quotient Law
$8^3 \div 8^2 = \dfrac{8 \cdot 8 \cdot 8}{8 \cdot 8}$ $= 8^1$ or 8^{3-2}	$a^3 \div a^2 = \dfrac{a \cdot a \cdot a}{a \cdot a}$ $= a^1$ or a^{3-2}	$a^m \div a^n = \dfrac{a^m}{a^n} = a^{m-n}$ $(a \neq 0)$
		Power of a Product Law
$(8 \cdot 7)^3 = (8 \cdot 7)(8 \cdot 7)(8 \cdot 7)$ $= (8 \cdot 8 \cdot 8)(7 \cdot 7 \cdot 7)$ $= 8^3 \cdot 7^3$	$(a \cdot b)^3 = (a \cdot b)(a \cdot b)(a \cdot b)$ $= (a \cdot a \cdot a)(b \cdot b \cdot b)$ $= a^3 b^3$	$(ab)^m = a^m b^m$
		Power of a Quotient Law
$\left(\dfrac{8}{7}\right)^3 = \left(\dfrac{8}{7}\right)\left(\dfrac{8}{7}\right)\left(\dfrac{8}{7}\right)$ $= \dfrac{8^3}{7^3}$	$\left(\dfrac{a}{b}\right)^3 = \left(\dfrac{a}{b}\right)\left(\dfrac{a}{b}\right)\left(\dfrac{a}{b}\right)$ $= \dfrac{a^3}{b^3}$	$\left(\dfrac{a}{b}\right)^n = \dfrac{a^n}{b^n}$ $(b \neq 0)$
		Power of a Power Law
$(8^3)^2 = (8^3)(8^3)$ $= (8 \cdot 8 \cdot 8)(8 \cdot 8 \cdot 8)$ $= 8^6$ or $8^{3 \times 2}$	$(a^3)^2 = (a^3)(a^3)$ $= (a \cdot a \cdot a)(a \cdot a \cdot a)$ $= a^6$ or $a^{3 \times 2}$	$(a^m)^n = a^{mn}$

9. $(x^2)(x^3) = (x \times x)(x \times x \times x) = (x \times x \times x \times x \times x) = x^5$
$(x^2)^3 = x^2 \times x^2 \times x^2 = x \times x \times x \times x \times x \times x = x^6$

10. a) a^6 b) m^9 c) s^{10} d) x^{11} e) y^{12}

11. a) t^6 b) x^2 c) p d) d^9 e) p^7

12. a) $x^5 y^5$ b) $m^4 n^4$ c) $27x^3$ d) $1000z^3$ e) $\frac{1}{4}c^2$
f) $16b^4$ g) $-x^3$ h) $81y^4$ i) $16p^2q^2$ j) $-64p^3q^3$

13. a) $\frac{x^2}{y^2}$ b) $\frac{a^6}{b^6}$ c) $\frac{625}{c^4}$ d) $\frac{b^3}{125}$ e) $\frac{z^{10}}{y^{10}}$

14. a) p^4 b) h^{20} c) b^{12} d) s^{90} e) z^{21}

15. a) 6 b) 4 c) 16 d) 8 e) 3 f) 1

16. a) x^9 b) $x^7 y^7$ c) t^9 d) t^6 e) y^{12} f) $\frac{a^{11}}{b^{11}}$ g) $\frac{d^3}{8}$ h) $64s^6 6$

17. a) g^{15} b) a^2 c) $81b^4c^4$ d) $\frac{25}{y^2}$ e) a^4 f) $\frac{1}{81}p^4q^4$ g) a^{12} h) x^6

18. a) $y^0 = 1$ b) $-a^5b^5$ c) m^{12} d) $r^0 = 1$ e) c^{18} f) a^6b^6 g) $\frac{1}{a^8}$ h) $2x^3y^3$

19. a) $2^3 \times 2^4 = 2^{12}$ b) $(4^3)^2 = 4^9$

The student multiplied 3 and 4 instead of adding 3 and 4.
$2^3 \times 2^4 = 2^7$

The student squared the exponent 3 instead of multiplying 3 and 2.
$(4^3)^2 = 4^6$

c) $3^4 \times 3^5 = 9^9$ d) $3^2 \times 2^3 = 6^5$

The student multiplied the bases together.
$3^4 \times 3^5 = 3^9$

The student multiplied the bases together. The exponent laws are only valid when the bases are the same. No simplification.

e) $(-5a^2b)^3 = -5a^6b^3$ f) $\left(\frac{1}{2}pq\right)\left(\frac{1}{2}pq\right) = p^2q^2$

The student did not cube the -5.
$(-5a^2b)^3 = -125a^6b^3$

The student added $\frac{1}{2}$ and $\frac{1}{2}$ instead of multiplying $\frac{1}{2}$ and $\frac{1}{2}$.
$\left(\frac{1}{2}\right)\left(\frac{1}{2}pq\right) = \frac{1}{4}p^2q^2$

Class Ex. #5
a) $3^4 \cdot 3^2$ b) $\dfrac{(-2)^5}{(-2)^3}$ c) $(5^2)^3 = 5^6$
$= 3^6$ $= (-2)^2$ $= 15625$
$= 729$ $= 4$

Class Ex. #6
a) $(a)^4(a)^3$ b) $x^6 x$ c) $b^7 \times b^0 \times b^4$ d) $\dfrac{x^8}{x^4}$ e) $\dfrac{y^{10}}{y^2}$ f) $(a^4)^3$
a^7 x^7 b^{11} x^4 y^8 a^{12}

g) $(y^5)^5$ h) $\left(\dfrac{x}{y}\right)^9$ i) $\left(\dfrac{c}{4}\right)^2$ j) $(sr)^6$ k) $(2a)^5$ l) $(-3pq)^4$
$\dfrac{x^{15}}{y^{15}}$ $\dfrac{x^9}{y^9}$ $\dfrac{c^2}{16}$ $s^6 t^6$ $32a^5$ $81p^4q^4$

Assignment

1. a) base 8, exponent 3 b) base k, exponent 15 c) base 2, exponent x
d) base -x, exponent 4 e) base $\frac{3}{4}$, exponent 6

2. a) 5 b) -6 c) 1 d) $\frac{1}{4}$ e) $\frac{5}{8}$

3. a) c^4 b) $5x^3$ c) $(ab)^2$ d) $(-5)^3$ e) s^2t
$c \times c \times c \times c$ $5 \times x \times x \times x$ $(-5)\times(-5)\times(-5)$ $s \times s \times t$
$= a \times b \times a \times b$

f) $2\left(\frac{5}{4}\right)^3$ g) $(4a)^2$ h) $3cd^2$ i) $3(cd)^2$ j) $(3cd)^2$
$2 \times \frac{5}{4} \times \frac{5}{4} \times \frac{5}{4}$ $4a \times 4a$ $3 \times c \times d \times d$ $3 \times c \times d \times c \times d$ $3 \times c \times d \times 3 \times c \times d$
$= 4 \times 4 \times a \times a$ $= 3 \times c \times c \times d \times d$ $= 3 \times 3 \times c \times c \times d \times d$

4. a) 6561 b) -25 c) 25 d) -125 e) -125 f) $\frac{27}{125}$

5. a) -100 b) 100 c) -1000 d) -1000

6. $-8^0 = -1$ since the exponent applies only to the base 8.
$(-8)^0 = 1$ since the exponent applies to the base -8.

7. a) 1 b) -1 c) 1 d) $\frac{1}{2}(1) = \frac{1}{2}$ e) $\frac{1}{2}(0) = \frac{1}{2}$

8. a) $9^3 \cdot 9^6$ b) $(7^2)^3$ c) $\dfrac{8^{15}}{8^{13}}$ d) $\left(\dfrac{2}{3}\right)\left(\dfrac{2}{3}\right)^3$
$= 9^9$ $= 7^6$ $= 8^2$ $= \left(\dfrac{2}{3}\right)^4 = \dfrac{16}{81}$
$= 387420489$ $= 117649$ $= 64$

e) $\dfrac{1.5^7}{1.5^5}$ f) $(-3^3)^2$ g) $(-5)^6 \times (-5)^2$ h) $4^3 \cdot 4^4 \cdot 4^2$
$= (1.5)^2$ $= (-1)^2 \, 3^6$ $= (-5)^8$ $= 4^9$
$= 2.25$ $= 3^6 = 729$ $= 390625$ $= 262144$

20.

Column 1		Column 2	
F	i) $(-a^2)^3$ $-a^6$	A.	a^4
C	ii) $(-a^3)^2$ a^6	B.	a^5
B	iii) $a^3 \times a^2$ a^5	C.	a^6
C	iv) $a^8 \div a^2$ a^{24}	D.	a^{24}
D	v) $a^{30} \div a^6$ a^6	E.	$-a^5$
F	vi) $-(a^2)^3$ $-a^6$	F.	$-a^6$
F	vii) $-(a^3)^2$ $-a^6$		

21. $(2^3)^P = 2^{12}$
$P = 4$

$\dfrac{4^{10}}{4^9} = 4^2 \quad Q = 8$

$2^r \cdot 2^r = 2^{16}$
$r = 8$

$(3^6)^2 = 1$
$S = 0$

$\boxed{4\ 8\ 8\ 0}$

22. $n + n + n = 27$
$3n = 27 \qquad n = 9$

$\boxed{9\ \ \ }$

Exponents Lesson #2:
Combining the Exponent Laws

Warm-Up #1

$(3 \cdot x \cdot x)(5 \cdot x \cdot x \cdot x) = 3 \cdot 5 \cdot x \cdot x \cdot x \cdot x \cdot x$
$= 15x^5$

Warm-Up #2

Use factors to explain why $6a^6 \div 3a^2 = 2a^4$.

$\dfrac{2 \cdot 6 \cdot a \cdot a \cdot a \cdot a \cdot a \cdot a}{3 \cdot a \cdot a} = 2a^4$

Laura is correct.

Class Ex. #1

a) $4x^5 \times 2x^3$ $8x^8$

b) $(-7a^8)(6a^{12})$ $-42a^{20}$

c) $\dfrac{20y^{20}}{5y^5}$ $4y^{15}$

d) $\dfrac{30b^{14}}{45b^{10}}$ $\dfrac{2}{3}b^4$

e) $(3a^4)(a^5)(6a^3)$ $18a^{12}$

f) $(-16n^5) \div (-2n)$ $8n^4$

Class Ex. #2

a) $x^5 y^8 x^3 y^4$ $x^8 y^{12}$

b) $\dfrac{x^5 y^8}{x^3 y^4}$ $x^2 y^4$

c) $(-3bc)(b^3 c^2)(-4b^2 c)$ $12b^6 c^4$

d) $\dfrac{10e^8 f^{12}}{4e^4 f^7}$ $\dfrac{5}{2}e^4 f^5$

Class Ex. #3

a) $(3x^2)^3$ $27x^6$

b) $(-2a^2 b^3)^2$ $4a^4 b^6$

c) $\dfrac{x^3 x^5}{x^2 x}$ $= \dfrac{x^8}{x^3} = x^5$

d) $\left(\dfrac{2a}{y^3}\right)^3$ $= \dfrac{-8a^3}{y^9}$

Class Ex. #4

a) $-(n^2)^5$ $-(n^{10}) = -n^{10}$

b) $\left(\dfrac{4y^3 \times 3x^6}{6x^5}\right)^4$ $\left(\dfrac{12x^6 y^3}{6x^5}\right)^4 = (2xy^3)^4 = 16x^4 y^{12}$

Class Ex. #5

a) $(-a)^6 \div (-a)^4$ $= (-a)^2 = a^2$

b) $-a^6 \div (-a)^4$ $= -a^6 \div a^4 = -a^2$

c) $-a^7 \div (-a)^3$ $= -a^7 \div -a^3 = a^4$

Class Ex. #6

a) $(-2a^2 b^3)^3 (4a^5 b^7)$ $= (-8a^6 b^9)(4a^5 b^7)$ $= -32a^{11}b^{16}$

b) $\dfrac{72x^4 y^{10}(-z^2)^4}{6(2xy^2)^3 z^8 y^3}$
$= \dfrac{72x^4 y^{10} z^8}{6(8x^3 y^6)z^8 y^3}$
$= \dfrac{72x^4 y^{10} z^8}{48x^3 y^9 z^8} = \dfrac{3}{2}xy$

d) $(5ab^6)^2 (4a^2 b)$ $= (25a^2 b^{12})(4a^2 b)$ $= 100a^4 b^{13}$

Extension

Class Ex. #7

a) $\dfrac{b^{4x+y}}{b^{x-2y}}$
$= b^{(4x+y)-(x-2y)}$
$= b^{4x+y-x+2y} = b^{3x+3y}$

b) $\dfrac{x^{5a+7b} \cdot x^{3a+b}}{x^a \cdot x^{2a-7b}}$ $= \dfrac{x^{5a+7b+3a+b}}{x^{a+2a-7b}}$
$= \dfrac{x^{8a+8b}}{x^{3a-7b}}$ $= x^{(8a+8b)-(3a-7b)}$
$= x^{8a+8b-3a+7b}$
$= x^{5a+15b}$

Assignment

1. a) $9a^7$ b) $30b^{15}$ c) $15a^6$ d) $-24x^{13}$ e) $7e^{15}$ f) $0.2c^4$

2. a) $2x^2$ b) $9e$ c) $3d^4$ d) $-10d^{72}$ e) $2e^5$ f) f

3. a) $15a^6 b^{11}$ b) $x^{11}y^4$ c) $3xy^5$ d) $5xy^5$ e) $\dfrac{1}{3}f^8 d^2$ f) $-14b^7 c^9$

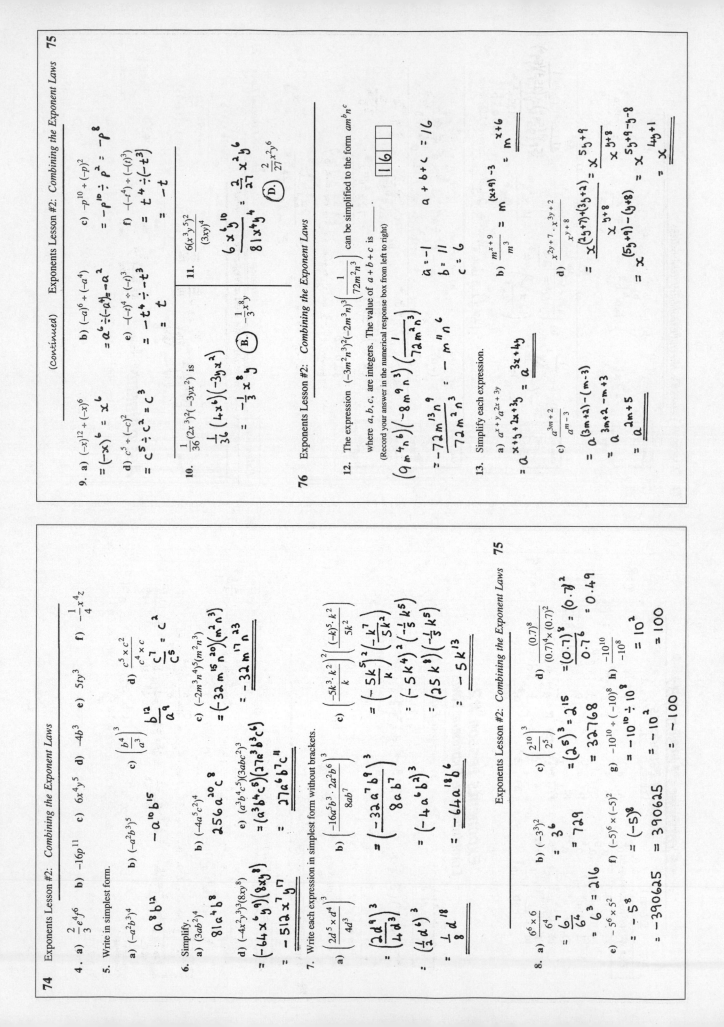

74   Exponents Lesson #2:   *Combining the Exponent Laws*

4. a) $\frac{2}{3}e^4f^6$ b) $-16p^{11}$ c) $6x^4y^5$ d) $-4b^3$ e) $5ry^3$ f) $-\frac{1}{4}x^4z$

5. Write in simplest form.

a) $(-a^2b^3)^4$ b) $(-a^2b^3)^5$ c) $\left(\dfrac{b^4}{a^3}\right)^3$ d) $\dfrac{c^5 \times c^2}{c^4 \times c}$

$81a^4b^8$ $-a^{10}b^{15}$ $\dfrac{b^{12}}{a^9}$ $\dfrac{c^7}{c^5} = c^2$

6. Simplify.

a) $(3ab^2)^4$ b) $(-4a^5c^2)^4$ c) $(-2m^3n^4)^5(m^2n^3)$

$81a^4b^8$ $256a^{20}c^8$ $=(-32m^{15}n^{20})(m^2n^3)$

$= -32m^{17}n^{23}$

d) $(-4x^2)^3(8xy^8)$ e) $(a^3b^4c^5)(3abc^2)^3$

$(-64x^6y^9)(8xy^8)$ $=(a^3b^4c^5)(27a^3b^3c^6)$

$= -512x^7y^{17}$ $= 27a^6b^7c^{11}$

7. Write each expression in simplest form without brackets.

a) $\left(\dfrac{2d^5 \times d^4}{4d^3}\right)^3$ b) $\left(\dfrac{-16a^5b^3 \cdot 2a^2b^6}{8ab^7}\right)^3$ c) $\left(\dfrac{-5k^3 \cdot k^2}{k}\right)^2\left(\dfrac{(-k)^5 \cdot k^2}{5k^2}\right)$

$\left(\dfrac{2d^9}{4d^3}\right)^3$ $\left(\dfrac{-32a^7b^9}{8ab^7}\right)^3$ $\left(\dfrac{-5k^5}{k}\right)^2\left(\dfrac{-k^7}{5k^2}\right)$

$= \left(\dfrac{1}{2}d^6\right)^3$ $= (-4a^6b^2)^3$ $= (-5k^4)^2\left(-\dfrac{1}{5}k^5\right)$

$= \dfrac{1}{8}d^{18}$ $= -64a^{18}b^6$ $= (25k^8)\left(-\dfrac{1}{5}k^5\right)$

$= -5k^{13}$

Exponents Lesson #2:   *Combining the Exponent Laws*   75

8. a) $\dfrac{6^6 \times 6}{6^4}$ b) $(-3^3)^2$ c) $\left(\dfrac{2^{10}}{2^5}\right)^3$ d) $\dfrac{(0.7)^8}{(0.7)^4 \times (0.7)^2}$

$= \dfrac{6^7}{6^4}$ $= 3^6$ $= (2^5)^3 = 2^{15}$ $= \dfrac{(0.7)^8}{(0.7)^6} = (0.7)^2$

$= 6^3 = 216$ $= 729$ $= 32768$ $\dfrac{0.7^8}{0.7^6} = 0.49$

e) $-5^6 \times (-5)^2$ f) $(-5)^6 \times (-5)^2$ g) $-10^{10} \div (-10)^8$ h) $\dfrac{-10^{10}}{-10^8}$

$= -5^8$ $= (-5)^8$ $= -10^{10} \div 10^8 = -10^2$ $= \dfrac{-10^{10}}{-10^8} = 10^2$

$= -390625$ $= 390625$ ≈ -100 $= 100$

---

75   *(continued)*   Exponents Lesson #2:   *Combining the Exponent Laws*

9. a) $(-x)^{12} + (-x)^6$ b) $(-a)^6 + (-a^4)$ c) $-p^{10} + (-p)^2$

$= (-x)^6 = x^6$ $= a^6 \div (-a^4) = a^2$ $= -p^{10} \div p^2 = -p^8$

d) $c^5 + (-c)^2$ e) $-(-t)^4 \div (-t)^3$ f) $-(-t^4) + (-(t)^3)$

$= c^5 \div c^2 = c^3$ $= -t^4 \div -t^3 = t$ $= t^4 \div -t^3 = -t$

10. $\dfrac{1}{36}(2x^3)^2(-3yx^2)$ is

$\dfrac{1}{36}(4x^6)(-3yx^2)$

$= -\dfrac{1}{3}x^8y$ B. $-\dfrac{1}{3}x^8y$

11. $\dfrac{6(x^3y^5)^2}{(3xy)^4}$

$\dfrac{6x^6y^{10}}{81x^4y^4} = \dfrac{2}{27}x^2y^6$

D. $\dfrac{2}{27}x^2y^6$

76   Exponents Lesson #2:   *Combining the Exponent Laws*

12. The expression $(-3m^2n^3)^2(-2m^3n)^3\left(\dfrac{1}{72m^2n^3}\right)$ can be simplified to the form am^bn^c

where a, b, c, are integers.   The value of $a + b + c$ is _____ .
(Record your answer in the numerical response box from left to right)

$(9m^4n^6)(-8m^9n^3)\left(\dfrac{1}{72m^2n^3}\right)$

$= -72m^{13}n^9 \left(\dfrac{1}{72m^2n^3}\right)$

$\dfrac{-72m^{13}n^9}{72m^2n^3} = -m^{11}n^6$

$a = -1$
$b = 11$ $a + b + c = 16$
$c = 6$

$\boxed{1\,|\,6}$

13. Simplify each expression.

a) $a^{x+y} \cdot a^{2x+3y}$ b) $\dfrac{m^{x+9}}{m^3} = m^{(x+9)-3} = m^{x+6}$

$= a^{x+y} \cdot a^{2x+3y} = a^{3x+4y}$

c) $\dfrac{a^{3m+2}}{a^{m-3}}$ d) $\dfrac{x^{2y+7} \cdot x^{3y+2}}{x^{y+8}}$

$= a^{(3m+2)-(m-3)}$ $= \dfrac{x^{(2y+7)+(3y+2)}}{x^{y+8}} = \dfrac{x^{5y+9}}{x^{y+8}}$

$= a^{3m+2-m+3}$ $= x^{(5y+9)-(y+8)}$

$= a^{2m+5}$ $= x^{5y+9-y-8}$

$= x^{4y+1}$

Class Ex. #3

a) $a^{-4} \times a^{-3}$

$= a^{-7} = \frac{1}{a^7}$

b) $6x^2 + 2x^7$

$3x^{-5} = \frac{3}{x^5}$

c) $\frac{y^6}{2y^{-5}}$

$= \frac{1}{2}y^{11}$

d) $(-2x)^{-3}$

$\frac{1}{(-2x)^3} = \frac{1}{-8x^3}$

$= -\frac{1}{8x^3}$

e) $\frac{8a^{-5}}{4b^{-3}}$

$= \frac{2b^3}{a^5}$

f) $\frac{(5p)^{-2}}{5q^4}$

$= \frac{1}{(5p)^2(5q^4)} = \frac{1}{(25p^2)(5q^4)}$

$= \frac{1}{125p^2q^4}$

Class Ex. #4

$5x^3y^{-8}z^{-2} \times \frac{x^4y\,z^2}{15x^8y^3z^{-1}}$

$5x^3y^{-8}z^{-2} + \frac{15x^8y^3z^{-1}}{x^5y^{-3}z^2}$

$= 5x^3y^{-8}z^{-2} \div 15x^3y^6z^{-3}$ or $= \frac{5x^{-8}y^{-11}}{15x^8y^3z^{-1}}$

$= \frac{1}{3}y^{-14}z \quad = \frac{z}{3y^{14}}$ $= \frac{z}{3y^{14}}$

Class Ex. #5

The exponent of -3 only applies to the variable p.

$2p^{-3} = 2^1 \cdot p^{-3} = 2^1 \cdot \frac{1}{p^3} = \frac{2}{p^3}$ not $\frac{1}{2p^3}$

Simplifying a Fractional Base with a Negative Exponent

a) $\left(\frac{2}{3}\right)^{-4} = \frac{1}{\left(\frac{2}{3}\right)^4} = \frac{1}{\left(\frac{16}{81}\right)} = 1 \times \frac{81}{16} = \frac{81}{16}$

b) $\frac{81}{16}$ c) true   d) $\left(\frac{2}{5}\right)^3 = \frac{8}{125}$

Exponents Lesson #3:
Integral Exponents

The Negative Exponent

a) $10^{-1} = \frac{1}{10} = \frac{1}{10^1}$ $3^{-1} = \frac{1}{3} = \frac{1}{3^1}$ $a^{-1} = \frac{1}{a}$

$10^{-2} = \frac{1}{100} = \frac{1}{10^2}$ $3^{-2} = \frac{1}{9} = \frac{1}{3^2}$ $a^{-2} = \frac{1}{a^2}$

$10^{-3} = \frac{1}{1000} = \frac{1}{10^3}$ $3^{-3} = \frac{1}{27} = \frac{1}{3^3}$ $a^{-3} = \frac{1}{a^3}$

b) Write the following with positive exponents.

i) $10^{-7} = \frac{1}{10^7}$ ii) $3^{-5} = \frac{1}{3^5}$ iii) $a^{-n} = \frac{1}{a^n}$

Using the Exponent Laws to Define the Negative Exponent

a) 0.008 or $\frac{1}{125}$

b) $5^4 \div 5^7 = \frac{5\cdot5\cdot5\cdot5}{5\cdot5\cdot5\cdot5\cdot5\cdot5\cdot5} = \frac{1}{5^3} = \frac{1}{125}$

c) $5^4 \div 5^7 = 5^{4-7} = 5^{-3}$ d) $a^{-p} = \frac{1}{a^p}$

e) i) $2^{-1} = \frac{1}{2^1} = \frac{1}{2}$ ii) $3^{-2} = \frac{1}{3^2} = \frac{1}{9}$ iii) $4^{-3} = \frac{1}{4^3} = \frac{1}{64}$

The Negative Exponent in the Denominator

$\frac{1}{4^{-3}} = \frac{1}{\frac{1}{4^3}} = 1 \times \frac{4^3}{1} = 4^3 = 64$ Confirmed by calculator.

Class Ex. #1

a) $4^5 \times 4^{-3}$ b) $3^2 \times 3^{-5}$ c) $\frac{1}{2^{-5}}$ d) $\frac{6^{-7}}{6^{-5}}$ e) $(2^3)^{-1} = 2^{-3}$

$= 4^2 = 16$ $= 3^{-3} = \frac{1}{3^3} = \frac{1}{27}$ $= 2^5 = 32$ $= \frac{1}{6^2} = \frac{1}{36}$ $= \frac{1}{2^3} = \frac{1}{8}$

Class Ex. #2

a) $\frac{8^3}{8^{-1}} = 8^4$ b) $\frac{8^3}{4^{-1}} = 2^4$ c) $a^{-3} = \frac{1}{a^3}$ d) $9a^{-3} = \frac{1}{9a^3}$

$8^{-(-1)}$ false   false   true $= 9\left(\frac{1}{a^3}\right) = \frac{9}{a^3}$ false

8^4 true

Assignment

1. a) $\dfrac{1}{x^3}$ b) $\dfrac{1}{y^9}$ c) $\dfrac{1}{4}$ d) a^5 e) 6^2

2. $\dfrac{3}{5^{-2}} = 3 \times 5^2 = 3 \times 25 = 75$

3. a) $\dfrac{1}{4^1} = \dfrac{1}{4}$ b) $\dfrac{1}{3^3} = \dfrac{1}{27}$ c) $7^2 = 49$ d) $\dfrac{1}{10^4} = \dfrac{1}{10\,000}$ e) $\dfrac{1}{3^4} = \dfrac{1}{81}$

4. a) $\dfrac{n^2}{m^5}$ b) $\dfrac{1}{c^2 x^5}$ c) $\dfrac{16}{h}$ d) $\dfrac{2}{3b^8}$ e) y^8

   f) $\dfrac{1}{4t^5}$ g) $\dfrac{x^9}{4}$ h) $4x^9$ i) a^2b^7 j) $\dfrac{1}{a^2b^7}$

5. a) $= -\dfrac{1}{3^2} = -\dfrac{1}{9}$ b) $= \dfrac{1}{(-3)^2} = \dfrac{1}{9}$ c) $= -7^2$; $\dfrac{8}{8} - \dfrac{49}{64}$ d) $= 1$ e) $= (-1)^{-2} = \dfrac{1}{(-1)^2} = 1$

6. a) $-\dfrac{1}{256}$ b) $-\dfrac{1}{343}$ c) $\dfrac{64}{27}$ d) 1600 e) $\dfrac{343}{64}$

7. a) T b) F c) T d) F e) F f) F g) T h) F

8. Simplify and write the answer with positive exponents.

a) $x^{10} \cdot x^{-5}$ $= x^5$

b) $m^5 + m^8$ $m^{-3} = m^3$

c) $b^{-1} \cdot b^{-3} = b^{-4} = \dfrac{1}{b^4}$

d) $-w^0 + w^5$ $-w^{-5} = -\dfrac{1}{w^5}$

9. a) $a^8 \times a^{-10}$ $= a^{-2} = \dfrac{1}{a^2}$

b) $10x^2 + 2x^{-1} = 5x^3$

c) $\dfrac{6y^{-6}}{2y^{-4}} = 3y^{-2} = \dfrac{3}{y^2}$

d) $\dfrac{2a^{-5}}{4b^6} = \dfrac{1}{2a^5b^6}$

e) $-7x^{-2} = \dfrac{-7}{x^2}$

f) $-(7x)^{-2} = -\dfrac{1}{(7x)^2} = -\dfrac{1}{49x^2}$

g) $(-7x)^{-2} = \dfrac{1}{(-7x)^2} = \dfrac{1}{49x^2}$

h) $\dfrac{(-7x)^{-2}}{-7x^{-2}} = \dfrac{1}{(-7x)^2} \cdot \dfrac{x^2}{(-7)} = \dfrac{1}{49x^2} \cdot \dfrac{x^2}{(-7)} = -\dfrac{1}{343}$

10. Simplify each expression, writing the answer with positive exponents.

a) $a^{-3}a^{-3}$ $= a^{-6} = \dfrac{1}{a^6}$

b) $(5b^8b^{-12})(-10b^3b^{-12})$
   $= (5b^{-4})(-10b^{-9})$
   $= -50b^{-13} = -\dfrac{50}{b^{13}}$

c) $(-7x^3x^{-5})(x^2x^{-3})$
   $= (-7x^{-2})(x^{-1})$
   $= -7x^{-3} = \dfrac{-7}{x^3}$

d) $(-2a^3)^{-3} \cdot 3a^{12}$
   $= \dfrac{1}{(-2a^3)^3} \cdot 3a^{12}$
   $= \dfrac{3a^{12}}{-8a^9} = -\dfrac{3}{8}a^3$

e) $\dfrac{16a^6b^{-3}}{-4a^6b^3}$
   $= -4b^{-6} = \dfrac{-4}{b^6}$

f) $(-3a^5b^{-3}c^0)^{-2}$
   $= \dfrac{1}{(-3a^5b^{-3})^2} = \dfrac{b^6}{9a^{10}}$

11. Simplify. Write the final answer with positive exponents.

a) $\dfrac{32a^2b^{-4}}{4a^{-8}b^{-2}} \times \dfrac{-8a^{-2}}{-3b^{-3}}$
   $= -256b^{-4}$
   $= -12a^{-2}b^{-5}$
   $= \dfrac{64\,a^8}{3b}$

b) $\dfrac{10(p^3q^2r^0)^{-3}}{(8p^{-3}q^5r^3)^{-2}}$
   $= \dfrac{10(8p^{-3}q^5r^0)^2}{(p^3q^2r^0)^3}$
   $= 640p^{-15}q^4r^6 = \dfrac{640q^4r^6}{p^{15}}$

c) $(-2x^5y^3z^8)^{-2} \cdot (-8x^4y^6z^{-24}z^{36})^3$
   $= \dfrac{1}{(-2x^5y^3z^8)^2} \cdot (-8x^4y^6z^{12})^3$
   $= \dfrac{-8x^4y^6z^{-24}z^{36}}{4x^{10}y^6z^{16}}$
   $= -2x^{-4}y^{-30}z^{20} = -\dfrac{2z^{20}}{x^4y^{30}}$

d) $(5a^3b^2)(-2a^{-2}b)^{-3} + (-5a^8b^{-9})^2$
   $= \dfrac{5a^3b^2}{(-2a^{-2}b)^3} \times \dfrac{1}{(-5a^8b^{-9})^2}$
   $= \dfrac{5a^3b^2}{-8a^{-6}b^3} \times \dfrac{1}{25a^{16}b^{-18}}$
   $= \dfrac{25a^{14}b^{-18}}{-8a^{-6}b^3}$
   $= -125a^{25}b^{-19} = -\dfrac{125a^{25}}{8b^{19}}$

12. Evaluate the following without using a calculator.

a) $\left(\dfrac{2}{3}\right)^{-3}$ b) $\left(\dfrac{1}{5}\right)^{-2}$ c) $\left(\dfrac{8}{5}\right)^{-1}$ d) $\left(\dfrac{3}{2}\right)^{-4}$

a) $= \left(\dfrac{3}{2}\right)^3 = \dfrac{27}{8}$

b) $= 5^2 = 25$

c) $= \dfrac{5}{8}$

d) $= \left(\dfrac{2}{3}\right)^4 = \dfrac{16}{81}$

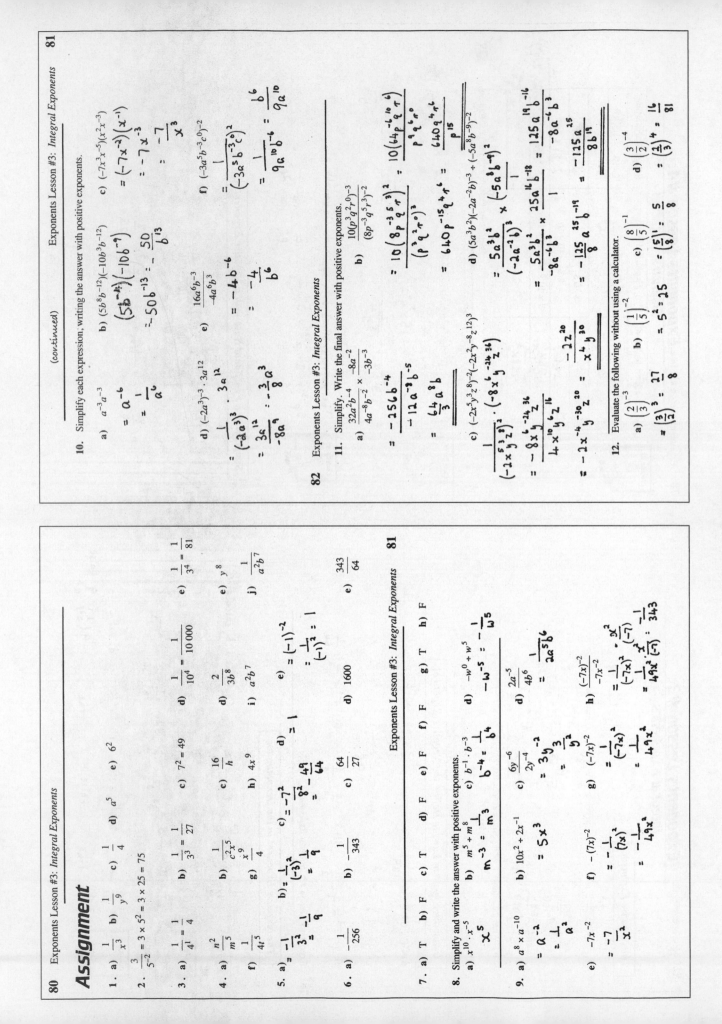

Class Ex. #1

Standard Notation	Expanded Form	Scientific Notation
61 500	$6.15 \times 10 \times 10 \times 10 \times 10$	6.15×10^4
500 000	$5 \times 10 \times 10 \times 10 \times 10 \times 10$	5×10^5
46.3	4.63×10	4.63×10^1
281	$2.81 \times 10 \times 10$	2.81×10^2
700 000	$7 \times 10 \times 10 \times 10 \times 10 \times 10$	7×10^5
920	$9.2 \times 10 \times 10$	9.2×10^2
1 400 000	$1.4 \times 10 \times 10 \times 10 \times 10 \times 10 \times 10$	1.4×10^6

a) The distance from Earth to the sun is approximately $\underline{9.3 \times 10^7}$ miles.

b) The speed of light is approximately $\underline{3 \times 10^8}$ metres/second.

c) The number of molecules of a gas per cubic metre is approximately $\underline{2.7 \times 10^{19}}$.

86 Exponents Lesson # 4 *Scientific Notation*

Class Ex. #3

a) 3.8×10^7 = 38 000 000

b) 2.51×10^{12} = 2 510 000 000 000

c) 2.9×10^3 = 2900

Class Ex. #4

a) $7.1 \times 10^2 \times 1000$
$= 7.1 \times 10^2 \times 10^3$
$= 7.1 \times 10^5$

b) $6.98 \times 10^7 \times 10$
$= 6.98 \times 10^8$

c) $\dfrac{5 \times 10^6}{1000} = \dfrac{5 \times 10^6}{10^3}$
$= 5 \times 10^3$

Class Ex. #5

Standard Notation	Expanded Form	Scientific Notation
0.000 53	$\dfrac{5.3}{10 \times 10 \times 10 \times 10}$	5.3×10^{-4}
0.000 000 07	$\dfrac{7}{10 \times 10 \times 10 \times 10 \times 10 \times 10 \times 10 \times 10}$	7×10^{-8}
0.0029	$\dfrac{2.9}{10 \times 10 \times 10}$	2.9×10^{-3}
0.000 0071	$\dfrac{7.1}{10 \times 10 \times 10 \times 10 \times 10 \times 10}$	7.1×10^{-6}
0.0031	$\dfrac{3.1}{10 \times 10 \times 10}$	3.1×10^{-3}
0.000 085	$\dfrac{8.5}{10 \times 10 \times 10 \times 10 \times 10}$	8.5×10^{-5}

---

82 Exponents Lesson #3: *Integral Exponents* (continued)

13. a) $\left(\dfrac{c}{d}\right)^{-3}$
$= \left(\dfrac{d}{c}\right)^3 = \dfrac{d^3}{c^3}$

b) $\left(\dfrac{x}{4}\right)^{-3}$
$= \left(\dfrac{4}{x}\right)^3 = \dfrac{64}{x^3}$

c) $\left(\dfrac{p^2}{r^4}\right)^{-3}$
$= \left(\dfrac{r^4}{p^2}\right)^3 = \dfrac{r^{12}}{p^6} = \dfrac{a^6}{b^{15}}$

d) $\left(\dfrac{a^{-2}}{b^{-5}}\right)^{-3}$

e) $\left(\dfrac{-12x^{-3}}{6y^{-8}}\right)^{-1} = -\dfrac{x^3}{2y^8}$

f) $\left(\dfrac{12x^3 y^{-1}}{-8x^{-1}y^5}\right)^{-2} = \left(\dfrac{-8x^{-1}y^5}{12x^3 y^{-1}}\right)^2$
$= \dfrac{64 x^{-2} y^{10}}{144 x^6 y^{-2}} = \dfrac{4y^{12}}{9x^8}$

83 Exponents Lesson #3: *Integral Exponents*

14. a) $\left(\dfrac{-x^3}{y}\right)^{-2} + \left(\dfrac{y^3}{x^5}\right)^2$
$= \dfrac{y^2}{x^6} \div \dfrac{y^6}{x^{10}}$
$= \dfrac{y^2}{x^6} \times \dfrac{x^{10}}{y^6}$
$= x^4 y^{-4}$
$= \dfrac{x^4}{y^4}$

b) $49\left(\dfrac{7w^3 x^{-5} z^4}{w^{-3} z}\right)^{-2} \times \dfrac{14(x^4 z^8)^0}{x^{-8} z^8}$
$= 49\left(\dfrac{w^{-3} z}{7w^3 x^{-5} z^4}\right)^2 \times \dfrac{14}{x^{-8} z^8}$
$= 49\left(\dfrac{1}{7} w^{-6} x^5 z^{-3}\right)^2 \times 14 x^8 z^{-8}$
$= 49 \left(\dfrac{1}{49} w^{-12} x^{10} z^{-6}\right) \times 14 x^8 z^{-8}$
$= 14 w^{-12} x^{18} z^{-14}$
$= \dfrac{14 x^{18}}{w^{12} z^{14}}$

15. $\dfrac{1^{-3} + 3^0}{2^{-1}}$ is **(B.)** 4
$= \dfrac{1+1}{\frac{1}{2}} = \dfrac{2}{\frac{1}{2}} = 4$

16. $\dfrac{6 \times 10^{-7} \times 2 \times 10^8}{3 \times 10^6} = \dfrac{12 \times 10}{3 \times 10^6} = 4 \times 10^{1-n}$
$n = 1 - 6 = -5$ **(A.)** -5

17. i) $3a^{-3} = \dfrac{1}{3a^3}$ X

ii) $8x^4 + 4x^7 = \dfrac{1}{2x^{-3}}$, $2x^{-3} = \dfrac{1}{2x^3}$ X

iii) $\dfrac{1}{2a} = 2a^{-1} = \dfrac{1}{2}a^{-1}$ X

(D.) none of the statements are true

Class Ex. #6

a) An inch is about $\underline{2.54 \times 10^{-5}}$ kilometres.

b) The mass of a particle of dust is about $\underline{7.5 \times 10^{-10}}$ kg.

c) The mass of an electron is about $\underline{9 \times 10^{-28}}$ g.

Class Ex. #7

a) Explain why 0.4×10^{-8} is not written in scientific notation.

0.4 is not between 1 and 10

b) Write 0.4×10^{-8} in scientific notation.

$$4 \times 10^{-1} \times 10^{-8} = 4 \times 10^{-9}$$

Class Ex. #8

a) 9.1×10^{14} b) 1.5×10^{-8}

Assignment

1. Complete the following table.

Standard Notation	Expanded Form	Scientific Notation
151 000	$1.51 \times 10 \times 10 \times 10 \times 10 \times 10$	1.51×10^5
23.4	2.34×10	2.34×10^1
32 000	$3.2 \times 10 \times 10 \times 10 \times 10$	3.2×10^4
830 000	$8.3 \times 10 \times 10 \times 10 \times 10 \times 10$	8.3×10^5
730	$7.3 \times 10 \times 10$	7.3×10^2
840	$8.4 \times 10 \times 10$	8.4×10^2
6 200	$6.2 \times 10 \times 10 \times 10$	6.2×10^3

2. a) 2.3×10^3 b) 7.58×10^6 c) 4.1×10^{10}
   d) 5.31×10^1 e) 4.32×10^{12} f) 7.6×10^0

3. a) 57.9×1000000
      $= 5.79 \times 10^1 \times 10^6$
      $= 5.79 \times 10^7$ km

   b) 1.4×100000000
      $= 1.4 \times 10^9$ km

4. a) 1 800 000 000 000   b) 673 000   c) 99 900 000
   d) 227 940 000   e) 4 500 000 000

5. a) $5.7 \times 10^3 \times 10\,000$
      $= 5.7 \times 10^3 \times 10^4$
      $= 5.7 \times 10^7$

   b) $9.843 \times 10^8 \times 10$
      9.843×10^9

   c) $\dfrac{6.1 \times 10^8}{10\,000} = \dfrac{6.1 \times 10^8}{10^4}$
      $= 6.1 \times 10^4$

   $\dfrac{20\,000}{4 \times 10^2} = \dfrac{2 \times 10^4}{4 \times 10^2}$
   $= 0.5 \times 10^2 = 5 \times 10^1$

6. Complete the following table.

Standard Notation	Expanded Form	Scientific Notation
0.000 000 9	$\dfrac{9}{10 \times 10 \times 10 \times 10 \times 10 \times 10 \times 10}$	9×10^{-7}
0.000 001	$\dfrac{1}{10 \times 10 \times 10 \times 10 \times 10 \times 10}$	1×10^{-6}
0.000 035	$\dfrac{3.5}{10 \times 10 \times 10 \times 10 \times 10}$	3.5×10^{-5}
0.99	$\dfrac{9.9}{10}$	9.9×10^{-1}
0.069	$\dfrac{6.9}{10 \times 10}$	6.9×10^{-2}
0.000 85	$\dfrac{8.5}{10 \times 10 \times 10 \times 10}$	8.5×10^{-4}

7. a) 1 to the left   b) 5 to the left   c) 3 to the right   d) 1 to the right   e) 8 to the left

8. a) 2.3×10^{-5} b) 5×10^{-3} c) 8.725×10^{-7} d) 7.93×10^4 e) 6×10^{-1}
   f) 7.89×10^8 g) 5.94×10^{-6} h) 2.51×10^{-2} i) 8.13×10^7

9. a) 0.002 7   b) 0.000 000 004 51   c) 0.000 128   d) 5 670 000   e) 89

10. a) 23.2×10^5
       $2.32 \times 10^1 \times 10^5$
       $= 2.32 \times 10^6$

    b) 0.7×10^3
       $7 \times 10^{-1} \times 10^3$
       $= 7 \times 10^2$

    c) 0.089×10^{-7}
       $8.9 \times 10^{-2} \times 10^{-7}$
       $= 8.9 \times 10^{-9}$

    d) 45.6×10^{-9}
       $4.56 \times 10^1 \times 10^{-9}$
       $= 4.56 \times 10^{-8}$

    e) 0.0032×10^{12}
       $3.2 \times 10^{-3} \times 10^{12}$
       $= 3.2 \times 10^9$

11. a) 1.512×10^4 b) 5.625×10^2 c) 8.9×10^{-14} d) 4.62×10^{-7}

12. a) 0.000 103 2   b) 108 000   c) 0.000 000 125   d) 0.000 000 8

13. C   14. B

15. $time = \dfrac{distance}{speed} = \dfrac{1.5 \times 10^n}{3 \times 10^8} = 0.5 \times 10^3 = 5 \times 10^{-1} \times 10^3 = 5 \times 10^2$

$a = 5$
$a + n = 7$
$n = 2$

$\boxed{7}$

Exponents Lesson #5:
Rational Exponents - Part One

Warm-Up #1   The Meaning of $a^{\frac{1}{n}}$

a) Complete and evaluate the following.

i) $\sqrt{5} \cdot \sqrt{5} = \sqrt{25} = 5$ ii) $5^{\frac{1}{2}} \cdot 5^{\frac{1}{2}} = 5^{\frac{1}{2}+\frac{1}{2}} = 5^{\boxed{1}} = 5$

Deduce a meaning for $5^{\frac{1}{2}}$. $= \sqrt{5}$

b) Complete and evaluate the following.

i) $\sqrt[3]{2} \cdot \sqrt[3]{2} \cdot \sqrt[3]{2} = \sqrt[3]{8} = 2$ ii) $2^{\frac{1}{3}} \cdot 2^{\frac{1}{3}} \cdot 2^{\frac{1}{3}} = 2^{\frac{1}{3}+\frac{1}{3}+\frac{1}{3}} = 2^{\boxed{1}} = 2$

Deduce a meaning for $2^{\frac{1}{3}}$. $= \sqrt[3]{2}$

c) Write the following in radical form and evaluate manually. Verify with a calculator.

i) $25^{\frac{1}{2}} = \sqrt{25} = 5$ ii) $64^{\frac{1}{3}} = \sqrt[3]{64} = 4$ iii) $81^{\frac{1}{4}} = \sqrt[4]{81} = 3$

d) Write the following in radical form.

i) $x^{\frac{1}{2}} = \sqrt{x}$ ii) $b^{\frac{1}{3}} = \sqrt[3]{b}$ iii) $p^{\frac{1}{10}} = \sqrt[10]{p}$ iv) $a^{\frac{1}{n}} = \sqrt[n]{a}$

Warm-Up #2   The Meaning of $a^{\frac{m}{n}}$

a) Complete and evaluate the following.

i) $\sqrt{5^3} \cdot \sqrt{5^3} = 5^3 = 125$ ii) $5^{\frac{3}{2}} \cdot 5^{\frac{3}{2}} = 5^{\frac{3}{2}+\frac{3}{2}} = 5^{\boxed{3}} = 125$

Deduce a meaning for $5^{\frac{3}{2}}$. $= \sqrt{5^3}$

b) Complete and evaluate the following.

i) $\sqrt[3]{2^2} \cdot \sqrt[3]{2^2} \cdot \sqrt[3]{2^2} = 2^2 = 4$ ii) $2^{\frac{2}{3}} \cdot 2^{\frac{2}{3}} \cdot 2^{\frac{2}{3}} = 2^{\frac{2}{3}+\frac{2}{3}+\frac{2}{3}} = 2^{\boxed{2}} = 4$

Deduce a meaning for $2^{\frac{2}{3}}$. $= \sqrt[3]{2^3}$

c) Write the following in radical form.

i) $x^{\frac{5}{3}} = \sqrt[3]{x^5}$ ii) $b^{\frac{4}{5}} = \sqrt[5]{b^4}$ iii) $p^{\frac{5}{2}} = \sqrt{p^5}$ iv) $a^{\frac{m}{n}} = \sqrt[n]{a^m}$

Warm-Up #3

a) Evaluate i) $2^2 = 4$ ii) $\sqrt[3]{64} = 4$ b) $(\sqrt[3]{8})^2$

c) i) $64^{\frac{3}{2}} = (\sqrt{64})^3 = 8^3 = 512$ ii) $4^{\frac{5}{2}} = (\sqrt{4})^5 = 2^5 = 32$ iii) $81^{\frac{3}{4}} = (\sqrt[4]{81})^3 = 3^3 = 27$

Warm-Up #4

a) $8^0 = 1$ b) $\dfrac{1}{8^{\frac{2}{3}}}$ Evaluate $8^{-\frac{2}{3}}$ without using a calculator.

$= \dfrac{1}{8^{2/3}} = \dfrac{1}{(\sqrt[3]{8})^2} = \dfrac{1}{2^2} = \dfrac{1}{4}$

Class Ex. #1

a) $25^{\frac{3}{2}} = (\sqrt{25})^3 = 5^3 = 125$

b) $1000^{\frac{4}{3}} = (\sqrt[3]{1000})^4 = 10^4 = 10000$

c) $27^{-\frac{2}{3}} = \dfrac{1}{27^{2/3}} = \dfrac{1}{(\sqrt[3]{27})^2} = \dfrac{1}{3^2} = \dfrac{1}{9}$

d) $16^{-\frac{3}{4}} = \dfrac{1}{16^{3/4}} = \dfrac{1}{(\sqrt[4]{16})^3} = \dfrac{1}{2^3} = \dfrac{1}{8}$

e) $(-8)^{\frac{2}{3}} = (\sqrt[3]{-8})^2 = (-2)^2 = 4$

f) $-8^{\frac{2}{3}} = -(\sqrt[3]{8})^2 = -(2)^2 = -4$

g) $(3^2 + 4^2)^{\frac{1}{2}} = (9+16)^{\frac{1}{2}} = (25)^{\frac{1}{2}} = \sqrt{25} = 5$

Class Ex. #2

a) $\left(\dfrac{9}{4}\right)^{\frac{3}{2}} = \left(\sqrt{\dfrac{9}{4}}\right)^3 = \left(\dfrac{3}{2}\right)^3 = \dfrac{27}{8}$

b) $\left(\dfrac{9}{4}\right)^{-\frac{3}{2}} = \left(\dfrac{4}{9}\right)^{\frac{3}{2}} = \left(\sqrt{\dfrac{4}{9}}\right)^3 = \left(\dfrac{2}{3}\right)^3 = \dfrac{8}{27}$

Class Ex. #3

a) $r^{\frac{1}{3}} = \sqrt[3]{r}$ b) $s^{\frac{4}{7}} = \sqrt[7]{s^4}$ c) $r^{-\frac{1}{6}} = \dfrac{1}{r^{1/6}} = \dfrac{1}{\sqrt[6]{r}}$ d) $v^{-\frac{3}{2}} = \dfrac{1}{v^{3/2}} = \dfrac{1}{\sqrt{v^3}}$

Class Ex. #4

A $64^{\frac{2}{3}} = (\sqrt[3]{64})^2$ B $(-64)^{\frac{2}{3}} = (\sqrt[3]{-64})^2$ C $64^{\frac{3}{2}} = (\sqrt{64})^3$ D $(-64)^{\frac{3}{2}} = (\sqrt{-64})^3$

D involves the square root of a negative number which has no meaning.

Class Ex. #5

a) $\ell = 60^{\frac{1}{3}}$ m   b) $SA = 6\ell^2 = 6(60^{\frac{1}{3}})^2 = 6(60^{\frac{2}{3}})$ m²

c) edge length = 3.9 m   surface area = 92.0 m²

Class Ex. #6

a) $100^{-\frac{1}{2}}$ b) $1000^{-\frac{1}{3}}$

Assignment

1. Evaluate without the use of a calculator.

a) $4^{\frac{1}{2}} = \sqrt{4} = 2$

b) $100^2 = \sqrt{100} = 10$

c) $64^{\frac{1}{3}} = \sqrt[3]{64} = 4$

d) $9^{\frac{3}{2}} = (\sqrt{9})^3 = 3^3 = 27$

e) $49^{\frac{3}{2}} = (\sqrt{49})^3 = 7^3 = 343$

f) $16^{\frac{3}{4}} = (\sqrt[4]{16})^3 = 2^3 = 8$

g) $8^{\frac{2}{3}} = (\sqrt[3]{8})^2 = 2^2 = 4$

h) $125^{\frac{1}{3}} = \sqrt[3]{125} = 5$

i) $(6^2 + 8^2)^{\frac{3}{2}} = (36+64)^{\frac{3}{2}} = (\sqrt{100})^3 = 10^3 = 1000$

j) $(0.04)^{0.5} = \sqrt{0.04} = 0.2$

2. Determine the exact value without using a calculator.

a) $9^{-\frac{1}{2}} = \frac{1}{9^{\frac{1}{2}}} = \frac{1}{\sqrt{9}} = \frac{1}{3}$

b) $4^{-\frac{7}{2}} = \frac{1}{4^{\frac{7}{2}}} = \frac{1}{(\sqrt{4})^7} = \frac{1}{2^7} = \frac{1}{128}$

c) $25^{-\frac{3}{2}} = \frac{1}{25^{\frac{3}{2}}} = \frac{1}{(\sqrt{25})^3} = \frac{1}{5^3} = \frac{1}{125}$

d) $1000^{-\frac{2}{3}} = \frac{1}{1000^{\frac{2}{3}}} = \frac{1}{(\sqrt[3]{1000})^2} = \frac{1}{10^3} = \frac{1}{1000}$

e) $64^{-\frac{5}{6}} = \frac{1}{64^{\frac{5}{6}}} = \frac{1}{(\sqrt[6]{64})^5} = \frac{1}{2^5} = \frac{1}{32}$

f) $8^{-\frac{4}{3}} = \frac{1}{8^{\frac{4}{3}}} = \frac{1}{(\sqrt[3]{8})^4} = \frac{1}{2^4} = \frac{1}{16}$

g) $49^{-\frac{3}{2}} = \frac{1}{49^{\frac{3}{2}}} = \frac{1}{(\sqrt{49})^3} = \frac{1}{7}$

h) $32^{-\frac{4}{5}} = \frac{1}{32^{\frac{4}{5}}} = \frac{1}{(\sqrt[5]{32})^4} = \frac{1}{2^4} = \frac{1}{16}$

i) $(5^2 - 3^2)^{-\frac{5}{4}} = 16^{-\frac{5}{4}} = \frac{1}{(\sqrt[4]{16})^5} = \frac{1}{2^5} = \frac{1}{32}$

j) $(0.09)^{-\frac{3}{2}} = \frac{1}{(0.09)^{\frac{3}{2}}} = \frac{1}{(\sqrt{0.09})^3} = \frac{1}{(0.3)^3} = \frac{1000}{27} = 0.027$

3. Determine the exact value without using a calculator.

a) $\left(\frac{1}{25}\right)^{-\frac{1}{2}} = \sqrt{25} = 5$

b) $\left(\frac{1}{4}\right)^{-\frac{1}{2}} = 4^{\frac{1}{2}} = \sqrt{4} = 2$

c) $\left(\frac{1}{8}\right)^{-\frac{1}{3}} = (\sqrt[3]{8})^1 = 2$

d) $\left(\frac{1}{16}\right)^{-\frac{1}{4}} = \left(\frac{1}{3}\right)^{-4} = 3^4 = 81$

e) $\left(\frac{16}{81}\right)^{-\frac{3}{4}} = \left(\frac{81}{16}\right)^{\frac{3}{4}} = \left(\sqrt[4]{\frac{81}{16}}\right)^3 = \left(\frac{3}{2}\right)^3 = \frac{27}{8}$

4. Determine the exact value without using a calculator.

a) $(-8)^{\frac{1}{3}} = \sqrt[3]{-8} = -2$

b) $(-27)^{\frac{2}{3}} = (\sqrt[3]{-27})^2 = (-3)^2 = 9$

c) $-25^{-\frac{1}{2}} = -\frac{1}{25^{\frac{1}{2}}} = -\frac{1}{\sqrt{25}} = -\frac{1}{5}$

d) $-(-32)^{-\frac{4}{5}} = -\frac{1}{(-32)^{\frac{4}{5}}} = -\frac{1}{(\sqrt[5]{-32})^4} = -\frac{1}{(-2)^4} = -\frac{1}{16}$

e) $(-0.008)^{\frac{2}{3}} = (\sqrt[3]{-0.008})^2 = (-0.2)^2 = 0.04$

5. Use a calculator to evaluate the following to the nearest hundredth.

a) $4^{\frac{2}{3}}$ 2.52

b) $7^{\frac{3}{4}}$ 4.30

c) $(-5)^{\frac{3}{6}}$ 6.90

d) $6^{-\frac{4}{3}}$ 0.64

e) $-(-0.8)^{\frac{2}{3}}$ -0.86

6. a) $\sqrt[4]{a}$ b) $\sqrt{b}$ c) $\sqrt[5]{c}$ d) $\frac{1}{\sqrt{d}}$ e) $\frac{1}{\sqrt[6]{e}}$ f) $(\sqrt[3]{f})^2$ g) $(\sqrt[3]{g})^4$ h) $(\sqrt{h})^5$

7. b) and d) have no meaning → the even root of a negative number is not possible.

---

8. a) $(216)^{\frac{1}{3}}$ b) area of one face $= (216^{\frac{1}{3}})^2 = (216)^{\frac{2}{3}}$ cm^2

surface area $= 6(216)^{\frac{2}{3}}$ cm^2

c) edge length : $(216)^{\frac{1}{3}} = 6$ cm.

surface area : $6(216)^{\frac{2}{3}} = 216$ cm^2

9. a) edge length $= V^{\frac{1}{3}} = \sqrt[3]{V}$

b) $(V^{\frac{1}{3}})^2 = V^{\frac{2}{3}} = (\sqrt[3]{V})^2$ or $\sqrt[3]{V^2}$

10. a) $5 = 25^{\frac{1}{2}}$ b) $8 = 512^{\frac{1}{3}}$ c) $-3 = (-27)^{\frac{1}{3}}$ d) $\frac{1}{4} = 16^{-\frac{1}{2}}$ e) $6 = \left(\frac{1}{36}\right)^{-\frac{1}{2}}$ f) $100 = 1000^{\frac{2}{3}}$

11. $\left(\frac{16}{9}\right)^{0.5} = \sqrt{\frac{16}{9}} = \frac{4}{3}$

(B.) $\frac{4}{3}$

12. $(-4)^{1.5} = (-4)^{\frac{3}{2}} = (\sqrt{-4})^3$ not possible

(D.) has no meaning

13. Calculation 1. $-(27)^{-\frac{2}{3}} = -\left(\frac{1}{3}\right)^2 = -\frac{1}{9}$

Calculation 2. $\left(\frac{1}{27}\right)^{\frac{1}{3}} = \sqrt[3]{\frac{1}{27}} = \frac{1}{3}$

Calculation 3. $(-27)^{\frac{2}{3}} = (\sqrt[3]{-27})^2 = (-3)^2 = 9$

Calculation 4. $\left(\frac{1}{-27}\right)^{-\frac{1}{3}} = (-27)^{\frac{1}{3}} = \sqrt[3]{-27} = -3$

$\boxed{3\ 2\ 1\ 4}$

Exponents Lesson #6: Rational Exponents - Part Two

Review   Complete the following as a review.

Product Law $x^m \cdot x^n = x^{m+n}$ Quotient Law $x^m \div x^n = x^{m-n}$

Power of a Power $(x^m)^n = x^{mn}$ Power of a Product $(xy)^m = x^m y^m$

Power of a Quotient $\left(\dfrac{x}{y}\right)^m = \dfrac{x^m}{y^m}$, $y \neq 0$

Integral Exponent Rule $x^{-m} = \dfrac{1}{x^m}$, where $x \neq 0$

Rational Exponents $x^{\frac{m}{n}} = \sqrt[n]{x^m}$ or $(\sqrt[n]{x})^m$

Class Ex. #1

a) $x^{\frac{1}{6}} = \sqrt[6]{x}$

b) $-y^{\frac{5}{4}} = -\sqrt[4]{y^5}$

c) $(-z)^{\frac{5}{3}} = \sqrt[3]{(-z)^5}$

d) $(-z)^{-\frac{5}{3}} = \dfrac{1}{\sqrt[3]{(-z)^5}}$

e) $5t^{\frac{3}{4}} = 5\sqrt[4]{t^3}$

f) $(5t)^{\frac{3}{4}} = \sqrt[4]{(5t)^3}$

Class Ex. #2

a) $x^{\frac{3}{2}} \times x = x^{\frac{5}{2}} = \sqrt{x^5}$

b) $y^{\frac{3}{4}} \div y^{\frac{5}{3}} = y^{-\frac{11}{12}} = \dfrac{1}{\sqrt[12]{y^{11}}}$

c) $(a^{\frac{1}{2}})^{\frac{2}{3}} = a^{\frac{1}{3}} = \sqrt[3]{a}$

d) $\left(\dfrac{x^2}{y}\right)^{-\frac{1}{2}} = \dfrac{y^{\frac{1}{2}}}{x} = \sqrt{\dfrac{y}{x^2}}$

Class Ex. #3

a) $4x^{\frac{3}{4}} \times 3x^{-\frac{1}{8}} = 12x^{\frac{5}{8}} = 12\sqrt[8]{x^5}$

b) $\dfrac{5x^{\frac{3}{5}}}{25x^{-\frac{2}{5}}} = \frac{1}{5}x = \frac{1}{5}\sqrt[5]{x^6}$

c) $(8a^{\frac{1}{2}})^{\frac{4}{3}} = 8^{\frac{4}{3}} a^{\frac{2}{3}} = 16a^{\frac{2}{3}} = 16\sqrt[3]{a^2}$

Class Ex. #4

a) $\sqrt[3]{a^5}$
$= a^{\frac{5}{3}}$

b) $\sqrt[5]{a^2}$
$= a^{\frac{2}{5}}$

c) $\sqrt{a^9}$
$= a^{\frac{9}{2}}$

d) $\frac{1}{\sqrt{a^7}} = a^{-\frac{7}{2}}$
$= a^{-\frac{7}{2}}$

Class Ex. #5

a) $\sqrt{1296}$
$= ((1296)^2)^{\frac{1}{2}}$
$= 1296^{\frac{1}{2}} = 6$

b) $\frac{1}{\sqrt{169}} = \frac{1}{169^{\frac{1}{2}}}$
$= 169^{-\frac{1}{2}} = \frac{1}{13}$

c) $\sqrt[3]{\sqrt{64}}$
$= ((64)^{\frac{1}{2}})^{\frac{1}{3}}$
$= 64^{\frac{1}{6}} = 2$

Class Ex. #6

a) $\sqrt[3]{8x^5}$
$= \sqrt[3]{8}\sqrt[3]{x^5}$
$= 2x^{\frac{5}{3}}$

b) $\sqrt[5]{32x^3}$
$= \sqrt[5]{32}\sqrt[5]{x^3}$
$= 2x^{\frac{3}{5}}$

c) $\sqrt{900x}$
$= \sqrt{900}\sqrt{x}$
$= 30x^{\frac{1}{2}}$

d) $\sqrt[3]{x^5}(\sqrt[3]{x})$
$= x^{\frac{5}{3}}\cdot x^{\frac{1}{3}}$
$= x^2$

e) $2\sqrt{x}\times\sqrt[3]{x}$
$= 2x^{\frac{1}{2}}\cdot x^{\frac{1}{3}}$
$= 2x^{\frac{5}{6}}$

Class Ex. #7

a) $\sqrt{\sqrt{a^3}}$
$= (a^{\frac{3}{2}})^{\frac{1}{2}}$
$= a^{\frac{3}{4}}$

b) $\sqrt[5]{\sqrt[3]{64v^6}}$
$= ((64v^6)^{\frac{1}{3}})^{\frac{1}{2}}$
$= (64v^6)^{\frac{1}{6}}$
$= 2v$

c) $(\sqrt[4]{x^5y^3})^{\frac{3}{2}}$
$= ((x^5y^3)^{\frac{1}{4}})^{\frac{3}{2}}$
$= (x^5y^3)^{\frac{3}{8}}$
$= x^{\frac{15}{8}}y^{\frac{9}{8}}$

Assignment

1. a) $\sqrt[5]{a^4}$ b) $\sqrt{b^3}$ c) $\sqrt[4]{c}$ d) $\frac{1}{\sqrt[5]{x^2}}$ e) $\frac{1}{\sqrt[3]{y}}$ f) $5\sqrt[3]{h^2}$

g) $\sqrt[3]{(5h)^2}$ h) $-\sqrt[4]{r^5}$ i) $\sqrt[4]{(-r)^5}$ j) $\frac{2}{\sqrt{x}}$

2. a) $x^{\frac{7}{2}}\times x$
$= x^{\frac{9}{2}}$
$= \sqrt{x^9}$

b) $y^{\frac{6}{5}}+y^{\frac{4}{5}}$
$= y^{\frac{2}{5}}$
$= \sqrt[5]{y^2}$

c) $(a^{\frac{2}{5}})^{\frac{3}{4}}$
$= a^{\frac{3}{10}}$
$= \sqrt[10]{a^3}$

d) $(e^3f)^{\frac{3}{2}} = (\sqrt{e^3f})^3$
$= e^{\frac{9}{2}}f^{\frac{3}{2}}$
$= \sqrt{e^9f^3}$
$= \sqrt{e^9f^3}^3$

e) $x^{\frac{1}{2}}\times x^{-1}$
$= x^{-\frac{1}{2}}$
$= \frac{1}{x^{\frac{1}{2}}} = \frac{1}{\sqrt{x}}$

f) $y^{\frac{2}{7}}+y^{\frac{5}{7}}$
$= y^{-\frac{3}{7}} = \frac{1}{y^{\frac{3}{7}}}$
$= \frac{1}{\sqrt[7]{y^3}}$

g) $\left(\frac{x}{y^4}\right)^{\frac{1}{2}} = \frac{x^{\frac{1}{2}}}{y^2}$
$= \frac{\sqrt{x}}{y^2}$

h) $\left(\frac{x^2}{y}\right)^{-\frac{3}{2}} = \left(\frac{y}{x^2}\right)^{\frac{3}{2}}$
$= \frac{y^{\frac{3}{2}}}{x^3} = \frac{\sqrt{y^3}}{x^3}$

3. a) $2x^{\frac{3}{8}}\times 5x^{-\frac{1}{8}}$
$= 10x^{-\frac{1}{4}}$
$= 10\sqrt[4]{x}$

b) $64(a^{\frac{1}{2}})^{\frac{1}{3}}$
$= 64a^{\frac{1}{6}}$
$= 64\sqrt[6]{a}$

c) $((64a)^{\frac{1}{3}})^{\frac{1}{2}}$
$= (64a)^{\frac{1}{6}}$
$= 2a^{\frac{1}{6}}$
$= 2\sqrt[6]{a}$

d) $(64a^{\frac{2}{3}})^{\frac{1}{2}}$
$= 64^{\frac{1}{2}}a^{\frac{1}{3}}$
$= 8a^{\frac{1}{3}}$
$= 8\sqrt[3]{a}$

e) $\frac{y^2}{y^4}\frac{y^2}{1}$
$= \frac{y^7}{y^6}$
$= y^{\frac{1}{12}}$
$= \sqrt[12]{y}$

f) $\frac{a^3b^2}{b^3(a^{\frac{1}{2}})^2}$
$= \frac{a^3b^{\frac{1}{2}}}{b^3a^3} = b^{-\frac{5}{2}}$
$= \frac{1}{b^{\frac{5}{2}}}$
$= \frac{1}{\sqrt{b^5}}$

g) $\frac{10x^{-\frac{3}{5}}}{5x^{\frac{2}{5}}}$
$= 2x^{-\frac{4}{5}}$
$= \frac{2}{x^{\frac{4}{5}}}$
$= \frac{2}{\sqrt[5]{x^4}}$

h) $\frac{(a^4)^{\frac{1}{3}}}{9}+\frac{a}{81^{\frac{3}{4}}}$
$= \frac{a^{\frac{4}{3}}}{9}\times\frac{81}{a}$
$= \frac{27a^{\frac{4}{3}}}{9a}$
$= 3a^{\frac{1}{3}} = 3\sqrt[3]{a}$

4. a) $\sqrt[5]{a^3}$
$a^{\frac{3}{5}}$

b) $\sqrt[5]{a^4}$
$a^{\frac{4}{5}}$

c) $\sqrt{a^5}$
$a^{\frac{5}{2}}$

d) $\frac{1}{\sqrt[4]{a}}$
$\frac{1}{a^{\frac{1}{4}}} = a^{-\frac{1}{4}}$

e) $\frac{1}{\sqrt[4]{a^5}}$
$\frac{1}{a^{\frac{5}{4}}} = a^{-\frac{5}{4}}$

5. a) $\sqrt{\sqrt{64}}$
$= ((64)^{\frac{1}{3}})^{\frac{1}{2}}$
$= 64^{\frac{1}{6}}$
$= 2$

b) $\frac{1}{\sqrt[4]{625}}$
$= (625)^{-\frac{1}{4}}$
$= 625^{-\frac{1}{4}}$
$= \frac{1}{5}$

c) $\sqrt{\sqrt{2401}}$
$= ((2401)^{\frac{1}{2}})^{\frac{1}{2}}$
$= 2401^{\frac{1}{4}}$
$= 7$

6. a) $\sqrt[3]{\sqrt{x}}\sqrt[3]{x^7}$
$= \sqrt[3]{x^{\frac{7}{2}}}$
$= 3x^{\frac{7}{6}}$
$= 3x^{\frac{7}{6}}$

b) $\sqrt[4]{81}\sqrt[4]{x^5}$
$= 3x^{\frac{5}{4}}$
$= 3x^{\frac{3}{4}}$

c) $\sqrt[3]{-64}\sqrt[3]{x}$
$= -4x^{\frac{1}{3}}$
$= -4x^{\frac{1}{3}}$

d) $x^{\frac{3}{4}}\cdot x^{\frac{1}{2}}$
$= x^{\frac{5}{4}}$

e) $3x^{\frac{1}{3}}\times 3x^{\frac{1}{3}}$
$= 3\cdot x^{\frac{1}{3}}\times 3x^{\frac{1}{3}}$
$= 9x^{\frac{1}{3}}$

f) $\left(\frac{25x^{\frac{5}{3}}}{5x^{\frac{1}{3}}}\right)^2$
$= (5x^{\frac{4}{3}})^2$
$= 25x^{\frac{8}{3}}$

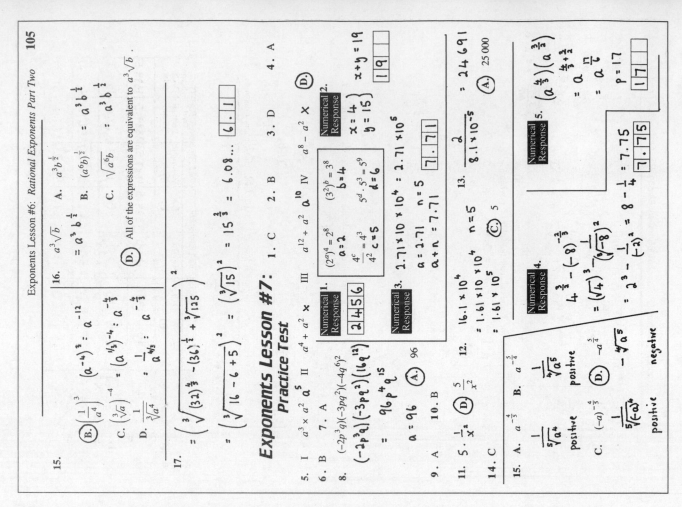

16. $a^3 \sqrt{b}$ A. $a^3 b^{\frac{1}{2}}$

$= a^3 b^{\frac{1}{2}}$ B. $(a^6 b)^{\frac{1}{2}}$ $= a^3 b^{\frac{1}{2}}$

C. $\sqrt{a^6 b}$ $= a^3 b^{\frac{1}{2}}$

(D.) All of the expressions are equivalent to $a^3 \sqrt{b}$.

15.

(B.) $\left(\frac{1}{a^4}\right)^3$

$(a^{-4})^3 = a^{-12}$

C. $\frac{\sqrt[3]{a}}{\sqrt[3]{a^4}}$ $= (a^{1/3})^{-4} = a^{-\frac{4}{3}}$

D. $\frac{1}{\sqrt[3]{a^4}}$ $= a^{-\frac{4}{3}}$

17. $= \left(\sqrt[3]{(32)^{\frac{4}{5}} - (36)^{\frac{1}{2}} + \sqrt[3]{125}}\right)^2$

$= \left(\sqrt[3]{16 - 6 + 5}\right)^2 = \left(\sqrt[3]{15}\right)^2 = 15^{\frac{2}{3}} = 6.08\ldots$ $\boxed{6 . 11}$

Exponents Lesson #7:
Practice Test

1. C   2. B   3. D   4. A

5. I $a^3 \times a^2$ II $a^4 + a^2 \times$ III $a^{12} \div a^2$ IV $a^8 - a^2 \times$ (D.)

6. B   7. A

Numerical 1.
Response
$\boxed{2\ 4\ 5\ 6}$

$(2^a)^4 = 2^8$
$a = 2$

$\frac{4^c}{4^2} = 4^3$
$c = 5$

Numerical 2.
Response
$(3^2)^b = 3^8$
$b = 4$

$5^d \cdot 5^3 = 5^9$
$d = 6$

$x + y = 19$
$\boxed{1\ 9}$
$\left.\begin{array}{l} x = 4 \\ y = 15 \end{array}\right\}$

8. $(-2p^3 q)(-3pq^2)(-4q^6)^2$

$(-2p^3 q)(-3pq^2)(16q^{12})$

$= 96 p^4 q^{15}$

(A.) 96 $a = 96$

Numerical 3.
Response
$2.71 \times 10^4 = 2.71 \times 10^5$
$2.71 \times 10 \times 10^4 = 2.71 \times 10^5$
$a = 2.71$ $n = 5$
$a + n = 7.71$
$\boxed{7 . 71}$

9. A   10. B

11. $5 \cdot \frac{1}{x^2}$ (D) $\frac{5}{x^2}$

12. 16.1×10^4
$= 1.61 \times 10 \times 10^4$
$= 1.61 \times 10^5$
$n = 5$ (C.) 5

13. $\frac{2}{8.1 \times 10^{-5}} = 24691$

(A.) 25 000

14. C

Numerical 4.
Response
$4^{\frac{3}{2}} - (-8)^{-\frac{2}{3}}$

$= (\sqrt{4})^3 - \frac{1}{(\sqrt[3]{-8})^2}$

$= 2^3 - \frac{1}{(-2)^2} = 8 - \frac{1}{4} = 7.75$

$\boxed{7 . 75}$

Numerical 5.
Response
$\left(a^{\frac{4}{3}}\right)\left(a^{\frac{3}{2}}\right)$

$= a^{\frac{4}{3} + \frac{3}{2}}$

$= a^{\frac{17}{6}}$

$p = 17$

$\boxed{1\ 7}$

15. A. $a^{-\frac{4}{5}}$ $\frac{1}{\sqrt[5]{a^4}}$ positive
B. $a^{-\frac{5}{4}}$ $\frac{1}{\sqrt[4]{a^5}}$ positive
C. $(-a)^{-\frac{4}{5}}$ $\frac{1}{\sqrt[5]{(-a)^4}}$ positive
(D.) $-a^{\frac{5}{4}}$ $-\sqrt[4]{a^5}$ negative

---

7. a) $\sqrt{\sqrt{x^5}}$

$= \left((x^5)^{\frac{1}{2}}\right)^{\frac{1}{2}}$

$= x^{\frac{5}{4}}$

b) $\sqrt[3]{\sqrt{a^8}}$

$= \left((a^8)^{\frac{1}{2}}\right)^{\frac{1}{3}}$

$= a^{\frac{4}{3}}$

c) $\sqrt[3]{\sqrt{729 y^{12}}}$

$= \left((729 y^{12})^{\frac{1}{2}}\right)^{\frac{1}{3}}$

$= (729 y^{12})^{\frac{1}{6}} = 3y^2$

d) $\sqrt[3]{\sqrt[4]{x^{\frac{2}{3}}}}$

$= \left(x^{\frac{2}{3}}\right)^{-\frac{1}{4}}$

$= x^{\frac{1}{18}}$

e) $\left(\sqrt[4]{2y - 3}\right)^{-3}$

$= \frac{1}{\left(\sqrt[4]{2y-3}\right)^3} = \frac{1}{(2y-3)^{\frac{3}{4}}}$

f) $\left(\sqrt[4]{x^4 y^3}\right)^{\frac{3}{2}}$

$= (x^4 y^3)^{\frac{3}{8}}$

$= (x^4 y^3)^{\frac{3}{8}}$

$= x^{\frac{3}{2}} y^{\frac{9}{8}}$

g) $-\sqrt[3]{\sqrt{x^2}}$

$= -x^{\frac{2}{3}}$

h) $\sqrt[3]{(-x)^2}$

$= (-x)^{\frac{2}{3}}$

Column 1 **Column 2**

(D) **8.** $\left(\frac{p}{q}\right)^{\frac{4}{3}} = \sqrt[3]{\left(\frac{p}{q}\right)^4} = \sqrt[3]{\frac{p^4}{q^4}}$ A. $\sqrt[4]{\frac{q^3}{p^3}}$

B **9.** $\left(\frac{p}{q}\right)^{\frac{3}{4}} = \sqrt[4]{\left(\frac{p}{q}\right)^3} = \sqrt[4]{\frac{p^3}{q^3}}$ B. $\sqrt[4]{\frac{p^3}{q^3}}$

(D) **10.** $\left(\frac{q}{p}\right)^{-\frac{4}{3}} = \left(\frac{p}{q}\right)^{\frac{4}{3}}$ Same as #8. C. $-\sqrt[4]{\frac{p^3}{q^3}}$

A **11.** $\left(\frac{p}{q}\right)^{-\frac{3}{4}} = \left(\frac{q}{p}\right)^{\frac{3}{4}} = \sqrt[4]{\left(\frac{q}{p}\right)^3} = \sqrt[4]{\frac{q^3}{p^3}}$ D. $\sqrt[3]{\frac{p^4}{q^4}}$

A **12.** $\left(\frac{q}{p}\right)^{\frac{3}{4}}$ Same as #11 E. $\sqrt[3]{\frac{q^4}{p^4}}$

E **13.** $\left(\frac{p}{q}\right)^{-\frac{4}{3}} = \sqrt[3]{\left(\frac{q}{p}\right)^4} = \sqrt[3]{\frac{q^4}{p^4}}$ F. $-\sqrt[3]{\frac{q^4}{p^4}}$

14. $(-x^3)^{-\frac{5}{3}}$

$= \frac{1}{(-x^3)^{\frac{5}{3}}}$

$= \frac{1}{(-1)^{\frac{5}{3}} (x^3)^{\frac{5}{3}}}$

$= \frac{1}{(-1)^5 x^5}$

$= -\frac{1}{x^5}$

(D.) $-\frac{1}{x^5}$

Class Ex. #6

−11

Class Ex. #7

a) $v = 12$, calculate t

$60 = vt$
$60 = (12)t$
$\frac{60}{12} = \frac{12t}{12}$
$t = 5$

b) $S = 100$, calculate r

$S = 4\pi r$
$\frac{100}{4\pi} = \frac{4\pi r}{4\pi}$
$r = 8.0$

c) $V = 95$, calculate r

$V = \frac{4}{3}\pi r^3$
$95 = \frac{4}{3}\pi r^3$
$\frac{3 \times 95}{4\pi} = \frac{4\pi r^3}{4\pi}$
$r = \sqrt[3]{\frac{3 \times 95}{4\pi}}$
$r = 2.8$

Class Ex. #8

a) If $S = \frac{\pi r}{4}$, solve for r and calculate the value of r when $S = 75$.

$\frac{4S}{\pi} = \frac{\pi r}{\pi}$
$r = \frac{4S}{\pi}$
$r = \frac{4(75)}{\pi} = 95.5$

b) If $A = \pi r^2$, solve for r and calculate the value of r when $A = 72$.

$\frac{A}{\pi} = \frac{\pi r^2}{\pi}$
$r^2 = \frac{A}{\pi}$
$r = \sqrt{\frac{A}{\pi}}$
$r = \sqrt{\frac{72}{\pi}} = 4.8$

c) If $V = \frac{1}{3}\pi r^2 h$, solve for h and calculate the value of h when $V = 20$ and $r = 9$.

$\frac{3V}{\pi r^2} = \frac{\pi r^2 h}{\pi r^2}$
$h = \frac{3V}{\pi r^2}$
$h = \frac{3(20)}{\pi (9)^2} = 0.2$

Measurement Lesson #1: Assignment Pages 118 to 122 Measurement Lesson #1

Assignment

1.

Round to the nearest Number	One	Ten	Hundred	Tenth	Hundredth	First Decimal Place	Second Decimal Place
1 389.5263	1390	1390	1400	1389.5	1389.53	1389.5	1389.53
$\frac{73}{7}$	10	10	✕	10.4	10.43	10.4	10.43
547.77	548	550	500	547.8	547.77	547.8	547.77
$\sqrt{3750}$	61	60	100	61.2	61.24	61.2	61.24

Written Response - 5 marks

1. • $\frac{4.00 \times 10^7}{1.65}$ = 24242424 = 24000000

   • $(1.25 \times 10^5)(6.80 \times 10^9)$ = 8.50×10^{14}

   • $\frac{3.30 \times 10^{23}}{9.11 \times 10^{-31}}$ = 3.62×10^{53}

   • $\frac{1.99 \times 10^{30}}{(5.98 \times 10^{24} + 3.30 \times 10^{23})}$ = 315372 = 315000

Measurement Lesson #1:
Review and Preview

114 Measurement Lesson #1: *Review and Preview*

Class Ex. #1 Complete the following table.

Round to the nearest Number	One	Ten	Hundred	Tenth	Hundredth	First Decimal Place	Second Decimal Place
538.5968	539	540	500	538.6	538.60	538.6	538.60
10 964.893	10965	10960	11000	10964.9	10964.89	10964.9	10964.89

Class Ex. #2
a) 10.622   b) 15.38
c) 22.2   d) 9.13

Class Ex. #3
a) 7.5×10^7
b) 3.9×10^{-5}

116 Measurement Lesson #1: *Review and Preview*

Class Ex. #4
a) 2.2×10^{-3}
b) 1.7×10^8
c) 2.7×10^3

Class Ex. #5

a) $y^2 - 7x - 3$
$= (-3)^2 - 7(2) - 3$
$= 9 - 14 - 3$
$= -8$

b) $9x^2 - y + y^3$
$= 9(2)^2 - (-3) + (-3)^3$
$= 9(4) + 3 + (-27)$
$= 36 + 3 - 27$
$= 12$

2.

Number (Round to the nearest)	Tenth	Ten	Hundredth	Three Decimal Places	Integer	One Decimal Place
75.5825	75.6	80	75.58	75.583	76	75.6
$83\frac{2}{3}$	83.7	80	83.67	83.667	84	83.7
-252.7839	-252.8	-250	-252.78	-252.784	-253	-252.8
$\sqrt{8563}$	92.5	90	92.54	92.536	93	92.5
25	25.0	30	25.00	25.000	25	25.0

3. a) 2.4×10^3 b) 6.8×10^8 c) 7.8×10^{-5}
  d) 9.0×10^{-2} e) 1.0×10^1 f) 4.3×10^{-3}

4. a) 3.87×10^{-3} b) 5.69×10^7 c) 1.23×10^{11}

5. a) 3.80×10^{10} b) 6.93×10^{13} c) 1.96×10^3
  d) 4.34×10^{-3} e) 2.65×10^5 f) 5.12×10^{-5}

6. a) 108.2×1000000
    $= 1.1 \times 10^8$ km
  b) 2.875×1000000000
    $= 2.9 \times 10^9$ km

7. a) 779 million   b) 150 million

8. a) 157 400   b) 5 800

9. a) $c - b$
    $= 2 - (-3)$
    $= 2 + 3$
    $= 5$
  b) $2c - 5b$
    $= 2(2) - 5(-3)$
    $= 4 + 15$
    $= 19$
  c) $c^4 b^2$
    $= (2)^4(-3)^2$
    $= (16)(9)$
    $= 144$
  d) $2c^3 + 20$
    $= 2(2)^3 + 20$
    $= 2(8) + 20$
    $= 16 + 20$
    $= 36$
  e) $\frac{1}{2} c^2 b^3$
    $= \frac{1}{2}(2)^2(-3)^3$
    $= \frac{1}{2}(4)(-27)$
    $= -54$
  f) $\sqrt{2cb^2}$
    $= \sqrt{2(2)(-3)^2}$
    $= \sqrt{36}$
    $= 6$

10. a) 9   b) 41   c) -2000   d) -700   e) -39.2 or $-\frac{196}{5}$ f) 100

11.
a) $h = 15$, calculate b
  $75 = bh$
  $\frac{75}{15} = \frac{b(15)}{15}$
  $b = 5$

b) $C = 175$, calculate r
  $C = 2\pi r$
  $\frac{175}{2\pi} = \frac{2\pi r}{2\pi}$
  $r = 27.9$

c) $A = 60$ and $b = 7$, calculate h
  $A = \frac{bh}{2}$
  $60 = \frac{(7)h}{2}$
  $\frac{120}{7} = \frac{7h}{7}$
  $h = 17.1$

d) $V = 512$, calculate s
  $V = s^3$
  $512 = s^3$
  $\sqrt[3]{512} = s$
  $s = 8$

e) $V = 270$, and $h = 3$, calculate r
  $V = \frac{1}{3}\pi r^2 h$
  $270 = \frac{1}{3}\pi r^2(3)$
  $\frac{810}{3\pi} = \frac{3\pi r^2}{3\pi}$
  $r^2 = \frac{270}{\pi}$ $r = \sqrt{\frac{270}{\pi}}$
  $r = 9.3$

f) $r = 6.5$, calculate A
  $A = \pi r^2$
  $A = \pi(6.5)^2$
  $A = 132.7$

12.
a) $S = \sqrt{A}$
  $S = \sqrt{441}$
  $S = 21$

b) $b = \frac{V}{\ell h}$
  $b = \frac{75}{(10)(6)}$
  $b = 1.3$

c) $\frac{S}{2\pi} = \frac{2\pi r^2}{2\pi}$
  $r^2 = \frac{S}{2\pi}$ $r = \sqrt{\frac{S}{2\pi}}$

d) $\frac{3V}{\pi r^2} = \frac{\pi r^2 h}{\pi r^2}$
  $h = \frac{3V}{\pi r^2}$
  $h = \frac{3(20)}{\pi(9)^2}$
  $h = 0.2$

e) $\frac{3V}{4\pi} = \frac{4\pi r^3}{4\pi}$
  $r^3 = \frac{3V}{4\pi}$ $r = \sqrt[3]{\frac{3V}{4\pi}}$
  $r = \sqrt[3]{\frac{3(512)}{4\pi}} = 5.0$

13.
i) $25.745 + 4.051 = 6.3552\ldots$ ✗
ii) $\frac{2.985 \times 10^{-4}}{4.702 \times 10^{-3}} = 6.3500\ldots$ ✓
iii) $(2.501 \times 10^{-6})(2.539 \times 10^6)$
    0.06348 ✗

A. i) only
B. ii) only
C. iii) only ⟵ (circled)
D. i), ii) and iii)

14.
  $\frac{S - 2\pi r^2}{2\pi r} = \frac{2\pi r h}{2\pi r}$
  $h = \frac{S - 2\pi r^2}{2\pi r} = \frac{1435 - 2\pi(4.87)^2}{2\pi(4.87)} = 42.026\ldots$
  $= \boxed{42.0}$

Measurement Lesson #2:
Referents in Measurement

Class Ex. #1
a) pace
b) thumb
c) hand or span

Class Ex. #2 Calculate the sum of the measurements of the sides of the house in paces.

125 Measurement Lesson #2: Referents in Measurements

Class Ex. #3
a) Identify a referent which could be used to measure the length in SI units.
   the width of a fingernail – pinky finger
b) Identify a referent which could be used to measure the length in imperial units.
   the width of a thumb across the joint
c) Explain the process of measuring the length in imperial units.

Place one thumb at the left edge of the paper. Place the other thumb to the right of the first thumb so that the joints are touching.

Remove the first thumb and place it to the right of the second thumb so that the joints are touching. Continue the process until the right edge of the paper is reached.

The number of "thumbs" used is an estimate of the length in inches.

126 Measurement Lesson #2: Referents in Measurement

Class Ex. #4
Take a piece of string and wrap it around the circumference of the DVD. Cut or mark the piece of string so that the length of the string is equal to the circumference. Straighten out the string and estimate the length using the width of a pinky fingernail as equivalent to 1cm.

Class Ex. #5
a) SI units   imperial units.
   7.6cm   3in
b) $7.6 \times 2 = 15.2$cm $3 \times 2 = 6$in
c) It could be used as a referent for $\frac{1}{2}$ ft in the imperial system.

Class Ex. #6
A football field is about 100 m so ten football fields end to end could be used as a referent for 1 kilometre.

Assignment

1. Answers may vary
   a) adult foot or cubit   b) adult foot or cubit   c) thumb

2. a) Ask one player to measure the distances by using his/her foot (heel to toe). If you still cannot determine which is closer, use a smaller measurement like the width of your hand.
   b) Ask one player to measure the distances by using the width of finger(s) or thumb(s)

3. i) E   ii) I   iii) F   iv) B   v) K   vi) H
   vii) G   viii) D   ix) C   x) A   xi) J

4. Use the width of your pinky fingernail as a personal referent for 1 cm. The length is approximately 19 cm.

5. Answers may vary
   a) width of pencil lead   b) diameter of a pen   c) distance from the floor to your navel
   d) width of the face of a watch   e) distance from your elbow to your wrist
   f) half the distance between the tips of your fingers when your arms are outstretched.

6. Wrap a piece of string around the circumference of the ball, then straighten out the string and measure it using the width of your thumb across the joint as a referent for one inch.

7. The blocks are of equal length.

8. C   9. D   10. C   11. A

12. C   13. A   14. D   15. $\frac{1000}{25} = 40$ $\boxed{40}$

Measurement Lesson #3:
Measuring Devices

133   Measurement Lesson #3: *Measuring Devices*

Class Ex. #1
a) $1.5 + 0.49$ b) $9.5 + 0.09$
= 1.99 mm   = 9.59 mm

136   Measurement Lesson #3: *Measuring Devices*

Class Ex. #2
a) $8.6 + 0.02 = 8.62$ cm
$3\frac{6}{16} + \frac{7}{128} = 3\frac{55}{128}$ in

b) $60 + 0.45 = 60.45$ mm
$2\frac{6}{16} + \frac{1}{128} = 2\frac{49}{128}$ in

Measurement Lesson #4: Conversion Within the SI System (continued)

Class Ex. #3

a) 12 km to mm

12×10^6

$= 1.2 \times 10^7$ mm

b) 580 μg to grams

580×10^{-6}

$= 5.8 \times 10^{-4}$ g

c) 15 700 cL to ML

15700×10^{-8}

$= 1.57 \times 10^{-4}$ ML

Measurement Lesson #4: Conversion Within the SI System

Class Ex. #4

Alice

$x = 3$ m

Jim

$\dfrac{(1\ m)(300\ cm)}{100\ cm} = x$

$x = 3$ m

Rema

$x = 3$ m

$300\ cm = 3$ m

m	cm
1	100
x	300

$\dfrac{1}{x} = \dfrac{100}{300}$

$300 = 100x$

$x = 3$

OR

	m	cm
	1	100
	x	300

$\dfrac{1}{100} = \dfrac{x}{300}$

$300\ cm = 3\ m$

- An alternative approach is to leave the units as headings, and to carry out the cross product as shown below.

Notice that in each case x is measured in metres.

Measurement Lesson #4: Conversion Within the SI System

Class Ex. #5

Scale (cm)	actual (m)
3.5	0.6
x	

$\dfrac{1}{3.5} = \dfrac{0.6}{x}$

$x = (3.6)(0.6) = 2.1$

actual length = 2.1 m

Class Ex. #6

beans (mL)	rice (mL)
175	650
70	x

$\dfrac{175}{70} = \dfrac{650}{x}$

$175x = (70)(650)$

$x = \dfrac{(70)(650)}{175} = 260$

She should add 260 mL of rice.

Measurement Lesson #4: Conversion Within the SI System

Class Ex. #7

a) 12 kilometres = _12000_ m

$12\ km \times \dfrac{1000\ m}{1\ km}$

$= 12000$ m

b) 2730 nanometres = 0.00000273 m

$2730\ nm \times \dfrac{1\ m}{10^9\ nm}$

$= 2.73 \times 10^{-6}$ or 0.00000273

Assignment

Measurement Lesson #3: Assignment Pages **127 to 140** Measurement Lesson #3

1. Determine the micrometer readings in metric units.

a) $17 + 0.15 = 11.91$ mm   b) $11.5 + 0.41 = 11.91$ mm

c) $6 + 0.00 = 6.00$ mm   d) $5.5 + 0.00 = 5.50$ mm

e) $12 + 0.01 = 12.01$ mm   f) $11 + 0.49 = 11.49$ mm

g) $12.5 + 0.35 = 12.85$ mm   h) $1 + 0.23 = 1.23$ mm

2. Answers may vary slightly.

a) 9.77 mm $3\frac{105}{128}$ in.   b) 5.05 cm $1\frac{63}{64}$ in.   c) 6.15 cm $2\frac{53}{128}$ in.   d) 11.21 cm $4\frac{53}{128}$ in.

3. Answers may vary slightly.

a) 41.65 mm $1\frac{41}{64}$ in.   b) 60.55 mm $2\frac{25}{64}$ in.   c) 13.30 mm $\frac{67}{128}$ in.   d) 62.05 mm $2\frac{57}{128}$ in.

4. Answers may vary depending on the accuracy of the measuring instrument.

5. Answers may vary depending on the accuracy of the measuring instrument.

6. a) tape measure   b) ruler   c) micrometer   d) tape measure   e) trundle wheel

7. B   8. A   9. D   10. C

Measurement Lesson #4:
Conversion Within the SI System

Conversion of Units Within the International System of Units (SI)

1 gigametre (Gm) = 1 000 000 000 m   1 centimetre (cm) = 0.01 m

1 megametre (Mm) = 1 000 000 m   1 millimetre (mm) = 0.001 m

1 kilometre (km) = 1 000 m   1 micrometre (μm) = 0.000 001 m

   1 nanometre (nm) = 0.000 000 001 m

1 litre (L) = 1 000 millilitres (mL)   1 millilitre (mL) = 0.001 L

1 gram (g) = 1 000 milligrams (mg)   1 milligram (mg) = 0.001 g

1 kilogram (kg) = 1 000 grams (g)   1 gram (g) = 0.001 kg

Measurement Lesson #4: Conversion Within the SI System

Class Ex. #1

a) 1 m = 10^2 cm

1 m = 100 cm

b) 1 mm = 10^{-3} m

1 mm = 0.001 m

c) 1 L = 10^3 mL

1 L = 1000 mL

Class Ex. #2

a) 7.5×10^2

$= 750$ cm

b) 72350×10^{-6}

$= 0.07235$ kg

c) 325×10^3

$= 325\,000$ nm

Note

Complete the unit analysis calculation started below.

$$\frac{2.4\ \text{km}}{1} \times \frac{1000\ \text{m}}{1\ \text{km}} \times \frac{1000\ \text{mm}}{1\ \text{m}} = 2\,400\,000\ \text{mm}$$

$$\frac{0.25\ \text{Gm}}{1} \times \frac{10^9\ \text{m}}{1\ \text{Gm}} \times \frac{1\ \text{Mm}}{10^6\ \text{m}} = \underline{250\ \text{Mm}}$$

Class Ex. #8

a) What conversions will Zimmer need to know to solve this problem?

The number of metres in one kilometre.

The number of seconds in one minute.

b) Complete Zimmer's work below to solve the problem. Show the cancellation in units.

$$\frac{50\ \text{m}}{s} \times \frac{1\ \text{km}}{1000\ \text{m}} \times \frac{60\ s}{1\ \text{min}} = \frac{3000}{1000} = \underline{3\ \text{km/min}}$$

Class Ex. #9

Assignment

1. a) 6780 cm = __67.8__ m
   6780 ×10⁻²

   b) 0.91 km = __910__ m
   0.91×10³

   c) 14 km = __1 400 000__ cm
   14 ×10⁵

   d) 87 mm = __8.7__ cm
   87×10⁻¹

   e) 65.23 m = __6523__ cm
   65.23×10²

   f) 0.04 mm = __0.000 04__ m
   0.04×10⁻³

   g) 0.88 m = __0.000 88__ km
   0.88 ×10⁻³

   h) 27.39 cm = __273.9__ mm
   27.39 ×10¹

   i) 0.736 μm = __0.000 736__ mm
   0.736 ×10⁻³

   j) 29 Gm = __29 000 000__ km
   29×10⁶

   k) 5830 nm = __5.83__ μm
   5830×10⁻³

   l) 2.17 Mm = __0.00 217__ Gm
   2.17×10⁻³

2. a) 52 kL = __52 000__ L
   52×10³

   b) 891 ml = __0.891__ L
   891×10⁻³

   c) 85.2 L = __8520__ cL
   85.2 ×10²

   d) 27 mg = __2.7__ cg
   27×10⁻¹

   e) 0.9875 kg = __987.5__ g
   0.9875×10³

   f) 4257 g = __4.257__ kg
   4257×10⁻³

   g) 89 gigajoules = __89 000__ megajoules
   89×10³

   h) 67 230 nm = __0.006 723__ cm
   67230 ×10⁻⁷

---

3. $82 \times 10^{-1} = $ __8.2__ Bels

4. a) 15 km = __15000__ m

km	m
1	1000
15	x

$\frac{1}{15} = \frac{1000}{x}$

$x = 15(1000)$

$x = 15000$

   b) 28500 cm = __285__ m

cm	m
100	1
28500	x

$\frac{100}{28500} = \frac{1}{x}$

$100x = 28500$

$x = 285$

   c) 0.35 mm = __0.035__ cm

mm	cm
10	1
0.35	x

$\frac{10}{0.35} = \frac{1}{x}$

$10x = 0.35$

$x = 0.035$

   d) 112 cm = __1120__ mm

cm	mm
1	10
112	x

$\frac{1}{112} = \frac{10}{x}$

$x = 10(112) = 1120$

   e) 857.8 m = __85780__ cm

m	cm
1	100
857.8	x

$\frac{1}{857.8} = \frac{100}{x}$

$x = (857.8)(100)$

$= 85780$

   f) 0.03 mm = __0.00003__ m

mm	m
1000	1
0.03	x

$\frac{1000}{0.03} = \frac{1}{x}$

$1000x = 0.03$

$x = 0.00003$

   g) 5 200 m = __5.2__ km

m	km
1000	1
5200	x

$\frac{1000}{5200} = \frac{1}{x}$

$1000 x = 5200$

$x = 5.2$

   h) 0.014 megawatts = __14000__ watts

MW	W
1	10⁶
0.014	x

$\frac{1}{0.014} = \frac{10^6}{x}$

$x = 0.014 \times 10^6$

$= 14000$

   i) 59 000 μm = __0.059__ m

μm	m
10⁶	1
59000	x

$\frac{10^6}{59000} = \frac{1}{x}$

$10^6 \cdot x = 59000$

$x = 0.059$

   j) 6.7GHz = __6 700 000 000__ Hz
   (gigahertz)

GHz	Hz
1	10⁹
6.7	x

$\frac{1}{6.7} = \frac{10^9}{x}$

$x = 6.7 \times 10^9$

$x = 6700000000$

   k) 29 080 nm = __0.002 908__ cm

nm	cm
10⁷	1
29080	x

$\frac{10^7}{29080} = \frac{1}{x}$

$10^7 \cdot x = 29080$

$x = 0.002908$

   l) 5.15 Mm = __0.00515__ Gm

Mm	Gm
1000	1
5.15	x

$\frac{1000}{5.15} = \frac{1}{x}$

$1000x = 5.15$

$x = 0.00515$

5.

map (cm)	actual (km)
4	62
x	217

$\frac{4}{x} = \frac{62}{217}$

$(4)(217) = 62x$

$\frac{(4)(217)}{62} = 14$

$x = \frac{(4)(217)}{62} = 14$

$\underline{\text{distance} = 14\ \text{km}}$

Multiple Choice 10. (C.) $1\ Mg = 1000\ Gg$ $1\ Gg = 1000\ Mg$

Matching Match each question number on the left with the equivalent letter on the right.

E	11. 9000 millimetres	9	A.	9 million kilometres
D	12. 0.9 cm	9×10^{-3}	B.	9 micrometres
A	13. 9 Gm	9×10^{9}	C.	9×10^{5} metres
B	14. 9000 nm	9×10^{-6}	D.	9000 micrometres
C	15. 0.9 Mm	9×10^{5}	E.	9 metres

Convert all measurements to metres

Numerical Response 16. $\dfrac{1.4\ m}{1} \times \dfrac{100\,cm}{1\ m} = 140\ cm$

$\boxed{1\ 4\ 0}$

Measurement Lesson #5:
Conversion Within and Between the SI and Imperial Systems

Convert the following:

a) 6 ft 7 in to inches
$(6\times12)+7 = 79$ in

b) 5 yds 2 ft to feet
$(5\times3)+2 = 17$ ft

c) 1 mi 255 yds to yards
$(1\times1760)+255 = 2015$ yds

d) 51 in to feet and inches
$\dfrac{51}{12} = 4\tfrac{3}{12} = 4$ ft 3 in

e) 73 ft to yards and feet
$\dfrac{73}{3} = 24\tfrac{1}{3} = 24$ yds 1 ft

f) 4215 yds to miles and yards
$\dfrac{4215}{1760} = 2\tfrac{695}{1760} = 2$ mi 695 yds

Convert 0.4 miles to inches by the following methods:

Proportional Reasoning | Unit Analysis

miles	feet
1	5280
0.4	x

$\dfrac{1}{5280} = \dfrac{0.4}{x}$ $x = (0.4)(5280) = 2112\ ft$

feet	inches
1	12
2112	y

$\dfrac{1}{12} = \dfrac{2112}{y}$ $y = 12(2112) = 25344\ in$

Unit Analysis:
$\dfrac{0.4\ mi}{1} \times \dfrac{5280\,ft}{1\ mi} \times \dfrac{12\,in}{1\ ft} = 25344\ in$

0.4 miles $= 25344$ inches

6.

C$	euros
900	1400
720	x

$\dfrac{900}{720} = \dfrac{1400}{x}$

$900x = (720)(1400)$

$x = \dfrac{(720)(1400)}{900}$

$x = 1120$

Josh should receive 1200 euros

7. a) 3.7 km = **3700** m
$\dfrac{3.7\ km}{1} \times \dfrac{1000\,m}{1\ km} = 3700\ m$

b) 77 500 cm = **775 000** mm
$\dfrac{77500\ cm}{1} \times \dfrac{10\,mm}{1\ cm} = 775000\ mm$

c) 920 mL = **0.92** L
$\dfrac{920\ mL}{1} \times \dfrac{1\,L}{1000\,mL} = 0.92\ L$

d) 33.1 m = **33100** mm
$\dfrac{33.1\ m}{1} \times \dfrac{1000\,mm}{1\ m} = 33100\ mm$

8. a) 29 km = **2 900 000** cm
$\dfrac{29\ km}{1} \times \dfrac{1000\,m}{1\ km} \times \dfrac{100\,cm}{1\ m} = 2900000\ cm$

b) 34 200 mm = **0.0342** km
$\dfrac{34200\ mm}{1} \times \dfrac{1\,m}{1000\,mm} \times \dfrac{1\,km}{1000\,m} = 0.0342\ km$

c) 950 mm = **950 000** μm
$\dfrac{950\ mm}{1} \times \dfrac{1\,m}{1000\,mm} \times \dfrac{10^{6}\,\mu m}{1\ m} = 950000\ \mu m$

d) 162.8 Mm = **0.1628** Gm
$\dfrac{162.8\ Mm}{1} \times \dfrac{10^{6}\,m}{1\ Mm} \times \dfrac{1\,Gm}{10^{9}\,m} = 0.1628\ Gm$

9. a) 240 m/s = **14.4** km/min
$\dfrac{240\ m}{1\ s} \times \dfrac{1\,km}{1000\,m} \times \dfrac{60\,s}{1\,min} = 14.4\ km/min$

b) 8.4 m/s = **30.24** km/h
$\dfrac{8.4\ m}{1\ s} \times \dfrac{1\,km}{1000\,m} \times \dfrac{60\,s}{1\,min} \times \dfrac{60\,min}{1\ h} = 30.24\ km/h$

c) 120 m/h = **2000** mm/min
$\dfrac{120\ m}{1\ h} \times \dfrac{1000\,mm}{1\ m} \times \dfrac{1\,h}{60\,min} = 2000\ mm/min$

d) 2 m/min = **0.12** km/h
$\dfrac{2\ m}{1\ min} \times \dfrac{1\,km}{1000\,m} \times \dfrac{60\,min}{1\ h} = 0.12\ km/h$

e) 72 km/h = **20** m/sec
$\dfrac{72\ km}{1\ h} \times \dfrac{1000\,m}{1\ km} \times \dfrac{1\,h}{60\,min} \times \dfrac{1\,min}{60\,sec} = 20\ m/sec$

f) 35 mm/s = **0.126** km/h
$\dfrac{35\ mm}{1\ s} \times \dfrac{1\,m}{1000\,mm} \times \dfrac{1\,km}{1000\,m} \times \dfrac{60\,s}{1\,min} \times \dfrac{60\,min}{1\ h} = 0.126\ km/h$

Class Ex. #3

Step 1
$$\frac{2.54 \text{ cm}}{1 \text{ in}} \cdot \frac{12 \text{ in}}{1 \text{ ft}} \cdot \frac{1 \text{ m}}{100 \text{ cm}}$$

Step 2
$$= \frac{2.54 \text{ cm}}{1 \text{ in}} \cdot \frac{12 \text{ in}}{1 \text{ ft}} \cdot \frac{1 \text{ m}}{100 \text{ cm}} = 0.3048 \text{ m/ft}$$

$$\underline{1 \text{ foot} = 0.3048 \text{ metres}}$$

Class Ex. #4

a) 5 ft 10 in = $\underline{1.778}$ m (to three decimal places).

= (5×12)+10 = 70 in

$$\frac{70 \text{ in}}{1} \times \frac{2.54 \text{ cm}}{1 \text{ in}} \times \frac{1 \text{ m}}{100 \text{ cm}} = 1.778 \text{ m}$$

b) 2.0573 m = $\underline{6}$ ft $\underline{9}$ in (to the nearest inch).

$$\frac{2.0573 \text{ m}}{1} \times \frac{100 \text{ cm}}{1 \text{ m}} \times \frac{1 \text{ in}}{2.54 \text{ cm}} = 81 \text{ in}$$

$$\frac{75}{12} = 6\frac{3}{12} = 6 \text{ ft } 3 \text{ in} \qquad \frac{81}{12} = 6\frac{9}{12} = 6 \text{ ft } 9 \text{ in}$$

Class Ex. #5

$$\frac{2183 \text{ m}}{1} \times \frac{1 \text{ ft}}{0.3048 \text{ m}}$$
$$= 7162.07... \text{ ft}$$

$$\frac{7162.07...}{1500} = 4.77...$$

$$\underline{5 \text{ DVD's needed}}$$

Assignment

1. a) 3 ft 11 in to inches
   (3×12)+11 = 47 in

   b) 7 yds 1 ft to feet
   (7×3)+1 = 22 ft

   c) 2 mi 325 yds to yards
   (2×1760)+325 = 3845 yds

   d) 75 in to feet and inches
   $$\frac{75}{12} = 6\frac{3}{12} = 6 \text{ ft } 3 \text{ in}$$

   e) 82 ft to yards and feet
   $$\frac{82}{3} = 27\frac{1}{3} = 27 \text{ yds } 1 \text{ ft}$$

   f) 18 480 feet to miles and feet
   $$\frac{18480}{5280} = 3\frac{2640}{5280} = 3 \text{ mi } 2640 \text{ ft}$$

   g) 4 yds 2 ft 6 in to inches
   $$[(4×3)+2]×12 + 6$$
   = 174 in

   h) 100 in to yards, feet and inches
   $$\frac{100}{12} = 8\frac{4}{12} = 8 \text{ ft } 4 \text{ in}$$
   $$\frac{8}{3} = 2\frac{2}{3} = 2 \text{ yds } 2 \text{ ft}$$
   100 in = 2 yds 2 ft 4 in

2. a) 2.3 mi to in
   $$\frac{2.3 \text{ mi}}{1} \times \frac{5280 \text{ ft}}{1 \text{ mi}} \times \frac{12 \text{ in}}{1 \text{ ft}}$$
   = 145 728 in

   b) 200 000 in. to mi (to the nearest hundredth of a mile)
   $$\frac{200000 \text{ in}}{1} \times \frac{1 \text{ ft}}{12 \text{ in}} \times \frac{1 \text{ mi}}{5280 \text{ ft}}$$
   = 3.16 mi

3. a) yards
   (26×1760)+385
   = 46145 yds

   b) feet
   46145 × 3
   = 138435 ft

   c) inches
   138435 × 12
   = 1661220 in

4. a) 1 yd = $\underline{0.9144}$ m
   $$\frac{1 \text{ yd}}{1} \times \frac{3 \text{ ft}}{1 \text{ yd}} \times \frac{0.3048 \text{ m}}{1 \text{ ft}} = 0.9144 \text{ m}$$

   b) 1 mi = 1.6093 km
   $$\frac{1 \text{ mi}}{1} \times \frac{5280 \text{ ft}}{1 \text{ mi}} \times \frac{0.3048 \text{ m}}{1 \text{ ft}} \times \frac{1 \text{ km}}{1000 \text{ m}} = 1.6093 \text{ km}$$

   c) 1 m = $\underline{3.2808}$ ft
   $$\frac{1 \text{ m}}{1} \times \frac{1 \text{ ft}}{0.3048 \text{ m}} = 3.2808 \text{ ft}$$

   d) 1 m = 1.0936 yds
   $$\frac{1 \text{ m}}{1} \times \frac{1 \text{ ft}}{0.3048 \text{ m}} \times \frac{1 \text{ yd}}{3 \text{ ft}} = 1.0936 \text{ yds}$$

   e) 1 km = $\underline{0.6214}$ mile
   $$\frac{1 \text{ km}}{1} \times \frac{1000 \text{ m}}{1 \text{ km}} \times \frac{1 \text{ ft}}{0.3048 \text{ m}} \times \frac{1 \text{ mi}}{5280 \text{ ft}} = 0.6214 \text{ mi}$$

5. a) 17 ft 4 in = $\underline{5.28}$ m (two decimal places)
   (17×12)+4
   = 208 in

   $$\frac{208 \text{ in}}{1} \times \frac{2.54 \text{ cm}}{1 \text{ in}} \times \frac{1 \text{ m}}{100 \text{ cm}}$$

   b) 4.25 m = $\underline{13}$ ft $\underline{11}$ in (nearest inch)
   $$\frac{4.25 \text{ m}}{1} \times \frac{100 \text{ cm}}{1 \text{ m}} \times \frac{1 \text{ in}}{2.54 \text{ cm}} = 167 \text{ in}$$
   167÷12 = 13 ft 11 in

6. a) (3×12)+3 = 39 in
   $$\frac{39 \text{ in}}{1} \times \frac{2.54 \text{ cm}}{1 \text{ in}} \times \frac{1 \text{ m}}{100 \text{ cm}} = 0.99 \text{ m}$$

   b) (5×12)+7 = 67 in
   $$\frac{67 \text{ in}}{1} \times \frac{2.54 \text{ cm}}{1 \text{ in}} \times \frac{1 \text{ m}}{100 \text{ cm}} = 1.70 \text{ m}$$

   c) (6×12)+3 = 75 in
   $$\frac{75 \text{ in}}{1} \times \frac{2.54 \text{ cm}}{1 \text{ in}} \times \frac{1 \text{ m}}{100 \text{ cm}} = 1.91 \text{ m}$$

7. a) $$\frac{1.67 \text{ m}}{1} \times \frac{100 \text{ cm}}{1 \text{ m}} \times \frac{1 \text{ in}}{2.54 \text{ cm}} = 66 \text{ in} = 5 \text{ ft } 6 \text{ in}$$

   b) $$\frac{2.28 \text{ m}}{1} \times \frac{100 \text{ cm}}{1 \text{ m}} \times \frac{1 \text{ in}}{2.54 \text{ cm}} = 90 \text{ in} = 7 \text{ ft } 6 \text{ in}$$

   c) $$\frac{1.80 \text{ m}}{1} \times \frac{100 \text{ cm}}{1 \text{ m}} \times \frac{1 \text{ in}}{2.54 \text{ cm}} = 71 \text{ in} = 5 \text{ ft } 11 \text{ in}$$

$$\frac{71 \text{ lbs}}{1} \times \frac{1 \text{ kg}}{2.2 \text{ lbs}} = \underline{32 \text{ kg}}$$
$$\frac{118 \text{ lbs}}{1} \times \frac{1 \text{ kg}}{2.2 \text{ lbs}} = \underline{53 \text{ kg}}$$
$$\frac{195 \text{ lbs}}{1} \times \frac{1 \text{ kg}}{2.2 \text{ lbs}} = \underline{89 \text{ kg}}$$

$$\frac{58.1 \text{ kg}}{1} \times \frac{2.2 \text{ lbs}}{1 \text{ kg}} = \underline{128 \text{ lbs}}$$
$$\frac{170 \text{ kg}}{1} \times \frac{2.2 \text{ lbs}}{1 \text{ kg}} = \underline{374 \text{ lbs}}$$
$$\frac{91 \text{ kg}}{1} \times \frac{2.2 \text{ lbs}}{1 \text{ kg}} = \underline{200 \text{ lbs}}$$

8. $$\frac{1 \text{ mi}}{1} \times \frac{1.6093 \text{ km}}{1 \text{ mi}} \times \frac{1000 \text{ m}}{1 \text{ km}} = 1609.3 \text{ m}$$

   1609.3 - 1500 = 109.3 m

   $$\underline{1 \text{ mile is longer by } 109 \text{ m}}$$

   $$\frac{109.3 \text{ m}}{1} \times \frac{1.0936 \text{ yds}}{1 \text{ m}} = 119.53... \text{ yds}$$

   $$\underline{1 \text{ mile is longer by } 120 \text{ yds}}$$

Measurement Lesson #6:

Conversion in the SI and Imperial Systems: Square Units & Cubic Units

Conversion in the SI and Imperial Systems: Square Units & Cubic Units

| Investigation #1 | Conversions between Units of Area in the Metric System |

a) Calculate the area of the square in m^2.

$$area = 1 \ m^2$$

1 m × 1 m

b) Convert the sides of the square in a) to cm and mm and write them below.
- Calculate the area in cm^2 and mm^2.

100 cm, 1000 mm

$area = 10000 \ cm^2$

$area = 1000000 \ mm^2$

c) From a) and b) we can determine that $1 m^2 = 10000 \ cm^2$ and $1 m^2 = 1000000 \ mm^2$.

d) Calculate the area of the rectangle in m^2.

4 m × 2 m

$A = 8 \ m^2$

e) Convert the sides of the rectangle in d) to cm and mm and write them below.
- Calculate the area in cm^2 and mm^2.

400 cm, 200 cm, 4000 mm, 2000 mm

$A = 80000 \ cm^2$

$A = 8 \ 000 \ 000 \ mm^2$

f) Use the ratios in c) to confirm the area of the rectangle in e) in cm^2 and mm^2.

$8(10000) : 80000 \ cm^2$

$8(1000000) = 8000000 \ mm^2$

g) Whereas length involves one dimension, area involves two dimensions. The area conversion between any two square units is the square of the length conversion between the linear units. e.g. to convert from km^2 to m^2 multiply by 1000×1000 or 1000^2.

Converting 2.5 km to m, we multiply by 10^3. On the metric unit number line we move 3 places to the right and hence move the decimal point 3 places to the right in the conversion. 2.5 km = 2500 m.

Converting $2.5 \ km^2$ to m^2, we multiply by $(10^3)^2 = 10^6$ and move the decimal point 6 places to the right and hence move the decimal point 6 places to the right. $2.5 \ km^2 = 2 \ 500 \ 000 \ m^2$

$3 \times 2 = 6$ places to the right.

G   M   k   h   da   Unit   d   c   m   μ   n

Class Ex. #1 Convert the following. Express the answers in standard and scientific notation.

a) $12 \ m^2$ to mm^2

$12 \times (10^3)^2 \ mm$

$= 12 \times 10^6 \ mm^2$

$= 12 \ 000 \ 000 \ mm^2$

$= 1.2 \times 10^7 \ mm^2$

b) $41 \ 500 \ cm^2$ to km^2

$41500 \times (10^{-5})^2 \ km^2$

$= 41500 \times 10^{-10} \ km^2$

$= 0.000 \ 00 \ 415 \ km^2$

$= 4.15 \times 10^{-6} \ km^2$

c) $389 \ 275 \ km^2$ to Mm^2

$389275 \times (10^{-3})^2 \ Mm^2$

$= 389275 \times 10^{-6} \ Mm^2$

$= 0.389275 \ Mm^2$

$= 3.89275 \times 10^{-1} \ Mm^2$

Measurement Lesson #5: Assignment Pages **153 to 156** Measurement Lesson #5

9. $\dfrac{\frac{1}{4} \ mi}{1} \times \dfrac{1.6093 \ km}{1 \ mi} \times \dfrac{1000 \ m}{1 \ km} = 402.325 \ m$

$402.325 - 400 = 2.325 \ m$

$\dfrac{2.325 \ m}{1} \times \dfrac{1 \ yd}{0.9144 \ m} = 2.54... \ yds$

Quarter mile is longer by 2m

Quarter mile is longer by 3 yds

10. $\dfrac{299 \ 792 \ 458}{1000}$

$= 300 \ 000 \ km/s$

11. $\dfrac{299 \ 792 \ 458 \ m}{1 \ s} \times \dfrac{1 \ km}{1000 \ m} \times \dfrac{0.6214 \ mi}{1 \ km}$

$= 186 \ 291 \ mi/s$ **A.** 186 000

12. $\dfrac{186 \ 000 \ mi}{1 \ sec} \times \dfrac{60 \ sec}{1 \ min} \times \dfrac{60 \ min}{1 \ hr} \times \dfrac{24 \ hr}{1 \ day} \times \dfrac{365\frac{1}{4} \ days}{1 \ year} \times \dfrac{100 \ 000 \ years}{1} = 5.9 \times 10^{17} \ mi$

D. 5.9×10^{17}

13. $3 \ yds = 3 \times 3 = 9 \ ft$

$9 \ ft \ and \ 7 \ in = (9 \times 12) + 7 = 115 \ in$ **B.** 115

14. $\dfrac{85 \ km}{1 \ h} \times \dfrac{1 \ mi}{1.6093 \ km} = 52.8... \ miles \ per \ hour$ | 5 | 3 |

15. $\dfrac{510 \ mi}{1 \ h} \times \dfrac{1.6093 \ km}{1 \ mi} = 820.7... \ kilometres \ per \ hour$ | 8 | 2 | 1 |

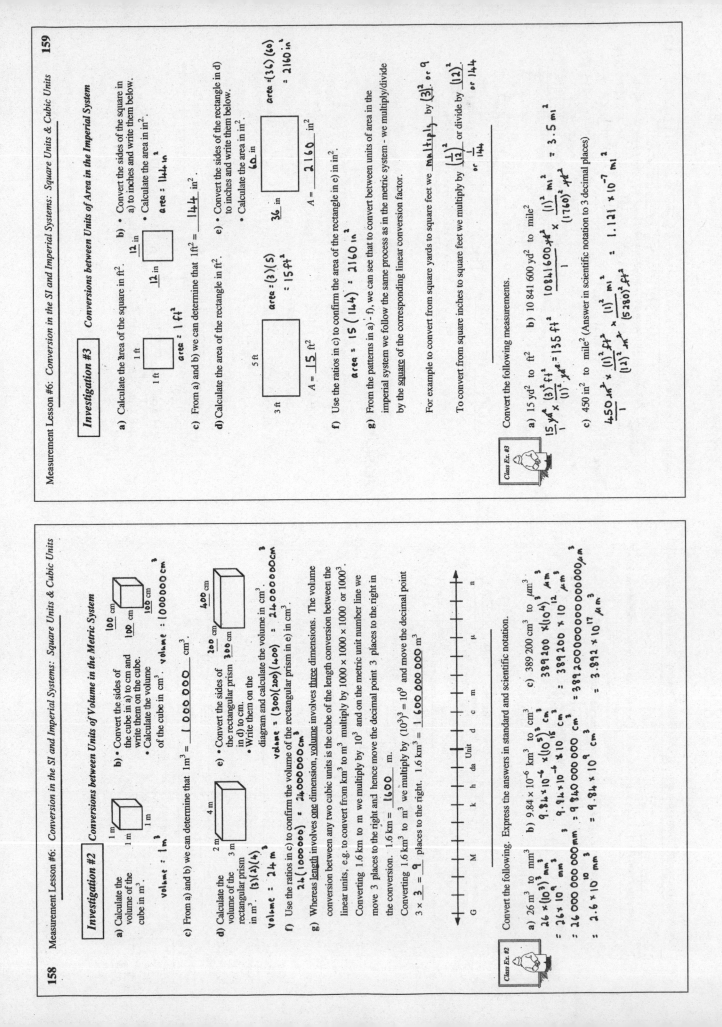

Investigation #3 — *Conversions between Units of Area in the Imperial System*

a) Calculate the area of the square in ft².

1 ft × 1 ft

area = 1 ft²

b) • Convert the sides of the square in a) to inches and write them below.
• Calculate the area in in².

12 in × 12 in

area = 144 in²

c) From a) and b) we can determine that 1ft² = **144** in².

d) Calculate the area of the rectangle in ft².

3 ft × 5 ft

area = (3)(5) = 15 ft²

A = **15** ft²

e) • Convert the sides of the rectangle in d) to inches and write them below.
• Calculate the area in in².

36 in × 60 in

area = (36)(60) = 2160 in²

A = **2160** in²

f) Use the ratios in c) to confirm the area of the rectangle in e) in in².

area = 15 (144) = 2160 ft²

g) From the patterns in a) - f), we can see that to convert between units of area in the imperial system we follow the same process as in the metric system - we multiply/divide by the square of the corresponding linear conversion factor.

For example to convert from square yards to square feet we **multiply** by (3)² or divide by (1/3)².

To convert from square inches to square feet we multiply by (1/12)² or divide by (12)²
or 1/144 or 144

Class Ex. #3 Convert the following measurements.

a) 15 yd² to ft²

15 yd²/1 × (3)²ft²/(1)² yd² = 135 ft²

b) 10 841 600 yd² to mile²

10841600 yd²/1 × (1)² mi²/(1760)² yd² = 3.5 mi²

c) 450 in² to mile² (Answer in scientific notation to 3 decimal places)

450 in²/1 × (1)² ft²/(12)² in² × (1)² mi²/(5280)² ft² = 1.121 × 10⁻⁷ mi²

Investigation #2 — *Conversions between Units of Volume in the Metric System*

a) Calculate the volume of the cube in m³.

1 m × 1 m × 1 m

volume = 1 m³

b) • Convert the sides of the cube in a) to cm and write them on the cube.
• Calculate the volume of the cube in cm³.

100 cm × 100 cm × 100 cm

volume = 1 000 000 cm³

c) From a) and b) we can determine that 1m³ = **1 000 000** cm³.

d) Calculate the volume of the rectangular prism in m³. (3)(2)(4)

2 m × 3 m × 4 m

volume = 24 m³

e) • Convert the sides of the rectangular prism in d) to cm.
• Write them on the diagram and calculate the volume in cm³.

200 cm × 300 cm × 400 cm

volume = (300)(200)(400) = 24 000 000 cm³

f) Use the ratios in c) to confirm the volume of the rectangular prism in e) in cm³.

24 (1 000 000) = 24 000 000 cm³

g) Whereas length involves one dimension, volume involves three dimensions. The volume conversion between any two cubic units is the cube of the length conversion between the linear units, e.g. to convert from km³ to m³ multiply by 1000 × 1000 × 1000 or 1000³.

Converting 1.6 km to m we multiply by 10³ and on the metric unit number line we move 3 places to the right and hence move the decimal point 3 places to the right in the conversion. 1.6 km = **1600** m.

Converting 1.6 km³ to m³ we multiply by (10³)³ = 10⁹ and move the decimal point 3 × 3 = **9** places to the right. 1.6 km³ = **1 600 000 000** m³

(metric unit number line)
G   M   k   h   da   Unit   d   c   m   μ   n

Class Ex. #2 Convert the following. Express the answers in standard and scientific notation.

a) 26 m³ to mm³

26 × (10³)³ mm³
= 26 × 10⁹ mm³
= 26 000 000 000 mm³
= 2.6 × 10¹⁰ mm³

b) 9.84 × 10⁻⁶ km³ to cm³

9.84 × 10⁻⁶ × ((10⁵)³ cm³
9.84 × 10⁻⁶ × 10¹⁵ cm³
= 9 840 000 000 cm³
= 9.84 × 10⁹ cm³

c) 389 200 cm³ to μm³

389 200 × (10⁴)³ μm³
= 389 200 × 10¹² μm³
= 389 200 000 000 000 000 μm³
= 3.892 × 10¹⁷ μm³

Investigation #4

Conversions between Units of Volume in the Imperial System

a) Calculate the volume of the cube in ft³.

[cube: 1 ft × 1 ft × 1 ft]

volume = 1 ft³

b) • Convert the sides of the cube in a) to inches and write them on the cube.

[cube: 12 in × 12 in × 12 in]

• Calculate the volume of the cube in in³.

volume = $(12)^3$ = 1728 in³

c) From a) and b) we can determine that 1 ft³ = __1728__ in³.

d) Calculate the volume of the rectangular prism in ft³.

[rectangular prism: 3 ft × 4 ft × 5 ft]

volume = $(4)(3)(5)$ = 60 ft³

e) • Convert the sides of the rectangular prism in d) to inches and write them on the diagram.

[rectangular prism: 36 in, 48 in, 60 in]

• Calculate the volume of the rectangular prism in in³.

volume = $(48)(36)(60)$ = 103680 in³

f) Use the ratios in c) to confirm the volume of the rectangular prism in e) in in³.

volume = $60(1728)$ = 103680 in³

g) From the patterns in a) - f), we can see that to convert between units of volume in the imperial system we follow the same process as in the metric system - we multiply/divide by the __cube__ of the corresponding linear conversion factor.

For example, to convert from cubic yards to cubic inches we __multiply__ by __$(36)^3$__.

To convert from cubic yards to cubic miles we divide by __$(1760)^3$__.

Convert the following measurements.

a) 233 280 in³ = __5__ yd³

$$\frac{233280 \text{ in}^3}{1} \times \frac{(1)^3 \text{ yd}^3}{(36)^3 \text{ in}^3}$$

b) 40.5 ft³ = __1.5__ yd³

$$\frac{40.5 \text{ ft}^3}{1} \times \frac{(1)^3 \text{ yd}^3}{(3)^3 \text{ ft}^3}$$

Class Ex. #5

Convert 5 cubic miles into cubic inches. Answer in scientific notation to two decimal places.

$$\frac{5 \text{ mi}^3}{1} \times \frac{(5280)^3 \text{ ft}^3}{(1)^3 \text{ mi}^3} \times \frac{(12)^3 \text{ in}^3}{(1)^3 \text{ ft}^3} = 1.27 \times 10^{15} \text{ in}^3$$

Class Ex. #6

a) determine, to the nearest cm³, which box has the greater volume and by how much.

box 1: $V = (0.8)(0.6)(0.6) = 0.288 \text{ m}^3$

$$\frac{0.288 \text{ m}^3}{1} \times \frac{(100)^3 \text{ cm}^3}{(1)^3 \text{ m}^3} = 288\,000 \text{ cm}^3$$

box 2: $V = (2.5)(2)(2) = 10 \text{ ft}^3$

$$\frac{10 \text{ ft}^3}{1} \times \frac{(12)^3 \text{ in}^3}{(1)^3 \text{ ft}^3} \times \frac{(2.54)^3 \text{ cm}^3}{(1)^3 \text{ in}^3} = 283168 \text{ cm}^3$$

$288000 - 283168 = 4832$ First box has greater volume by 4832 cm³

b) determine, to the nearest in², which box has the greater surface area and by how much.

box 1: $SA = 4(0.8 \times 0.6) + 2(0.6 \times 0.6) = 2.64 \text{ m}^2$

box 2: $SA = 4(2.5 \times 2) + 2(2 \times 2) = 28 \text{ ft}^2$

$$\frac{2.64 \text{ m}^2}{1} \times \frac{(1)^2 \text{ ft}^2}{(0.3048)^2 \text{ m}^2} \times \frac{(12)^2 \text{ in}^2}{(1)^2 \text{ ft}^2} = 4092 \text{ in}^2$$

$$\frac{28 \text{ ft}^2}{1} \times \frac{(12)^2 \text{ in}^2}{(1)^2 \text{ ft}^2} = 4032 \text{ in}^2$$

$4092 - 4032 = 60$

First box has greater surface area by 60 in²

Measurement Lesson #6: Assignment Pages 161 to 164 Measurement Lesson #6

Assignment

1. Convert the following to the indicated measurements.

a) 53 m² = __530 000__ cm²

$53 \times (10^2)^2 = 53 \times 10^4$

b) 1326 mm² = __13.26__ cm²

$1326 \times (10^{-1})^2 = 1326 \times 10^{-2}$

c) 890 000 mm² = __0.89__ m²

$890000 \times (10^{-3})^2 = 890000 \times 10^{-6}$

d) 0.611 km² = __611 000__ m²

$0.611 \times (10^3)^2 = 0.611 \times 10^6$

e) 78 cm³ = __78 000__ mm³

$78 \times (10)^3$

f) 0.003 58 cm² = __0.358__ mm²

$0.00358 \times (10)^2$

g) 92 400 m³ = __0.000 0924__ km³

$92400 \times (10^{-3})^3 = 92400 \times 10^{-9}$

h) 0.07 m³ = __70 000 000__ mm³

$0.07 \times (10^3)^3 = 0.07 \times 10^9$

i) 415 cm³ = __0.000 415__ m³

$415 \times (10^{-2})^3 = 415 \times 10^{-6}$

j) 415 m³ = __415 000 000__ cm³

$415 \times (10^2)^3 = 415 \times 10^6$

5. a) 24.5 ft² to mi²

$$\frac{24.5 \text{ ft}^2}{1} \times \frac{(1)^2 \text{ mi}^2}{(5280)^2 \text{ ft}^2}$$
$$= 8.79 \times 10^{-7} \text{ mi}^2$$

b) 440 yds³ to mi³

$$\frac{440 \text{ yds}^3}{1} \times \frac{(1)^3 \text{ mi}^3}{(1760)^3 \text{ yds}^3}$$
$$= 8.07 \times 10^{-8} \text{ mi}^3$$

c) 60 yds² to in²

$$\frac{60 \text{ yds}^2}{1} \times \frac{(3)^2 \text{ ft}^2}{(1)^2 \text{ yds}^2} \times \frac{(12)^2 \text{ in}^2}{(1)^2 \text{ ft}^2}$$
$$= 7.78 \times 10^4 \text{ in}^2$$

d) 24.5 ft³ to yds³

$$\frac{24.5 \text{ ft}^3}{1} \times \frac{(1)^3 \text{ yds}^3}{(3)^3 \text{ ft}^3}$$
$$= 9.07 \times 10^{-1} \text{ yds}^3$$

e) 78.9 in³ to ft³

$$\frac{78.9 \text{ in}^3}{1} \times \frac{(1)^3 \text{ ft}^3}{(12)^3 \text{ in}^3}$$
$$= 4.57 \times 10^{-2} \text{ ft}^3$$

f) 0.4 mi² to in²

$$\frac{0.4 \text{ mi}^2}{1} \times \frac{(5280)^2 \text{ ft}^2}{(1)^2 \text{ mi}^2} \times \frac{(12)^2 \text{ in}^2}{(1)^2 \text{ ft}^2}$$
$$= 1.61 \times 10^9 \text{ in}^2$$

Use the Conversion Factor 2.54 cm = 1 in for the remainder of this assignment.

6. a) square centimetres

area = (90)(60)
= 5400 cm²

b) square inches

$$\frac{5400 \text{ cm}^2}{1} \times \frac{(1)^2 \text{ in}^2}{(2.54)^2 \text{ cm}^2}$$
= 837 in²

c) square feet

$$\frac{837 \text{ in}^2}{1} \times \frac{(1)^2 \text{ ft}^2}{(12)^2 \text{ in}^2}$$
= 6 ft²

7. a) Determine, to the nearest ft³, which container has the greater volume, and by how much.

Container 1: V = (4.8)(3)(2.5) = 36 m³ $\frac{36 \text{ m}^3}{1} \times \frac{(1)^3 \text{ ft}^3}{(0.3048)^3 \text{ m}^3}$ = 1271.3... ft³

Container 2: V = (15)(12)(7) = 1260 ft³

The first container has a greater volume by 11 ft³.

1271.3... - 1260 = 11.3...

b) Determine, to the nearest cm², which container has the greater surface area, and by how much.

Container 1: SA = 2(4.8×3) + 2(3×2.5) + 2(4.8×2.5) = 67.8 m²

Container 2: SA = 2(15×12) + 2(12×7) + 2(15×7) = 738 ft²

Container 1: $\frac{67.8 \text{ m}^2}{1} \times \frac{(100)^2 \text{ cm}^2}{(1)^2 \text{ m}^2}$ = 678000 cm²

Container 2: $\frac{738 \text{ ft}^2}{1} \times \frac{(0.3048)^2 \text{ m}^2}{(1)^2 \text{ ft}^2} \times \frac{(100)^2 \text{ cm}^2}{(1)^2 \text{ m}^2}$ = 685624.4... cm²

The second container has greater surface area by 7264 cm².

8. 2.5 km = 2500 m   Volume = (2500)(14)(0.08)

8 cm = 0.08 m   = 2800 m³

9. $\frac{2800 \text{ m}^3}{1} \times \frac{(100)^3 \text{ cm}^3}{(1)^3 \text{ m}^3} \times \frac{(1)^3 \text{ in}^3}{(2.54)^3 \text{ cm}^3} \times \frac{(1)^3 \text{ ft}^3}{(12)^3 \text{ in}^3}$ = 98881.06... ft³

Cost = $3.50 × 98881.06 = $349100

Measurement Lesson #6: Assignment Pages **161 to 164** Measurement Lesson #6

2. a) 2.1 m² = 2.1 × 10⁻⁶ km²

$$\frac{2.1}{(10^{-3})^2}$$
$$= 2.1 \times 10^{-6}$$

b) 0.289 km² = 2.89 × 10⁹ cm²

0.289 × (10⁵)²
= 0.289 × 10¹⁰

c) 7450 mm² = 7.45 × 10⁻³ m²

7450 × (10⁻³)²
= 7450 × 10⁻⁶

d) 0.37 km³ = 3.7 × 10⁸ m³

0.37 × (10³)³
= 0.37 × 10⁹

e) 50 000 Mm² = 5 × 10⁻² Gm²

50000 × (10⁻³)²
= 50000 × 10⁻⁶

f) 920 mm² = 9.2 × 10¹⁴ nm²

920 × (10⁶)²
= 920 × 10¹²

g) 0.289 km² = 2.89 × 10⁻¹³ Gm²

0.289 × (10⁻⁶)²
= 0.289 × 10⁻¹²

h) 2.14 × 10⁴ mm² = 2.14 × 10¹⁰ μm²

2.14 × 10⁴ × (10³)²
= 2.14 × 10⁴ × 10⁶

i) 560 000 μm³ = 5.6 × 10⁻⁴ mm³

560000 × (10⁻³)³
= 560000 × 10⁻⁹

j) 780 cm³ = 7.8 × 10⁻¹ dm³

780 × (10⁻¹)³
= 780 × 10⁻³

3. a) 720 in² = 5 ft²

$\frac{720 \text{ in}^2}{1} \times \frac{(1)^2 \text{ ft}^2}{(12)^2 \text{ in}^2}$ = 5

b) 0.5 mi² = 1 548 800 yds²

$\frac{0.5 \text{ mi}^2}{1} \times \frac{(1760)^2 \text{ yds}^2}{(1)^2 \text{ mi}^2}$ = 1548800

c) 8 145 ft² = 905 yds²

$\frac{8145 \text{ ft}^2}{1} \times \frac{(1)^2 \text{ yds}^2}{(3)^2 \text{ ft}^2}$ = 905

d) 4.2 ft² = 604.8 in²

$\frac{4.2 \text{ ft}^2}{1} \times \frac{(12)^2 \text{ in}^2}{(1)^2 \text{ ft}^2}$ = 604.8

e) 7 mi² = 195 148 800 ft²

$\frac{7 \text{ mi}^2}{1} \times \frac{(5280)^2 \text{ ft}^2}{(1)^2 \text{ mi}^2}$ = 195148800

f) 123 904 yds² = 0.04 mi²

$\frac{123904 \text{ yds}^2}{1} \times \frac{(1)^2 \text{ mi}^2}{(1760)^2 \text{ yds}^2}$ = 0.04

g) 3.5 yds² = 4536 in²

$\frac{3.5 \text{ yds}^2}{1} \times \frac{(3)^2 \text{ ft}^2}{(1)^2 \text{ yds}^2} \times \frac{(12)^2 \text{ in}^2}{(1)^2 \text{ ft}^2}$ = 4536

h) 1 944 in² = 1.5 yds²

$\frac{1944 \text{ in}^2}{1} \times \frac{(1)^2 \text{ ft}^2}{(12)^2 \text{ in}^2} \times \frac{(1)^2 \text{ yds}^2}{(3)^2 \text{ ft}^2}$ = 1.5

4. a) 7.1 ft³ to in³

$\frac{7.1 \text{ ft}^3}{1} \times \frac{(12)^3 \text{ in}^3}{(1)^3 \text{ ft}^3}$
= 12268.8 in³

b) 5.4 ft³ to yds³

$\frac{5.4 \text{ ft}^3}{1} \times \frac{(1)^3 \text{ yds}^3}{(3)^3 \text{ ft}^3}$
= 0.2 yds³

c) 0.05 miles³ to yds³

$\frac{0.05 \text{ mi}^3}{1} \times \frac{(1760)^3 \text{ yds}^3}{(1)^3 \text{ mi}^3}$
= 272588800 yds³

d) 24 yds³ to ft³

$\frac{24 \text{ yds}^3}{1} \times \frac{(3)^3 \text{ ft}^3}{(1)^3 \text{ yds}^3}$
= 648 ft³

e) 1 123.2 in³ to ft³

$\frac{1123.2 \text{ in}^3}{1} \times \frac{(1)^3 \text{ ft}^3}{(12)^3 \text{ in}^3}$
= 0.65 ft³

f) 2 yds³ to in³

$\frac{2 \text{ yds}^3}{1} \times \frac{(3)^3 \text{ ft}^3}{(1)^3 \text{ yds}^3} \times \frac{(12)^3 \text{ in}^3}{(1)^3 \text{ ft}^3}$
= 93312 in³

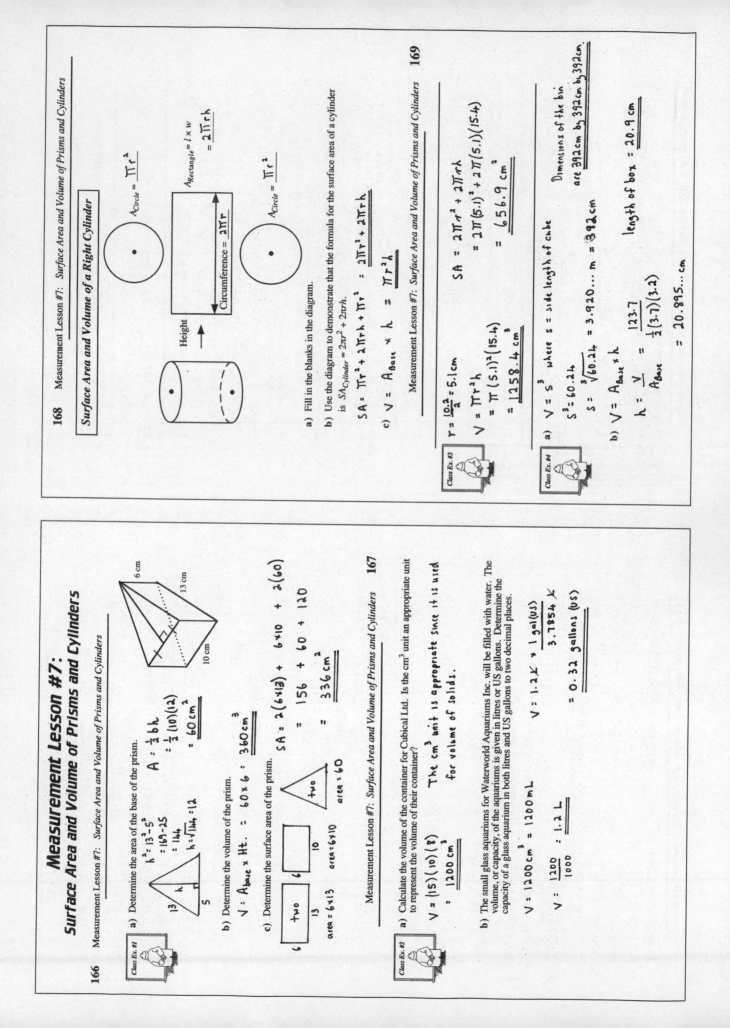

Measurement Lesson #7:
Surface Area and Volume of Prisms and Cylinders

166 Measurement Lesson #7: *Surface Area and Volume of Prisms and Cylinders*

Class Ex. #1

a) Determine the area of the base of the prism.

$h^2 = 13^2 - 5^2$ $A = \frac{1}{2} bh$

$= 169 - 25$ $= \frac{1}{2}(10)(12)$

$= 144$ $= \underline{60 \text{ cm}^2}$

$h = \sqrt{144} = 12$

b) Determine the volume of the prism.

$V = A_{Base} \times Ht. = 60 \times 6 = \underline{360 \text{ cm}^3}$

c) Determine the surface area of the prism.

$SA = 2(6 \times 12) + 6 \times 10 + 2(60)$

$= 156 + 60 + 120$

$= \underline{336 \text{ cm}^2}$

area = 6×13   area = 6×10   area = 60

Measurement Lesson #7: *Surface Area and Volume of Prisms and Cylinders*   **167**

Class Ex. #2

a) Calculate the volume of the container for Cubical Ltd. Is the cm³ unit an appropriate unit to represent the volume of their container?

$V = (15)(10)(8)$ The cm³ unit is appropriate since it is used for volume of solids.

$= \underline{1200 \text{ cm}^3}$

b) The small glass aquariums for Waterworld Aquariums Inc. will be filled with water. The volume, or capacity, of the aquariums is given in litres or US gallons. Determine the capacity of a glass aquarium in both litres and US gallons to two decimal places.

$V = 1200 \text{ cm}^3 = 1200 \text{ mL}$ $V = 1.2 L \times 1 gal(US)$ / $3.7854 L$

$V = \frac{1200}{1000} = \underline{1.2 \text{ L}}$ $= \underline{0.32 \text{ gallons (US)}}$

---

168 Measurement Lesson #7: *Surface Area and Volume of Prisms and Cylinders*

Surface Area and Volume of a Right Cylinder

$A_{Circle} = \underline{\pi r^2}$

$A_{Rectangle} = l \times w = \underline{2 \pi r h}$

Circumference $= \underline{2 \pi r}$

$A_{Circle} = \underline{\pi r^2}$

a) Fill in the blanks in the diagram.

b) Use the diagram to demonstrate that the formula for the surface area of a cylinder is $SA_{Cylinder} = 2\pi r^2 + 2\pi rh$.

$SA = \pi r^2 + 2\pi rh + \pi r^2 = \underline{2 \pi r^2 + 2 \pi r h}$

c) $V = A_{Base} \times h = \underline{\pi r^2 h}$

Measurement Lesson #7: *Surface Area and Volume of Prisms and Cylinders*   **169**

Class Ex. #3

$r = \frac{10.2}{2} = 5.1 \text{cm}$

$V = \pi r^2 h$

$= \pi (5.1)^2 (15.4)$

$= \underline{1258.4 \text{ cm}^3}$

$SA = 2\pi r^2 + 2\pi rh$

$= 2\pi(5.1)^2 + 2\pi(5.1)(15.4)$

$= \underline{656.9 \text{ cm}^2}$

Class Ex. #4

a) $V = s^3$ where s = side length of cube

$s^3 = 60.24$

$s = \sqrt[3]{60.24} = 3.920... \text{ m} = 392 \text{ cm}$

Dimensions of the bin are 392cm by 392cm by 392cm.

b) $V = A_{Base} \times h$

$h = \frac{V}{A_{Base}} = \frac{123.7}{\frac{1}{2}(3.7)(3.2)}$

$= 20.895... \text{ cm}$

length of box = $\underline{20.9 \text{ cm}}$

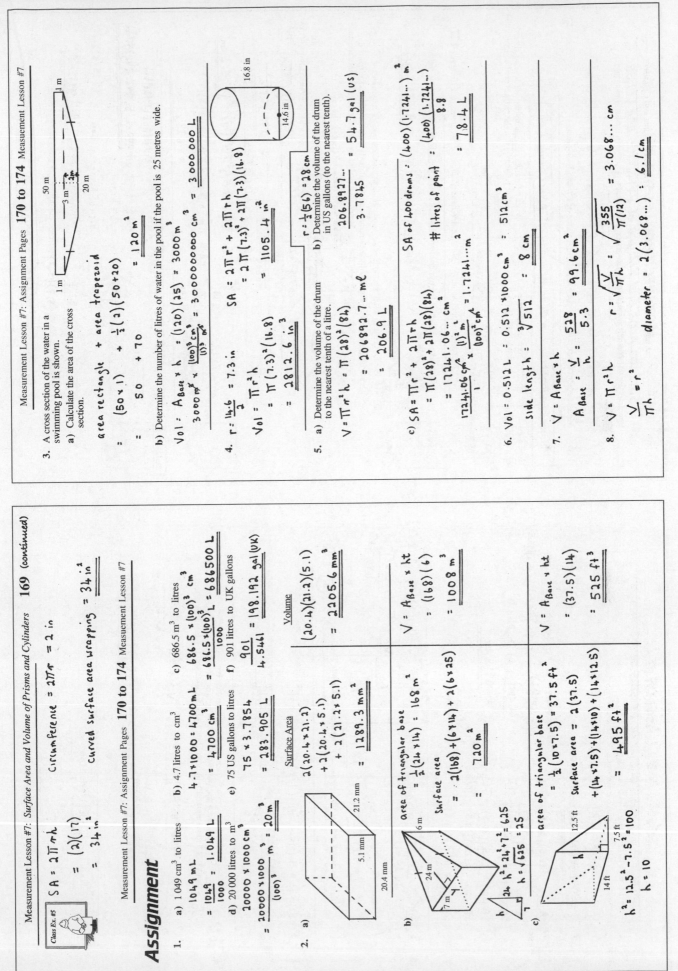

3. A cross section of the water in a swimming pool is shown.

a) Calculate the area of the cross section.

area rectangle + area trapezoid

$= (50 \times 1) + \frac{1}{2}(2)(50+20)$

$= 50 + 70$

$= 120 \text{ m}^2$

b) Determine the number of litres of water in the pool if the pool is 25 metres wide.

$Vol = A_{Base} \times h = (120)(25) = 3000 \text{ m}^3$

$3000 \text{ m}^3 \times \frac{(100)^3 \text{cm}^3}{(1)^3 \text{m}^3} = 3000000000 \text{ cm}^3 = \underline{3\ 000\ 000 \text{ L}}$

4. $r = \frac{14.6}{2} = 7.3 \text{ in}$ $SA = 2\pi r^2 + 2\pi r h$

$Vol = \pi r^2 h$ $= 2\pi(7.3)^2 + 2\pi(7.3)(16.8)$

$= \pi(7.3)^2(16.8)$ $= \underline{1105.4 \text{ in}^2}$

$= \underline{2812.6 \text{ in}^3}$

5. a) Determine the volume of the drum to the nearest tenth of a litre.

$r = \frac{1}{2}(56) = 28 \text{ cm}$

$V = \pi r^2 h = \pi(28)^2(84)$

$= 206892.7... \text{ mℓ}$

$= \underline{206.9 \text{ L}}$

b) Determine the volume of the drum in US gallons (to the nearest tenth).

$\frac{206.8927...}{3.7845} = \underline{54.7 \text{ gal (US)}}$

c) $SA = \pi r^2 + 2\pi r h$

$= \pi(28)^2 + 2\pi(28)(84)$

$= 17241.06... \text{ cm}^2$

$\frac{17241.06 \text{ cm}^2}{1} \times \frac{(1)^2 \text{ m}^2}{(100)^2 \text{cm}^2} = 1.7241...\text{ m}^2$

SA of 400 drums $= (400)(1.7241...) = (400)(1.7241...) \text{ m}^2$

litres of paint $= \frac{(400)(1.7241...)}{8.8} = \underline{78.4 \text{ L}}$

6. $Vol = 0.512 \text{ L} = 0.512 \times 1000 \text{ cm}^3 = 512 \text{ cm}^3$

side length $= \sqrt[3]{512} = \underline{8 \text{ cm}}$

7. $V = A_{Base} \times h$

$A_{Base} = \frac{V}{h} = \frac{528}{5.3} = \underline{99.6 \text{ cm}^2}$

8. $V = \pi r^2 h$

$\frac{V}{\pi h} = r^2$

$r = \sqrt{\frac{V}{\pi h}} = \sqrt{\frac{355}{\pi(12)}} = 3.068...$ $= \underline{6.1 \text{ cm}}$

diameter $= 2(3.068...) = \underline{6.1 \text{ cm}}$

Class Ex. #5

$SA = 2\pi r \cdot h$ Circumference $= 2\pi r = 2 \text{ in}$

$= (2)(17)$

$= 34 \text{ in}^2$ Curved surface area wrapping $= \underline{34 \text{ in}^2}$

Assignment

1. a) 1049 cm³ to litres   b) 4.7 litres to cm³   c) 686.5 m³ to litres

1049 mL $4.7 \times 1000 = 4700 \text{ mL}$ $686.5 \times (100)^3 \text{ cm}^3$

$= \frac{1049}{1000} = \underline{1.049 \text{ L}}$ $= \frac{4700}{1000}$ $= \frac{686.5 \times (100)^3}{1000} \text{ L} = \underline{686500 \text{ L}}$

$= \underline{4700 \text{ cm}^3}$

d) 20 000 litres to m³   e) 75 US gallons to litres   f) 901 litres to UK gallons

$20000 \times 1000 \text{ cm}^3$ 75×3.7854 $\frac{901}{4.5461} = \underline{198.192 \text{ gal (UK)}}$

$= \frac{20000 \times 1000}{(100)^3} \text{ m}^3 = \underline{20 \text{ m}^3}$ $= \underline{283.905 \text{ L}}$

2. a)

Surface Area

$2(20.4 \times 21.2)$
$+ 2(20.4 \times 5.1)$
$+ 2(21.2 \times 5.1)$
$= \underline{1289.3 \text{ mm}^2}$

Volume

$(20.4)(21.2)(5.1)$
$= \underline{2205.6 \text{ mm}^3}$

b)

$h^2 = 24^2 + 7^2 = 625$
$h = \sqrt{625} = 25$

area of triangular base

$= \frac{1}{2}(24 \times 14) = 168 \text{ m}^2$

Surface area

$= 2(168) + (6 \times 14) + 2(6 \times 25)$
$= \underline{720 \text{ m}^2}$

$V = A_{Base} \times ht$
$= (168)(6)$
$= \underline{1008 \text{ m}^3}$

c)

$h^2 = 12.5^2 - 7.5^2 = 100$
$h = 10$

area of triangular base

$= \frac{1}{2}(10 \times 7.5) = 37.5 \text{ ft}^2$

Surface area $= 2(37.5)$
$+ (14 \times 7.5) + (14 \times 10) + (14 \times 12.5)$
$= \underline{495 \text{ ft}^2}$

$V = A_{Base} \times ht$
$= (37.5)(14)$
$= \underline{525 \text{ ft}^3}$

Measurement Lesson #8:
Surface Area and Volume of Pyramids and Cones

How does the volume of a pyramid compare to the volume of a prism with identical base and height?

The volume of the pyramid is $\frac{1}{3}$ of the volume of the prism.

Volume of a Right Circular Cone

How does the volume of a cone compare to the volume of a cylinder with identical base and height?

The volume of the cone is $\frac{1}{3}$ of the volume of the cylinder.

Right Circular Cone

Write a formula connecting the vertical height (h), the slant height (s) and the radius (r) of a right circular cone.

$$s^2 = h^2 + r^2$$

a) Make a sketch of the pyramid and calculate the volume to the nearest cubic metre.

$$V = \frac{1}{3} A_{Base} h = \frac{1}{3}(440)^2(147) = 9\ 486\ 400\ m^3$$

Class Ex. #1

b) Make a sketch of the net of the pyramid and calculate the surface area to the nearest square metre. Explain why the base is not included in the calculation of the surface area.

The base is not included because it is not exposed.

$s^2 = 147^2 + 220^2$
$s^2 = 70009$
$s = \sqrt{70009} = 264.59...$

$$SA_{Pyramid} = \text{area of 4 triangular faces}$$
$$= 4\left(\frac{1}{2}(440)(\sqrt{70009})\right)$$
$$= 232\ 841\ m^2$$

Class Ex. #2

$h = 15$
$r = 8$

$$V = \frac{1}{3}\pi r^2 h = \frac{1}{3}\pi(8)^2(15) = 1005.3\ cm^3$$

$$SA = \pi r^2 + \pi r s = \pi(8)^2 + \pi(8)(17)$$
$$= 628.3\ cm^2$$

$s^2 = 15^2 + 8^2$
$= 289$
$s = \sqrt{289}$
$= 17\,cm$

Class Ex. #3

a) the hexagonal base consists of six equilateral triangles

area of one triangle $= \frac{1}{2}bh = \frac{1}{2}(10)(5\sqrt{3})$
$= 25\sqrt{3}\ cm^2$

area of hexagonal base $= 6(25\sqrt{3})\ cm^2$
$= 150\sqrt{3}\ cm^2$ or $260\ cm^2$

$h^2 = 10^2 - 5^2 = 75$
$h = \sqrt{75} = \sqrt{25}\sqrt{3}$
$h = 5\sqrt{3}$

b) The pyramid is filled with water. Determine the volume of water to the nearest ml.

$$V = \frac{1}{3}A_{Base}h = \frac{1}{3}(150\sqrt{3})(20) = 1000\sqrt{3} = 1732\ ml$$

---

9. a) Interior measurements 14.5 by 18.5 by $27.5\,cm$

$V = (14.5)(18.5)(27.5)$
$= 7376.9\ cm^3$

b) Surface area to be painted

$SA_{back} = (21.5)(30.5)$
$SA_{lid} = (17.5)(21.5)$
$SA_{inside lid} = (17.5)(21.5)$
$SA_{left} = (17.5)(30.5) - \pi(3.5)^2$
$SA_{right} = (17.5)(30.5) - \pi(3.5)^2$
$SA_{base} = (17.5)(21.5) - 2\pi(3)^2$

$= 3(17.5)(21.5) + 2(17.5)(30.5) + (21.5)(30.5)$
$\quad - 2\pi(3.5)^2 - 2\pi(3)^2$
$= 2718\ cm^2$

10. $8.15\,m^3 \times \dfrac{(1)^3\ ft^3}{(0.3048)^3\ m^3} = 287.81...\ ft^3$

$V = A_{Base} \times h$

$h = \dfrac{V}{A_{Base}} = \dfrac{287.81...}{16} = 18\ ft$

11. **B.** $\pi r^2 + 2\pi r h$

12. $V = (11)(7)(4) = 308\ ft^3$

$\dfrac{308\ ft^3}{1} \times \dfrac{(0.3048)^3\ m^3}{(1)^3\ ft^3} = 8.7\ m^3$

B. $8.7\ m^3$

13. $SA = 2(11 \times 7) + 4(11 \times 4) + 4(7 \times 4) = 442\ ft^2$

$\dfrac{442\ ft^2}{1} \times \dfrac{(0.3048)^2\ m^2}{(1)^2\ ft^2} = 41.1\ m^2$ $\boxed{41.1}$

14. $10\,m^3 \times \dfrac{(1)^3\ ft^3}{(0.3048)^3\ m^3} = 353.146...\ ft^3$

$h = \dfrac{V}{A_{Base}} = \dfrac{353.146}{11 \times 7} = 4.5863...\ ft$

$0.5863...ft = 0.5863...\times 12\ in$
$= 7\ in$

height $= 4\,ft\ 7\,in$
$a = 4$ $b = 7$
$a + b = 11$ $\boxed{11}$

15. $1\,pint \times \dfrac{1\,gal}{8\,pints} \times \dfrac{4.5461\,L}{1\,gal} \times \dfrac{1000\ mL}{L}$

$= 568\ mL$ $\boxed{568}$

Class Ex. #4

a) Explain how Problem 1 can be solved using mental math. State the answer.

Volume of a cone = $\frac{1}{3}\pi r^2 h$

Volume of first cone = $\frac{1}{3}\pi r^2 (5)$

Volume of second cone = $\frac{1}{3}\pi r^2 (20)$

The second cone has a volume 4 times the volume of the first cone.

Volume of second cone = 4(10) = **40 cm³**

b) Explain how Problem 2 can be solved using mental math. State the answer.

Volume of first cone = $\frac{1}{3}\pi (5)^2 h$

Volume of second cone = $\frac{1}{3}\pi (20)^2 h$

The second cone has a volume 4^2 times the volume of the first cone.

Volume of second cone = $(4^2)(10)$ = $(16)(10)$ = **160 cm³**

Assignment

1. a) $\frac{1}{3}(27)$ = 9 ft³   b) 3(6) = 18 m³   c) $\frac{1}{3}(300)$ = 100 in³   d) 3(39) = 117 mm³

2. a) a cone with base radius 8 mm and height 10 mm

$V = \frac{1}{3}\pi r^2 h$

$= \frac{1}{3}\pi (8)^2 (10)$

= **670 mm³**

b) a square based pyramid with side 18 cm and height 12 cm

$V = \frac{1}{3}Ah$

$= \frac{1}{3}(18^2)(12)$

= **1296 cm³**

c) a cone with base diameter 12 ft and slant height 10 ft

$h^2 = 10^2 - 6^2 = 64$

$h = \sqrt{64} = 8$

$V = \frac{1}{3}\pi r^2 h$

$= \frac{1}{3}\pi (6)^2 (8)$

= **302 ft³**

d) a cone with slant height 51 in and vertical height 45 in

$r^2 = 51^2 - 45^2 = 576$

$r = \sqrt{576} = 24$

$V = \frac{1}{3}\pi r^2 h$

$= \frac{1}{3}\pi (24)^2 (45)$

= **27143 in³**

e) a triangular based pyramid with base area 35 m² and height 8.4 m

$V = \frac{1}{3}Ah = \frac{1}{3}(35)(8.4)$

= **98 m³**

---

3. Calculate the surface area of the figures in #1 a) -c) above. Answer to the nearest whole number.

a) $s^2 = 10^2 + 8^2 = 164$

$s = \sqrt{164}$

$SA = \pi r^2 + \pi rs$

$= \pi (8)^2 + \pi(8)(\sqrt{164})$ = **523 mm²**

b) $s^2 = 12^2 + 9^2 = 225$

$s = \sqrt{225} = 15$

area of one triangular face

$= \frac{1}{2}bh = \frac{1}{2}(18)(15) = 135 cm²$

c) Surface area = area of 4 triangular faces + area of base

$= 4(135) + (18)^2$ = **864 cm²**

$SA = \pi r^2 + \pi rs$

$= \pi (6)^2 + \pi(6)(10)$ = **302 ft²**

4. a)

b) $SA = 2\left[\frac{1}{2}(13)(8)\right] + 2\left[\frac{1}{2}(10)(15)\right] + (18)(10)$

= **564 in²**

c) $h^2 = 15^2 - 9^2$

Height: 12 in

$= 144$

$h = 12$

$V = \frac{1}{3}Ah$

$= \frac{1}{3}(18)(10)(12)$ Vol = **720 in³**

$= 720 in³$

b) $s^2 = 14^2 + 6^2 = 232$

$s = \sqrt{232}$

$L =$

$r =$

$V = \frac{1}{3}\pi r^2 h = \frac{1}{3}\pi (6)^2 (14)$

= **527.8 m³**

$SA = \pi r^2 + \pi rs$

$= \pi (6)^2 + \pi (6)(\sqrt{232})$

= **400.2 m²**

5. a) $r^2 = 25^2 - 24^2$

$= 49$

$r = 7$

$V = \frac{1}{3}\pi r^2 h = \frac{1}{3}\pi (7)^2 (24)$

= **1231.5 yds³**

$SA = \pi r^2 + \pi rs$

$= \pi (7)^2 + \pi (7)(25)$

= **703.7 yds²**

6. a) Determine the slant height of a paper cup to the nearest 0.1 cm.

$s^2 = 7^2 + 3^2 = 58$

$s = \sqrt{58} = 7.6\ cm$

slant ht = 7.6 cm

b) To the nearest whole number, how many ml of water will a paper cup hold?

$V = \frac{1}{3}\pi r^2 h = \frac{1}{3}\pi(3)^2(7)$

$= 66\ cm^3$

Cup will hold 66 mL

c) Determine how much paper is required, to the nearest square cm, to make a cup.

$SA = \pi r s = \pi(3)(\sqrt{58})$

$= 72\ cm^2$

72 cm² is required to make a cup

7. a) $V = \frac{1}{3}(9)^3 = 243\ cm^3$

b) $V = \frac{1}{3}\pi r^2 h = \frac{1}{3}\pi(4.5)^2(9) = 191\ cm^3$

8. $V = \frac{1}{3}Ah = \frac{1}{3}(450)^2(66) = 4\ 455\ 000\ m^3$

9. $V = \frac{1}{3}Ah$

$3V = Ah$

$A = \frac{3V}{h}$

area of base $= \frac{3(2\,570\,000)}{147}$

side of base $= \sqrt{\frac{3(2570000)}{147}} = 229\ m$

10. Determine the exact volume and surface area of a right pyramid with a height of $\sqrt{3}$ feet and a hexagonal base with six sides of 2 feet.

hexagonal base

$H^2 = 2^2 - 1^2 = 3$

$H = \sqrt{3}$

area of 1 triangle $= \frac{1}{2}bh = \frac{1}{2}(2)\sqrt{3} = \sqrt{3}$

area of 6 triangles $= 6\sqrt{3}$

area of hexagonal base $= 6\sqrt{3}\ ft^2$

Vol. of pyramid $= \frac{1}{3}Ah = \frac{1}{3}(6\sqrt{3})(\sqrt{3}) = 6\ ft^3$

Surface area = hexagonal base + six triangular faces

triangular face: $s^2 = (\sqrt{3})^2 + (\sqrt{3})^2 = 6$ $s = \sqrt{6}$

$SA = 6\sqrt{3} + 6\left(\left(\frac{1}{2}\right)(2)(\sqrt{6})\right)$

$= 6\sqrt{3} + 6\sqrt{6}\ ft^2$

---

11. a) To the nearest hundred square feet, how many square feet of glass is in the pyramid at the Louvre?

$s^2 = 70^2 + (57.5)^2$

$= 8206.25$

$s = \sqrt{8206.25}$

Area of 4 triangular faces $= 4\left(\frac{1}{2}(115)(\sqrt{8206.25})\right)$

$= 20800$

20 800 ft² of glass

b) How many times as great as the volume of the pyramid in Edmonton is the volume of the pyramid at the Louvre? Answer to the nearest tenth.

$V_L = \frac{1}{3}Ah = \frac{1}{3}(115)^2(70) = 308583\frac{1}{3}\ ft^3$

$V_m = \frac{1}{3}Ah = \frac{1}{3}(19.5)^2(18.0) = 2281.5\ m^3 \times \frac{11^3\ ft^3}{(0.3048)^3\ m^3} = 80570.4...\ ft^3$

ratio $\frac{V_L}{V_m} = \frac{308583.3...}{80570.4...} = 3.8\ times$

12. r: $\frac{23.0}{2} = 11.5\ ft$ $V = \frac{1}{3}\pi r^2 h = \frac{1}{3}\pi(11.5)^2(9.2) = 1274.1...\ ft^3$

$\frac{1274.1...\ ft^3}{1} \times \frac{(0.3048)^3\ m^3}{(1)^3\ ft^3} = 36.08\ m^3$

13. $V = \frac{1}{3}Ah = \frac{1}{3}s^2 h$ new V $= \frac{1}{3}(2s)^2 h = \frac{4}{3}s^2 h$

$\frac{orig.}{new} = \frac{\frac{1}{3}s^2 h}{\frac{4}{3}s^2 h} = \frac{1}{4}$ (C.) $\frac{1}{4}$

14. $V = \frac{1}{3}\pi r^2 h$ new V $= \frac{1}{3}\pi(2r)^2\left(\frac{1}{2}h\right) = \frac{2}{3}\pi r^2 h$ (B.)

15. $V = \frac{1}{3}\pi r^2 h$ $h = \frac{3(3800)}{\pi(10)^2}$

$3V = \pi r^2 h$ $= 36.3\ m$

$h = \frac{3V}{\pi r^2}$ [36.3]

16. $V = \frac{1}{3}A_{Base}h$

$3V = Ah$

$A = \frac{3V}{h}$

$A_{Base} = \frac{3(160)}{12} = 40\ ft^2$

$A_{Base} = length \times width$

$width = \frac{A_{Base}}{length} = \frac{40}{5} = 8\ ft$

$\frac{8\ ft}{1} \times \frac{12\ in}{1\ ft} \times \frac{2.54\ cm}{1\ in} = 243.84 = 244\ cm$ [244]

Surface Area and Volume of Spheres

Volume of a Sphere

b) ii) $= \frac{4}{3}\pi(5)^3 = \frac{500}{3}\pi = 523.6 \text{ cm}^3$

c) ii) $= \frac{4}{3}\pi r^3$

186 Measurement Lesson #9: *Surface Area and Volume of Spheres*

Class Ex. #1

a) The volume of a hemisphere is $\frac{2}{3}\pi r^3$

b) The surface area of a hemisphere = curved surface area + area of circular base
$$= 2\pi r^2 + \pi r^2 = 3\pi r^2$$

c) The surface area of a hemisphere = $2\pi r^2$ if the base is **not** included.

Measurement Lesson #9: *Surface Area and Volume of Spheres*   187

Class Ex. #2

a) $r = \frac{2302}{2} = 1151 \text{ km}$
$$SA = 4\pi r^2 = 4\pi(1151)^2$$
$$= 1.7 \times 10^7 \text{ km}^2$$

b) $V = \frac{4}{3}\pi r^3$
$$= \frac{4}{3}\pi(1151)^3$$
$$= 6.4 \times 10^9 \text{ km}^3$$

Class Ex. #3

Circumference = 108 cm
$2\pi r = 108$
$r = \frac{108}{2\pi} = \frac{54}{\pi} \text{ cm}$

Vol. $= \frac{4}{3}\pi r^3 = \frac{4}{3}\pi\left(\frac{54}{\pi}\right)^3$
$$= 21272.6 \text{ cm}^3$$

Class Ex. #4

a) $r = \frac{4\pi}{2} = 2\pi$
$$SA = 3\pi r^2 = 3\pi(2\pi)^2$$
$$= 12\pi^3 \text{ unit}^3$$

b) $SA = 2\pi r^2 = 2\pi(2\pi)^2 = 8\pi^3 \text{ unit}^3$

Class Ex. #5

$V = \frac{4}{3}\pi r^3$
$3V = 4\pi r^3$
$r^3 = \frac{3V}{4\pi}$
$r = \sqrt[3]{\frac{3V}{4\pi}}$

$r = \sqrt[3]{\frac{3(433.5)}{4\pi}} = 4.694... \text{ in}$

$\frac{4.694 \text{ in}}{1} \times \frac{2.54 \text{ cm}}{1 \text{ in}} = 11.92... = 12$

Assignment

1. a) the surface area of a soccer ball with a diameter of 21 cm $r = 10.5$ cm
$$SA = 4\pi r^2 = 4\pi(10.5)^2$$
$$= 1385.4 \text{ cm}^2$$

b) the volume of a spherical ornament with a radius of 12 in
$$V = \frac{4}{3}\pi r^3 = \frac{4}{3}\pi(12)^3$$
$$= 7238.2 \text{ in}^3$$

c) the volume and surface area of the earth, in scientific notation, if the shape of the earth is spherical and the diameter of the earth is about 12 756 km $r = 6378$ km
$$V = \frac{4}{3}\pi r^3 = \frac{4}{3}\pi(6378)^3 = 1.1 \times 10^{12} \text{ km}^3$$
$$SA = 4\pi r^2 = 4\pi(6378)^2 = 5.1 \times 10^8 \text{ km}^2$$

d) the volume and surface area of a hemisphere of radius 4.2 ft
$$V = \frac{2}{3}\pi r^3 = \frac{2}{3}\pi(4.2)^3 = 155.2 \text{ ft}^3$$
$$SA = 3\pi r^2 = 3\pi(4.2)^2 = 166.3 \text{ ft}^2$$

2. Volume of liquid = Volume$_{\text{cylinder}}$ − Volume$_{\text{hemisphere}}$
$$V = \pi r^2 h - \frac{2}{3}\pi r^3$$
$$= \pi(3.1)^2(7.3) - \frac{2}{3}\pi(3.1)^3$$
$$= 157.99... \text{ mL}$$
Volume = 158 mL

3. a) Solve the equation $V = \frac{4}{3}\pi r^3$ for r. Write the answer as a radical and as a power.
$V = \frac{4}{3}\pi r^3$
$3V = 4\pi r^3$
$\frac{3V}{4\pi} = r^3$
$r = \sqrt[3]{\frac{3V}{4\pi}}$
$r = \left(\frac{3V}{4\pi}\right)^{\frac{1}{3}}$

b) The volume of a beach ball is 50 965 cm³. Calculate the radius to the nearest tenth of a cm.
$r = \sqrt[3]{\frac{3V}{4\pi}} = \sqrt[3]{\frac{3(50965)}{4\pi}}$
radius $= 23.0$ cm

4. a) diameter is 0.35 cm
$r = \frac{0.35}{2} = 0.175$ cm

vol. of sphere + cylinder + hemisphere
$= \frac{4}{3}\pi(0.175)^3 + \pi(0.15)^2(10.3) + \frac{2}{3}\pi(0.15)^3$
$= 0.76 \text{ cm}^3$

b) SA of sphere − base of cylinder + curved surface of cylinder + hemisphere
$= 4\pi(0.175)^2 - \pi(0.15)^2 + 2\pi(0.15)(10.3) + 2\pi(0.15)^2$
$= 10.16 \text{ cm}^2$

9.
A. 2.5 cm
B. 4 cm
C. 5 cm *(circled)*
D. 6 cm

$Vol = 65 \text{ cm}^3$

$V = \frac{4}{3}\pi r^3$

$3V = 4\pi r^3$

$r^3 = \frac{3V}{4\pi}$

$r^3 = \frac{3(65)}{4\pi}$

$r = \sqrt[3]{\frac{3(65)}{4\pi}}$

$r = 2.494\ldots \text{ cm}$

$diameter = 2(2.494\ldots)$
$= 4.998\ldots$

10.
$4\pi r^2 = 255$

$r^2 = \frac{255}{4\pi}$

$r = \sqrt{\frac{255}{4\pi}}$

$diameter = 2(4.50\ldots)$
$= 9.0 \text{ m}$ C. 9.0

11.
$V = \frac{4}{3}\pi r^3$
$= \frac{4}{3}\pi (15)^3$
$= 4500\,\pi$

C. 4500π

12.
$V_{\text{water in jar}} = \pi r^2 h = \pi(3.5)^2(5) = 192.42\ldots \text{ cm}^3$

$V_{\text{sphere}} = \frac{4}{3}\pi r^3 = \frac{4}{3}\pi(1.5)^3 = 14.13\ldots \text{ cm}^3$

$\text{Total volume} = 192.42\ldots + 14.13\ldots = 206.55\ldots \text{ cm}^3$

$V = \pi r^2 h$

$h = \frac{V}{\pi r^2}$

$\text{new water depth} = \frac{206.55\ldots}{\pi(3.5)^2} = 5.367\ldots \text{ cm}$

[5.4]

13.
$\text{water in sphere A} = 0.8 \times \frac{4}{3}\pi(6)^3 = 230.4\,\pi$

$\text{water in sphere B} = 0.2 \times \frac{4}{3}\pi R^3 = \frac{4}{15}\pi R^3$

$\frac{4}{15}\pi R^3 = 230.4\,\pi$

$R^3 = \frac{230.4\,\pi}{\frac{4}{15}\pi} = 864$

$R = \sqrt[3]{864} = 9.52\ldots \text{ cm}$

$diameter = 2(9.52\ldots) = 19.0 \text{ cm}$

[19.0]

14.

$V_{\text{cylinder}} + V_{\text{sphere}}$
$= \pi(3)^2(8) + \frac{4}{3}\pi(3)^3 = 339.29\ldots \text{ m}^3$

[339]

15.
$V_{\text{hemisphere}} + V_{\text{cone}} = \frac{2}{3}\pi(0.31)^3 + \frac{1}{3}\pi(0.31)^2(0.62) = 0.1247\ldots \text{ cm}^3$

radius of hemisphere = 3.1 mm = 0.31 cm
height of cone = 0.62 cm

$Mass = (19.3)(0.1247\ldots)$
$= 2.408\ldots \text{ g}$ [2.4]

16.
$SA_{\text{hemisphere}} + SA_{\text{cone}} = 2\pi(3.1)^2 + \pi(3.1)(\sqrt{48.05})$
$= 127.88\ldots \text{ mm}^2$

$s^2 = 6.2^2 + 3.1^2$
$= 48.05$
$s = \sqrt{48.05}$

(no base to hemisphere or cone)

[128]

---

5. a) Calculate the surface area of each case to one decimal place. The diameter of the case is 20 cm. $r = 10$ cm

$SA = 3\pi r^2 = 3\pi(10)^2 = 942.5 \text{ cm}^2$

b) How much will it cost to make 500 pencil cases?

$SA(500 \text{ cases}) = 500(942.5) \text{ cm}^2$

$\text{Cost of fabric} = 500(942.5) \times \dfrac{\$0.04}{100} = \$188.50$

$\text{Cost of zippers} = 500 \times \$0.05 = \$25$

Total cost
$= \$213.50$

6.
$V = \frac{4}{3}\pi r^3$

$3V = 4\pi r^3$

$r^3 = \frac{3V}{4\pi}$

$r = \sqrt[3]{\frac{3V}{4\pi}} = \sqrt[3]{\frac{3(1.53\times10^{15})}{4\pi}} = 71482.69\ldots \text{ km}$

$SA = 4\pi r^2 = 4\pi(71482.69\ldots)^2 = 6.42 \times 10^{10} \text{ km}^2$

7.
$SA = 4\pi r^2 = 277.6$

$r^2 = \frac{277.6}{4\pi}$

$r = \sqrt{\frac{277.6}{4\pi}}$

$r = 4.70\ldots$

$V = \frac{4}{3}\pi r^3$
$= \frac{4}{3}\pi(4.70\ldots)^3$
$= 434.9 \text{ in}^3$

8. a) Calculate the surface area of the miniature silver ball, to the nearest cm². Container is a cube with volume 1728 cm³.

$\text{side length} = \sqrt[3]{1728} = 12 \text{ cm}$

$SA = 4\pi r^2 = 4\pi(6)^2$
$= 452.38\ldots \text{ cm}^2$

diameter of ball = 12 cm
radius of ball = 6 cm

Surface area of ball = 452 cm²

b) Determine the volume of bubble wrap used to the nearest cm³.

$V_{\text{ball}} = \frac{4}{3}\pi r^3 = \frac{4}{3}\pi(6)^3 = 904.77\ldots \text{ cm}^3$

$V_{\text{space}} = V_{\text{container}} - V_{\text{ball}}$
$= 1728 - 904.77\ldots$
$= 823.22\ldots \text{ cm}^3$

Volume of bubble wrap
$= 80\% \text{ of } 823.22\ldots = 659 \text{ cm}^3$

Measurement Lesson #10: Practice Test

1. (D.) inch

2. $1.39 m \times 1000 = 1390 mm$
   $83 cm \times 10 = 830 mm$
   Difference = 560 mm
   (C.) 560

3. $0.028 cm \times \frac{1 m}{100 cm} \times \frac{1 km}{1000 m}$
   $= 0.00000028$
   (A.) 0.000 000 28

4. zero

5. $16\frac{1}{2} \times 4 = 66 in$
   $\frac{66}{12} = 5\frac{6}{12} = 5\frac{1}{2} ft$
   (C.) $5\frac{1}{2}$ feet

6. (B.) vernier caliper

7. $1216 \frac{km}{h} \times \frac{5 mi}{8 km} = 760 \frac{mi}{h}$
   (B.) 760

8. $1.5 + 0.49 = 1.99 mm$
   (C.) 1.99 mm

9. $660 km \times \frac{1000 m}{km} \times \frac{100 cm}{m} = 6 \times 10^7 cm$

map (cm)	actual (cm)
1	2 000 000
x	6×10^7

   $\frac{1}{x} = \frac{2\,000\,000}{6\times10^7}$
   $6\times10^7 = (2\times10^6) \times x$
   $x = \frac{6\times10^7}{2\times10^6} = 30 cm$
   (D.) 30 cm

10. $9 mm \times \frac{1 cm}{10 mm} \times \frac{1 in}{2.54 cm} = 0.354... in$
    $10 mm \times \frac{1 cm}{10 mm} \times \frac{1 in}{2.54 cm} = 0.393... in$
    $\frac{5}{16} = 0.3125$ $\frac{3}{8} = 0.375$ $\frac{7}{16} = 0.4375$
    (B.) $\frac{3}{8}$ in

11. $\frac{1}{2} in \times \frac{2.54 cm}{1 in} = 12.7 mm$
    $\frac{9}{16} in \times \frac{2.54 cm}{1 in} \times \frac{10 mm}{1 cm} = 14.2875 mm$
    (C.) 14 mm

12. $s^2 = 24^2 + 7^2 = 625$
    $s = \sqrt{625} = 25 cm$
    $SA_{cone} = \pi r^2 + \pi r s$
    $= \pi(7)^2 + \pi(7)(25)$
    $= 224\pi$
    A. 49π
    B. 175π
    C. 217π
    D. 224π ✓

13. $r = \frac{23}{2} = 11.5 in$
    $SA = 4\pi r^2$
    $= 4\pi(11.5)^2$
    $= 1662$
    (A.) 1662
    A. 1897
    B. 1026
    C. 814
    D. 10

14. $V = \frac{1}{3} A_{base}\, h$
    $H^2 = 10^2 - 5^2 = 75$
    $H = \sqrt{75} = \sqrt{25}\sqrt{3} = 5\sqrt{3}$
    $= \frac{1}{3}\left(\frac{1}{2}(10)(5\sqrt3)\right)(12)$
    $= 100\sqrt3 \; m^3$
    (B.) $100\sqrt3$

15. $V = \frac{1}{3}\pi r^3$
    $3V = 2\pi r^3$
    $r^3 = \frac{3V}{2\pi}$
    $r = \sqrt[3]{\frac{3V}{2\pi}} = \sqrt[3]{\frac{3(2260.5)}{2\pi}}$
    $= 10.2576... m$
    $= 1025.76... cm$

---

1. $6 yds \times \frac{3 ft}{1 yd} \times \frac{12 in}{1 ft} = 216 in$ $\frac{216}{13\frac12} = 16$ #tiles = (16)(12)
   $4\frac12 yds \times \frac{3 ft}{1 yd} \times \frac{12 in}{1 ft} = 162 in$ $\frac{162}{13\frac12} = 12$ = 192
   [192]

2. $V = (78.2)(42.5)(25.2) = 83752.2 cm^3$
   $83752.2 cm^3 \times \frac{1 L}{1000 cm^3} \times \frac{3 drops}{10 L} = 25.12... drops$
   [25]

3. $8 yds \times \frac{3 ft}{1 yd} \times \frac{12 in}{1 ft} \times \frac{1 plants}{11 in} = 26.18...$
   [26]

4. $\frac{100 m}{9.58 s} \times \frac{1 km}{1000 m} \times \frac{60 s}{1 min} \times \frac{60 min}{1 h} = 37.6$
   [37.6]

5. $r = \frac{7.4}{2} = 3.7 cm$
   $SA = 2\pi r h$
   $= 2\pi(3.7)(10.9)$
   $= 253.4... cm^2$
   [253]

1. • Answer in m³ correct to one decimal place.
   h = 6.3 m
   diam. = 4(6.3) = 25.2 m
   $r = \frac{1}{2}(25.2) = 12.6 m$
   $V = \frac13 \pi r^2 h$
   $= \frac13 \pi (12.6)^2(6.3)$
   $= 1047.4 m^3$
   [1047.4 m³]

   • How many trucks are needed?
   $V_{cylinder} = \pi r^2 h$
   $= \pi(2)^2(10)$
   $= 125.66... m^3$
   #trucks = $\frac{1047.4}{125.66...} = 8.3$
   9 trucks are needed

   • Answer in metres correct to one decimal place.
   $r = \frac{14}{2} = 7 m$
   $V = \frac13 \pi r^2 h$
   $3V = \pi r^2 h$
   $h = \frac{3V}{\pi r^2}$
   $h = \frac{3(1047.4)}{\pi(7)^2}$
   $= 20.4 m$
   height = 20.4 m

   • $1047.4 m^3 \times (100)^3 \frac{cm^3}{m^3} \times \frac{(1)^3 in^3}{(2.54)^3 cm^3} \times \frac{(1)^3 ft^3}{(12)^3 in^3} = 36988.6 ft^3$

   LMT → $(120\times9) + (5.20\times1047.4) = C\$6526.48$ $C\$6526.48$
   TT → $(100\times9) + (0.14\times36988.6) = C\$6753.78$
   $\frac{6078.40}{0.96} = C\$6753.78$ $6078.40 = US\$6078.40$

   It is cheaper to use Lower Mainland Transportation

Trigonometry Lesson #1: Trigonometric Ratios

Warm-Up #1

$$\frac{A_1B_1}{OA_1} = \frac{1.4}{2} = 0.7$$

$$\frac{A_2B_2}{OA_2} = \frac{2.8}{4} = 0.7$$

$$\frac{A_3B_3}{OA_3} = \frac{4.2}{6} = 0.7$$

$$\frac{A_4B_4}{OA_4} = \frac{5.6}{8} = 0.7$$

We can conclude that the ratio $\frac{0.7}{1}$ is somehow connected to the angle of 35°.

Warm-Up #2

$$\frac{A_1B_1}{OA_1} = \frac{2.4}{1.5} = 1.6$$

$$\frac{A_2B_2}{OA_2} = \frac{4.8}{3} = 1.6$$

$$\frac{A_3B_3}{OA_3} = \frac{7.2}{4.5} = 1.6$$

$$\frac{A_4B_4}{OA_4} = \frac{9.6}{6} = 1.6$$

We can conclude that the ratio $\frac{1.6}{1}$ is somehow connected to the angle of 58°.

200 Trigonometry Lesson #1: *Trigonometric Ratios*

Class Ex. #1

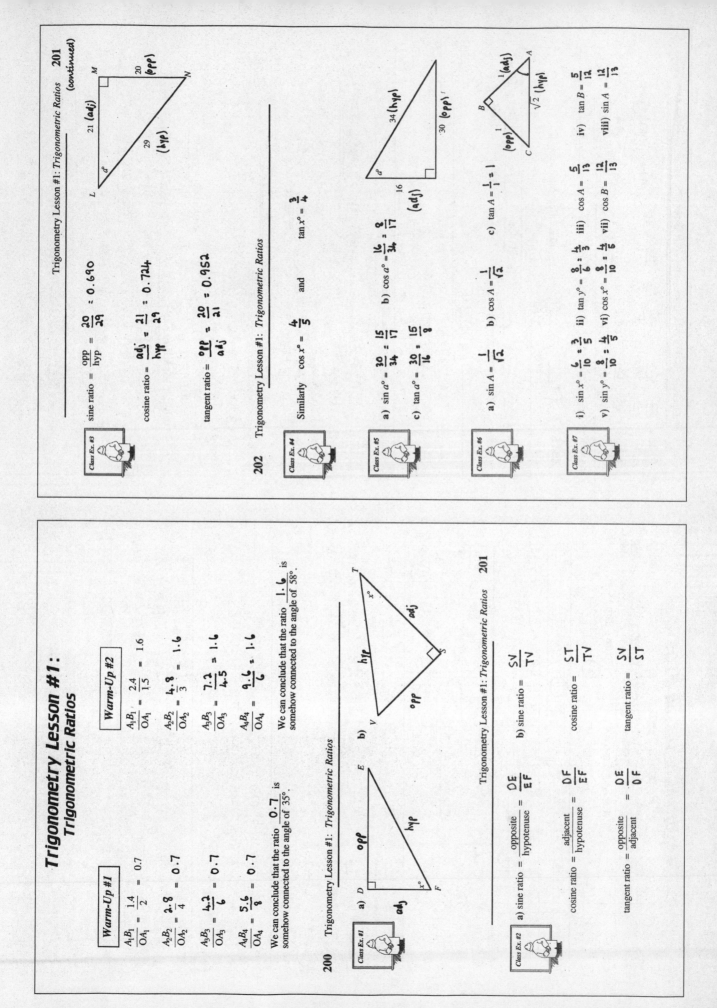

201 Trigonometry Lesson #1: *Trigonometric Ratios*

Class Ex. #2

a) sine ratio $= \dfrac{\text{opposite}}{\text{hypotenuse}} = \dfrac{DE}{EF}$ b) sine ratio $= \dfrac{SV}{TV}$

cosine ratio $= \dfrac{\text{adjacent}}{\text{hypotenuse}} = \dfrac{DF}{EF}$ cosine ratio $= \dfrac{ST}{TV}$

tangent ratio $= \dfrac{\text{opposite}}{\text{adjacent}} = \dfrac{DE}{OF}$ tangent ratio $= \dfrac{SV}{ST}$

Trigonometry Lesson #1: *Trigonometric Ratios* 201
(continued)

Class Ex. #3

sine ratio $= \dfrac{\text{opp}}{\text{hyp}} = \dfrac{20}{29} = 0.690$

cosine ratio $= \dfrac{\text{adj}}{\text{hyp}} = \dfrac{21}{29} = 0.724$

tangent ratio $= \dfrac{\text{opp}}{\text{adj}} = \dfrac{20}{21} = 0.952$

202 Trigonometry Lesson #1: *Trigonometric Ratios*

Class Ex. #4

Similarly $\cos x° = \dfrac{4}{5}$ and $\tan x° = \dfrac{3}{4}$

Class Ex. #5

a) $\sin a° = \dfrac{30}{34} = \dfrac{15}{17}$ b) $\cos a° = \dfrac{16}{34} = \dfrac{8}{17}$

c) $\tan a° = \dfrac{30}{16} = \dfrac{15}{8}$

Class Ex. #6

a) $\sin A = \dfrac{1}{\sqrt{2}}$ b) $\cos A = \dfrac{1}{\sqrt{2}}$ c) $\tan A = \dfrac{1}{1} = 1$

Class Ex. #7

i) $\sin x° = \dfrac{6}{10} = \dfrac{3}{5}$ ii) $\tan y° = \dfrac{8}{6} = \dfrac{4}{3}$ iii) $\cos A = \dfrac{5}{13}$ iv) $\tan B = \dfrac{5}{12}$

v) $\sin y° = \dfrac{8}{10} = \dfrac{4}{5}$ vi) $\cos x° = \dfrac{8}{10} = \dfrac{4}{5}$ vii) $\cos B = \dfrac{12}{13}$ viii) $\sin A = \dfrac{12}{13}$

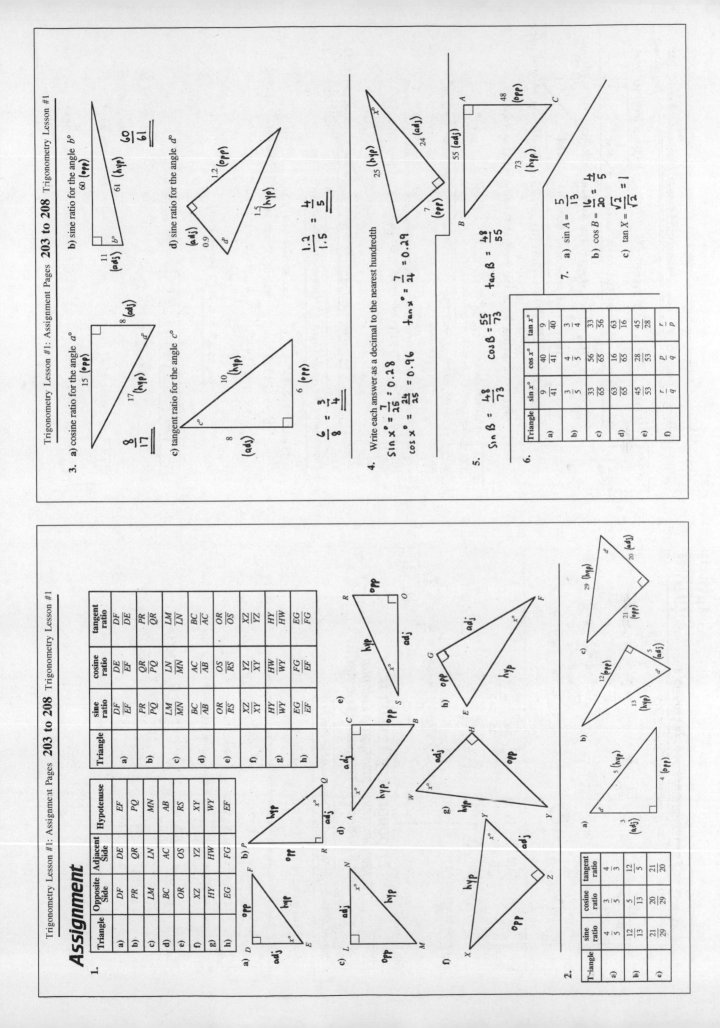

Assignment

1.

Triangle	Opposite Side	Adjacent Side	Hypotenuse
a)	DF	DE	EF
b)	PR	QR	PQ
c)	LM	LN	MN
d)	BC	AC	AB
e)	OR	OS	RS
f)	XZ	YZ	XY
g)	HY	HW	WY
h)	EG	FG	EF

Triangle	sine ratio	cosine ratio	tangent ratio
a)	$\frac{DF}{EF}$	$\frac{DE}{EF}$	$\frac{DF}{DE}$
b)	$\frac{PR}{PQ}$	$\frac{QR}{PQ}$	$\frac{PR}{QR}$
c)	$\frac{LM}{MN}$	$\frac{LN}{MN}$	$\frac{LM}{LN}$
d)	$\frac{BC}{AB}$	$\frac{AC}{AB}$	$\frac{BC}{AC}$
e)	$\frac{OR}{RS}$	$\frac{OS}{RS}$	$\frac{OR}{OS}$
f)	$\frac{XZ}{XY}$	$\frac{YZ}{XY}$	$\frac{XZ}{YZ}$
g)	$\frac{HY}{WY}$	$\frac{HW}{WY}$	$\frac{HY}{HW}$
h)	$\frac{EG}{EF}$	$\frac{FG}{EF}$	$\frac{EG}{FG}$

2.

Triangle	sine ratio	cosine ratio	tangent ratio
a)	$\frac{4}{5}$	$\frac{3}{5}$	$\frac{4}{3}$
b)	$\frac{12}{13}$	$\frac{5}{13}$	$\frac{12}{5}$
c)	$\frac{21}{29}$	$\frac{20}{29}$	$\frac{21}{20}$

---

3. a) cosine ratio for the angle $a°$

$$\frac{8}{17}$$

b) sine ratio for the angle $b°$

$$\frac{60}{61}$$

c) tangent ratio for the angle $c°$

$$\frac{6}{8} = \frac{3}{4}$$

d) sine ratio for the angle $d°$

$$\frac{1.2}{1.5} = \frac{4}{5}$$

4. Write each answer as a decimal to the nearest hundredth

$$\sin x° = \frac{7}{25} = 0.28$$

$$\cos x° = \frac{24}{25} = 0.96$$

$$\tan x° = \frac{7}{24} = 0.29$$

5.

$$\sin \beta = \frac{48}{73} \qquad \cos \beta = \frac{55}{73} \qquad \tan \beta = \frac{48}{55}$$

6.

Triangle	sin $x°$	cos $x°$	tan $x°$
a)	$\frac{9}{41}$	$\frac{40}{41}$	$\frac{9}{40}$
b)	$\frac{3}{5}$	$\frac{4}{5}$	$\frac{3}{4}$
c)	$\frac{33}{65}$	$\frac{56}{65}$	$\frac{33}{56}$
d)	$\frac{63}{65}$	$\frac{16}{65}$	$\frac{63}{16}$
e)	$\frac{45}{53}$	$\frac{28}{53}$	$\frac{45}{28}$
f)	$\frac{r}{q}$	$\frac{p}{q}$	$\frac{r}{p}$

7. a) $\sin A = \frac{5}{13}$

b) $\cos B = \frac{16}{20} = \frac{4}{5}$

c) $\tan X = \frac{\sqrt{2}}{\sqrt{2}} = 1$

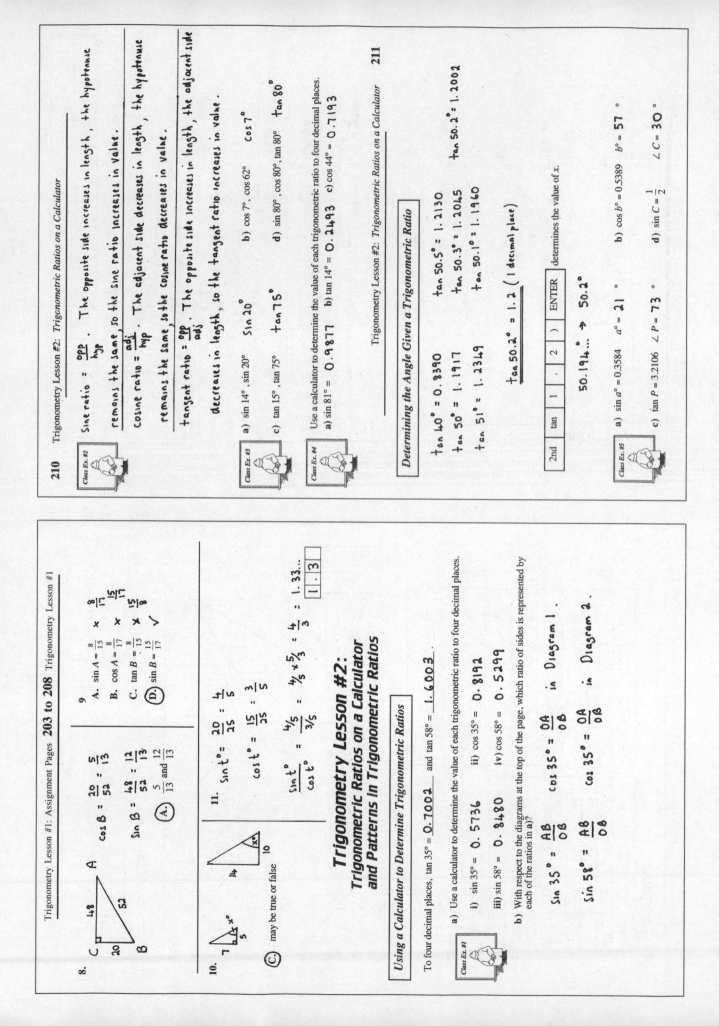

8.

cos B = $\frac{20}{52}$ = $\frac{5}{13}$

sin B = $\frac{48}{52}$ = $\frac{12}{13}$

Ⓐ. $\frac{5}{13}$ and $\frac{12}{13}$

9.

A. sin A = $\frac{8}{15}$ ✗

B. cos A = $\frac{8}{17}$ ✗

C. tan B = $\frac{8}{15}$ ✗

Ⓓ. sin B = $\frac{15}{17}$ ✓

10.

Ⓒ. may or false

11.

sin t° = $\frac{20}{25}$ = $\frac{4}{5}$

cos t° = $\frac{15}{25}$ = $\frac{3}{5}$

$\dfrac{\sin t°}{\cos t°}$ = $\dfrac{4/5}{3/5}$ = $\dfrac{4}{5} \times \dfrac{5}{3}$ = $\dfrac{4}{3}$ = 1.33...

[1].[3]

Trigonometry Lesson #2:
Trigonometric Ratios on a Calculator and Patterns In Trigonometric Ratios

Using a Calculator to Determine Trigonometric Ratios

To four decimal places, tan 35° = 0.7002 and tan 58° = 1.6003 .

Class Ex. #1

a) Use a calculator to determine the value of each trigonometric ratio to four decimal places.

i) sin 35° = 0.5736   ii) cos 35° = 0.8192

iii) sin 58° = 0.8480   iv) cos 58° = 0.5299

b) With respect to the diagrams at the top of the page, which ratio of sides is represented by each of the ratios in a)?

sin 35° = $\frac{AB}{OB}$ cos 35° = $\frac{OA}{OB}$ in Diagram 1.

sin 58° = $\frac{OA}{OB}$ cos 35° = $\frac{OA}{OB}$ in Diagram 2.

Class Ex. #2

Sine ratio = $\frac{opp}{hyp}$. The opposite side increases in length, the hypotenuse remains the same, so the sine ratio increases in value.

Cosine ratio = $\frac{adj}{hyp}$. The adjacent side decreases in length, the hypotenuse remains the same, so the cosine ratio decreases in value.

tangent ratio = $\frac{opp}{adj}$. The opposite side increases in length, the adjacent side decreases in length, so the tangent ratio increases in value.

Class Ex. #3

a) sin 14°, sin 20°   b) cos 7°, cos 62°   Cos 7°

c) tan 15°, tan 75°   Sin 20°   tan 75°

d) sin 80°, cos 80°, tan 80°   tan 80°

Class Ex. #4

Use a calculator to determine the value of each trigonometric ratio to four decimal places.

a) sin 81° = 0.9877   b) tan 14° = 0.2493   c) cos 44° = 0.7193

Determining the Angle Given a Trigonometric Ratio

tan 40° = 0.8390   tan 50.5° = 1.2130

tan 50° = 1.1917   tan 50.3° = 1.2045   tan 50.2° = 1.2002

tan 51° = 1.2349   tan 50.1° = 1.1960

tan 50.2° = 1.2 (1 decimal place)

50.194...° → 50.2°

[2nd] [tan] [1] [.] [2] [ )] [ENTER]   determines the value of x.

Class Ex. #5

a) sin a° = 0.3584   a° = 21 °   b) cos b° = 0.5389   b° = 57 °

c) tan P = 3.2106   ∠P = 73 °   d) sin C = $\frac{1}{2}$ ∠C = 30 °

$\sin a° = \dfrac{y}{r}$

Similarly $\cos a° = \dfrac{x}{r}$

and $\tan a° = \dfrac{y}{x}$

If $a = 0$, then the opposite side $y = 0$ and the adjacent side $x = r$.

So $\sin 0° = \dfrac{y}{r} = \dfrac{0}{r} = 0$ $\cos 0° = \dfrac{x}{r} = \dfrac{r}{r} = 1$ $\tan 0° = \dfrac{y}{x} = \dfrac{0}{r} = 0$

If $a = 90$, then the adjacent side $x = 0$ and the opposite side $y = r$.

So $\sin 90° = \dfrac{y}{r} = \dfrac{r}{r} = 1$ $\cos 90° = \dfrac{x}{r} = \dfrac{0}{r} = 0$ $\tan 90° = \dfrac{y}{x} = \dfrac{r}{0} =$ undefined

Class Ex. #6

Trigonometry Lesson #2: *Trigonometric Ratios on a Calculator*   213

Angle x°	0°	10°	20°	30°	40°	50°	60°	70°	80°	90°
sin x°	0	0.17	0.34	0.5	0.64	0.77	0.87	0.94	0.98	1

Complete the following statement:

As the angle $x°$ increases from 0° to 90°, $\sin x°$ increases from __0__ to __1__ .

Class Ex. #7

Draw a right triangle *LMN* in which $\angle L = 90°$ and $\angle N = x°$.

a) Write an expression for the measure of $\angle M$ in terms of x.

$\angle M = (90-x)°$

b) Explain using ratios why $\sin x° = \cos(90-x)°$.

$\sin x° = \sin N = \dfrac{LM}{MN}$

$\cos(90-x)° = \cos M = \dfrac{LM}{MN}$

$\sin x°$ and $\cos(90-x)°$ both are equal to $\dfrac{LM}{MN}$.

c) Complete the following using an angle between 0° and 90°.

i) $\sin 20° = \cos$ __70__°

ii) $\sin 8° = \cos$ __82__°

Assignment

1. a) 0.9272   b) 0.5774   c) 0.9455   d) 0.9272   e) 114301   f) 0.1219
   g) 1.7321   h) 0.3090   i) 0.3090   j) 0.7071   k) 0.7071   l) 1

2. a) 0.6143   b) 0.0840   c) 0.1184   d) 0.9951   e) 2.0145   f) 0.2990

3. a) 50°   b) 57°   c) 51°   d) 19°   e) 60°   f) 45°   g) 45°   h) 30°

4. a) 42.8°   b) 82.9°   c) 28.8°   d) 5.2°   e) 73.0°   f) 53.1°   g) 72.5°   h) 88.9°   i) 56.4°

5. Draw two triangles where the hypotenuse does not change.

   Sine ratio = $\dfrac{opp}{hyp}$

   The side opposite the angle of 20° is smaller than the side opposite the angle of 40°.

   The sine ratio is therefore smaller for an angle of 20° than for an angle of 40°.

6. Draw two triangles where the hypotenuse does not change.

   cosine ratio = $\dfrac{adj}{hyp}$

   The side adjacent to the angle of 30° is greater than the side adjacent to the angle of 70°.

   The cosine ratio is therefore greater for an angle of 30° than for an angle of 70°.

7. Draw two triangles where the hypotenuse does not change.

   tangent ratio = $\dfrac{opp}{adj}$

   The side opposite the angle of 15° is smaller than the side opposite the angle of 50°.

   The side adjacent to the angle of 15° is greater than the side adjacent to the angle of 50°.

   The tangent ratio is therefore smaller for an angle of 15° than for an angle of 50°.

8. a) sin 58°   b) cos 35°   c) tan 86°   d) cos 29°   e) sin 74°   f) tan 60°

9.

Angle x°	0°	10°	20°	30°	40°	50°	60°	70°	80°	90°
cos x°	1	0.98	0.94	0.87	0.77	0.64	0.5	0.34	0.17	0

Trigonometry Lesson #3:
Calculating The Length of a Side in a Right Triangle

Class Ex. #1

a) $x^2 = 2.5^2 + 3.7^2$
$= 19.94$
$x = \sqrt{19.94}$
$= 4.5$ cm

b) $AB^2 = 122^2 - 120^2$
$= 484$
$AB = \sqrt{484}$
$= 22$ mm

Trigonometry Lesson #3: *Calculating the Length of a Side*

We use the __sine__ ratio.   Cross multiply to get $14.2 \sin 52° = x$

$\sin 52° = \dfrac{x}{14.2}$

To 1 decimal place, $x = 11.2$ cm.

Class Ex. #2

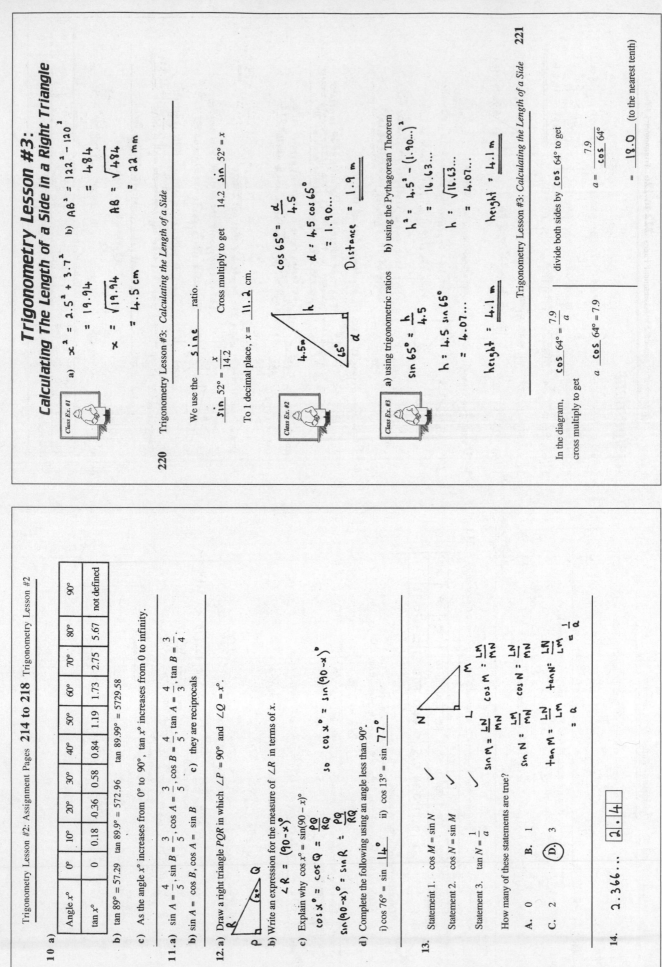

$\cos 65° = \dfrac{d}{4.5}$
$d = 4.5 \cos 65°$
$= 1.90...$

Distance $= 1.9$ m

Class Ex. #3

a) using trigonometric ratios

$\sin 65° = \dfrac{h}{4.5}$
$h = 4.5 \sin 65°$
$= 4.07...$
height $= 4.1$ m

b) using the Pythagorean Theorem

$h^2 = 4.5^2 - (1.90...)^2$
$= 16.63...$
$h = \sqrt{16.63...}$
$= 4.07...$
height $= 4.1$ m

Trigonometry Lesson #3: *Calculating the Length of a Side*

In the diagram, $\cos 64° = \dfrac{7.9}{a}$ divide both sides by $\cos 64°$ to get
cross multiply to get

$a \cos 64° = 7.9$

$a = \dfrac{7.9}{\cos 64°}$

$= 18.0$ (to the nearest tenth)

Trigonometry Lesson #2: Assignment Pages **214 to 218** Trigonometry Lesson #2

10 a)

Angle x°	0°	10°	20°	30°	40°	50°	60°	70°	80°	90°
tan x°	0	0.18	0.36	0.58	0.84	1.19	1.73	2.75	5.67	not defined

b) tan 89° = 57.29   tan 89.9° = 572.96   tan 89.99° = 5729.58

c) As the angle x° increases from 0° to 90°, tan x° increases from 0 to infinity.

11. a) $\sin A = \dfrac{4}{5}$, $\sin B = \dfrac{3}{5}$, $\cos A = \dfrac{3}{5}$, $\cos B = \dfrac{4}{5}$, $\tan A = \dfrac{4}{3}$, $\tan B = \dfrac{3}{4}$.

b) $\sin A = \cos B$, $\cos A = \sin B$ c) they are reciprocals

12. a) Draw a right triangle PQR in which $\angle P = 90°$ and $\angle Q = x°$.

b) Write an expression for the measure of $\angle R$ in terms of x.
$\angle R = (90-x)°$

c) Explain why $\cos x° = \sin(90 - x)°$

$\cos x° = \dfrac{PQ}{RQ}$ $\cos Q = \dfrac{PQ}{RQ}$

$\sin(90-x)° = \sin R = \dfrac{PQ}{RQ}$ so $\cos x° = \sin(90-x)°$

d) Complete the following using an angle less than 90°.
i) $\cos 76° = \sin \underline{14}°$ ii) $\cos 13° = \sin \underline{77}°$

13.

Statement 1. $\cos M = \sin N$ ✓
Statement 2. $\cos N = \sin M$ ✓
Statement 3. $\tan N = \dfrac{1}{a}$ ✓

$\sin M = \dfrac{LN}{MN}$ $\cos M = \dfrac{LM}{MN}$

$\sin N = \dfrac{LM}{MN}$ $\cos N = \dfrac{LN}{MN}$

$\tan M = \dfrac{LN}{LM}$ $\tan N = \dfrac{LM}{LN} = \dfrac{1}{a}$
$= a$

How many of these statements are true?

A. 0   B. 1   C. 2   (D.) 3

14. $2.366... = \boxed{2.4}$

Class Ex. #4

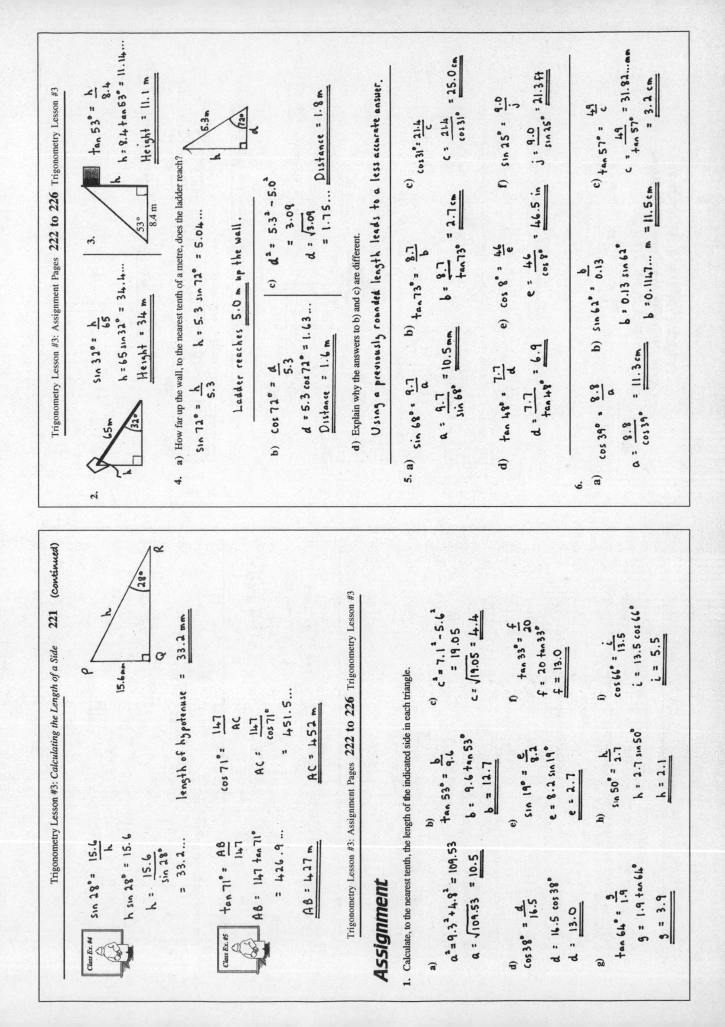

$\sin 28° = \dfrac{15.6}{h}$

$h \sin 28° = 15.6$

$h = \dfrac{15.6}{\sin 28°}$

$= 33.2...$

length of hypotenuse $= \underline{33.2 \text{ mm}}$

Class Ex. #5

$\tan 71° = \dfrac{AB}{147}$

$AB = 147 \tan 71°$

$= 426.9...$

$\underline{AB = 4.27 \text{ m}}$

$\cos 71° = \dfrac{147}{AC}$

$AC = \dfrac{147}{\cos 71°}$

$= 451.5...$

$\underline{AC = 452 \text{ m}}$

Assignment

1. Calculate, to the nearest tenth, the length of the indicated side in each triangle.

a) $a^2 = 9.3^2 + 4.8^2 = 104.53$

$a = \sqrt{104.53} = \underline{10.5}$

b) $\tan 53° = \dfrac{b}{9.6}$

$b = 9.6 \tan 53°$

$\underline{b = 12.7}$

c) $c^2 = 7.1^2 - 5.6^2$

$= 19.05$

$c = \sqrt{19.05} = \underline{4.4}$

d) $\cos 38° = \dfrac{d}{16.5}$

$d = 16.5 \cos 38°$

$\underline{d = 13.0}$

e) $\sin 19° = \dfrac{e}{8.2}$

$e = 8.2 \sin 19°$

$\underline{e = 2.7}$

f) $\tan 33° = \dfrac{f}{20}$

$f = 20 \tan 33°$

$\underline{f = 13.0}$

g) $\tan 64° = \dfrac{g}{1.9}$

$g = 1.9 \tan 64°$

$\underline{g = 3.9}$

h) $\sin 50° = \dfrac{h}{2.7}$

$h = 2.7 \sin 50°$

$\underline{h = 2.1}$

i) $\cos 66° = \dfrac{i}{13.5}$

$i = 13.5 \cos 66°$

$\underline{i = 5.5}$

2. $\sin 32° = \dfrac{h}{65}$

$h = 65 \sin 32° = 34.4...$

$\underline{\text{Height} = 34 \text{ m}}$

3. $\tan 53° = \dfrac{h}{8.4}$

$h = 8.4 \tan 63° = 11.14...$

$\underline{\text{Height} = 11.1 \text{ m}}$

4. a) How far up the wall, to the nearest tenth of a metre, does the ladder reach?

$\sin 72° = \dfrac{h}{5.3}$

$h = 5.3 \sin 72° = 5.04...$

$\underline{\text{Ladder reaches } 5.0 \text{ m up the wall.}}$

b) $\cos 72° = \dfrac{d}{5.3}$

$d = 5.3 \cos 72° = 1.63...$

$\underline{\text{Distance} = 1.6 \text{ m}}$

c) $d^2 = 5.3^2 - 5.0^2$

$= 3.09$

$d = \sqrt{3.09}$

$= 1.75...$

$\underline{\text{Distance} = 1.8 \text{ m}}$

d) Explain why the answers to b) and c) are different.

Using a previously rounded length leads to a less accurate answer.

5. a) $\sin 68° = \dfrac{9.7}{a}$

$a = \dfrac{9.7}{\sin 68°} = \underline{10.5 \text{ mm}}$

b) $\tan 73° = \dfrac{8.7}{b}$

$b = \dfrac{8.7}{\tan 73°} = \underline{2.7 \text{ cm}}$

c) $\cos 31° = \dfrac{21.4}{c}$

$c = \dfrac{21.4}{\cos 31°} = \underline{25.0 \text{ cm}}$

d) $\tan 48° = \dfrac{7.7}{d}$

$d = \dfrac{7.7}{\tan 48°} = \underline{6.9}$

e) $\cos 8° = \dfrac{46}{e}$

$e = \dfrac{46}{\cos 8°} = \underline{46.5 \text{ in}}$

f) $\sin 25° = \dfrac{9.0}{j}$

$j = \dfrac{9.0}{\sin 25°} = \underline{21.3 \text{ ft}}$

6. a) $\cos 39° = \dfrac{8.8}{a}$

$a = \dfrac{8.8}{\cos 39°} = \underline{11.3 \text{ cm}}$

b) $\sin 61° = \dfrac{b}{0.13}$

$b = 0.13 \sin 61°$

$b = 0.1147... \text{ m} = \underline{11.5 \text{ cm}}$

c) $\tan 57° = \dfrac{49}{c}$

$c = \dfrac{49}{\tan 57°} = 31.81...\text{mm}$

$= \underline{3.2 \text{ cm}}$

Trigonometry Lesson #4:
Calculating the Measure of an Angle in a Right Triangle

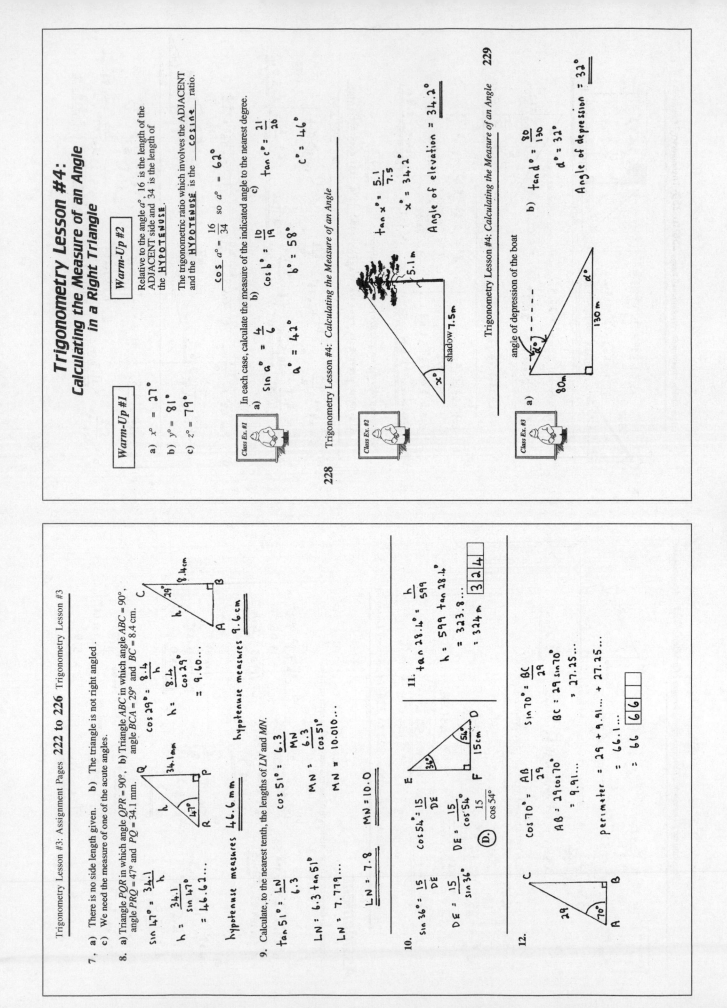

Warm-Up #1

a) $x° = 27°$

b) $y° = 81°$

c) $z° = 79°$

Warm-Up #2

Relative to the angle $a°$, 16 is the length of the ADJACENT side and 34 is the length of the **HYPOTENUSE**.

The trigonometric ratio which involves the ADJACENT and the **HYPOTENUSE** is the **COSINE** ratio.

$\cos a° = \dfrac{16}{34}$ so $a° = 62°$

Class Ex. #1 In each case, calculate the measure of the indicated angle to the nearest degree.

a) $\sin a° = \dfrac{4}{6}$

$a° = 42°$

b) $\cos b° = \dfrac{10}{19}$

$b° = 58°$

c) $\tan c° = \dfrac{21}{20}$

$c° = 46°$

Class Ex. #2

$\tan x° = \dfrac{5.1}{7.5}$

$x° = 34.2°$

Angle of elevation $= 34.2°$

5.1 m

shadow 7.5m

Class Ex. #3

a) angle of depression of the boat

b) $\tan d° = \dfrac{80}{130}$

$d° = 32°$

Angle of depression $= 32°$

80m   130 m $d°$

Trigonometry Lesson #3: Assignment Pages **222 to 226** Trigonometry Lesson #3

7. a) There is no side length given. b) The triangle is not right angled.
   c) We need the measure of one of the acute angles.

8. a) Triangle PQR in which angle $QPR = 90°$, angle $PRQ = 47°$ and $PQ = 34.1$ mm. b) Triangle ABC in which angle $ABC = 90°$, angle $BCA = 29°$ and $BC = 8.4$ cm.

a)
$\sin 47° = \dfrac{34.1}{h}$

$h = \dfrac{34.1}{\sin 47°}$

$= 46.62...$

hypotenuse measures **46.6 mm**

b)
$\cos 29° = \dfrac{8.4}{h}$

$h = \dfrac{8.4}{\cos 29°}$

$= 9.60...$

hypotenuse measures **9.6 cm**

9. Calculate, to the nearest tenth, the lengths of LN and MN.

$\tan 51° = \dfrac{LN}{6.3}$

$LN = 6.3 \tan 51°$

$LN = 7.779...$

$LN = 7.8$

$\cos 51° = \dfrac{6.3}{MN}$

$MN = \dfrac{6.3}{\cos 51°}$

$MN = 10.010...$

$MN = 10.0$

10.
$\sin 36° = \dfrac{15}{DE}$

$DE = \dfrac{15}{\sin 36°}$

$\cos 54° = \dfrac{15}{DE}$

$DE = \dfrac{15}{\cos 54°}$

D.

11.
$\tan 28.4° = \dfrac{h}{599}$

$h = 599 \tan 28.4...$

$= 323.8...$

$= 324 \text{ m}$ **324**

12.
$\cos 70° = \dfrac{AB}{29}$

$AB = 29 \cos 70°$

$= 9.91...$

$\sin 70° = \dfrac{BC}{29}$

$BC = 29 \sin 70°$

$= 27.25...$

perimeter $= 29 + 9.91... + 27.25...$

$= 66.1...$

$= 66$ **66**

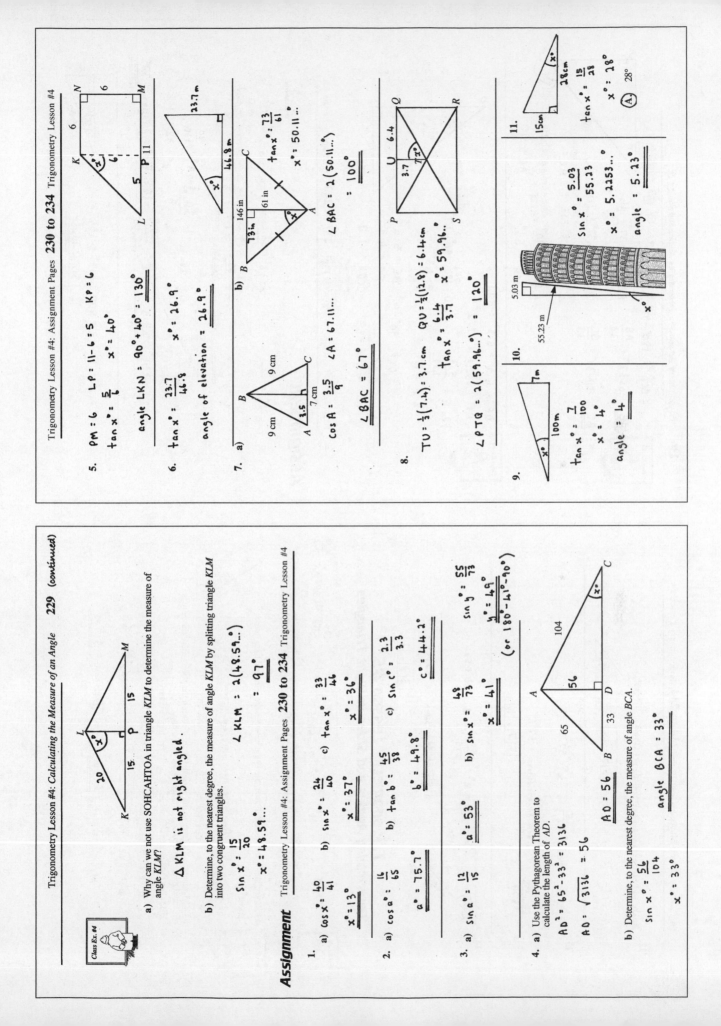

Class Ex. #4

a) Why can we not use SOHCAHTOA in triangle *KLM* to determine the measure of angle *KLM*?

△KLM is not right angled.

b) Determine, to the nearest degree, the measure of angle *KLM* by splitting triangle *KLM* into two congruent triangles.

$\sin x° = \frac{15}{20}$

$x° = 48.59...$

$\angle KLM = 2(48.59...°)$
$= 97°$

Assignment   Trigonometry Lesson #4: Assignment Pages **230 to 234** Trigonometry Lesson #4

1. a) $\cos x° = \frac{40}{41}$

   $x° = 13°$

   b) $\sin x° = \frac{24}{40}$

   $x° = 37°$

   c) $\tan x° = \frac{33}{46}$

   $x° = 36°$

2. a) $\cos a° = \frac{16}{65}$

   $a° = 75.7°$

   b) $\tan b° = \frac{45}{38}$

   $b° = 49.8°$

   c) $\sin c° = \frac{2.3}{3.3}$

   $c° = 44.2°$

3. a) $\sin a° = \frac{12}{15}$

   $a° = 53°$

   b) $\sin x° = \frac{48}{73}$

   $x° = 41°$

   $\sin y = \frac{55}{73}$
   $y = 49°$
   (or $180 - 41° - 90°$)

4. a) Use the Pythagorean Theorem to calculate the length of *AD*.

   $AD^2 = 65^2 - 33^2 = 3136$

   $AD = \sqrt{3136} = 56$

   $AD = 56$

   b) Determine, to the nearest degree, the measure of angle *BCA*.

   $\sin x° = \frac{56}{104}$

   $x° = 33°$

   angle BCA = 33°

---

5. $PM = 6$ $LP = 11 - 6 = 5$ $KP = 6$

   $\tan x° = \frac{5}{6}$ $x° = 40°$

   angle LKN = $90° + 40° = 130°$

6. $\tan x° = \frac{23.7}{46.8}$ $x° = 26.9°$

   angle of elevation = 26.9°

7. a) $\cos A = \frac{3.5}{9}$

   $\angle BAC = 67.11...$

   $\angle BAC = 67°$

   b) $\tan x° = \frac{73}{61}$

   $x° = 50.11...°$

   $\angle BAC = 2(50.11...°)$
   $= 100°$

8. $TU = \frac{1}{2}(7.4) = 3.7cm$ $QU = \frac{1}{2}(12.8) = 6.4cm$

   $\tan x° = \frac{6.4}{3.7}$ $x° = 59.96...°$

   $\angle PTQ = 2(59.96...°) = 120°$

9. $\tan x° = \frac{7}{100}$

   $x° = 4°$

   angle = 4°

10. $\sin x° = \frac{5.03}{55.23}$

    $x° = 5.2253...°$

    angle = 5.23°

11. $\tan x° = \frac{15}{28}$

    $x° = 28°$

    Ⓐ 28°

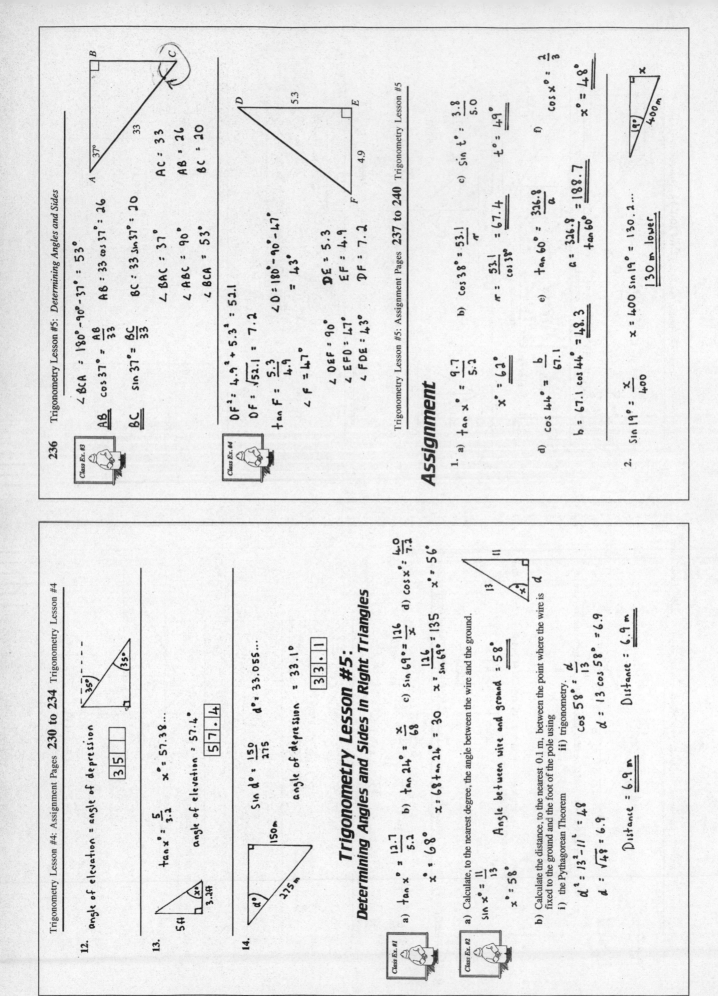

236 Trigonometry Lesson #5: Determining Angles and Sides

Class Ex. #3

$\angle BCA = 180° - 90° - 37° = 53°$

$\dfrac{AB}{33} \quad \cos 37° = \dfrac{AB}{33} \quad AB = 33\cos 37° = 26$

$\dfrac{BC}{33} \quad \sin 37° = \dfrac{BC}{33} \quad BC = 33\sin 37° = 20$

$\angle BAC = 37°$

$\angle ABC = 90°$

$\angle BCA = 53°$

$AC = 33$

$AB = 26$

$BC = 20$

Class Ex. #4

$DF^2 = 4.9^2 + 5.3^2 = 52.1$

$DF = \sqrt{52.1} = 7.2$

$\tan F = \dfrac{5.3}{4.9}$

$\angle F = 47°$

$\angle D = 180° - 90° - 47° = 43°$

$\angle DEF = 90°$

$\angle EFD = 47°$

$\angle FDE = 43°$

$DE = 5.3$

$EF = 4.9$

$DF = 7.2$

Assignment

Trigonometry Lesson #5: Assignment Pages 237 to 240 Trigonometry Lesson #5

1. a) $\tan x° = \dfrac{9.7}{5.2}$
   $x° = 62°$

   b) $\cos 38° = \dfrac{53.1}{r}$
   $r = \dfrac{53.1}{\cos 38°} = 67.4$

   c) $\sin t° = \dfrac{3.8}{5.0}$
   $t° = 49°$

   d) $\cos 44° = \dfrac{b}{67.1}$
   $b = 67.1\cos 44° = 48.3$

   e) $\tan 60° = \dfrac{326.8}{a}$
   $a = \dfrac{326.8}{\tan 60°} = 188.7$

   f) $\cos x° = \dfrac{2}{3}$
   $x° = 48°$

2. $\sin 19° = \dfrac{x}{400}$
   $x = 400\sin 19° = 130.2...$
   130 m lower

Trigonometry Lesson #4: Assignment Pages 230 to 234 Trigonometry Lesson #4

12. angle of elevation = angle of depression |3|5|

13. $\tan x° = \dfrac{5}{3.2}$
    $x° = 57.38...$
    angle of elevation = 57.4° |57.4|

14. $\sin d° = \dfrac{150}{275}$
    $d° = 33.055...$
    angle of depression = 33.1° |33.1|

Trigonometry Lesson #5:
Determining Angles and Sides In Right Triangles

Class Ex. #1

a) $\tan x° = \dfrac{12.7}{5.2}$
   $x° = 68°$

b) $\tan 24° = \dfrac{x}{68}$
   $x = 68\tan 24° = 30$

c) $\sin 69° = \dfrac{126}{x}$
   $x = \dfrac{126}{\sin 69°} = 135$

d) $\cos x° = \dfrac{4.0}{7.2}$
   $x° = 56°$

Class Ex. #2

a) Calculate, to the nearest degree, the angle between the wire and the ground.

$\sin x° = \dfrac{11}{13}$

$x° = 58°$ Angle between wire and ground = 58°

b) Calculate the distance, to the nearest 0.1 m, between the point where the wire is fixed to the ground and the foot of the pole using

i) the Pythagorean Theorem

$d^2 = 13^2 - 11^2 = 48$

$d = \sqrt{48} = 6.9$

Distance = 6.9 m

ii) trigonometry.

$\cos 58° = \dfrac{d}{13}$

$d = 13\cos 58° = 6.9$

Distance = 6.9 m

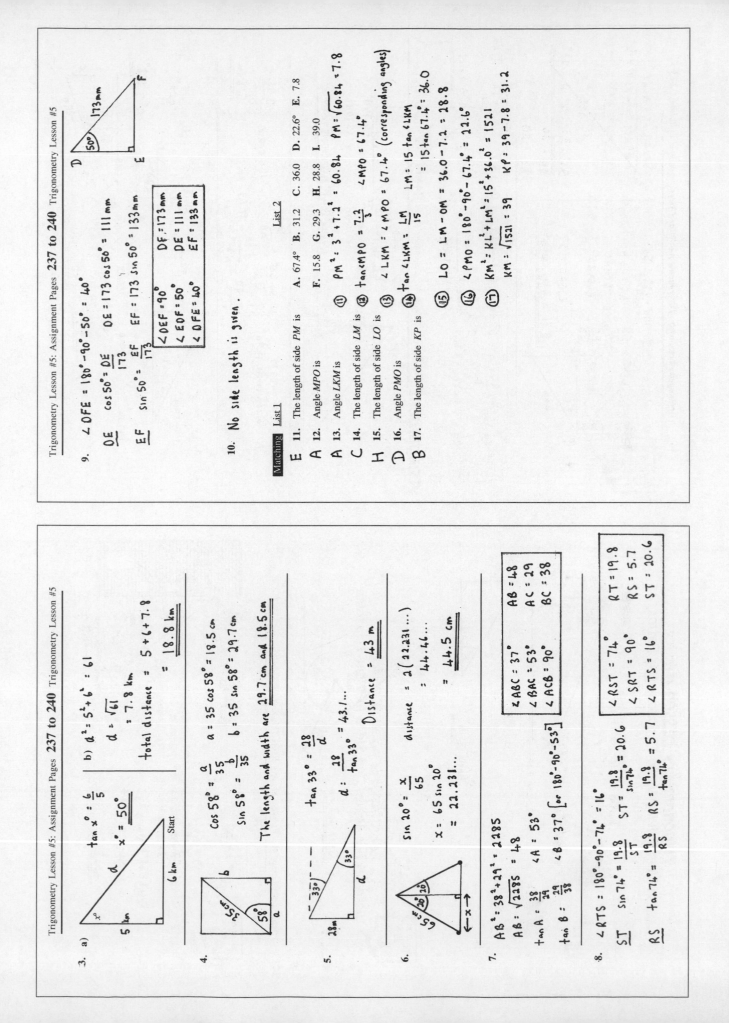

9. $\angle DFE = 180° - 90° - 50° = 40°$

$\cos 50° = \dfrac{DE}{173}$ $DE = 173 \cos 50° = 111 \text{ mm}$

$\sin 50° = \dfrac{EF}{173}$ $EF = 173 \sin 50° = 133 \text{ mm}$

$\angle DEF = 90°$	$DF = 173 \text{ mm}$
$\angle EOF = 50°$	$DE = 111 \text{ mm}$
$\angle DFE = 40°$	$EF = 133 \text{ mm}$

10. No side length is given.

Matching   List 1   List 2

E **11.** The length of side *PM* is   A. 67.4° B. 31.2 C. 36.0 D. 22.6° E. 7.8

A **12.** Angle *MPO* is   F. 15.8 G. 29.3 H. 28.8 I. 39.0

A **13.** Angle *LKM* is

C **14.** The length of side *LM* is

H **15.** The length of side *LO* is

D **16.** Angle *PMO* is

B **17.** The length of side *KP* is

⑪ $PM^2 = 3^2 + 7.2^2 = 60.84$ $PM = \sqrt{60.84} \approx 7.8$

⑫ $\tan \angle MPO = \dfrac{7.2}{3}$ $\angle MPO = 67.4°$

⑬ $\angle LKM = \angle MPO = 67.4°$ (corresponding angles)

⑭ $\tan \angle LKM = \dfrac{LM}{15}$ $LM = 15 \tan \angle LKM = 15 \tan 67.4° = 36.0$

⑮ $LO = LM - OM = 36.0 - 7.2 = 28.8$

⑯ $\angle PMO = 180° - 90° - 67.4° = 22.6°$

⑰ $KM^2 = KL^2 + LM^2 = 15^2 + 36.0^2 = 1521$ $KM = \sqrt{1521} = 39$ $KP = 39 - 7.8 = 31.2$

---

3. a) $\tan x° = \dfrac{6}{5}$ $x° = 50°$

b) $a^2 = 5^2 + 6^2 = 61$ $a = \sqrt{61} = 7.8 \text{ km}$

total distance $= 5 + 6 + 7.8 = 18.8 \text{ km}$

4. $\cos 58° = \dfrac{a}{35}$ $a = 35 \cos 58° = 18.5 \text{ cm}$

$\sin 58° = \dfrac{b}{35}$ $b = 35 \sin 58° = 29.7 \text{ cm}$

The length and width are 29.7 cm and 18.5 cm

5. $\tan 33° = \dfrac{28}{d}$ $d = \dfrac{28}{\tan 33°} = 43.1...$

Distance = 43 m

6. $\sin 20° = \dfrac{x}{65}$ $x = 65 \sin 20° = 22.231...$

distance $= 2(22.231...) = 44.46... = 44.5 \text{ cm}$

7. $AB^2 = 38^2 + 29^2 = 2285$ $AB = \sqrt{2285} = 48$

$\tan A = \dfrac{38}{29}$ $\angle A = 53°$

$\tan B = \dfrac{29}{38}$ $\angle B = 37°$ [or $180° - 90° - 53°$]

$\angle ABC = 37°$	$AB = 48$
$\angle BAC = 53°$	$AC = 29$
$\angle ACB = 90°$	$BC = 38$

8. $\angle RTS = 180° - 90° - 74° = 16°$

$\sin 74° = \dfrac{19.8}{ST}$ $ST = \dfrac{19.8}{\sin 74°} = 20.6$

$\tan 74° = \dfrac{19.8}{RS}$ $RS = \dfrac{19.8}{\tan 74°} = 5.7$

$\angle RST = 74°$	$RT = 19.8$
$\angle SRT = 90°$	$RS = 5.7$
$\angle RTS = 16°$	$ST = 20.6$

Trigonometry Lesson #6:
Problem Solving Using Trigonometric Ratios

Class Ex. #1

a)
height of tree = 11.1 + 1.8
= 12.9 m

$\tan 12° = \dfrac{x}{52}$

$x = 52 \tan 12°$

$= 11.1$

b)
$\tan x° = \dfrac{12.9}{52}$

$x° = 14°$

Angle = 14°

Class Ex. #2

$\sin 15° = \dfrac{20}{OC}$

$OC = \dfrac{20}{\sin 15°} = 47.3...$

$OC = 47 \text{ mm}$

242 Trigonometry Lesson #6: Problem Solving Using Trigonometric Ratios

Class Ex. #3

$\tan 62° = \dfrac{x}{12}$

$x = 12 \tan 62°$

$= 22.56...$

height of building
= 22.56... + 5.2 + 6
= 33.8 ft

Trigonometry Lesson #6: Problem Solving Using Trigonometric Ratios 243

Class Ex. #4

a)
$\cos 30° = \dfrac{PR}{6}$

$PR = 6 \cos 30°$

$= 5.2$

R is 5.2 km east of P

b) bearing of S from P
= ∠ NPS = ∠ PSR = x°

$\tan x° = \dfrac{5.2}{12}$

$x° = 23°$

bearing is 23° or 023°

c) $\sin 30° = \dfrac{RQ}{6}$

$RQ = 6 \sin 30° = 3 \text{ km}$

total distance = PQ + QR + RS = 6 + 3 + 12 = 21 km

$\text{time} = \dfrac{\text{distance}}{\text{speed}} = \dfrac{21}{9} = 2\frac{1}{3} = 2.3 \text{ hours}$

Assignment Trigonometry Lesson #6: Assignment Pages **244 to 248** Trigonometry Lesson #6

1.
$\tan 34.1° = \dfrac{1063}{x}$

$x = \dfrac{1063}{\tan 34.1°}$

$= 1570 \text{ ft.}$

length of shadow = 1570 ft

2. a) The angle in a semicircle is 90°

b) $\sin 38° = \dfrac{7.1}{AB}$

$AB = \dfrac{7.1}{\sin 38°} = 11.53... \text{ cm}$

radius = $\dfrac{11.53...}{2}$ = 5.8 cm

3. a)
$\tan 16° = \dfrac{h}{300}$

$h = 300 \tan 16°$

$= 86.0...$

height = 86 m

b) 300 - 75 = 225

$\tan x° = \dfrac{86.0...}{225}$

$x° = 21°$

angle of elevation = 21°

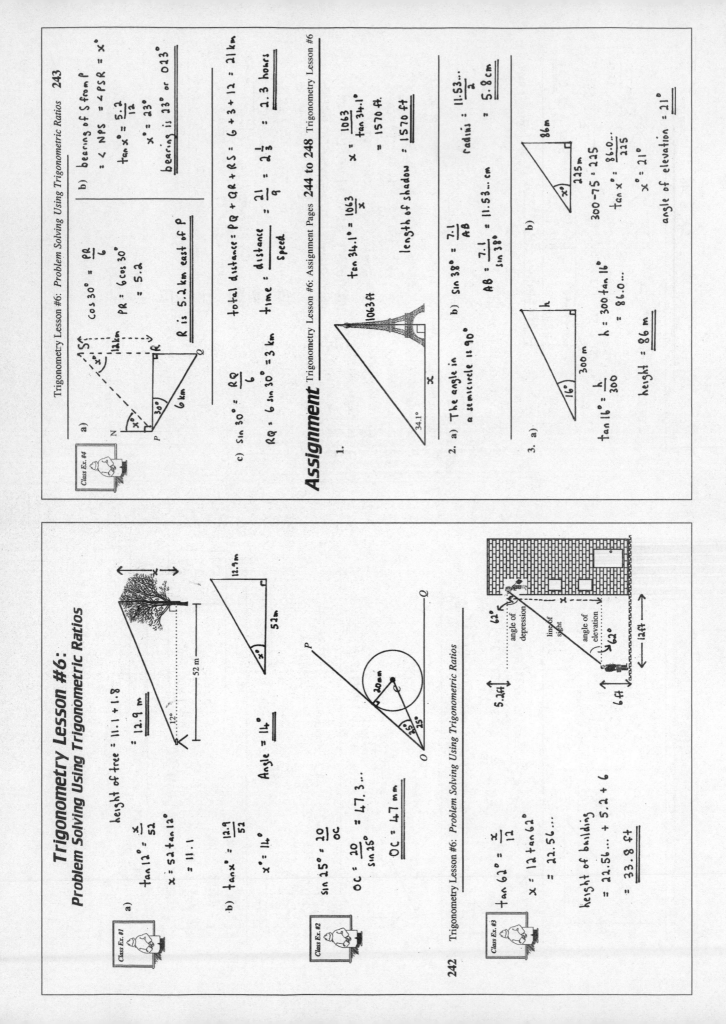

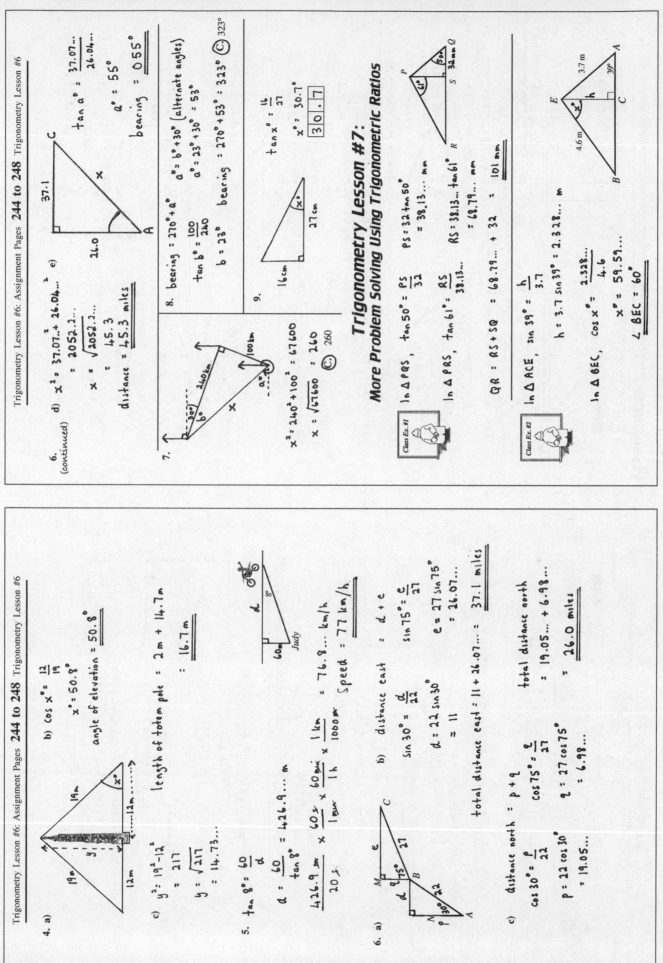

6.
(continued)

d) $x^2 = 37.07...^2 + 26.04...^2$ e)
$= 2052.2...$
$x = \sqrt{2052.2...}$
$= 45.3$
distance $= 45.3$ miles

$\tan a° = \dfrac{37.07...}{26.04...}$
$a° = 55°$
bearing $= \underline{055°}$

8. bearing $= 270° + a°$
$\tan b° = \dfrac{100}{240}$
$b = 23°$

$a° = b° + 30°$ (alternate angles)
$a° = 23° + 30° = 53°$
bearing $= 270° + 53° = 323°$ C. 323°

7. $x^2 = 240^2 + 100^2 = 67600$
$x = \sqrt{67600} = 260$ C. 260

9. $\tan x° = \dfrac{16}{27}$
$x° = 30.7°$
$\boxed{30.7}$

Trigonometry Lesson #7:
More Problem Solving Using Trigonometric Ratios

Class Ex. #1

In $\triangle PQS$, $\tan 50° = \dfrac{PS}{32}$
$PS = 32 \tan 50°$
$= 38.13...$ mm

In $\triangle PRS$, $\tan 61° = \dfrac{RS}{38.13...}$
$RS = 38.13... \tan 61°$
$= 68.79...$ mm

$QR = RS + SQ = 68.79... + 32 = \underline{101 \text{ mm}}$

Class Ex. #2

In $\triangle ACE$, $\sin 39° = \dfrac{h}{3.7}$
$h = 3.7 \sin 39° = 2.328...$ m

In $\triangle BEC$, $\cos x° = \dfrac{2.328...}{4.6}$
$x° = 59.59...$
$\angle BEC = \underline{60°}$

---

4. a)
b) $\cos x° = \dfrac{12}{19}$
$x° = 50.8°$
angle of elevation $= \underline{50.8°}$

c) $y^2 = 19^2 - 12^2$
$= 217$
$y = \sqrt{217}$
$= 14.73...$
length of totem pole $= 2m + 14.7m = \underline{16.7 \text{ m}}$

5. $\tan 8° = \dfrac{60}{d}$
$d = \dfrac{60}{\tan 8°} = 426.9... \text{ m}$

$\dfrac{426.9 \text{ m}}{20 \text{ s}} \times \dfrac{60 \text{ s}}{1 \text{ min}} \times \dfrac{60 \text{ min}}{1 \text{ h}} \times \dfrac{1 \text{ km}}{1000 \text{ m}} = 76.8... \text{ km/h}$
Speed $= \underline{77 \text{ km/h}}$

6. a)
b) distance east $= d + e$
$\sin 30° = \dfrac{d}{22}$
$d = 22 \sin 30°$
$= 11$

$\sin 75° = \dfrac{e}{27}$
$e = 27 \sin 75°$
$= 26.07...$

total distance east $= 11 + 26.07... = \underline{37.1 \text{ miles}}$

c) distance north $= p + q$
$\cos 30° = \dfrac{p}{22}$ $\cos 75° = \dfrac{q}{27}$
$p = 22 \cos 30°$ $q = 27 \cos 75°$
$= 19.05...$ $= 6.98...$

total distance north
$= 19.05... + 6.98...$
$= \underline{26.0 \text{ miles}}$

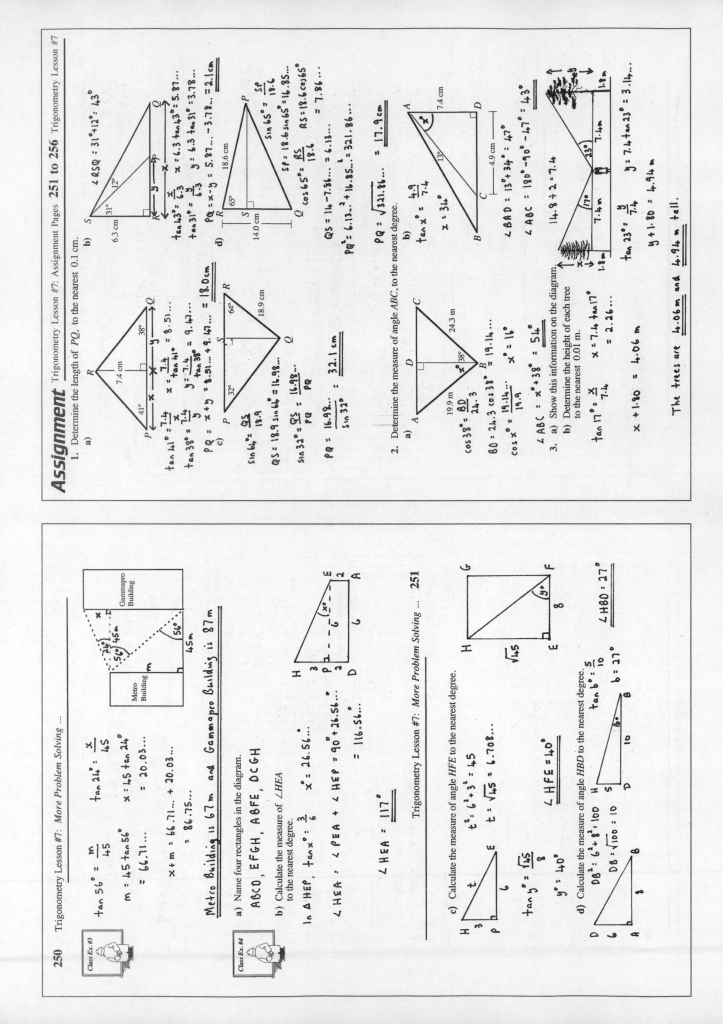

1. Determine the length of PQ, to the nearest 0.1 cm.

a)

$\tan 41° = \dfrac{7.4}{x}$ $x = \dfrac{7.4}{\tan 41°} = 8.51...$

$\tan 38° = \dfrac{7.4}{y}$ $y = \dfrac{7.4}{\tan 38°} = 9.47...$

$PQ = x + y = 8.51... + 9.47... = 18.0 \text{ cm}$

b)

$\angle RSQ = 31° + 12° = 43°$

$\tan 43° = \dfrac{x}{6.3}$ $x = 6.3 \tan 43° = 5.87...$

$\tan 31° = \dfrac{y}{6.3}$ $y = 6.3 \tan 31° = 3.78...$

$PQ = x - y = 5.87... - 3.78... = 2.1 \text{ cm}$

c)

$\sin 64° = \dfrac{QS}{18.9}$

$QS = 18.9 \sin 64° = 16.98...$

$\sin 32° = \dfrac{QS}{PQ} = \dfrac{16.98}{PQ}$

$PQ = \dfrac{16.98...}{\sin 32°} = 32.1 \text{ cm}$

d)

$\sin 65° = \dfrac{SP}{18.6}$

$SP = 18.6 \sin 65° = 16.85...$

$\cos 65° = \dfrac{RS}{18.6}$ $RS = 18.6 \cos 65° = 7.86...$

$QS = 14 - 7.86... = 6.13...$

$PQ^2 = 6.13...^2 + 16.85...^2 = 321.86...$

$PQ = \sqrt{321.86...} = 17.9 \text{ cm}$

2. Determine the measure of angle ABC, to the nearest degree.

a)

$\cos 38° = \dfrac{BD}{24.3}$

$BD = 24.3 \cos 38° = 19.14...$

$\cos x° = \dfrac{19.14...}{19.9}$ $x° = 16°$

$\angle ABC = x° + 38° = 54°$

b)

$\tan x° = \dfrac{4.9}{7.4}$

$x = 34°$

$\angle BAD = 13° + 34° = 47°$

$\angle ABC = 180° - 90° - 47° = 43°$

3. a) Show this information on the diagram.
   b) Determine the height of each tree to the nearest 0.01 m.

$14.8 \div 2 = 7.4$

$\tan 23° = \dfrac{x}{7.4}$ $x = 7.4 \tan 17°$ $y = 7.4 \tan 23°$

$\tan 17° = \dfrac{x}{7.4}$ $= 2.26...$ $y = 4.94 \text{ m}$

$x + 1.80 = 4.06 \text{ m}$ $y + 1.80 = 4.94 \text{ m}$

The trees are __4.06 m__ and __4.94 m tall.__

Class Ex. #3

Gammapro Building
Metro Building

$\tan 56° = \dfrac{m}{45}$ $\tan 24° = \dfrac{x}{45}$

$m = 45 \tan 56°$ $x = 45 \tan 24°$

$= 66.71...$ $= 20.03...$

$x + m = 66.71... + 20.03...$

$= 86.75...$

Metro Building is 67 m and Gammapro Building is 87 m

Class Ex. #4

a) Name four rectangles in the diagram.

$ABCD, EFGH, ABFE, DCGH$

b) Calculate the measure of $\angle HEA$ to the nearest degree.

In $\triangle HEP$, $\tan x° = \dfrac{3}{6}$ $x° = 26.56...°$

$\angle HEA = \angle PEA + \angle HEP = 90° + 26.56...°$

$= 116.56...°$

$\angle HEA = 117°$

c) Calculate the measure of angle HFE to the nearest degree.

$t^2 = 6^2 + 3^2 = 45$

$t = \sqrt{45} = 6.708...$

$\tan y° = \dfrac{\sqrt{45}}{8}$

$y° = 40°$

$\angle HFE = 40°$

d) Calculate the measure of angle HBD to the nearest degree.

$DB^2 = 6^2 + 8^2 = 100$

$DB = \sqrt{100} = 10$

$\tan b° = \dfrac{5}{10}$

$b = 27°$

$\angle HBD = 27°$

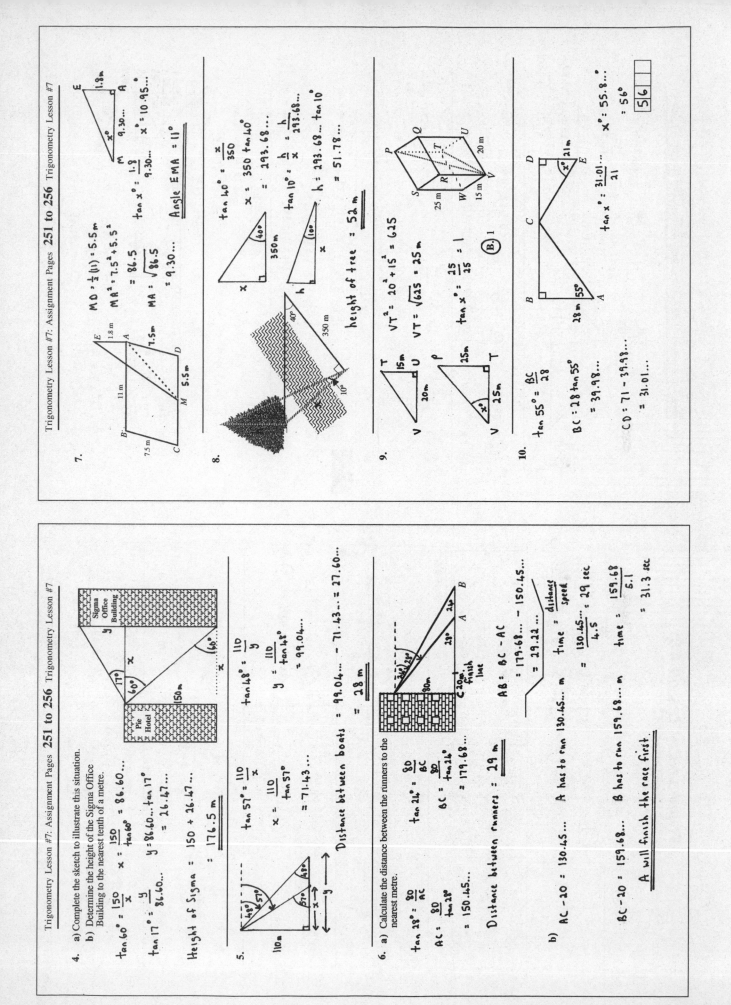

4. a) Complete the sketch to illustrate this situation.

b) Determine the height of the Sigma Office Building to the nearest tenth of a metre.

$\tan 60° = \dfrac{150}{x}$ $x = \dfrac{150}{\tan 60°} = 86.60...$

$\tan 17° = \dfrac{y}{86.60...}$ $y = 86.60...\tan 17° = 26.47...$

Height of Sigma $= 150 + 26.47...$

$= 176.5 \text{ m}$

5. $\tan 57° = \dfrac{110}{x}$

$x = \dfrac{110}{\tan 57°} = 71.43...$

$\tan 48° = \dfrac{110}{y}$

$y = \dfrac{110}{\tan 48°} = 99.04...$

Distance between boats $= 99.04... - 71.43... = 27.60... = 28 \text{ m}$

6. a) Calculate the distance between the runners to the nearest metre.

$\tan 28° = \dfrac{80}{AC}$ $AC = \dfrac{80}{\tan 28°} = 150.45...$

$\tan 24° = \dfrac{80}{BC}$ $BC = \dfrac{80}{\tan 24°} = 179.68...$

$AB = BC - AC = 179.68... - 150.45... = 29.22... = 29 \text{ m}$

Distance between runners $= 29 \text{ m}$

b) $AC - 20 = 130.45...$ A has to run $130.45...$ m $time = \dfrac{distance}{speed}$

$= \dfrac{130.45...}{4.5} = 29 \text{ sec}$

$BC - 20 = 159.68...$ B has to run $159.68...$ m $time = \dfrac{159.68...}{5.1}$

$= 31.3 \text{ sec}$

A will finish the race first.

7. $MD = \frac{1}{2}(11) = 5.5 \text{ m}$

$MA^2 = 7.5^2 + 5.5^2$

$= 86.5$

$MA = \sqrt{86.5}$

$= 9.30...$

$\tan x° = \dfrac{1.8}{9.30...}$

$x° = 10.95...$

Angle EMA = 11°

8. $\tan 40° = \dfrac{x}{350}$

$x = 350 \tan 40°$

$= 293.68...$

$\tan 10° = \dfrac{h}{x}$ $h = 293.68... \tan 10°$

$h = 51.78...$

height of tree = 52 m

9. $VT^2 = 20^2 + 15^2 = 625$

$VT = \sqrt{625} = 25 \text{ m}$

$\tan x° = \dfrac{15}{25} = 1$

B. 1

10. $\tan 55° = \dfrac{BC}{28}$

$BC = 28 \tan 55°$

$= 39.98...$

$CD = 71 - 39.98...$

$= 31.01...$

$\tan x° = \dfrac{31.01...}{21}$

$x° = 55.8...$

$= 56°$

56

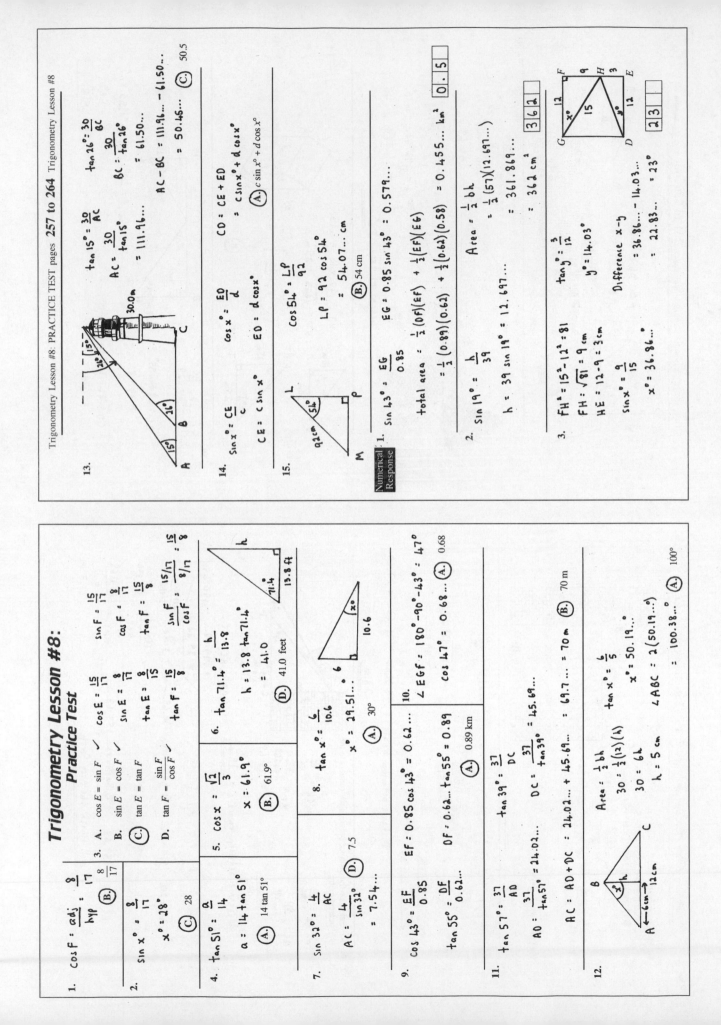

Trigonometry Lesson #8:
Practice Test

1. $\cos F = \dfrac{adj.}{hyp} = \dfrac{8}{17}$

(B.) $\dfrac{8}{17}$

2. $\sin x° = \dfrac{8}{17}$

$x° = 28°$

(C.) 28

3. A. $\cos E = \sin F$ ✓ $\cos E = \dfrac{15}{17}$ $\sin F = \dfrac{15}{17}$

B. $\sin E = \cos F$ ✓ $\sin E = \dfrac{8}{17}$ $\cos F = \dfrac{8}{17}$

(C.) $\tan E = \tan F$ $\tan E = \dfrac{8}{15}$ $\tan F = \dfrac{15}{8}$

D. $\tan F = \dfrac{\sin F}{\cos F}$ ✓ $\tan F = \dfrac{15}{8}$ $\dfrac{\sin F}{\cos F} = \dfrac{15/17}{8/17} = \dfrac{15}{8}$

4. $\tan 51° = \dfrac{a}{14}$

$a = 14 \tan 51°$

(A.) $14 \tan 51°$

5. $\cos x = \dfrac{\sqrt{2}}{3}$

$x = 61.9°$

(B.) $61.9°$

6. $\tan 71.4° = \dfrac{h}{13.8}$

$h = 13.8 \tan 71.4°$

$= 41.0$

(D.) 41.0 feet

7. $\sin 32° = \dfrac{4}{AC}$

$AC = \dfrac{4}{\sin 32°}$

$= 7.54...$

(D.) 7.5

8. $\tan x° = \dfrac{6}{10.6}$

$x° = 29.51...°$

(A.) $30°$

9. $\cos 43° = \dfrac{EF}{0.85}$

$EF = 0.85 \cos 43° = 0.62...$

$\tan 55° = \dfrac{DF}{0.62...}$

$DF = 0.62... \tan 55° = 0.89$

(A.) 0.89 km

10. $\angle EGF = 180° - 90° - 43° = 47°$

$\cos 47° = 0.68... \approx$ (A.) 0.68

11. $\tan 57° = \dfrac{37}{AD}$

$AD = \dfrac{37}{\tan 57°} = 24.02...$

$\tan 39° = \dfrac{37}{DC}$

$DC = \dfrac{37}{\tan 39°} = 45.69...$

$AC = AD + DC = 24.02... + 45.69... = 69.7... = 70m$ (B.) 70 m

12. Area $= \dfrac{1}{2}bh$

$30 = \dfrac{1}{2}(12)(h)$

$30 = 6h$

$h = 5$ cm

$\tan x° = \dfrac{6}{5}$

$x° = 50.19...°$

$\angle ABC = 2(50.19...°)$

$= 100.38...° \approx$ (A.) $100°$

13. $\tan 15° = \dfrac{30}{AC}$

$AC = \dfrac{30}{\tan 15°} = 111.96...$

$\tan 26° = \dfrac{30}{BC}$

$BC = \dfrac{30}{\tan 26°} = 61.50...$

$AC - BC = 111.96... - 61.50...$

$= 50.45...$ (C.) 50.5

14. $\sin x° = \dfrac{CE}{c}$

$CE = c \sin x°$

$\cos x° = \dfrac{ED}{d}$

$ED = d \cos x°$

$CD = CE + ED$

$= c \sin x° + d \cos x°$

(A.) $c \sin x° + d \cos x°$

15. $\cos 54° = \dfrac{LP}{92}$

$LP = 92 \cos 54°$

$= 54.07...$ cm

(B.) 54 cm

Numerical Response

1. $\sin 43° = \dfrac{EG}{0.85}$ $EG = 0.85 \sin 43° = 0.579...$

total area $= \dfrac{1}{2}(DF)(EF) + \dfrac{1}{2}(EF)(EG)$

$= \dfrac{1}{2}(0.89)(0.62) + \dfrac{1}{2}(0.62)(0.58) = 0.455...$ km^2

0.5

2. $\sin 19° = \dfrac{h}{39}$

$h = 39 \sin 19° = 12.697...$

Area $= \dfrac{1}{2}bh$

$= \dfrac{1}{2}(57)(12.697...)$

$= 361.869...$

$= 362$ cm^2

362

3. $FH^2 = 15^2 - 12^2 = 81$ $\tan y° = \dfrac{3}{12}$

$FH = \sqrt{81} = 9$ cm $y° = 14.03°$

$HE = 12 - 9 = 3$ cm

$\sin x° = \dfrac{9}{15}$ Difference $x - y$

$x° = 36.86...°$ $= 36.86... - 14.03...$

$= 22.83... = 23°$

23

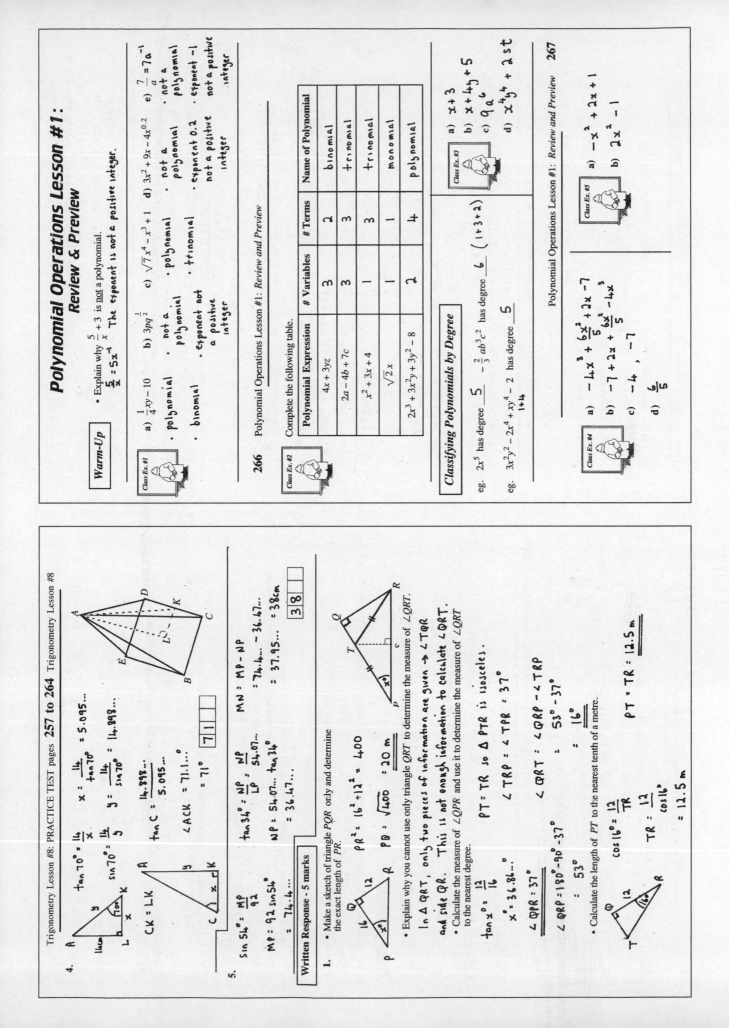

Polynomial Operations Lesson #1: Review & Preview

• Explain why $\frac{5}{x} + 3$ is <u>not</u> a polynomial.

$\frac{5}{x} = 5x^{-1}$ The exponent is not a positive integer.

Class Ex. #1

a) $\frac{1}{4}xy - 10$
- polynomial
- binomial

b) $3pq^{\frac{1}{2}}$
- not a polynomial
- exponent not a positive integer

c) $\sqrt{7}x^4 - x^3 + 1$
- polynomial
- trinomial

d) $3x^2 + 9x - 4x^{0.2} + 1$
- not a polynomial
- exponent 0.2 not a positive integer

e) $\frac{7}{a} = 7a^{-1}$
- not a polynomial
- exponent -1 not a positive integer

266 Polynomial Operations Lesson #1: *Review and Preview*

Class Ex. #2

Complete the following table.

Polynomial Expression	# Variables	# Terms	Name of Polynomial
$4x + 3yz$	3	2	binomial
$2a - 4b + 7c$	3	3	trinomial
$x^2 + 3x + 4$	1	3	trinomial
$\sqrt{2}x$	1	1	monomial
$2x^3 + 3x^2y + 3y^2 - 8$	2	4	polynomial

Classifying Polynomials by Degree

eg. $2x^5$ has degree 5 $-\frac{2}{3}ab^3c^2$ has degree 6 $(1+3+2)$

eg. $3x^2y^2 - 2x^4 + xy^4 - 2$ has degree 5 $(1+4)$

Class Ex. #3

a) $x + 3$
b) $x + 4y + 5$
c) $9a^6$
d) $x^4y^4 + 2st$

Polynomial Operations Lesson #1: *Review and Preview* **267**

Class Ex. #4

a) $-4x^3 + \frac{6x^2}{5} + 2x - 7$
b) $-7 + 2x + \frac{6x^2}{5} - 4x^3$
c) $-4, \ -7,$
d) $\frac{6}{5}$

Class Ex. #5

a) $-x^2 + 2x + 1$
b) $2x^2 - 1$

Trigonometry Lesson #8: PRACTICE TEST pages **257 to 264** Trigonometry Lesson #8

4.

$\tan 70° = \frac{14}{x}$ $x = \frac{14}{\tan 70°} = 5.095...$

$\sin 70° = \frac{14}{y}$ $y = \frac{14}{\sin 70°} = 14.898...$

$CK = LK$

$\tan C = \frac{14.898...}{5.095...}$

$\angle ACK = 71.1...°$
$= 71°$ [7 1]

5.

$\sin 54° = \frac{MP}{92}$

$MP = 92 \sin 54$
$= 74.4...$

$\tan 34° = \frac{NP}{LP} = \frac{NP}{54.07...}$

$NP = 54.07... \tan 34$
$= 36.47...$

$MN = MP - NP$
$= 74.4... - 36.47...$
$= 37.95... = 38cm$
[3 8]

Written Response - 5 marks

1. • Make a sketch of triangle PQR only and determine the exact length of PR.

$PR^2 = 16^2 + 12^2 = 400$

$PR = \sqrt{400} = 20$ m

• Explain why you cannot use only triangle QRT to determine the measure of ∠QRT.

In Δ QRT, only two pieces of information are given → ∠TQR and side QR. This is not enough information to calculate ∠QRT.

• Calculate the measure of ∠QPR and use it to determine the measure of ∠QRT to the nearest degree.

$PT = TR$ so Δ PTR is isosceles.

$\tan x° = \frac{12}{16}$ $\angle TRP = \angle TPR = 37°$

$x° = 36.86...$

$\angle QPR = 37°$

$\angle QRT = \angle QRP - \angle TRP$

$\angle QRP = 180° - 90° - 37°$
$= 53°$

$= 53° - 37°$
$= 16°$ [16°]

• Calculate the length of PT to the nearest tenth of a metre.

$\cos 16° = \frac{12}{TR}$

$TR = \frac{12}{\cos 16°}$
$= 12.5$ m

$PT = TR = 12.5$ m

Page 268

268 Polynomial Operations Lesson #1: *Review and Preview*

Class Ex. #6
$$3x^2 - 2x - 2$$

Class Ex. #7
$$-3x^2 + 4x - 1$$

Simplify the following polynomials by collecting like terms.

a) $(3a - 4b + c) + (3b - 5c - 3a)$

$3a - 4b + c + 3b - 5c - 3a$

$= -b - 4c$

b) $\quad (4x^2 - 9x + 6)$
$\quad - (2x^2 - 3x - 1)$
$\quad\overline{\quad 2x^2 - 6x + 7}$

Polynomial Operations Lesson #1: *Review and Preview* **269**

Class Ex. #9
Simplify

a) $4x - 2x^2 + 3 - 6x^2 + 5 - x$

$= -8x^2 + 3x + 8$

b) $a^2b - ab^2 + 4a^3b - 7ab^2 + 5a^2b$

$= 4a^3b + 6a^2b - 8ab^2$

Polynomial Operations Lesson #1: Assignment Pages **269 to 274** Polynomial Operations Lesson #1

Assignment

1. a) binomial b) monomial c) trinomial

2. a) 1 b) 4 c) 0 d) 4 e) 6

3. a) yes c) yes e) yes
   d) no, $\dfrac{7}{x^3} = 7x^{-3}$, which is a negative exponent.
   f) no, the exponent 1.5 is not a positive integer.

4.

Polynomial expression	# variables	# terms	name of polynomial	degree
$2y^3 + y^4 - y + 13$	1	4	polynomial	4
$9ab - 4x + 11c$	4	3	trinomial	2
25	0	1	monomial	0
$\frac{3}{5}x^3yz^5 + 3x^2yz^4$	3	2	binomial	9

5.

Polynomial expression	leading coefficient	constant term	degree
$y^4 - y + 13$	1	13	4
$0.2t^3 - 0.3t^2 + 0.4t - 0.5$	0.2	-0.5	3
$\sqrt{5} - x^6$	-1	$\sqrt{5}$	6
$\pi x^2 - 7 - 3x$	π	-7	2
$-\frac{1}{10}c^2$	$-\frac{1}{10}$	0	2

6. answers may vary a) $x^2 - x + 30$ b) $abcd + 6$ c) $-2xy^2$ d) 10

7. a) $2w^3 + 6w^2 - 9w + 5$ b) $-\frac{2}{3}a^3 + \frac{1}{4}a^2 - a - 1$ c) $-4z^6 + z^3 + z - 3$

8. a) $5 - 9w + 6w^2 - 2w^3$ b) $-7 + 9x + 3x^2 - 4x^3 - 2x^4 - 4x^5$ c) $8 - 8x + 8x^3$

Page (269 to 274)

Polynomial Operations Lesson #1: Assignment Pages **269 to 274** Polynomial Operations Lesson #1

9. a) true b) false degree is 6 c) false coefficient is $\frac{6}{5}$
   d) true e) false not a polynomial f) true
   g) false (descending) h) true

10. a) $-2x + 1$ b) $2x^2 - x + 3$ c) $-x - 2$ 11. a) $2x^2 - 3x - 6$ b) $2x^2 - 1$

12. a) $-x^2 - 4x - 4$ b) $1 + x - 2x^2$

13. a) $4p - 10q$ b) $-11x^2 + 7x$ c) $2x + 15$ d) $-3a^2 + a$ e) $-4x + 11y + 8z - 6$

14. a) $(5a - 9b - 2c) + (c - 7b - 3a)$
$= 5a - 9b - 2c + c - 7b - 3a$
$= 2a - 16b - c$

b) $(3 - a - 2a^2) + (9 - 4a + 5a^2)$
$= 3 - a - 2a^2 + 9 - 4a + 5a^2$
$= 3a^2 - 5a + 12$

c) $(2x^2 + 5x - 1) + (3x - 6 - 6x^2) + (4 - 5x + x^2)$
$= 2x^2 + 5x - 1 + 3x - 6 - 6x^2 + 4 - 5x + x^2$
$= -3x^2 + 3x - 3$

d) $(4a - 6b) - (5a - 2b)$
$= 4a - 6b - 5a + 2b$
$= -a - 4b$

e) $\quad (5x^2 - 8x + 3)$
$\quad - (3x^2 - 3x - 1)$
$\quad\overline{\quad 2x^2 - 5x + 4}$

f) $\quad (7x^2 + 2x - 1)$
$\quad - (-5x^2 - 3x - 1)$
$\quad\overline{\quad 12x^2 + 5x}$

g) $\quad (-4x^2 + 2x - 6)$
$\quad - (3x + 6 - 2x^2)$
$\quad\overline{\quad -2x^2 - x - 12}$

15. a) Subtract $3x^2 - 2x + 7$ from $6x^2 - 5x - 2$.

$(6x^2 - 5x - 2) - (3x^2 - 2x + 7)$

$= 6x^2 - 5x - 2 - 3x^2 + 2x - 7 \quad = \quad 3x^2 - 3x - 9$

b) Subtract the sum of $2x^3 - 7x^2 - 6x + 1$ and $8 - 3x + 5x^2 - 4x^3$ from $2x^3 - 7x + 9$.

$(2x^3 - 7x^2 - 6x + 1) + (8 - 3x + 5x^2 - 4x^3) = -2x^3 - 2x^2 - 9x + 9$

$2x^3 - 7x + 9 - (-2x^3 - 2x^2 - 9x + 9) = 2x^3 - 7x + 9 + 2x^3 + 2x^2 + 9x - 9$

$= 4x^3 + 2x^2 + 2x$

16. a) $(6m + n) - (2m - 3n) - (3n + 2m)$
$= 6m + n - 2m + 3n - 3n - 2m$
$= 2m + n$ cm.

b) $2m - 3n = 2(4) - 3(-1) = 11$ cm
$3n + 2m = 3(-1) + 2(4) = 5$ cm
$2m + n = 2(4) + (-1) = 7$ cm

17. **D.**

18. A. $(3x^2 - 3x) - (2x + 3x^2)$ $\quad 3x^2 - 3x - 2x - 3x^2 = -5x$
    B. $5x - (2x^2 - 2x) + (2x^2 + 2x)$ $\quad 5x - 2x^2 + 2x + 2x^2 + 2x = 9x$
    C. (circled) $8 + (4 - 2x) - (12 - 7x)$ $\quad 8 + 4 - 2x - 12 + 7x = 5x$
    D. $(2x^2 - 2x + 6) - (2x^2 - 2x) + (9x - 6)$ $\quad 2x^2 - 2x + 6 - 2x^2 + 2x + 9x - 6 = 9x$

19. 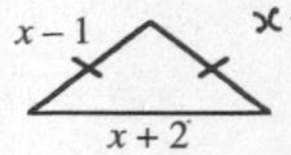 [triangle with sides $x-1$, $x+2$]

20. $a = 3$
$b = -5$
$c = 4$

$3a - 2b - c$
$= 3(3) - 2(-5) - 4$
$= 15$

(A.) a monomial

$\boxed{15}$

Polynomial Operations Lesson #2:
Multiplying a Polynomial by a Monomial

Class Ex. #1

a) $2x + 2$ b) $x^2 + 3x$ c) $-3x + 3$

d) $2x^2 - 4x$ e) $2x^2 - 2x$

276

Polynomial Operations Lesson #2: *Multiplying a Polynomial by a Monomial*

Class Ex. #2

a) $2x^2 - x$ b) $x(2x-1)$ c) $-x(-2x+1)$

d) $x(2x-1) = 2x^2 - x$

$-x(-2x+1) = 2x^2 - x$

e) LS: $3(2x-1) = 15$ RS: $2(3)^2 - 3 = 15$

LS: $3(2(3)-1) = 15$ RS: $2(3)^2 - 3 = 15$

LS: $-3(-2(3)+1) = 15$ RS: $2(3)^2 - 3 = 15$

verified

The Distributive Property

$2(x+1) = \underline{2x+2},\quad x(x+3) = \underline{x^2+3x},\quad 2x(x-2) = \underline{2x^2-4x},$

$-3(x-1) = \underline{-3x+3},\quad$ and $(x-1)(2x) = \underline{2x^2-2x}.$

Class Ex. #4

a) $6 - 4(8x+1)$ b) $4(2x-3) - 2(x-6)$ c) $5x(3x^2-7x+1) - (4x+3x^2)$

$= 6 - 32x - 4$ $= 8x - 12 - 2x + 12$ $= 15x^3 - 35x^2 + 5x - 4x - 3x^2$

$= 2 - 32x$ $= 6x$ $= 15x^3 - 38x^2 + x$

Class Ex. #5

[diagram with $4x$, $3x+2$, $2x$, $x+5$]

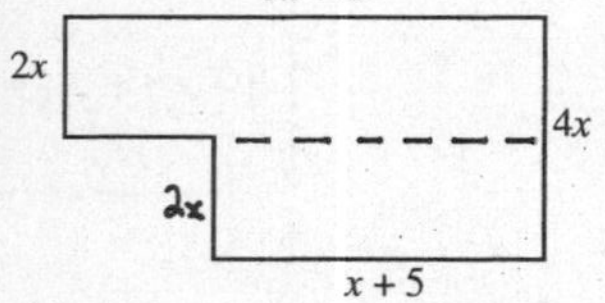

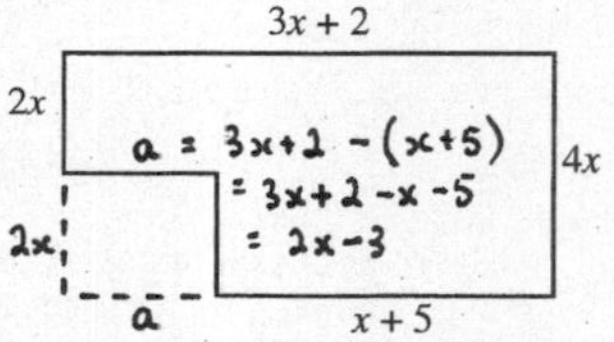

area $= 2x(3x+2) + 2x(x+5)$

$= 6x^2 + 4x + 2x^2 + 10x$

$= 8x^2 + 14x$

[diagram with $4x$, $3x+2$, $2x$, $x+5$]

$a = 3x+1 - (x+5)$

$= 3x+1 - x - 5$

$= 2x - 3$

area $= 4x(3x+2) - 2x(2x-3)$

$= 12x^2 + 8x - 4x^2 + 6x$

$= 8x^2 + 14x$

Polynomial Operations Lesson #2: *Multiplying a Polynomial by a Monomial*   **277**

Assignment

1. a) $3(2x+1) = 6x+3$ b) $x(x+2) = x^2+2x$ c) $-2(x-1) = -2x+2$

d) $(x+1)(x) = x^2+x$ e) $-3x(2-x) = -6x+3x^2$

2. a) $x(x+1) = x^2+x$ b) $3(x-1) = 3x-3$ c) $(x-1)(x) = x^2-x$

d) $x(2x+1) = 2x^2+x$ e) $2x(x-2) = 2x^2-4x$ f) $(x-2)(2x) = 2x^2-4x$

3. a) i) [diagram]   b) i) [diagram]

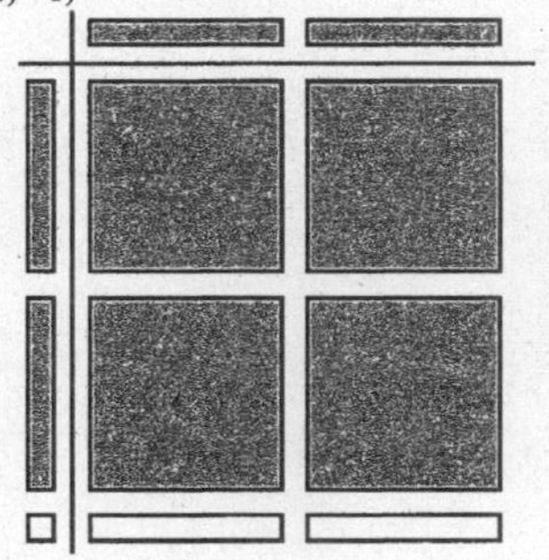

ii) $2x(2x-1) = 4x^2 - 2x$

ii)
Left Side	Right Side
$(2 \times 4)((2 \times 4)-1)$	$4(4^2)-2(4)$
$= (8)((7))$	$= 64 - 8$
$= 56$	$= 56$

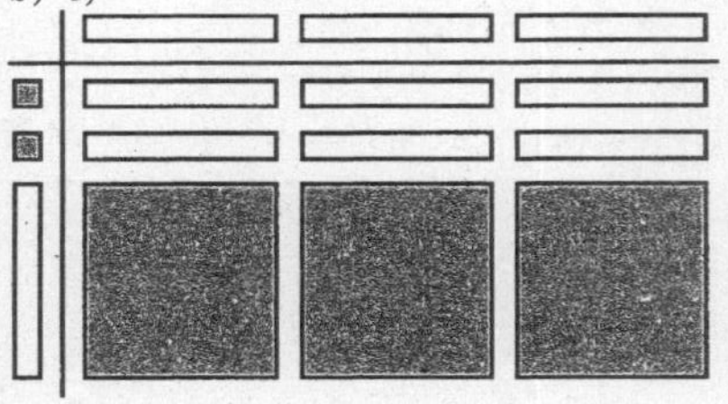

ii) $-3x(2-x) = -6x + 3x^2$

iii)
Left Side	Right Side
$(-3 \times 4)(2-4)$	$(-6 \times 4)+3(4^2)$
$= (-12)((-2))$	$= -24 + 48$
$= 24$	$= 24$

4. a) $42x - 18$ b) $-16x - 36$ c) $8xy + 32xz$

d) $-x^2 + 5xy$ e) $3x - 6y + 9z$ f) $-2ab + 2ac - 10ad$

g) $3x^2 + 9x$ h) $2x^2 - 10xy + 8xz$ i) $x^2 - 2x^3 + 3x^4$ j) $-8x^3 - 4x^2 + 24x$

5. a) $3(x+5) - 7$ b) $8 - 2(5x+11)$ c) $6(x-2) + x$

$= 3x + 15 - 7$ $= 8 - 10x - 22$ $= 6x - 12 + x$

$= 3x + 8$ $= -10x - 14$ $= 7x - 12$

d) $2(x+3) + 4(2x-1)$ e) $2(x+3) - 4(2x-1)$ f) $-2(x+1) + 7(3x-2)$

$= 2x + 6 + 8x - 4$ $= 2x + 6 - 8x + 4$ $= -2x - 2 + 21x - 14$

$= 10x + 2$ $= -6x + 10$ $= 19x - 16$

g) $5(-x+12) - 5(x-8)$ h) $(2-x) - 2(2x-10)$ i) $6(-x+4) - (x-15)$

$= -5x + 60 + 5x - 40$ $= 2 - x - 4x + 20$ $= -6x + 24 - x + 15$

$= 20$ $= -5x + 22$ $= -7x + 39$

6. a) $3x(2x+y) = 6x + 3xy$ b) $x^2(x^3-2x+7) = x^6 - 2x^3 + 7x^2$

$3x(2x) = 6x^2$ not $6x$ $x^2(x^3) = x^5$ not x^6

$3x(2x+y) = 6x^2 + 3xy$ $x^2(x^3-2x+7) = x^5 - 2x^3 + 7x^2$

9.
A. $2x(x+3)$ $2x^2+6x$
B. $-2x(x+3)$ $-2x^2-6x$
C. $2x(x-3)$ $2x^2-6x$
D. $-2x(x-3)$ $-2x^2+6x$ (circled)

10.
A. $-2x^2(3x+2) = -6x^3-4x^2$ ✓
B. $-4x(2-x) = -8x+4x^2$
C. $-5x(x^2-3) = -5x^3-15x$ $-5x^3+15x$ (circled C)
D. $7x^2(x^2+3) = 7x^4+21x^2$

11.
$8x-6x^2 + 10x^2-5x -12x-6$
$= 4x^2-9x-6$

$a = 4$
$b = -9$
$c = -6$

$a+b+c = 4+(-9)+6 = 1$

	1

Polynomial Operations Lesson #3:
Multiplication of Two Binomials

Class Ex. #1

a) $(x+3)(x+2) = x^2+5x+6$
b) $(x+4)(2x+1) = 2x^2+9x+4$
c) $(x-3)(x-2) = x^2-5x+6$
d) $(2x-1)(x+2) = 2x^2+3x-2$

Class Ex. #2

a) $(5x-6)(2x+1) = 10x^2-7x-6$

	$5x$	-6
$2x$	$10x^2$	$-12x$
1	$5x$	-6

b) $(a^2-5)(a^2-8) = a^4-13a^2+40$

	a^2	-5
a^2	a^4	$-5a^2$
-8	$-8a^2$	40

c) $(3p+2q)(p+9q)=3p^2+29pq+18q^2$

	$3p$	$2q$
p	$3p^2$	$2pq$
$9q$	$27pq$	$18q^2$

d) $(a+b)(c+d) = ac+bc+ad+bd$

	a	b
c	ac	bc
d	ad	bd

Class Ex. #3

Use an area diagram and no calculator to determine the following products.

a) 43×51

	40	3
50	2000	150
1	40	3

$1000+150+40+3$
$= 2193$

b) 76×82

	70	6
80	5600	480
2	140	12

$5600+480+140+12$
$= 6232$

---

6. Continued

c) $4(x-2)-2(x-3)$
$=4x-8-2x-6$
$=2x-14$

d) $2(2t-3)-4(t+5)$
$=4t-3-4t-5$
$=-8$

e) $5(a+b)-(a+b)$
$=5a+5b-a+b$
$=4a+6b$

$-2(-3) = 6$ not -6 The negative multiplies both terms in the binomial.

$4(x-2)-2(x-3)$
$= 4x-8-2x+6$
$= 2x-2$

The monomials 2 and -4 multiply both terms a and b.

$2(2t-3)-4(t+5)$
$= 4t-6-4t-20$
$= -26$

$5(a+b)-(a+b)$
$= 5a+5b-a-b$
$= 4a+4b$

7.
a) $2a(a+3)-4a(2a-1)$
$= 2a^2+6a-8a^2+4a$
$= -6a^2+10a$

b) $4(x^2+3)-(2x^2-1)$
$= 4x^2+12-2x^2+1$
$= 2x^2+13$

c) $2(x+3)-x-1$
$= 2x+6-x-1$
$= x+5$

d) $2(z^3+3)-(3z+7)$
$2z^3+3z-3z-7$
$= z^3-7$

e) $5(8x-3y)+2(4y+x)$
$= 40x-15y+8y+2x$
$= 42x-7y$

f) $-2x(x^4+3x^3)-7x(2x^4-x^3)$
$= -2x^5-6x^4-14x^5+7x^4$
$= -16x^5+x^4$

g) $3a(2a^2b-ab+b^2)-6b(a^3+3ab-5b^2)$
$= 6a^3b-3a^2b+3ab^2-6a^3b-18ab^2+30b^3$
$= -3a^2b-15ab^2+30b^3$

h) $3x(x-3)-2x(x-1)+x(2x-2)$
$= 3x^2-9x-2x^2+2x+2x^2-2x$
$= 3x^2-9x$

i) $(p^2-3p)(4p)-(3+5p)(-2p^2)$
$= 4p^3-12p^2+6p^2+10p^3$
$= 14p^3-6p^2$

j) $a(b-c)+b(c-a)+c(a-b)$
$= ab-ac+bc-ab+ac-bc$
$= 0$

k) $20x^3y^3-4x^3y^2(3x+5y-xy)$
$= 20x^3y^3-12x^4y^2-20x^3y^3+4x^4y^3$
$= -12x^4y^2+4x^4y^3$

8.
a)

$6a(3a+1)-4a(a+1)$
$= 18a^2+6a-4a^2-4a$
$= 14a^2+2a$

b)

$4x(2x+5)-x(x+2)$
$= 8x^2+20x-x^2-2x$
$= 7x^2+18x$

3.

a) 23×21

	20	3
20	400	60
1	20	3

= 483

b) 34×12

	30	4
10	300	40
2	60	8

= 408

c) 74×32

	70	4
30	2100	120
2	140	8

= 2368

d) 65×73

	60	5
70	4200	350
3	180	15

= 4745

e) 49×55

	40	9
50	2000	450
5	200	45

= 2695

f) 86×86

	80	6
80	6400	480
6	480	36

= 7396

4.

a) $(x+4)(x+7)$
$= x(x+7)+4(x+7)$
$= x^2+7x+4x+28$
$= x^2+11x+28$

b) $(a+7)(3a-5)$
$= a(3a-5)+7(3a-5)$
$= 3a^2-5a+21a-35$
$= 3a^2+16a-35$

c) $(p-2)(p-8)$
$= p(p-8)-2(p-8)$
$= p^2-8p-2p+16$
$= p^2-10p+16$

d) $(x+6y)(x-2y)$
$= x(x-2y)+6y(x-2y)$
$= x^2-2xy+6xy-12y^2$
$= x^2+4xy-12y^2$

e) $(4a+9b)(2a+3b)$
$= 4a(2a+3b)+9b(2a+3b)$
$= 8a^2+12ab+18ab+27b^2$
$= 8a^2+30ab+27b^2$

f) $(6-y)(1+4y)$
$= 6(1+4y)-y(1+4y)$
$= 6+24y-y-4y^2$
$= 6+23y-4y^2$

g) $(2a-1)(6b-1)$
$= 2a(6b-1)-1(6b-1)$
$= 12ab-2a-6b+1$

h) $(7x^2-3)(7x^2-3)$
$= 7x^2(7x^2-3)-3(7x^2-3)$
$= 49x^4-21x^2-21x^2+9$
$= 49x^4-42x^2+9$

i) $(2y^2-3)(5y^5+1)$
$= 2y^2(5y^5+1)-3(5y^5+1)$
$= 10y^7+2y^2-15y^5-3$
$= 10y^7-15y^5+2y^2-3$

5.

a) $(x+3)(x+6)$
$= x^2+6x+3x+18$
$= x^2+9x+18$

b) $(y+4)(y+9)$
$= y^2+9y+4y+36$
$= y^2+13y+36$

c) $(x+1)(x-8)$
$= x^2-8x+x-8$
$= x^2-7x-8$

d) $(a-7)^2=(a-7)(a-7)$
$= a^2-7a-7a+49$
$= a^2-14a+49$

e) $(x+2)(5x+4)$
$= 5x^2+4x+10x+8$
$= 5x^2+14x+8$

f) $(3y-5)(2y+9)$
$= 6y^2+27y-10y-45$
$= 6y^2+17y-45$

g) $(6x+1)(x-6)$
$= 6x^2-36x+x-6$
$= 6x^2-35x-6$

h) $(6-5b)(6-5b)$
$= 36-30b-30b+25b^2$
$= 36-60b+25b^2$

i) $(x+3y)(x+4y)$
$= x^2+4xy+3xy+12y^2$
$= x^2+7xy+12y^2$

j) $(a-7b)(3a+4b)$
$= 3a^2+4ab-21ab-28b^2$
$= 3a^2-17ab-28b^2$

k) $(5x+z)(5x-z)$
$= 25x^2-5xz+5xz-z^2$
$= 25x^2-z^2$

l) $(9-a^2)(5-a^2)$
$= 45-9a^2-5a^2+a^4$
$= 45-14a^2+a^4$

Class Ex. #4

a) $(x+3)(x+2)$
$= x(x+2)+3(x+2)$
$= x^2+2x+3x+6$
$= x^2+5x+6$

b) $(a-7)(2a-1)$
$= a(2a-1)-7(2a-1)$
$= 2a^2-a-14a+7$
$= 2a^2-15a+7$

c) $(p-8)(q-8)$
$= p(q-8)-8(q-8)$
$= pq-8p-8q+64$

d) $(x+4y)(x-5y)$
$= x(x-5y)+4y(x-5y)$
$= x^2-5xy+4xy-20y^2$
$= x^2-xy-20y^2$

e) $(9a^2-1)(5a^3+6)$
$= 9a^2(5a^3+6)-1(5a^3+6)$
$= 45a^5+54a^2-5a^3-6$
$= 45a^5-5a^3+54a^2-6$

Class Ex. #5

a) $(x+6)(x+4)$
$= x^2+4x+6x+24$
$= x^2+10x+24$

b) $(y-7)(y+2)$
$= y^2+2y-7y-14$
$= y^2-5y-14$

c) $(3x+1)(x-5)$
$= 3x^2-15x+x-5$
$= 3x^2-14x-5$

d) $(6a-5b)^2=(6a-5b)(6a-5b)$
$= 36a^2-30ab-30ab+25b^2$
$= 36a^2-60ab+25b^2$

Assignment

1.
a) $(x+1)(x+1)$
$= x^2+2x+1$

b) $(2x+1)(x+3)$
$= 2x^2+7x+3$

c) $(x-1)(x-2)$
$= x^2-3x+2$

d) $(x-2)(x+2)$
$= x^2-4$

e) $(1+3x)(1-x)$
$= 1+2x-3x^2$

2.

a) $(x+6)(x-2)$

	x	6
x	x^2	$6x$
-2	$-2x$	-12

$x^2+4x-12$

b) $(2x-3)(2x+7)$

	2x	3
2x	$4x^2$	$6x$
7	$14x$	21

$4x^2+20x+21$

c) $(2x-y)(4x+y)$

	2x	-y
4x	$8x^2$	$-4xy$
y	$2xy$	$-y^2$

$8x^2-2xy-y^2$

d) $(3d-5)(6d-9)$

	3d	-5
6d	$18d^2$	$-30d$
-9	$-27d$	45

$18d^2-57d+45$

c) $(y-3)(4y+1)$

	4y	1
y	$4y^2$	y
-3	$-12y$	-3

$4y^2-11y-3$

f) $(3p-8q)(p-5q)$

	3p	-8q
p	$3p^2$	$-8pq$
-5q	$-15pq$	$40q^2$

$3p^2-23pq+40q^2$

g) $(a^2+8)(a^2-8)$

	a²	8
a²	a^4	$8a^2$
-8	$-8a^2$	-64

a^4-64

h) $(t^3-2s)(t^3+2s)$

	t³	2s
t³	t^6	$2st^3$
2s	$2st^3$	$4s^2$

$t^6+4st^3+4s^2$

i) $(a+b)(a+c)$

	a	b
a	a^2	ab
c	ac	bc

$a^2+ab+ac+bc$

6. Area = length × width = $(2a+5)(a+4)$

(i) use a diagram.

$2a^2 + 13a + 20$

	2a	5
2a	$2a^2$	5a
4	8a	20

(ii) use the distributive property

$(2a+5)(a+4)$
$= 2a(a+4) + 5(a+4)$
$= 2a^2 + 8a + 5a + 20$
$= 2a^2 + 13a + 20$

(iii) use FOIL

$(2a+5)(a+4)$
$: 2a^2 + 8a + 5a + 20$
$= 2a^2 + 13a + 20$

7. a) $(7x-2)(3x+5)$
$= 21x^2 + 35x - 6x - 10$
$= 21x^2 + 29x - 10$

b) $(2h-3)(2h-1)$
$= 4h^2 - 2h - 6h + 3$
$= 4h^2 - 8h + 3$

c) $(3z+4)(3z+5)$
$= 9z^2 + 15z + 12z + 20$
$= 9z^2 + 27z + 20$

d) $(4x-3)(3x-4)$
$= 12x^2 - 16x - 9x + 12$
$= 12x^2 - 25x + 12$

e) $(8x-3y)(2x+y)$
$= 16x^2 + 8xy - 6xy - 3y^2$
$= 16x^2 + 2xy - 3y^2$

f) $(1+3b)^2 = (1+3b)(1+3b)$
$= 1 + 3b + 3b + 9b^2$
$= 1 + 6b + 9b^2$

g) $(x-2)(6y-1)$
$= 6xy - x - 12y + 2$

h) $(1+3y^2)(1-3y^2)$
$= 1 - 3y^2 + 3y^2 - 9y^4$
$= 1 - 9y^4$

i) $(x^2+7y^2)(2x^2-5y^2)$
$= 2x^4 - 5x^2y^2 + 14x^2y^2 - 35y^4$
$= 2x^4 + 9x^2y^2 - 35y^4$

8. $(x+3)(2x+1) = 2x^2 + x + 6x + 3 = 2x^2 + 7x + 3$

$b=2 \quad q=7 \quad r=3 \quad \boxed{273}$

9. $(3x-c)(x-3) = 3x^2 - 9x - cx + 3c$

leading coefficient = 3
constant term = 3c

$3c = 12$
$c = 4 \quad \boxed{4}$

Polynomial Operations Lesson #4:
Multiplication of Polynomials - Part One

Three Important Products

i) $(a+b)^2 = (a+b)(a+b)$
$= a^2 + ab + ab + b^2$
$= a^2 + 2ab + b^2$

ii) $(a-b)^2 = (a-b)(a-b)$
$= a^2 - ab - ab + b^2$
$= a^2 - 2ab + b^2$

iii) $(a-b)(a+b) = (a-b)(a+b)$
$= a^2 + ab - ab - b^2$
$= a^2 - b^2$

Class Ex. #1

a) $(x+7)^2$
$= x^2 + 2(7)(x) + 49$
$= x^2 + 14x + 49$

b) $(3x-1)^2$
$= 9x^2 - 2(1)(3x) + 1$
$= 9x^2 - 6x + 1$

c) $(2m-3n)^2$
$= 4m^2 - 2(2m)(3n) + 9n^2$
$= 4m^2 - 12mn + 9n^2$

d) $(4-7x)(4+7x)$
$= (4)^2 - (7x)^2$
$= 16 - 49x^2$

e) $(5a+3b)(5a-3b)$
$= (5a)^2 - (3b)^2$
$= 25a^2 - 9b^2$

e) $(2p-9q)(2p-9q)$
$= (2p)^2 - 2(2p)(9q) + 81q^2$
$= 4p^2 - 2(2p)(9q) + 81q^2$
$= 4p^2 - 36pq + 81q^2$

Class Ex. #2

a) $5(2x-3)(x-6)$
$= 5(2x^2 - 12x - 3x + 18)$
$= 5(2x^2 - 15x + 18)$
$= 10x^2 - 75x + 90$

b) $-8(7p+3)^2$
$= -8(49p^2 + 42p + 9)$
$= -392p^2 - 336p - 72$

Class Ex. #3

a) $(x+5)(x-5) - (x+2)(x+8)$
$= x^2 - 25 - (x^2 + 8x + 2x + 16)$
$= x^2 - 25 - x^2 - 8x - 2x - 16$
$= -10x - 41$

b) $(9a+4)(4a-9) - (6a-5)^2$
$= 36a^2 - 81a + 16a - 36 - (36a^2 - 60a + 25)$
$= 36a^2 - 81a + 16a - 36 - 36a^2 + 60a - 25$
$= -5a - 61$

Class Ex. #4

a) $5x(3x^2-7x+1) - (4x+3x^2)(5x-8)$
$= 15x^3 - 35x^2 + 5x - (20x^2 - 32x + 15x^3 - 24x^2)$
$= 15x^3 - 35x^2 + 5x - 20x^2 + 32x - 15x^3 + 24x^2$
$= -31x^2 + 37x$

b) $4(2x-7)(3x+2) - 8(x-1)(3x-1)$
$= 4(6x^2 + 4x - 21x - 14) - 8(3x^2 - x - 3x + 1)$
$= 24x^2 + 16x - 84x - 56 - 24x^2 + 8x + 24x - 8$
$= -36x - 64$

Class Ex. #5

$(x+a)(x+a) + b$
$= x^2 + 2ax + a^2 \cdot b$
$= x^2 + 20x + 50$

$2a = 20$
$\underline{a = 10}$

$a^2 + b = 50$
$10^2 + b = 50$
$100 + b = 50$
$\underline{b = -50}$

Assignment

1. a) $x^2 - 16x + 64$
   b) $x^2 - 81$
   c) $9x^2 - 6xy + y^2$
   d) $25x^2 + 20xy + 4y^2$
   e) $9x^2 - 4$
   f) $4y^2 - 4y + 1$
   g) $4p^2 + 28p + 49$
   h) $16m^2 - 9n^2$
   i) $25a^2 - 60ab + 36b^2$
   j) $81 - 25x^4$
   k) $36a^2 - 84ab + 49b^2$
   l) $4a^6 - 49$

2. a) $2(4x-3)(3x-4)$
   $= 2(12x^2 - 16x - 9x + 12)$
   $= 2(12x^2 - 25x + 12)$
   $= 24x^2 - 50x + 24$

   b) $7(5x-2)(6x+1)$
   $= 7(30x^2 + 5x - 12x - 2)$
   $= 7(30x^2 - 7x - 2)$
   $= 210x^2 - 49x - 14$

   c) $-3(a+8)(2a+9)$
   $= -3(2a^2 + 9a + 16a + 72)$
   $= -3(2a^2 + 25a + 72)$
   $= -6a^2 - 75a - 216$

   d) $5(4x+1)^2$
   $= 5(16x^2 + 8x + 1)$
   $= 80x^2 + 40x + 5$

   e) $6(8x-3y)(2x+y)$
   $= 6(16x^2 + 8xy - 6xy - 3y^2)$
   $= 6(16x^2 + 2xy - 3y^2)$
   $= 96x^2 + 12xy - 18y^2$

   f) $-4(a+3b)(2a-5b)$
   $= -4(2a^2 - 5ab + 6ab - 15b^2)$
   $= -4(2a^2 + ab - 15b^2)$
   $= -8a^2 - 4ab + 60b^2$

3. a) $(x-3)(x-6) + (x+2)(x+7)$
$= (x^2 - 6x - 3x + 18) + (x^2 + 7x + 2x + 14)$
$= x^2 - 9x + 18 + x^2 + 9x + 14$
$= 2x^2 + 32$

b) $(x-5)(x+4) - (x+1)(x-8)$
$= (x^2 + 4x - 5x - 20) - (x^2 - 8x + x - 8)$
$= (x^2 - x - 20) - (x^2 - 7x - 8)$
$= x^2 - x - 20 - x^2 + 7x + 8$
$= 6x - 12$

c) $(x-3)^2 + (x+3)^2$
$= (x^2 - 6x + 9) + (x^2 + 6x + 9)$
$= x^2 - 6x + 9 + x^2 + 6x + 9$
$= 2x^2 + 18$

d) $(x-y)(x-4y) - (x+y)(x-y)$
$= (x^2 - 4xy - xy + 4y^2) - (x^2 - y^2)$
$= x^2 - 5xy + 4y^2 - x^2 + y^2$
$= -5xy + 5y^2$

4. a) $(3x-1)(x-3) - 2x(x-1)$
$= (3x^2 - 9x - x + 3) - 2x^2 + 2x$
$= 3x^2 - 10x + 3 - 2x^2 + 2x$
$= x^2 - 8x + 3$

b) $(4x+1)(2x+3) - (3x-7)(2x-5)$
$= (8x^2 + 12x + 2x + 3) - (6x^2 - 15x - 14x + 35)$
$= 8x^2 + 14x + 3 - (6x^2 - 29x + 35)$
$= 8x^2 + 14x + 3 - 6x^2 + 29x - 35$
$= 2x^2 + 43x - 32$

c) $(9x-1)(x-4) - (3x+1)(3x-1)$
$= (9x^2 - 36x - x + 4) - (9x^2 - 1)$
$= 9x^2 - 37x + 4 - 9x^2 + 1$
$= -37x + 5$

d) $8(5-3x)(2+5x) - 3(1+x)^2$
$= 8(10 + 25x - 6x - 15x^2) - 3(1 + 2x + x^2)$
$= 8(10 + 19x - 15x^2) - 3 - 6x - 3x^2$
$= 80 + 152x - 120x^2 - 3 - 6x - 3x^2$
$= 77 + 146x - 123x^2$

e) $5(2x-3)(2x+5) + 3(x+7)(x+2)$
$= 5(4x^2 + 10x - 6x - 15) + 3(x^2 + 2x + 7x + 14)$
$= 5(4x^2 + 4x - 15) + 3(x^2 + 9x + 14)$
$= 20x^2 + 20x - 75 + 3x^2 + 27x + 42$
$= 23x^2 + 47x - 33$

f) $4(2p+3q)^2 - (5p-q)(7p+11q)$
$= 4(4p^2 + 12pq + 9q^2) - (35p^2 + 55pq - 7pq - 11q^2)$
$= 16p^2 + 48pq + 36q^2 - (35p^2 + 48pq - 11q^2)$
$= 16p^2 + 48pq + 36q^2 - 35p^2 - 48pq + 11q^2$
$= -19p^2 + 47q^2$

5. a) $(x+4)^2 + (x+2)^2$
$= (x^2 + 8x + 16) + (x^2 + 4x + 4)$
$= x^2 + 8x + 16 + x^2 + 4x + 4$
$= 2x^2 + 12x + 20$

b) $(3a-b)^2 - (2a+5b)^2$
$= (9a^2 - 6ab + b^2) - (4a^2 + 20ab + 25b^2)$
$= 9a^2 - 6ab + b^2 - 4a^2 - 20ab - 25b^2$
$= 5a^2 - 26ab - 24b^2$

c) $3(y-1)^2 - 2(2y-1)^2$
$= 3(y^2 - 2y + 1) - 2(4y^2 - 4y + 1)$
$= 3y^2 - 6y + 3 - 8y^2 + 8y - 2$
$= -5y^2 + 2y + 1$

d) $9 - 2(x^2 + 6x - 7) + (2x-5)(x-3)$
$= 9 - 2(x^2 + 6x - 7) + (2x^2 - 6x - 5x + 15)$
$= 9 - 2(x^2 + 6x - 7) + (2x^2 - 11x + 15)$
$= 9 - 2x^2 - 12x + 14 + 2x^2 - 11x + 15$
$= -23x + 38$

e) $3(1+3y)(4-y) - (3y-2)(3y-5)$
$= 3(4 - y + 12y - 3y^2) - (9y^2 - 15y - 6y + 10)$
$= 3(4 + 11y - 3y^2) - (9y^2 - 21y + 10)$
$= 12 + 33y - 9y^2 - 9y^2 + 21y - 10$
$= -18y^2 + 54y + 2$

---

6. A student provides the following expansions for four binomial products.

$(x+3)^2 = x^2 + 9$ ✗ $(3x-y)(3x-y) = 9x^2 - 6xy - y^2$ ✗
$\qquad\qquad x^2 + 6x + 9$ $\qquad\qquad\qquad 9x^2 - 6xy + y^2$ ✗

$(2x+y)(2x-y) = 2x^2 - y^2$ ✗ $(5x+7)^2 = 25x^2 + 35x + 49$ ✗
$\qquad\qquad\quad 4x^2 - y^2$ $\qquad\qquad 25x^2 + 70x + 49$

D. Four

7. $(x-a)^2 + b \qquad\qquad 2a = 10 \qquad a^2 + b = 39$
$= x^2 - 2ax + a^2 + b \qquad a = 5 \qquad 25 + b = 39$
$\therefore x^2 - 10x + 39 \qquad\qquad\qquad\qquad b = 14$
$= x^2 - 10x + 39$

[1|4]

Polynomial Operations Lesson #5:
Multiplication of Polynomials - Part Two

Area = length × width = $(5x+2)(x^2 + 2x + 1)$

Class Ex. #1

i) use a diagram

	$5x$	2
x^2	$5x^3$	$2x^2$
$2x$	$10x^2$	$4x$
1	$5x$	2

$5x^3 + 12x^2 + 9x + 2$

ii) use the distributive property

$(5x+2)(x^2 + 2x + 1)$
$= 5x(x^2 + 2x + 1) + 2(x^2 + 2x + 1)$
$= 5x^3 + 10x^2 + 5x + 2x^2 + 4x + 2$
$= 5x^3 + 12x^2 + 9x + 2$

Class Ex. #2

a) $(x^2 - 4)(2x^3 + x - 5)$
$= x^2(2x^3 + x - 5) - 4(2x^3 + x - 5)$
$= 2x^5 + x^3 - 5x^2 - 8x^3 - 4x + 20$
$= 2x^5 - 7x^3 - 5x^2 - 4x + 20$

b) $(2y^2 - 3y - 7)(y - 6)$
$= 2y^2(y-6) - 3y(y-6) - 7(y-6)$
$= 2y^3 - 12y^2 - 3y^2 + 18y - 7y + 42$
$= 2y^3 - 15y^2 + 11y + 42$

Class Ex. #3

$= 4[a(a^2 - 3a - 6) - 4(a^2 - 3a - 6)] - (16a^2 - 9)$
$= 4[a^3 - 3a^2 - 6a - 4a^2 + 12a + 24] - 16a^2 + 9$
$= 4a^3 - 12a^2 - 24a - 16a^2 + 48a + 96 - 16a^2 + 9$
$= 4a^3 - 44a^2 + 24a + 105$

300 Polynomial Operations Lesson #5: Multiplication of Polynomials – Part Two

Class Ex. #4

a) $(x+1)(x+2)(x+5)$

b) $V = (x+1)(x+5)$ cm³

$= (x+1)(x^2 + 7x + 10)$
$= x(x^2 + 7x + 10) + 1(x^2 + 7x + 10)$
$= x^3 + 7x^2 + 10x + x^2 + 7x + 10$
$V = x^3 + 8x^2 + 17x + 10$

Class Ex. #5

Polynomial Operations Lesson #5: *Multiplication of Polynomials - Part Two* *(continued)*

a) $(x-3)(x+4)(2x-1)$

$= (x-3)\left[2x^2 - x + 8x - 4\right]$

$= (x-3)\left(2x^2 + 7x - 4\right)$

$= x\left(2x^2 + 7x - 4\right) -3\left(2x^2 + 7x - 4\right)$

$= 2x^3 + 7x^2 - 4x - 6x^2 - 21x + 12$

$= 2x^3 + x^2 - 25x + 12$

b) $(2x-1)(x-3)(x+4)$

$= (2x-1)\left[x^2 + 4x - 3x - 12\right]$

$= (2x-1)\left(x^2 + x - 12\right)$

$= 2x\left(x^2 + x - 12\right) -1\left(x^2 + x - 12\right)$

$= 2x^3 + 2x^2 - 24x - x^2 - x + 12$

$= 2x^3 + x^2 - 25x + 12$

c) Comment on the results to a) and b).

The results are the same. The order of multiplication does not matter.

Polynomial Operations Lesson #5: Assignment Pages **301 to 304** Polynomial Operations Lesson #5

Assignment

1. Use a diagram to determine the expansion.

a) $(y-5)(y^2 + 2y + 4)$

	y^2	$2y$	4
y	y^3	$2y^2$	$4y$
-5	$-5y^2$	$-10y$	-20

$= y^3 - 3y^2 - 6y - 20$

b) $(3m+7)(m^2 - 3m + 6)$

	$3m$	7
m^2	$3m^3$	$7m^2$
$-3m$	$-9m^2$	$-21m$
6	$18m$	42

$= 3m^3 - 2m^2 - 3m + 42$

2. Use the distributive law to determine the expansion.

a) $(x-4)(x^2 - 6x + 3)$

$= x\left(x^2 - 6x + 3\right) -4\left(x^2 - 6x + 3\right)$

$= x^3 - 6x^2 + 3x - 4x^2 + 24x - 12$

$= x^3 - 10x^2 + 27x - 12$

b) $(2a+5)(a^2 - 7a - 9)$

$= 2a\left(a^2 - 7a - 9\right) + 5\left(a^2 - 7a - 9\right)$

$= 2a^3 - 14a^2 - 18a + 5a^2 - 35a - 45$

$= 2a^3 - 9a^2 - 53a - 45$

3. Expand and simplify.

a) $(x^2 - 7)(2x^3 + 4x - 1)$

$= x^2\left(2x^3 + 4x - 1\right) -7\left(2x^3 + 4x - 1\right)$

$= 2x^5 + 4x^3 - x^2 - 14x^3 - 28x + 7$

$= 2x^5 - 10x^3 - x^2 - 28x + 7$

b) $(-m^2 - m + 1)(m + 1)$

$= -m^2(m+1) -m(m+1) +1(m+1)$

$= -m^3 - m^2 - m^2 - m + m + 1$

$= -m^3 - 2m^2 + 1$

c) $(a-3b)(4a^2 - 3ab - 2b^2)$

$= a\left(4a^2 - 3ab - 2b^2\right) -3b\left(4a^2 - 3ab - 2b^2\right)$

$= 4a^3 - 3a^2b - 2ab^2 - 12a^2b + 9ab^2 + 6b^3$

$= 4a^3 - 15a^2b + 7ab^2 + 6b^3$

d) $2(5x+2)(3x^2 + x - 4)$

$= 2\left[5x(3x^2 + x - 4) + 2(3x^2 + x - 4)\right]$

$= 2\left[15x^3 + 5x^2 - 20x + 6x^2 + 2x - 8\right]$

$= 2\left(15x^3 + 11x^2 - 18x - 8\right)$

$= 30x^3 + 22x^2 - 36x - 16$

Polynomial Operations Lesson #5: Assignment Pages **301 to 304** Polynomial Operations Lesson #5

4. Expand and simplify.

a) $(x+1)(x+2)(3x+5)$

$= (x+1)\left[3x^2 + 5x + 6x + 10\right]$

$= (x+1)\left(3x^2 + 11x + 10\right)$

$= x\left(3x^2 + 11x + 10\right) + 1\left(3x^2 + 11x + 10\right)$

$= 3x^3 + 11x^2 + 10x + 3x^2 + 11x + 10$

$= 3x^3 + 14x^2 + 21x + 10$

b) $(h-4)(2h-3)(3h-1)$

$= (h-4)\left[6h^2 - 2h - 9h + 3\right]$

$= (h-4)\left(6h^2 - 11h + 3\right)$

$= h\left(6h^2 - 11h + 3\right) -4\left(6h^2 - 11h + 3\right)$

$= 6h^3 - 11h^2 + 3h - 24h^2 + 44h - 12$

$= 6h^3 - 35h^2 + 47h - 12$

c) $(a+3b)(2a-5b)(2a+5b)$

$= (a+3b)\left[4a^2 + 10ab - 10ab - 25b^2\right]$

$= (a+3b)\left(4a^2 - 25b^2\right)$

$= a\left(4a^2 - 25b^2\right) + 3b\left(4a^2 - 25b^2\right)$

$= 4a^3 - 25ab^2 + 12a^2b - 75b^3$

d) $(3x+7y)(4x-3y)(x-4y)$

$= (3x+7y)\left[4x^2 - 16xy - 3xy + 12y^2\right]$

$= (3x+7y)\left(4x^2 - 19xy + 12y^2\right)$

$= 3x\left(4x^2 - 19xy + 12y^2\right) + 7y\left(4x^2 - 19xy + 12y^2\right)$

$= 12x^3 - 57x^2y + 36xy^2 + 28x^2y - 133xy^2 + 84y^3$

$= 12x^3 - 29x^2y - 97xy^2 + 84y^3$

5. Calculate the volume of the cube shown below.

$V = (2z+3)^3 = (2z+3)(2z+3)(2z+3)$

$= (2z+3)\left(4z^2 + 6z + 6z + 9\right)$

$= (2z+3)\left(4z^2 + 12z + 9\right)$

$= 2z\left(4z^2 + 12z + 9\right) + 3\left(4z^2 + 12z + 9\right)$

$= 8z^3 + 24z^2 + 18z + 12z^2 + 36z + 27$

$= 8z^3 + 36z^2 + 54z + 27$

6. Calculate the volume of the rectangular prism illustrated.

$V = (x-3)(2x+1)(2x+1)$

$= (x-3)\left(4x^2 + 2x + 2x + 1\right)$

$= (x-3)\left(4x^2 + 4x + 1\right)$

$= x\left(4x^2 + 4x + 1\right) -3\left(4x^2 + 4x + 1\right)$

$= 4x^3 + 4x^2 + x - 12x^2 - 12x - 3$

$= 4x^3 - 8x^2 - 11x - 3$

7. Simplify.

a) $-3(a^2+2)(3a^2 - a - 1)$

$= -3\left[a^2(3a^2 - a - 1) + 2(3a^2 - a - 1)\right]$

$= -3\left(3a^4 - a^3 - a^2 + 6a^2 - 2a - 2\right)$

$= -3\left(3a^4 - a^3 + 5a^2 - 2a - 2\right)$

$= -9a^4 + 3a^3 - 15a^2 + 6a + 6$

b) $(-2x^2 - 3x + 1)(x^2 - x - 3)$

	$-2x^2$	$-3x$	1
x^2	$-2x^4$	$-3x^3$	x^2
$-x$	$2x^3$	$3x^2$	$-x$
-3	$6x^2$	$9x$	-3

$= -2x^4 - x^3 + 10x^2 + 8x - 3$

c) $2(4x-1)^2 - (3x-2)^3$

$= 2\left[(16x^2 - 8x + 1) - \left[(3x-2)(9x^2 - 12x + 4)\right]\right.$

$= 2\left[5x(3x^2 + x - 4) + 2(3x^2 + x - 4)\right]$

$= 32x^2 - 16x + 2 - \left[3x(9x^2 - 12x + 4) - 2(9x^2 - 12x + 4)\right]$

$= 32x^2 - 16x + 2 - \left[27x^3 - 36x^2 + 12x - 18x^2 + 24x - 8\right]$

$= 32x^2 - 16x + 2 - 27x^3 + 36x^2 - 12x + 18x^2 - 24x + 8$

$= -27x^3 + 86x^2 - 52x + 10$

8. (**B.**) The student made an error in Line 2.

$$(a+2)(a+2)(a+2) \qquad \text{Line 1}$$
$$=(a+2)\left(\boxed{a^2+4}\right) \quad \text{X} \qquad \text{Line 2}$$
$$=a^3+2a^2+4a+8 \qquad \text{Line 3}$$

9. $(2x^3-7x^2-6)+(x^2+6x-3)-(3x-1)(2x^2-4x+3)$

$=2x^3-7x^2-6+x^2+6x-3-\left[3x(2x^2-4x+3)-1(2x^2-4x+3)\right]$

$=2x^3-6x^2+6x-9-\left[6x^3-12x^2+9x-2x^2+4x-3\right]$

$=2x^3-6x^2+6x-9-6x^3+12x^2-9x+2x^2-4x+3$

$=-4x^3+8x^2-7x-6$

$b=8 \quad c=-7$

$b-2c$

$=8-2(-7)=22$ [22]   [2 2]

Polynomial Operations Lesson #6:
Problem Solving with Polynomial Products

Class Ex. #1

a)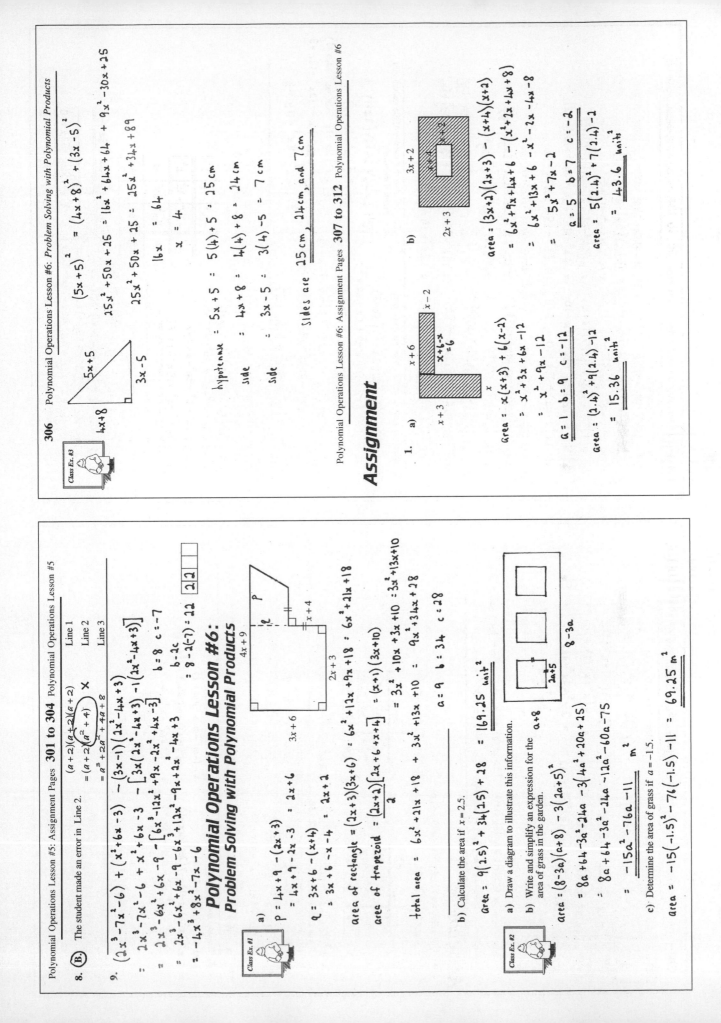

$p=4x+9-(2x+3)$
$=4x+9-2x-3=2x+6$

$q=3x+6-(x+4)$
$=3x+6-x-4=2x+2$

area of rectangle $=(2x+3)(3x+6)=6x^2+12x+9x+18=6x^2+21x+18$

area of trapezoid $=\dfrac{(2x+2)}{2}\left[2x+6+x+4\right]=(x+1)(3x+10)$
$=3x^2+10x+3x+10=3x^2+13x+10$

total area $=6x^2+21x+18+3x^2+13x+10=9x^2+34x+28$

$a=9 \quad b=34 \quad c=28$

b) Calculate the area if $x=2.5$.

Area $=9(2.5)^2+34(2.5)+28=169.25$ unit²

Class Ex. #2

a) Draw a diagram to illustrate this information.

b) Write and simplify an expression for the area of grass in the garden. $a+8$

area $=(8-3a)(a+8)-3(2a+5)^2$

$=8a+64-3a^2-24a-3(4a^2+20a+25)$

$=8a+64-3a^2-24a-12a^2-60a-75$

$=-15a^2-76a-11$ m²

c) Determine the area of grass if $a=-1.5$.

area $=-15(-1.5)^2-76(-1.5)-11=69.25$ m²

Class Ex. #3

$$(5x+5)^2=(4x+8)^2+(3x-5)^2$$
$$25x^2+50x+25=16x^2+64x+64+9x^2-30x+25$$
$$25x^2+50x+25=25x^2+34x+89$$
$$16x=64$$
$$x=4$$

hypotenuse $=5x+5=5(4)+5=25$ cm

side $=4x+8=4(4)+8=24$ cm

side $=3x-5=3(4)-5=7$ cm

Sides are 25 cm, 24 cm, and 7 cm

Assignment

1. a)

Area $=x(x+3)+6(x-2)$

$=x^2+3x+6x-12$

$=x^2+9x-12$

$a=1 \quad b=9 \quad c=-12$

Area $=(2.4)^2+9(2.4)-12=15.36$ unit²

b)

area $=(3x+2)(2x+3)-(x+4)(x+2)$

$=6x^2+9x+4x+6-(x^2+2x+4x+8)$

$=6x^2+13x+6-x^2-2x-4x-8$

$=5x^2+7x-2$

$a=5 \quad b=7 \quad c=-2$

area $=5(2.4)^2+7(2.4)-2=43.6$ unit²

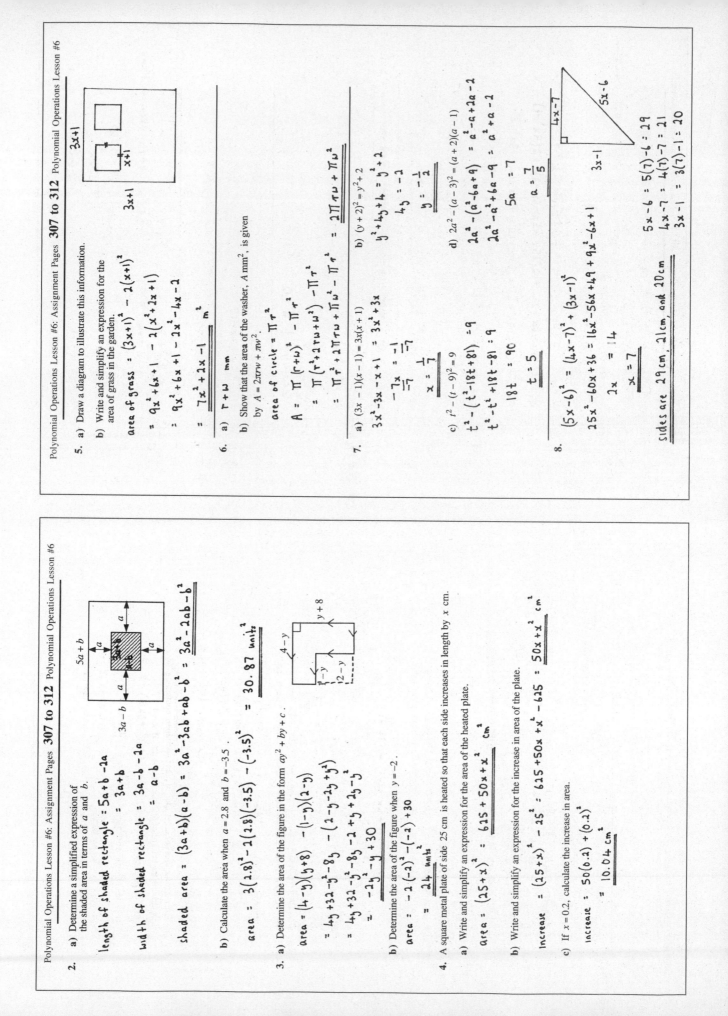

Polynomial Operations Lesson #6: Assignment Pages **307 to 312** Polynomial Operations Lesson #6

2. a) Determine a simplified expression of the shaded area in terms of a and b.

length of shaded rectangle = $5a+b -2a$
$= 3a+b$

width of shaded rectangle = $3a-b -2a$
$= a-b$

shaded area = $(3a+b)(a-b) = 3a^2-3ab+ab-b^2 = 3a^2-2ab-b^2$

b) Calculate the area when $a=2.8$ and $b=-3.5$.

Area = $3(2.8)^2 -2(2.8)(-3.5) -(-3.5)^2 = 30.87$ units²

3. a) Determine the area of the figure in the form $ay^2 + by + c$.

Area = $(4-y)(y+8) -(1-y)(2-y)$
$= 4y+32-y^2-8y - (2-y-2y+y^2)$
$= 4y+32-y^2-8y -2+y+2y-y^2$
$= -2y^2-y+30$

b) Determine the area of the figure when $y=-2$.

Area = $-2(-2)^2 -(-2) +30$
$= 24$ units²

4. A square metal plate of side 25 cm is heated so that each side increases in length by x cm.

a) Write and simplify an expression for the area of the heated plate.

Area = $(25+x)^2 = 625 + 50x + x^2$ cm²

b) Write and simplify an expression for the increase in area of the plate.

increase = $(25+x)^2 -25^2 = 625+50x+x^2 -625 = 50x+x^2$ cm²

c) If $x=0.2$, calculate the increase in area.

increase = $50(0.2) + (0.2)^2$
$= 10.04$ cm²

Polynomial Operations Lesson #6: Assignment Pages **307 to 312** Polynomial Operations Lesson #6

5. a) Draw a diagram to illustrate this information.

b) Write and simplify an expression for the area of grass in the garden.

Area of grass = $(3x+1)^2 - 2(x+1)^2$
$= 9x^2+6x+1 - 2(x^2+2x+1)$
$= 9x^2+6x+1 -2x^2-4x-2$
$= 7x^2+2x-1$ m²

6. a) $r+w$ mm

b) Show that the area of the washer, A mm², is given by $A = 2\pi rw + \pi w^2$.

area of circle = πr^2

$A = \pi(r+w)^2 - \pi r^2$
$= \pi(r^2+2rw+w^2) - \pi r^2$
$= \pi r^2 + 2\pi rw + \pi w^2 - \pi r^2 = 2\pi rw + \pi w^2$

7. a) $(3x-1)(x-1) = 3x(x+1)$
$3x^2-3x-x+1 = 3x^2+3x$
$-7x = -1$
$\dfrac{-7x}{-7} = \dfrac{-1}{-7}$
$x = \dfrac{1}{7}$

b) $(y+2)^2 = y^2+2$
$y^2+4y+4 = y^2+2$
$4y = -2$
$y = -\dfrac{1}{2}$

c) $t^2 -(t-9)^2 = 9$
$t^2 -(t^2-18t+81) = 9$
$t^2-t^2+18t-81 = 9$
$18t = 90$
$t = 5$

d) $2a^2 -(a-3)^2 = (a+2)(a-1)$
$2a^2 -(a^2-6a+9) = a^2-a+2a-2$
$2a^2-a^2+6a-9 = a^2+a-2$
$5a = 7$
$a = \dfrac{7}{5}$

8. $(5x-6)^2 = (4x-7)^2 + (3x-1)^2$
$25x^2-60x+36 = 16x^2-56x+49 + 9x^2-6x+1$
$2x = 14$
$x = 7$

$5x-6 = 5(7)-6 = 29$
$4x-7 = 4(7)-7 = 21$
$3x-1 = 3(7)-1 = 20$

sides are 29cm, 21cm, and 20cm

9. Consider a set of rectangles with sides $(4a-3)$ cm and $(2a+7)$ cm.

a) Write and simplify an expression in a for the area of one of these rectangles.

Area $= (4a-3)(2a+7) = 8a^2 + 28a - 6a - 21 = 8a^2 + 22a - 21$ cm²

b) If one of these rectangles has a perimeter of 50 cm, determine the length and width of this rectangle.

perimeter $= 2(4a-3) + 2(2a+7)$
$= 8a-6 + 4a+14$
$= 12a + 8$

$12a+8 = 50$
$12a = 42$
$a = \frac{42}{12}$
$a = \frac{7}{2}$

length $= 4\left(\frac{7}{2}\right) - 3 = \underline{11\,cm}$

width $= 2\left(\frac{7}{2}\right) + 7 = \underline{14\,cm}$

c) If another of these rectangles is a square, determine the length of each side.

$4a-3 = 2a+7$
$2a = 10$
$a = 5$

length $= 4(5) - 3 = \underline{17\ cm}$

10. A rectangle has length (x^2+4x-1) cm and width $(3x-2)$ cm.

a) Write and simplify an expression for the area of the rectangle in cm².

area $= (x^2+4x-1)(3x-2)$
$= x^2(3x-2) + 4x(3x-2) - 1(3x-2)$
$= 3x^3 - 2x^2 + 12x^2 - 8x - 3x + 2 = \underline{3x^3 + 10x^2 - 11x + 2\ cm^2}$

b) If $x=2.5$, calculate the area of the rectangle.

area $= 3(2.5)^3 + 10(2.5)^2 - 11(2.5) + 2 = \underline{83.875\ cm^2}$

11. Dice for a children's board game are cubes with an edge length of $(3x-2)$ mm.

a) Write and simplify an expression for the volume of a die in mm³.

Volume $= (3x-2)^3 = (3x-2)(3x-2)(3x-2)$
$= (3x-2)(9x^2-12x+4)$
$= 3x(9x^2-12x+4) - 2(9x^2-12x+4)$
$= 27x^3-36x^2+12x - 18x^2+24x-8$
$= \underline{27x^3 - 54x^2 + 36x - 8\ mm^3}$

b) The manufacturer packages dice in cubic containers containing 64 dice. Determine the volume of the container in cm³ if $x=4$.

volume of one die $= 27(4)^3 - 54(4)^2 + 36(4) - 8 = 1000$ mm³
side length of one die $= \sqrt[3]{1000} = 10mm = 1cm$
64 dice will be packaged $4 \times 4 \times 4$
side length of package $= 4cm$
volume of package $= 4^3 = \underline{64\ cm^3}$

12. a) Volume $= (5x-2)(3x-1)(3x+1)$
$= (5x-2)(9x^2-1)$
$= 45x^3 - 5x - 18x^2 + 2$
$= \underline{45x^3 - 18x^2 - 5x + 2\ cm^3}$

b) Surface area $= 2(5x-2)(3x-1) + 2(5x-2)(3x+1) + 2(3x-1)(3x+1)$
$= 2(15x^2-5x-6x+2) + 2(15x^2+5x-6x-2) + 2(9x^2-1)$
$= 30x^2-10x-12x+4 + 30x^2+10x-12x-4 + 18x^2-2$
$= \underline{78x^2 - 24x - 2\ cm^2}$

c) If $x=4$, calculate the volume and surface area of the rectangular prism.

volume $= 45(4)^3 - 18(4)^2 - 5(4) + 2 = \underline{2574\ cm^3}$

Surface area $= 78(4)^2 - 24(4) - 2 = \underline{1150\ cm^2}$

13. length $= y$ cm   width $= y-2$ cm   height $= y+2$ cm

$V = y(y-2)(y+2)$
$= y(y^2-4)$
$= y^3-4y$

14. $a=1 \quad b=0 \quad c=-4 \quad d=0 \quad \text{(C.)} \quad 2$

$x^2 = (x-3)(x+5)$
$x^2 = x^2+5x-3x-15$
$15 = 2x$
$x = 7.5 \quad \boxed{7.5}$

15. $x^2 = (x-8)^2 + 20^2$
$x^2 = x^2-16x+64+400$
$16x = 464$
$x = 29$

$x-8 = 29-8 = 21$

Sides are 29 cm, 21 cm and 20 cm

perimeter $= 29+21+20$
$= 70cm$
$\boxed{70.0}$

Polynomial Operations Lesson #7: Practice Test

1. (B.) $x+1$

2. a^3b $3+1=4$ (B.) 4

3. I $5x$ degree 1   II $3x^5-2x^6$ degree 6   III $3x^4-3x^2+5x^5$ (2) not a polynomial   IV $3x^2y^3$ degree $2+3=5$ (A.) IV only

4. (C.) $2x(x-3)$

5. $x^2-xy+xy-y^2$
   $= x^2-y^2$ (B.) 2

6. $A = (6-a)(8-a)$
   $= 48-6a-8a+a^2$
   $= 48-14a+a^2$ (D.) $48-14a+a^2$

7. $-6x^5-10x^2$
   $-14x+21x^2$
   $-20x^3-5x^4$
   $-9x^2+9x^3$ (D.) $-9x^2(1-x)=-9x^2+9x^3$

8. $A = \tfrac{1}{2}bh = \tfrac{1}{2}(2x+8)(2x+8)$
   $= \tfrac{1}{2}(4x^2+16x+16x+64)$
   $= \tfrac{1}{2}(4x^2+32x+64)$
   $R = 2x^2+16x+32$
   $b=16$ (B.) 16

9. $Area = (4x+3)(2x+4) - (x+3)^2$
   $= 8x^2+16x+6x+12 - (x^2+6x+9)$
   $= 8x^2+22x+12 -x^2-6x-9$
   $= 7x^2+16x+3$ (C.) $7x^2+16x+3$

10. $6t(2t^2-7t-1) -1(2t^2-7t-1)$
    $= 12t^3-42t^2-6t -2t^2+7t+1$
    $= 12t^3-44t^2+t+1$

11. $(3x^2+3x-2)+(3x^2+2x-4)-(2x-3)(3x+2)$
    $= 6x^2+5x-6 - (6x^2+4x-9x-6)$
    $= 6x^2+5x-6 -6x^2-4x+9x+6$
    $= 10x$ $p=0$ $q=10$ $r=0$ (C.) 2

12. $= (a+3)(2a^2+a-12a-6)$
    $= (a+3)(2a^2-11a-6)$
    $= a(2a^2-11a-6) + 3(2a^2-11a-6)$
    $= 2a^3-11a^2-6a + 6a^2-33a-18$
    $= 2a^3-5a^2-39a-18$ (A.)

13. Response 1: x^6+x
    Response 2: $6x^3+6y^3$ degree 3
    Response 3: $4a^2b^4+2a^3$ $2+4=6$ degree 3
    Response 4: y^5z $5+1=6$ but not a binomial ✓   B

14. Which of the following polynomial products contains a term of degree one?
    Response 1 $(x-3)(x-2)$ $= x^2-2x-3x+6 = x^2-5x+6$ ✓
    Response 2 $(x-3)(x-3)$ $= x^2-3x-3x+9 = x^2-6x+9$ ✓
    Response 3 $(x-3)(x+3)$ $= x^2+3x-3x-9 = x^2-9$ ✗
    Response 4 $(x-3)(x-6)(x+2) = (x-3)(x^2+2x-6x-12) = (x-3)(x^2-4x-12) = x(x^2-4x-12)-3(x^2-4x-12) = x^3-4x^2-12x-3x^2+12x+36 = x^3-7x^2+36$

    A

15. (B.) $17-2x$ and $11-2x$

Numerical Response

1. $P=8$ $P-Q-R$
   $Q=4$ $= 8-4-(-9) = 13$ [1][3]
   $R=-9$

2. $6x(4-3x)-5x(x-4)-(9x+2)$
   $= 24x-18x^2-5x^2+20x-9x-2$
   $= -23x^2+35x-2$
   $a=-23$ $b=35$ $c=-2$
   $abc=(-23)(35)(-2) = 1610$ [1][6][1][0]

3. $x^2-2ax+a^2 = x^2-12x+c$
   Compare coefficients of x: $-2a=-12$ $a=6$
   Compare constant terms: $a^2+a=c$ $c=6^2+6=42$ [4][2]

4. $Volume = x(17-2x)(11-2x) = x(187-34x-22x+4x^2)$
   $= x(187-56x+4x^2)$
   $= 187x-56x^2+4x^3$
   $= 4x^3-56x^2+187x$
   $a=4$ $b=-56$ $c=187$ $a+c=4+187 = 191$ [1][9][1]

5. $(x-p)^2+q = x^2-14x+52$
   $x^2-2px+p^2+q = x^2-14x+52$
   $-2p=-14$ $p^2+q=52$
   $p=7$ $7^2+q=52$ $q=3$ [7][3]

Written Response

• Wendy's work contains one mathematical error. Describe in detail the error she made.
  In line 1 Wendy distributed the 5 before squaring. BEDMAS tells us to do exponents before multiplication.

• Cooper's work contains one mathematical error. Describe in detail the error he made.
  In line 1 Cooper expanded $(3y-1)^2$ incorrectly. The first term should be $(3y)(3y)=9y^2$

• Sahil's work contains one mathematical error. Describe in detail the error he made.
  In line 1 Sahil also expanded $(3y-1)^2$ incorrectly. The middle term should be $(3y)(-1)(2)=-6y$

• Determine the correct expansion of $5(3y-1)^2$.
  $5(3y-1)^2 = 5(9y^2-6y+1) = 45y^2-30y+5$

• Verify the expansion by substituting $y=-4$ in the original expression and in your expansion and confirming the same numerical value.
  $LS = 5(3(-4)-1)^2 = 5(-12-1)^2 = 5(-13)^2 = 5(169) = 845$
  $RS = 45(-4)^2-30(-4)+5 = 45(16)+120+5 = 720+120+5 = 845$
  $LS = RS$ so the expansion is verified.

Class Ex. #3

a) $20x - 6$
$= 2(10x-3)$

b) $16x^4 + 4x^2$
$= 4x^2(4x^2+1)$

c) $10a^3b^2 + 8ab^3 + 2ab^4 = 2ab^2(5a^2+4b+b^2)$

d) $12p^3 - 6p^2 + 15p$
$= 3p(4p^2-2p+5)$

e) $25xy^2z^3 - 20x^2y^4z^2 + 30x^4y^2z^5$
$= 5xy^2z^2(5z-4xy^2+6x^3z^3)$

Class Ex. #4

a) 7 b) $5x^2$

a) 5 b) $9p$

c) $(2n+3m)$

d) $(2xy^2-5y+1)$

Class Ex. #6

i) $A = \pi(2.60)^2 + \pi(2.60)(7.40)$
$= 81.68 \text{ cm}^2$

ii) $A = \pi r(r+s)$

iii) $A = \pi(2.60)(2.60+7.40)$
$= 81.68 \text{ cm}^2$

Factoring Polynomial ... Lesson #1: Assignment Pages   **324 to 328**   Factoring Polynomial ... Lesson #1

Assignment

1. $12a^3 = 2 \times 2 \times 3 \times a \times a \times a$
$30a^2 = 2 \times 3 \times 5 \times a \times a$ $GCF = 2 \times 3 \times a \times a = 6a^2$

2. $10xy^4 = 2 \times 5 \times x \times y \times y \times y \times y$
$25x^2y^3 = 5 \times 5 \times x \times x \times y \times y \times y$ $GCF = 5 \times x \times y \times y \times y = 5xy^3$

3. a) $7m$ b) $3x$ c) bc^2 d) ab e) $4x^3$ f) 3 g) $2pq$ h) $-5x^5z^4$ i) ab j) $2x$ k) $-2x^2y$ l) $-4q$

4. a) 12 b) p c) x d) 5 e) $2cd$ f) $3y$

5. a) $a+5$ b) $2p-q$ c) $2x-3$ d) $1+2ab$ e) $3+2y$ f) $4xmn^2-3n-1$

6. a) $6(m+n)$ b) $7(xy^2+7)$ c) $5(3pq-1)$ d) $4(2c+3d)$
   e) $y(x+1)$ f) $3x(2x-3)$ g) $3a(3b-4c)$ h) $24y^2(2-3y^3)$

7. a) $4(3x-2y+4z)$ b) $3p(3q+2r-5)$ c) $t(t^2+t+1)$ d) $5x(x-2y-4z)$
   e) $2ab(2c-d+4e)$ f) $7a^2b^2(2+3a-5b)$

8. a) $= 3x^2+6x$
   $= 3x(x+2)$
   b) $= 8y^2-12y-6$
   $= 2(4y^2-6y-3)$
   c) $= 6x^3y + 6x^2y^2 - 4xy^3$
   $= 2xy(3x^2+3xy-2y^2)$
   d) $= 2x^3-6x-4x^2+24x+5x^3-10x^2-4x$
   $= 7x^3-14x^2+14x$
   $= 7x(x^2-2x+2)$

9. a) $24x^3 - 60x^2$
   $= 12x^2(2x-5)$
   $12x^2(2x-5) = 24x^3-60x^2$
   b) $-8p^3 - 32p^2 - 8p$
   $= -8p(p^2+4p+1)$
   $-8p(p^2+4p+1) = -8p^3-32p^2-8p$

Factoring Polynomial Expressions Lesson #1: *Common Factors - Part One*

Expanding and Factoring

i) a monomial by a polynomial
e.g. $2x(x + 5) = 2x^2 + 10x$

ii) a binomial by a binomial to form a trinomial
e.g. $(x + 1)(x + 3) = x^2 + 4x + 3$
$x^2 + 3x + 1x + 3$

$(2x + 3)(x + 4) = 2x^2 + 11x + 12$
$2x^2 + 8x + 3x + 12$

iii) a binomial by a binomial to form a binomial
e.g. $(x - 5)(x + 5) = x^2 - 25$

Complete the following using the results obtained above.

i) factoring by removing a common factor
e.g. $2x^2 + 10x = 2x(x + 5)$

ii) factoring a trinomial.
e.g. $x^2 + 4x + 3 = (x+1)(x+3)$
$2x^2 + 11x + 12 = (2x+3)(x+4)$

iii) factoring a difference of squares
e.g. $x^2 - 25 = (x-5)(x+5)$

Greatest Common Factor

GCF of 48 and 72 is $2 \times 2 \times 2 \times 3 = 24$.

The same process can be used to determine the greatest common factor of two monomials like $6a^3$ and $9a^2b$.

$6a^3 = 2 \times 3 \times a \times a \times a$ and $9a^2b = 3 \times 3 \times a \times a \times b = 3a^2$

GCF of $6a^3$ and $9a^2b$ is $3 \times a \times a = 3a^2$

Class Ex. #1

$8x^2y^2 = 2 \times 2 \times 2 \times x \times x \times y \times y$
$20x^3y = 2 \times 2 \times 5 \times x \times x \times x \times y \times y \times y$
$GCF = 2 \times 2 \times x \times x \times y \times y = 4x^2y^2$

Class Ex. #2

a) $3ab$ b) $6x^3y^2$
c) ac^2 d) $-10a^2b$

Factoring Polynomial Expressions Lesson #2:
Common Factors - Part Two

Class Ex. #1

a) $(4x)(x+7)-(3)(x+7)$
$=(x+7)(4x-3)$

b) $7(3-2y)+2y(3-2y)$
$=(3-2y)(7+2y)$

c) $9a(4a+1)+(4a+1)$
$=(4a+1)(9a+1)$

Class Ex. #2

a) $(3y+2)(5y+1)+(3y+2)(4y)$
$(3y+2)(5y+1+4y)=(3y+2)(9y+1)$

b) $3a(a-6)-9(a-6)$
$=3(a-6)(a-3)$

c) $2x(x-5)+5(5-x)$
$=2x(x-5)-5(x-5)$
$=(x-5)(2x-5)$

d) $20x(x-3)-4(3-x)$
$=20x(x-3)+4(x-3)$
$=4(x-3)(5x+1)$

Class Ex. #3

a) $x^2+3x+6x+18$
$=x(x+3)+6(x+3)$
$=(x+3)(x+6)$

b) $8x^2-2x+12x-3$
$=2x(4x-1)+3(4x-1)$
$=(4x-1)(2x+3)$

c) $8a^2-4a-10a+5$
$=4a(2a-1)-5(2a-1)$
$=(2a-1)(4a-5)$

d) $6a^2-9a-2a+3$
$=3a(2a-3)-1(2a-3)$
$=(2a-3)(3a-1)$

e) $pq+pr-sq-sr$
$=p(q+r)-s(q+r)$
$=(q+r)(p-s)$

f) $5x^2+18y^2-15xy^2-6x$
$=5x^3-15xy^2-6x+18y^3$
$=5x(x^2-3y^3)-6(x^2-3y^3)$
$=(x-3y^3)(5x-6)$

330

Factoring Polynomial Expressions Lesson #2: *Common Factors - Part Two*

Class Ex. #4

a) $\frac{1}{3}x^2+4x=\frac{1}{3}x(x+12\ )$
$\frac{1}{3}x(x+12)=\frac{1}{3}x^2+4x$

b) $\frac{1}{4}a^2-4a=\frac{1}{4}a(\ a-16\ )$
$\frac{1}{4}a(a-16)=\frac{1}{4}a^2-4a$

c) $6x+\frac{2}{3}=\frac{2}{3}(9x+1\ )$
$\frac{2}{3}(9x+1)=6x+\frac{2}{3}$

d) $\frac{1}{2}a^2-\frac{3}{4}b^2=\frac{1}{4}(2a^2-3b^2)$
$\frac{1}{4}(2a^2-3b^2)=\frac{1}{2}a^2-\frac{3}{4}b^2$

Class Ex. #5

a) $a-\frac{1}{6}a^2=\frac{1}{6}a(6-a)$
$\frac{1}{6}a(6-a)=a-\frac{1}{6}a^2$

b) $\frac{1}{2}\pi r^2-2\pi r=\frac{1}{2}\pi r(r-4)$
$\frac{1}{2}\pi r(r-4)=\frac{1}{2}\pi r^2-2\pi r$

c) $4x^2+2x+\frac{2}{5}=\frac{2}{5}(10x^2+5x+\underline{\ 1\ })$
$\frac{2}{5}(10x^2+5x+1)=4x^2+2x+\frac{2}{5}$

Class Ex. #6

a) $2a+\frac{1}{4}a^3$
$=\frac{1}{4}a(8+a^2)$

b) $x^3+\frac{1}{3}x^2-\frac{1}{6}x$
$=\frac{1}{6}x(6x^2+2x-1)$

Factoring Polynomial ... Lesson #1: Assignment Pages 324 to 328 Factoring Polynomial ... Lesson #1

10. a) $r=\frac{11}{2}=5.5$ cm
b) $A=2\pi r(r+h)$

$A=2\pi(5.5)^2+2\pi(5.5)(14.5)$
$=691.15$ cm^2

c) $A=2\pi(5.5)(5.5+14.5)$
$=691.15$ cm^2

d) c)

11. a) $h=5t(6-t)$

b)

Time (t seconds)	0	1	2	3	4	5	6
Height (h metres)	0	25	40	45	40	25	0

c) At 2 seconds the arrow is on the way up and at 4 seconds it is on the way down.

d) $h=5(7)(6-7)=-35$. The arrow has already hit the ground at t=6. It does not travel 35m below the ground.

12. A square of side 2r cm has semicircles drawn externally on each of two opposite sides.

Find expressions in factored form for

a) the external perimeter of the shape   b) the area of the shape

Perimeter consists of the circumference of a circle of radius r and two straight lines each of length 2r.

$P=2\pi r+2(2r)$
$P=2\pi r+4r$
$\underline{P=2r(\pi+2)}$ cm

area consists of the area of a circle of radius r and the area of a square of side 2r.

$A=\pi r^2+(2r)^2$
$A=\pi r^2+4r^2$
$\underline{A=r^2(\pi+4)}$ cm^2

13. (D.) $\pi r(r^2+3)$ (D.) $3x^2-2x+1$

14. $3x^2(3x^2-2x+1)$

15. $x^3y(x^2y^2-y^2+x^4)$

$A=2\cdot1=3$
$B=4$
$a+b+c=14+7+(-2)=19$
$A+2B=3+2(4)=11$ [1 1]

$a=14$
$b=7$
$c=-2$

16. $14x(7x-3)$ $14+7+(-2)=19$ [1 9]

Assignment

1. a) $(3x)(x+5) - (7)(x+5)$
   $= (x+5)(3x-7)$

   b) $7y(x+4) + 2(x+4)$
   $= (x+4)(7y+2)$

   c) $x(x-1) - (x-1)$
   $= (x-1)(x-1)$ or $(x-1)^2$

   d) $(a+b)(x) - (a+b)(y)$
   $= (a+b)(x-y)$

   e) $4x(a+b) - 8y(a+b)$
   $= 4(a+b)(x-2y)$

   f) $2a(a+9) - 4(a+9)$
   $= 2(a+9)(a-4)$

   g) $21a(b+c) + 7d(b+c)$
   $= 7(b+c)(3a+d)$

   h) $x(5x-3) - 4(3-5x)$
   $= x(5x-3) + 4(5x-3)$
   $= (5x-3)(x+4)$

   i) $2(4-7p) + 3p(-4+7p)$
   $= 2(4-7p) - 3p(4-7p)$
   $= (4-7p)(2-3p)$

2. a) $x^2 + 2x + 6x + 12$
   $= x(x+2) + 6(x+2)$
   $= (x+2)(x+6)$

   b) $x^2 + 3x + 15x + 45$
   $= x(x+3) + 15(x+3)$
   $= (x+3)(x+15)$

   c) $m^2 - 5m + 2m - 10$
   $= m(m-5) + 2(m-5)$
   $= (m-5)(m+2)$

   d) $a^2 - 9a - 5a + 45$
   $= a(a-9) - 5(a-9)$
   $= (a-9)(a-5)$

   e) $x^2 - 15x - 4x + 60$
   $= x(x-15) - 4(x-15)$
   $= (x-15)(x-4)$

   f) $t^2 + 7t - 3t - 21$
   $= t(t+7) - 3(t+7)$
   $= (t+7)(t-3)$

3. a) $2x^2 + 2x + 3x + 3$
   $= 2x(x+1) + 3(x+1)$
   $= (x+1)(2x+3)$

   b) $3x^2 + x + 6x + 2$
   $= x(3x+1) + 2(3x+1)$
   $= (3x+1)(x+2)$

   c) $3m^2 + 9m + 5m + 15$
   $= 3m(m+3) + 5(m+3)$
   $= (m+3)(3m+5)$

   d) $6b^2 - 9b - 4b + 6$
   $= 3b(2b-3) - 2(2b-3)$
   $= (2b-3)(3b-2)$

   e) $2a^2 - 6a - a + 3$
   $= 2a(a-3) - 1(a-3)$
   $= (a-3)(2a-1)$

   f) $5x^2 + 2x - 25x - 10$
   $= x(5x+2) - 5(5x+2)$
   $= (5x+2)(x-5)$

   g) $16 + 4p + 4p + p^2$
   $= 4(4+p) + p(4+p)$
   $= (4+p)(4+p)$
   or $(4+p)^2$

   h) $15 - 3y - 5y + y^2$
   $= 3(5-y) - y(5-y)$
   $= (5-y)(3-y)$

   i) $a^2 + ax + ay + xy$
   $= a(a+x) + y(a+x)$
   $= (a+x)(a+y)$

4. a) $ab + x^2 - ax - bx$
   $= ab - ax - bx + x^2$
   $= a(b-x) - x(b-x)$
   $= (b-x)(a-x)$

   b) $4b^2 + 3a - 12b - ab$
   $= 4b^2 - 12b - ab + 3a$
   $= 4b(b-3) - a(b-3)$
   $= (b-3)(4b-a)$

   c) $4x^2 + 15y^2 - 12xy^2 - 5x$
   $= 4x^3 - 12xy^2 - 5x + 15y^3$
   $= 4x(x-3y^3) - 5(x-3y^3)$
   $= (x-3y^3)(4x-5)$

5. a) $\frac{1}{2}x - x^2 = \frac{1}{2}x(1-2x)$
   b) $3a^2 + \frac{2}{3}a = \frac{1}{3}a(9a+2)$
   c) $-\frac{1}{4}y^2 - y = -\frac{1}{4}y(y+4)$

6. a) $\frac{1}{5}n - \frac{2}{5} = \frac{1}{5}(n-2)$
   b) $\frac{1}{2}x^3 + \frac{1}{4}x = \frac{1}{4}x(2x^2+1)$
   c) $0.2a^3 - 0.5a = 0.1a(2a^2-5)$

7. a) $\frac{1}{2}(1+x)$
   b) $\frac{1}{2}(m-3)$
   c) $\frac{1}{4}h(3a-2b)$
   d) $\frac{2}{3}(x+9)$
   e) $\frac{1}{3}(3x^2-2)$
   f) $\frac{1}{5}(5z^2-z+2)$
   g) $\frac{4}{3}\pi r^2(r-3)$
   h) $\frac{1}{3}h(A+3\pi r^2)$

8. a) $s = \frac{1}{2}t(2v+at)$
   b) $s = \frac{1}{2}(0.1)\,(2(5)+(9.8)(0.1))$
   $= \underline{0.549\ \text{m}}$

9. a) $\frac{1}{2}x \ne \frac{1}{4}$ The common factor is $\frac{1}{4}x$. $\frac{1}{4}x(2x-1)$

   b) The second factor in the binomial should not contain π since π is part of the common factor. $\frac{1}{6}\pi r(r-3)$

   c) $t^2 - 4t - 24 + 6t = t(t-4) - 6(4-t) = (t-4)(t-6)$
   The last step does not follow from the previous one.
   $t-4$ is not a common factor unless the sign in the middle of the second step is changed $t(t-4) + 6(t-4) = (t-4)(t+6)$

10. $xy - 4xz + 3ty - 12tz$
    $= x(y-4z) + 3t(y-4z)$
    $= (y-4z)(x+3t)$
    Ⓒ $(y-4z)$

11. $p^2 + pq + p = p(p+q+1)$
    $\frac{2}{3}\pi r^3 + \pi r^2 h = \frac{1}{3}\pi r^2(2r+3h)$
    $t^2 + t^4 + t^6 = t^2(1+t^2+t^4)$
    Ⓐ 0

12. $x(x-2) - y(x-2)$
    $= (x-2)(x-y)$ Ⓑ $(x-2)(x-y)$

13. $3a^2 + 9a + 4a + c$
    $= 3a(a+3) + 4(a+3)$
    $= (a+3)(3a+4)$ c: 4×3
    $= 12$
    Ⓑ $3a+4$

14. $2x^2 + 3x + 8x + p$
    $= x(2x+3) + 4(2x+3)$
    $= (2x+3)(x+4)$ $p: 4\times3 = 12$

Factoring Polynomial Expressions Lesson #3:
Factoring Trinomials of the Form $x^2 + bx + c$ - Part One

Class Ex. #1

a) $x^2 + 5x + 4$ b) length = $x+4$, width = $x+1$ c) $x^2 + 5x + 4 = (x+4)(x+1)$

Class Ex. #2

a) $x^2 - 7x + 12$

b) $x^2 - 7x + 12 = (x-4)(x-3)$

Investigation: Factoring Trinomials by Inspection

• Expand the following binomials.

$(x+2)(x+4) = x^2 + 4x + 2x + 8 = x^2 + 6x + 8$.

$(x+3)(x+3) = x^2 + 3x + 3x + 9 = x^2 + 6x + 9$

$(x+1)(x+7) = x^2 + 7x + x + 7 = x^2 + 8x + 7$

$(x+5)(x+2) = x^2 + 2x + 5x + 10 = x^2 + 7x + 10$

$(x-5)(x-2) = x^2 - 2x - 5x + 10 = x^2 - 7x + 10$

$(x+8)(x-6) = x^2 - 6x + 8x - 48 = x^2 + 2x - 48$

• Consider the expansion $(x+p)(x+q) = x^2 + bx + c$.

In each of the examples above what is the connection between

i) the value of b and the values of p and q? $b = p + q$

ii) the value of c and the values of p and q? $c = pq$

Factoring $x^2 + bx + c$ by Inspection

In order to factor $x^2 + 8x + 12$ we need to find two numbers which multiply to __12__ and add to __8__.

In order to factor $x^2 - 13x + 12$ we need to find two numbers which multiply to __12__ and add to __-13__.

Class Ex. #3

$x^2 + qx + px + pq$

$= x^2 + px + qx + pq$

$= x^2 + (p+q)x + pq$

Sum	Product	Integers
12	20	2, 10
9	20	4, 5
4	4	2, 2
-9	18	-3, -6

Class Ex. #4

Sum	Product	Integers
-15	14	-1, -14
-1	-6	2, -3
2	-15	-3, 5
-26	48	-2, -24

Class Ex. #5

a) $x^2 + 8x + 12 = (x+2)(x+6)$

b) $x^2 + 13x + 12 = (x+1)(x+12)$

c) $x^2 - 13x + 12 = (x-1)(x-12)$

d) $a^2 - 11a + 10 = (a-1)(a-10)$

e) $y^2 + 3y + 4 =$ not possible

f) $x^2 + 27x + 50 = (x+2)(x+25)$

Class Ex. #6

a) $4x^2 - 32x + 48$
$= 4(x^2 - 8x + 12)$
$= 4(x-2)(x-6)$

b) $3x^3 + 21x^2 + 30x$
$= 3x(x^2 + 7x + 10)$
$= 3x(x+2)(x+5)$

Factoring Polynomial ... Lesson #3: Assignment Pages **338 to 342** Factoring Polynomial ... Lesson #3

Assignment

1. a) $x^2 + 4x + 3$ b) $x+3$, $x+1$,   c) $x^2 + 4x + 3 = (x+3)(x+1)$

2. a) $x^2 - 7x + 10$ b) $x-2$, $x-5$,   c) $x^2 - 7x + 10 = (x-2)(x-5)$

3. a) $(x+2)(x+3)$ b) $(x+1)(x+5)$ c) $(x-4)(x-2)$

4. a) 2, 3   c) 5, 6   d) -5, -6
   e) 1, 10   f) -3, -5   g) -7, -8   h) -4, -14

5. a) $(x+3)(x+4)$ b) $(x+1)(x+8)$ c) $(x-2)(x-5)$
   d) $(t-2)(t-12)$ e) $(z+5)(z+3)$ f) $(b-2)(b-10)$

6. a) $(x+1)(x+2)$ b) $(x-1)(x-2)$ c) $(x+3)(x+6)$
   d) $(x+2)(x+6)$ e) $(x-3)(x-7)$ f) $(x-3)(x-8)$

7. a) $(x+1)(x+10)$ b) not possible   c) $(n+4)(n+8)$
   d) $(y-4)(y-7)$ e) $(y+3)(y+14)$ f) $(f-3)(f-7)$
   g) $(p-2)(p-14)$ h) $(x+4)(x+20)$ i) $(c-2)(c-30)$
   j) not possible   k) $(d+3)(d+15)$ l) $(p-4)(p-25)$
   m) $(m+11)(m+11)$ n) $(n-6)(n-17)$ o) $(q-5)(q-23)$
   OR $(m+11)^2$

8. a) The expression $x^2 + bx + 12$ can be factored over the integers. Determine all possible values of b.

   We need 2 integers with a product of 12.   Add the integers

1	2	3	-1	-2	-3
12	6	4	-12	-6	-4

   $b = 13, 8, 7, -13, -8, -7$

   b) If the expression $x^2 + 6x + c$, where $c > 0$, can be factored over the integers, determine all possible values of c.

   We need 2 positive integers with a sum of 6.   Multiply the integers

1	2	3
5	4	3

   $c = 5, 8, 9$

9. A volleyball court has an area of $x^2 + 15x + 36$ square metres.

   a) Factor $x^2 + 15x + 36$ to find binomials that represent the length and width of the court.

   $x^2 + 15x + 36 = (x+12)(x+3)$ length = $x+12$ width = $x+3$

   b) If $x = 3$, determine the length and width of the court.

   length = $3+12 = 15$ m   width = $3+3 = 6$ m

Factoring Polynomial ... Lesson #3: Assignment Pages 338 to 342 Factoring Polynomial ... Lesson #3

10. Factor.

a) $2x^2 + 6x + 4$
$= 2(x^2 + 3x + 2)$
$= 2(x+1)(x+2)$

b) $4x^2 - 48x + 128$
$= 4(x^2 - 12x + 32)$
$= 4(x-4)(x-8)$

c) $-2a^2 - 30a - 108$
$= -2(a^2 + 15a + 54)$
$= -2(a+6)(a+9)$

d) $5x^2 - 20x + 15$
$= 5(x^2 - 4x + 3)$
$= 5(x-1)(x-3)$

e) $ax^2 - 14ax + 45a$
$= a(x^2 - 14x + 45)$
$= a(x-5)(x-9)$

f) $-10a^4 + 100a^3 - 240a^2$
$= -10a^2(a^2 - 10a + 24)$
$= -10a^2(a-4)(a-6)$

11. Consider the following in which each letter represents a whole number.

$x^2 + 5x + 6 = (x+A)(x+B)$ $x^2 + 10x + 21 = (x+B)(x+G)$ B = 3
$(x+2)(x+3)$ or $(x+3)(x+2)$ $(x+3)(x+7)$ or $(x+7)(x+3)$ A = 2
$x^2 - 9x + 20 = (x-T)(x-L)$ $2x^2 - 16x + 32 = 2(x-T)^2$ G = 7
$(x-4)(x-5)$ or $(x-5)(x-4)$ $= 2(x^2 - 8x + 16) = 2(x-4)^2$ T = 4 ; L = 5
$x^3 + 10x^2 + 9x = x(x+S)(x+E)$ $6x^2 - 54x + 48 = 6(x-I)(x-S)$ S = 1
$= x(x^2 + 10x + 9) = x(x+9)(x+1)$ $= 6(x^2 - 9x + 8) = 6(x-1)(x-8)$ E = 9
  or $x(x+1)(x+9)$ or $6(x-8)(x-1)$ I = 8

Determine the value of each letter and hence name the famous person represented by the following code.

(3) (8) (5) (5) (7) (2) (4) (9) (1)
 B   I   L   L   G   A   T   E   S

12. $3(m^2 - 9m + 18)$
$= 3(m-6)(m-3)$
(C) m - 9

13. A. $a^2 + 6a + 5$ $(a+5)(a+1)$
B. $a^2 + 11a + 30$ $(a+5)(a+6)$
C. $a^2 + 10a + 50$ x
D. $a^2 + 10a + 25$ $(a+5)^2$

14. A. -13   B. -8   C. 7   D. 11
$t^2 - 13t + 12$ $t^2 - 8t + 12$ $t^2 + 7t + 12$ $t^2 + 11t + 12$
$= (t-1)(t-12)$ $= (t-2)(t-6)$ $= (t+3)(t+4)$ x

15. $(x+1)(x+32) = x^2 + 33x + 32$ |3|3|

Factoring Polynomial Expressions Lesson #4:
Factoring Trinomials of the Form $x^2 + bx + c$ - Part Two

Review of Factoring By Inspection

In order to factor $x^2 + 6x + 9$, we need to find two numbers whose product is __9__ and whose sum is __6__.

In order to factor $x^2 + x - 12$, we need to find two numbers whose product is __-12__ and whose sum is __1__.

Class Ex. #1
a) $x^2 - x - 12$
$(x+3)(x-4)$
b) $x^2 + 3x - 18$
$(x-3)(x+6)$
c) $a^2 - 7a - 8$
$(a+1)(a-8)$

Class Ex. #2
a) $a^2 + 6a - 27$
$(a-3)(a+9)$
b) $2t^2 - 14t + 20$
$= 2(t^2 - 7t + 10) = 2(t-2)(t-5)$
c) $x^2 - 3x - 6$
not possible
d) $4x^4 - 16x^3 - 20x^2$
$= 4x^2(x^2 - 4x - 5)$
$= 4x^2(x+1)(x-5)$

344   Factoring Polynomial Expressions   Lesson #4:   Factoring Trinomials.... $x^2 + bx + c$ - Part Two

Factoring Trinomials of the form $x^2 + bxy + cy^2$

i) $(x+2)(x+4)$ can be expanded to $x^2 + 6x + 8$,
so $x^2 + 6x + 8$ can be factored to $(x+2)(x+4)$.

ii) $(x+2y)(x+4y)$ can be expanded to $x^2 + 6xy + 8y^2$,
so $x^2 + 6xy + 8y^2$ can be factored to $(x+2y)(x+4y)$.

Class Ex. #3
a) $x^2 + 13xy + 30y^2$
$(x+3y)(x+10y)$
b) $x^2 + 71xy - 72y^2$
$(x-y)(x+72y)$
c) $3a^2 - 15ab - 252b^2$
$= 3(a^2 - 5ab - 84b^2)$
$= 3(a+7b)(a-12b)$

Factoring Polynomial ... Lesson #4: Assignment Pages 344 to 346   Factoring Polynomial ... Lesson #4

Assignment

1.

	Sum	Product	Integers		Sum	Product	Integers
a)	8	-20	-2, 10	d)	3	-70	-7, 10
b)	-8	-20	2, -10	e)	-11	28	-4, -7
c)	-1	-20	4, -5	f)	0	-16	-4, 4

2. a) $(x-5)(x+3)$ b) $(x-6)(x+4)$ c) $(x+6)(x-4)$ d) $(x+3)(x-1)$
e) $(x+6)(x-5)$ f) $(x-5)(x+2)$

3. a) $(x+8)(x+2)$ b) $(x-9)(x-2)$ c) $(x+2)(x-4)$ d) $(x+6)(x-3)$
e) not possible   f) $(x-6)(x+2)$ g) $(x-5)^2$ h) $(x+5)(x-4)$
i) $(m+2)(m+19)$ j) $(a-14)(a-3)$ k) not possible   l) $(p-10)(p+1)$

Factoring Polynomial Expressions Lesson #5:
Difference of Squares

Investigation

a)

	Sum	Product	Integers	Polynomial	Factored Form
i)	-6	-16	$-8, 2$	$x^2 - 6x - 16$	$(x-8)(x+2)$
ii)	-15	-16	$-16, 1$	$x^2 - 15x - 16$	$(x-16)(x+1)$
iii)	0	-16	$-4, 4$	$x^2 + 0x - 16 = x^2 - 16$	$(x-4)(x+4)$
iv)	0	-64	$-8, 8$	$x^2 + 0x - 64 = x^2 - 64$	$(x-8)(x+8)$
v)	0	-25	$-5, 5$	$x^2 + 0x - 25 = x^2 - 25$	$(x-5)(x+5)$

b)
i) $x^2 - 9 =$
$(x-3)(x+3)$

ii) $x^2 - 49 =$
$(x-7)(x+7)$

iii) $x^2 - 36 =$
$(x-6)(x+6)$

iv) $x^2 - 1 =$
$(x-1)(x+1)$

v) $a^2 - 100 =$
$(a-10)(a+10)$

c) $(m-n)(m+n)$

$(m-n)(m+n) = m^2 + mn - mn - n^2$

$\qquad\qquad = m^2 - n^2$

d) i) Explain why the value of b is zero.

$(x-y)(x+y) = x^2 + xy - xy - y^2$

The two middle terms in the expansion are opposites of each other.
Their sum is zero so $b = 0$.

ii) Express c in terms of y.

$c = -y^2$

348   Factoring Polynomial Expressions Lesson #5: *Difference of Squares*

Class Ex. #1

a) $a^2 - 4$
$= (a-2)(a+2)$

b) $t^2 - 144$
$= (t-12)(t+12)$

c) $x^2 - y^2$
$= (x-y)(x+y)$

d) $p^2 - 7^2$
$= (p-7)(p+7)$

---

4. Factor.

a) $2x^2 + 14x + 24$
$= 2(x^2 + 7x + 12)$
$= 2(x+3)(x+4)$

b) $4x^2 - 28x - 32$
$= 4(x^2 - 7x - 8)$
$= 4(x-8)(x+1)$

c) $5x^2 - 20x + 15$
$= 5(x^2 - 4x + 3)$
$= 5(x-3)(x-1)$

d) $-2a^2 + 2a + 220$
$= -2(a^2 - a - 110)$
$= -2(a-11)(a+10)$

e) $b^2x^2 - 4b^2x - 45b^2$
$= b^2(x^2 - 4x - 45)$
$= b^2(x-9)(x+5)$

f) $2x^3 + 2x^2 - 40x$
$= 2x(x^2 + x - 20)$
$= 2x(x+5)(x-4)$

5. $x^2 + 4x - 5 = (x+A)(x-O)$
$\quad = (x+5)(x-1)$

$x^2 - 3x - 54 = (x-E)(x+I)$
$\quad = (x-9)(x+6)$

$x^3 + 2x^2 - 8x = x(x-Y)(x+P)$
$= x(x^2 + 2x - 8) = x(x-2)(x+4)$

$3x^2 - 48x + 192 = T(x-R)^2$
$= 3(x^2 - 16x + 64) = 3(x-8)^2$

$-5x^2 + 20x + 105 = -5(x+T)(x-H)$
$= -5(x^2 - 4x - 21) = -5(x+3)(x-7)$

Determine the value of each letter and hence name the fictional character represented by the following code. (7) (5) (8) (8) (2) (4) (1) (3) (3) (9) (8)

H A R R Y P O T T E R

6. a) $(x+15y)(x+3y)$
b) $(x-2y)(x+12y)$
c) $(a-6b)^2$
d) $(p-q)(p-11q)$
e) $(x-8y)(x+9y)$
f) $(x+2y)(x-56y)$

7. a) $4x^2 - 80xy + 144y^2$
$= 4(x^2 - 20xy + 36y^2)$
$= 4(x-18y)(x-2y)$

b) $3b^2 - 15bv - 72v^2$
$= 3(b^2 - 5bv - 24v^2)$
$= 3(b-8v)(b+3v)$

c) $2c^2 + 66cd - 140d^2$
$= 2(c^2 + 33cd - 70d^2)$
$= 2(c+35d)(c-2d)$

8. $x^2 - 10x + 21 = (x-3)(x-7)$
$x^2 - 4x - 21 = (x+3)(x-7)$ (A.) $x-7$

9. $= -m(m^2 + m - 6)$
$= -m(m+3)(m-2)$ (A.) $m-2$

10. $3(x^2 - 2xy - 3y^2)$
$= 3(x-3y)(x+y)$ (D.) $x+y$

11. $x^2 - 4x - 5 = (x-5)(x+1)$
$x^2 - 4x = x(x-4)$
$x^2 - 4x + 4 = (x-2)^2$
$x^2 - 4x + 5$ cannot be factored   (D.)   5

5. **a)** Write expressions in m and n for the length and width of the floor.

length $= 9m + 2n$ metres   width $= 9m - 2n$ metres

b) If the perimeter of the floor is 72 metres, form an equation in m and n and solve for m.

$$2(9m + 2n) + 2(9m - 2n) = 72$$
$$18m + 4n + 18m - 4n = 72$$
$$36m = 72$$
$$m = \frac{72}{36}$$
$$m = 2$$

c) Determine the length and width of the floor if the length is 25% greater the width.

$9m + 2n = 1.25(9m - 2n)$ $4.5n = 4.5$
$n = 1$

$14m = 2$, $18 + 2n = 1.25(18 - 2n)$
$18 + 2n = 22.5 - 2.5n$

length: $9(2) + 2(1) = \underline{20\,m}$
width: $9(2) - 2(1) = \underline{\underline{16\,m}}$

6. **a)** $8x^2 - 32$
$= 8(x^2 - 4)$
$= 8(x - 2)(x + 2)$

b) $4a^2 - 100y^2$
$= 4(a^2 - 25y^2)$
$= 4(a - 5y)(a + 5y)$

c) $3t^2 + 27s^2$
$= 3(t^2 + 9s^2)$

d) $7x^2 - 7y^2$
$= 7(x^2 - y^2)$
$= 7(x - y)(x + y)$

e) $9a^2b^2 - 36$
$= 9(a^2b^2 - 4)$
$= 9(ab - 2)(ab + 2)$

f) $8 - 50p^2q^2$
$= 2(4 - 25p^2q^2)$
$= 2(2 - 5pq)(2 + 5pq)$

g) $xy^2 - x^3$
$= x(y^2 - x^2)$
$= x(y - x)(y + x)$

h) $20a^2b^2 - 5a^4b^4$
$= 5a^2b^2(4 - a^2b^2)$
$= 5a^2b^2(2 - ab)(2 + ab)$

7. **a)** $(ab - 3)(ab + 3)$ **b)** $(c - de)(c + de)$ **c)** $(10x - yz)(10x + yz)$
d) $(pq - rs)(pq + rs)$ **e)** $(5xy - 1)(5xy + 1)$ **f)** $(cd - 2f)(cd + 2f)$
g) $(2xa - 7zt)(2xa + 7zt)$ **h)** $(4ac - 15bd)(4ac + 15bd)$

8. **a)** Write an expression for the shaded area.

area $= \pi R^2 - \pi r^2$

b) Write the expression in a) in factored form.

area $= \pi(R^2 - r^2) = \pi(R - r)(R + r)$

c) Determine the shaded area (as a multiple of π) if $R = 8.5$ and $r = 1.5$. Do not use a calculator.

area $= \pi(8.5 - 1.5)(8.5 + 1.5)$
$= \pi(7)(10)$
$= \underline{\underline{70\pi}}$

Factoring Polynomial Expressions Lesson #5: *Difference of Squares*   349

For example, $4x^2 - 25$ can be written as $(2x)^2 - (5)^2$

$\quad$ $9m^2 - 4n^2$ can be written as $(3m)^2 - (2n)^2$

$4x^2 - 25 = (2x - 5)(2x + 5)$ $\quad$ $9m^2 - 4n^2 = (3m - 2n)(3m + 2n)$

Class Ex. #2

a) $16t^2 - 49$
$(4t - 7)(4t + 7)$

b) $81a^2 - 1$
$(9a - 1)(9a + 1)$

c) $100 - y^2$
$(10 - y)(10 + y)$

d) $36p^2 - 25q^2$
$(6p - 5q)(6p + 5q)$

e) $4x^2 + 25$
not possible

f) $64 - 9a^2b^2$
$(8 - 3ab)(8 + 3ab)$

Class Ex. #3

a) Write expressions for the length and width of the floor.

length $= 5a + b$ ft   width $= 5a - b$ ft

b) The perimeter of the floor is 140 feet. Determine the length and width of the floor if the length is 1.8 times the width.

$2(5a + b) + 2(5a - b) = 140$
$10a + 2b + 10a - 2b = 140$
$20a = 140$
$a = 7$

$5a + b = 1.8(5a - b) = 140$
$5a + b = 9a - 1.8b$
$2.8b = 4a$
$2.8b = 4(7) = 28$
$b = \frac{28}{2.8}$
$b = 10$

length $= 5(7) + 10 = \underline{45\,ft}$
width $= 5(7) - 10 = \underline{25\,ft}$

350

Class Ex. #4

a) $2a^2 - 50$
$= 2(a^2 - 25)$
$= 2(a - 5)(a + 5)$

b) $3x^2 - 12y^2$
$= 3(x^2 - 4y^2)$
$= 3(x - 2y)(x + 2y)$

c) $144p^2q^2 - 4$
$= 4(36p^2q^2 - 1)$
$= 4(6pq - 1)(6pq + 1)$

d) $3x^3 - 27x$
$= 3x(x^2 - 9)$
$= 3x(x - 3)(x + 3)$

Assignment

1. **a)** $(x + 6)$ **b)** $(c - 11)$ **c)** $(j + k)$

2. **a)** $(x - 7)(x + 7)$ **b)** $(x - 1)(x + 1)$ **c)** $(x - 15)(x + 15)$ **d)** $(x - 20)(x + 20)$

3. A difference of squares can be regarded as a trinomial of the form $x^2 + bx + c$ in which $b = 0$ and c is negative. We need to find two numbers which multiply to c and add to zero.

4. **a)** $(m - n)(m + n)$ **b)** $(c - 7)(c - 7)$ **c)** $(1 - k)(1 + k)$
d) $(g - 8h)(g + 8h)$ **e)** $(5x - 12)(5x + 12)$ **f)** $(4a - 3b)(4a + 3b)$
g) not factorable   **h)** $(11a - 6b)(11a + 6b)$ **i)** not factorable using whole number exponent.
j) $(10 - 9b)(10 + 9b)$ **k)** $(1 + 5z)(1 - 5z)$ **l)** $(15a + b)(15a - b)$
m) $(13z - 2q)(13z + 2q)$ **n)** $(16 - y)(16 + y)$ **o)** not factorable   **p)** $(7a + 20)(7a - 20)$

Factoring Polynomial Expressions Lesson #6:

Warm-Up #1 Factoring $ax^2 + bx + c$ (where $a \neq 1$)

$(2x+1)(3x+4) = 6x^2 + 11x + 4$ so $6x^2 + 11x + 4$ factors to $(2x+1)(3x+4)$

$(3x-2)(4x+3) = 12x^2 + x - 6$ so $12x^2 + x - 6$ factors to $(3x-2)(4x+3)$

Class Ex. #1

a) $2x^2 + 7x + 6$　b) length : $2x+3$　c) $2x^2 + 7x + 6$

width : $x + 2$ 　　= $(2x+3)(x+2)$

356

Factoring Polynomial Expressions Lesson #6: *Factoring ax^2+bx+c (where $a\neq1$)*

Warm-Up #2 Review - Factoring by Grouping

Class Ex. #2

$5x^2 + 7x + 2$

$= (5x+2)(x+1)$

i) $6x^2 + 3x + 8x + 4$　　ii) $12x^2 + 9x - 8x - 6$

$= 3x(2x+1) + 4(2x+1)$　　$= 3x(4x+3) - 2(4x+3)$

$= (2x+1)(3x+4)$　　　　　$= (4x+3)(3x-2)$

357

Factoring Polynomial Expressions Lesson #6: *Factoring ax^2+bx+c (where $a\neq1$)*

In 2i) how are the numbers 8 and 3 connected to the value of a (i.e. 6), the value of b (i.e. 11) and the value of c (i.e. 4)?

$8 + 3 = 11$　　$8 \times 3 = 6 \times 4$　　$8 + 3 = b$

$8 + 3 = 11$　　$8 \times 3 = 6 \times 4$　　$8 \times 3 = ac$

In 2ii) how are the numbers 9 and -8 connected to the value of a (i.e. 12), the value of b (i.e. 1) and the value of c (i.e. -6)?

$9 + (-8) = 1$　　$9 \times (-8) = 12 \times (-6)$　　$9 + (-8) = b$

$9 + (-8) = 1$　　$9 \times (-8) = 12 \times (-6)$　　$9 \times (-8) = ac$

Class Ex. #3

a) $2x^2 + 7x + 6$

×	+
12	7

$4, 3$

$= 2x^2 + 4x + 3x + 6$

$= 2x(x+2) + 3(x+2)$

$= (x+2)(2x+3)$

b) $5x^2 + 7x + 2$

×	+
10	7

$2, 5$

$= 5x^2 + 2x + 5x + 2$

$= x(5x+2) + 1(5x+2)$

$= (5x+2)(x+1)$

Class Ex. #4 Factor.

a) $6x^2 + 17x - 3$

×	+
-18	17

$18, -1$

$= 6x^2 + 18x - x - 3$

$= 6x(x+3) - 1(x+3)$

$= (x+3)(6x-1)$

b) $3n^2 - 2n - 8$

×	+
-24	-2

$-6, 4$

$= 3n^2 - 6n + 4n - 8$

$= 3n(n-2) + 4(n-2)$

$= (n-2)(3n+4)$

c) $12x^2 - 8x + 1$

×	+
12	-8

$-2, -6$

$= 12x^2 - 2x - 6x + 1$

$= 2x(6x-1) - 1(6x-1)$

$= (6x-1)(2x-1)$

Class Ex. #5 Factor.

a) $15 - 7y - 2y^2$

×	+
-30	-7

$-10, 3$

$= 15 - 10y + 3y - 2y^2$

$= 5(3 - 2y) + y(3 - 2y)$

$= (3 - 2y)(5 + y)$

b) $15k^2 + 5k - 10$

×	+
-6	1

$-2, 3$

$= 5(3k^2 + k - 2)$

$= 5(3k^2 - 2k + 3k - 2)$

$= 5[k(3k-2) + 1(3k-2)]$

$= 5(3k-2)(k+1)$

---

9. a) Write the expression in factored form.

$= \frac{1}{2}m(v^2 - u^2) = \frac{1}{2}m(v-u)(v+u)$

b) Determine the value of the expression when $m = 10$, $v = 75$, and $u = 25$.
Do not use a calculator.

$\frac{1}{2}(10)(75-25)(75+25)$

$= \frac{1}{2}(10)(50)(100)$

$= 5(50)(100) = (250)(100) = \underline{25\,000}$

10. Consider the following in which each letter represents a whole number.

$64x^2 - y^2 = (Hx - y)(Hx + y)$　　$16x^2 - 4 = C(Ix + 1)(Ix - 1)$

$= (8x - y)(8x + y)$　　$= 4(x^2 - 1) = 4(x+1)(x-1)$

$7x^2 - 252y^2 = P(x - Ey)(x + Ey)$　　$Lx^2 - Ny^2 = (3x - 5y)(Sx + Ay)$

$= 7(x^2 - 36y^2) = 7(x - 6y)(x + 6y)$　　$9x^2 - 25y^2 = (3x - 5y)(3x + 5y)$

Determine the value of each letter and hence name the country represented by the following code.   (4) (8) (2) (9) (6)

　　　　　　C   H   I   L   E

H : 8	
C : 4	
I : 1	
S : 3	
A : 5	
L : 9	
N : 25	
P : 7	
E : 6	

11. a) Use the above process to evaluate:

i) 27×33

$= (30 - 3)(30 + 3)$

$= 30^2 - 3^2$

$= 900 - 9$

$= 891$

ii) 61×59

$= (60 + 1)(60 - 1)$

$= 60^2 - 1^2$

$= 3600 - 1$

$= 3599$

b) Explain why this process cannot be used to determine the product 66×72.

66×72 expressed as a difference of squares $(69^2 - 3^2)$ cannot easily be evaluated without a calculator or long multiplication.

c) Make up your own multiplication question which can be answered using this process.

Evaluate 42×38 without using long multiplication or a calculator.

$x^2 - y^2 = (x - y)(x + y)$

$42 \times 38 = (x-y)(x+y)$

$x - y = 5$　　$x + y = 9$

$x - 5 = 5$　　　$x = 7, \, y = 2$

12. A. $4 - m$　　$4(4 - m^2)$

B. $8 - 2m$　　$= 4(2 - m)(2 + m)$

C. $4 + m$

(D.) $2 + m$

13. A. 2　　$x^2 - y^2 = (x - y)(x + y)$

B. 5　　$45 = (x - y)(9)$

(C.) 7

D. impossible to determine

$x - y = 5$　　$x + y = 9$

$x = 7, \, y = 2$

$a^2 = 9$　$b^2 = 4$　$a^2 + b^2 = 9 + 4 = 13$

1	3

14. $(3x + 2y)(3x - 2y) = 9x^2 - 4y^2$

$a^2 = 9$　$b^2 = 4$　$a^2 + b^2 = 9 + 4 = 13$

1	3

Factor.

a) $2x^2 - 5xy + 2y^2$ (× 4, + −5; $(-1,-4)$)

$= 2x^2 - xy - 4xy + 2y^2$

$= x(2x-y) - 2y(2x-y)$

$= (2x-y)(x-2y)$

b) $2n^2 - 7nm - 15m^2$ (× −30, + −7; $(-10,3)$)

$= 2n^2 - 10nm + 3nm - 15m^2$

$= 2n(n-5m) + 3m(n-5n)$

$= (n-5m)(2n+3m)$

Assignment

1. a) $3x^2 + 7x + 2$ b) $3x + 1, x + 2$ c) $3x^2 + 7x + 2 = (3x + 1)(x + 2)$

2. a) $(2x + 3)(x + 1)$ b) $(2x + 1)(x + 3)$ c) $(3x + 2)(2x + 1)$ d) $(4x + 1)(x + 3)$

3. Factor the following expressions.

a) $10x^2 + 17x + 3$ (× 30, + 17)

$= 10x^2 + 2x + 15x + 3$

$= 2x(5x+1) + 3(5x+1)$

$= (5x+1)(2x+3)$

b) $9x^2 + 6x + 1$ (× 9, + 6)

$= 9x^2 + 3x + 3x + 1$

$= 3x(3x+1) + 1(3x+1)$

$= (3x+1)(3x+1)$ or $(3x+1)^2$

c) $3x^2 + 14x + 15$ (× 45, + 14)

$= 3x^2 + 5x + 9x + 15$

$= x(3x+5) + 3(3x+5)$

$= (3x+5)(x+3)$

d) $3a^2 - 23a - 8$ (× −24, + −23; $(1,-24)$)

$= 3a^2 + a - 24a - 8$

$= a(3a+1) - 8(3a+1)$

$= (3a+1)(a-8)$

e) $3a^2 + a - 2$ (× −6, + 1; $(-2,3)$)

$= 3a^2 - 2a + 3a - 2$

$= a(3a-2) + 1(3a-2)$

$= (3a-2)(a+1)$

f) $5x^2 - 23x - 10$ (× −50, + −23; $(2,-25)$)

$= 5x^2 + 2x - 25x - 10$

$= x(5x+2) - 5(5x+2)$

$= (5x+2)(x-5)$

g) $2p^2 - 19p + 9$ (× 18, + −19)

$= 2p^2 - p - 18p + 9$

$= p(2p-1) - 9(2p-1)$

$= (2p-1)(p-9)$

h) $6x^2 - 13x + 6$ (× 36, + −13; $(-4,-9)$)

$= 6x^2 - 4x - 9x + 6$

$= 2x(3x-2) - 3(3x-2)$

$= (3x-2)(2x-3)$

4. Factor.

a) $6x^2 + 5x - 6$ (× −36, + 5; $(9,-4)$)

$= 6x^2 + 9x - 4x - 6$

$= 3x(2x+3) - 2(2x+3)$

$= (2x+3)(3x-2)$

b) $2x^2 + x - 1$ (× −2, + 1; $(-1,2)$)

$= 2x^2 - x + 2x - 1$

$= x(2x-1) + 1(2x-1)$

$= (2x-1)(x+1)$

c) $3x^2 - 2x - 1$ (× −3, + −2; $(1,-3)$)

$= 3x^2 + x - 3x - 1$

$= x(3x+1) - 1(3x+1)$

$= (3x+1)(x-1)$

d) $8y^2 + 2y - 3$ (× −24, + 2; $(-4,6)$)

$= 8y^2 - 4y + 6y - 3$

$= 4y(2y-1) + 3(2y-1)$

$= (2y-1)(4y+3)$

e) $9t^2 - 24t + 16$ (× 144, + −24; $(-12,-12)$)

$= 9t^2 - 12t - 12t + 16$

$= 3t(3t-4) - 4(3t-4)$

$= (3t-4)(3t-4)$ or $(3t-4)^2$

f) $12m^2 - 11m - 5$ (× −60, + −11; $(4,-15)$)

$= 12m^2 + 4m - 15m - 5$

$= 4m(3m+1) - 5(3m+1)$

$= (3m+1)(4m-5)$

g) $12p^2 + 13p - 4$ (× −48, + 13; $(-3,16)$)

$= 12p^2 - 3p + 16p - 4$

$= 3p(4p-1) + 4(4p-1)$

$= (4p-1)(3p+4)$

h) $9x^2 - x - 10$ (× −90, + −1; $(-10,9)$)

$= 9x^2 - 10x + 9x - 10$

$= x(9x-10) + 1(9x-10)$

$= (9x-10)(x+1)$

5. A rectangular garden has an area of $2a^2 + 3a - 5$ m^2. (× −10, + 3; $(5,-2)$)

a) Write the area as the product of two binomials.

$2a^2 + 3a - 5$

$= 2a^2 + 5a - 2a - 5$

$= a(2a+5) - 1(2a+5) = (2a+5)(a-1)$

b) The garden is to be completely enclosed by a path 1m wide. Find and simplify an expression for the area of the path.

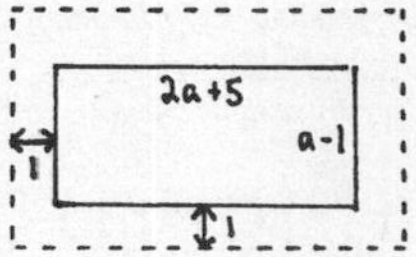

area of path $= (2a+7)(a+1) - (2a+5)(a-1)$

$= (2a^2+9a+7) - (2a^2+3a-5)$

$= 2a^2 + 9a + 7 - 2a^2 - 3a + 5 = 6a + 12$ m^2

c) The path is concrete, poured to a depth of 12 cm. Calculate the volume (in m^3) of concrete used if $a = 7$.

Volume $= (6a+12)(0.12) = (42+12)(0.12) = 6.48$ m^3

6. Factor the following expressions.

a) $12 + 8x + x^2$
$= 12 + 2x + 6x + x^2$
$= 2(6+x) + x(6+x)$
$= (6+x)(2+x)$

x	+
12	8

$(2, 6)$

b) $6 - 7x - 20x^2$
$= 6 + 8x - 15x - 20x^2$
$= 2(3+4x) - 5x(3+4x)$
$= (3+4x)(2-5x)$

x	+
−120	−7

$(8, -15)$

c) $3 + a - 10a^2$
$= 3 - 5a + 6a - 10a^2$
$= 1(3-5a) + 2a(3-5a)$
$= (3-5a)(1+2a)$

x	+
−30	1

$(-5, 6)$

d) $10a^2 + 25a - 15$
$= 5(2a^2 + 5a - 3)$
$= 5(2a^2 - a + 6a - 3)$
$= 5[a(2a-1) + 3(2a-1)]$
$= 5(2a-1)(a+3)$

x	+
−6	5

$(-1, 6)$

e) $12z^2 + 66z + 30$
$= 6(2z^2 + 11z + 5)$
$= 6(2z^2 + z + 10z + 5)$
$= 6[z(2z+1) + 5(2z+1)]$
$= 6(2z+1)(z+5)$

x	+
10	11

$(1, 10)$

f) $4x^3 - 7x^2 - 2x$
$= x(4x^2 - 7x - 2)$
$= x(4x^2 + x - 8x - 2)$
$= x[x(4x+1) - 2(4x+1)]$
$= x(4x+1)(x-2)$

x	+
−8	−7

$(8, -1)$

7. Consider the following in which each letter represents a whole number.

$10x^2 + 13x - 3 = (Ax + M)(Cx - P)$
$= 10x^2 + 15x - 2x - 3$
$= 5x(2x+3) - 1(2x+3)$
$= (2x+3)(5x-1)$
A : 2   M : 3   C : 5   p : 1

$7x^2 + 64x + 9 = (x + S)(Ox + P)$
$= 7x^2 + 63x + x + 9$
$= 7x(x+9) + 1(x+9)$
$= (x+9)(7x+1)$
S = 9   O = 7

$24x^2 - 90x + 54 = B(x - M)(Kx - M)$
$= 6(4x^2 - 15x + 9)$
$= 6(4x^2 - 12x - 3x + 9)$
$= 6[4x(x-3) - 3(x-3)]$
$= 6(x-3)(4x-3)$
B = 6   M = 3   K = 4

$64x^2 - 1 = (Lx - 1)(Lx + 1)$
$= (8x-1)(8x+1)$
L = 8

Determine the value of each letter and hence name the place in Canada represented by the following code.

(4)	(2)	(3)	(8)	(7)	(7)	(1)	(9)	(6)	(5)
K	A	M	L	O	O	P	S	B	C

---

8. a) Determine a polynomial expression for the volume of the wooden block.

volume of block = volume of tank − volume of water
$= 2x(3x+1)(5x+3) - (22x^3 + 18x^2 + 3x)$
$= 2x(15x^2 + 14x + 3) - 22x^3 - 18x^2 - 3x$
$= 30x^3 + 28x^2 + 6x - 22x^3 - 18x^2 - 3x = 8x^3 + 10x^2 + 3x$ m³

b) Factor the expression in a) to determine the dimensions of the wooden block.

$8x^3 + 10x^2 + 3x$
$= x(8x^2 + 10x + 3)$
$= x(8x^2 + 4x + 6x + 3)$
$= x[4x(2x+1) + 3(2x+1)]$
$= x(2x+1)(4x+3)$

Dimensions are $4x+3$ m, $2x+1$ m, and x m.

9. a) $8x^2 + 22xy + 5y^2$
$= 8x^2 + 20xy + 2xy + 5y^2$
$= 4x(2x+5y) + y(2x+5y)$
$= (2x+5y)(4x+y)$

b) $6x^2 + 11xy - 7y^2$
$= 6x^2 - 3xy + 14xy - 7y^2$
$= 3x(2x-y) + 7y(2x-y)$
$= (2x-y)(3x+7y)$

c) $4a^2 - 9ab - 9b^2$
$= 4a^2 + 3ab - 12ab - 9b^2$
$= a(4a+3b) - 3b(4a+3b)$
$= (4a+3b)(a-3b)$

d) $2m^2 - 19mn + 9n^2$
$= 2m^2 - mn - 18mn + 9n^2$
$= m(2m-n) - 9n(2m-n)$
$= (2m-n)(m-9n)$

e) $9x^2 + xy - 10y^2$
$= 9x^2 + 10xy - 9xy - 10y^2$
$= x(9x+10y) - y(9x+10y)$
$= (9x+10y)(x-y)$

f) $8x^2 + 7xy - 15y^2$
$= 8x^2 + 15xy - 8xy - 15y^2$
$= x(8x+15y) - y(8x+15y)$
$= (8x+15y)(x-y)$

10. $12x^2 + 10x - 8$
$= 2(6x^2 + 5x - 4)$
$= 2(6x^2 + 8x - 3x - 4)$
$= 2[2x(3x+4) - 1(3x+4)]$
$= 2(3x+4)(2x-1)$ (A.) $3x+4$

11. $4x^2 + 8x - 5$
$= 4x^2 - 2x + 10x - 5$
$= 2x(2x-1) + 5(2x-1)$
$= (2x-1)(2x+5)$

$12x^2 - 3$
$= 3(4x^2 - 1)$
$= 3(2x-1)(2x+1)$
(D.) $2x-1$

12. $3x^2 + 19x - 14$
$= 3x^2 + 21x - 2x - 14$
$= 3x(x+7) - 2(x+7)$
$= (x+7)(3x-2)$

$a = 7$ $b = 3$ $c = -2$
$b^c : \ 3^{-2} = \frac{1}{3^2} = \frac{1}{9} = 0.11\ldots$

$\boxed{0.\overline{111}}$

13. $15x^2 + 11x - 56$

$\times$	$+$
-840	11

$(35, -24)$

840
$10 \quad 84$
$2 \quad 5 \quad 4 \quad 2$
$\qquad 2 \quad 3 \quad 7$

$a = 5 \quad b = 8 \quad c = 3 \quad d = 7$

$= 15x^2 + 35x - 24x - 56$
$= 5x(3x+7) - 8(3x+7)$
$= (3x+7)(5x-8)$
$= (5x-8)(3x+7)$

14. a) $6\sin^2 x + \sin x - 2$
$= 6\sin^2 x + 4\sin x - 3\sin x - 2$
$= 2\sin x(3\sin x + 2) - 1(3\sin x + 2)$
$= (3\sin x + 2)(2\sin x - 1)$

b) $4\cos^2 x - 7\cos x + 3$
$= 4\cos^2 x - 3\cos x - 4\cos x + 3$
$= \cos x(4\cos x - 3) - 1(4\cos x - 3)$
$= (4\cos x - 3)(\cos x - 1)$

OR Let $A = \sin x$
$6A^2 + A - 2$
$= 6A^2 + 4A - 3A - 2$
$= 2A(3A+2) - 1(3A+2)$
$= (3A+2)(2A-1)$
$= (3\sin x + 2)(2\sin x - 1)$

OR Let $B = \cos x$
$4B^2 - 7B + 3$
$= 4B^2 - 3B - 4B + 3$
$= B(4B-3) - 1(4B-3)$
$= (4B-3)(B-1)$
$= (4\cos x - 3)(\cos x - 1)$

Factoring Polynomial Expressions Lesson #7: Further Factoring

Perfect Square Trinomials

$(p+q)^2 = p^2 + 2pq + q^2$ $\qquad$ $(p-q)^2 = p^2 - 2pq + q^2$

. The first term in the trinomial is the square of the __first__ term in the binomial.

. The last term in the trinomial is the square of the __last__ term in the binomial.

. The middle term in the trinomial is __twice__ the __product__ of the first and last terms in the binomial.

Class Ex. #1
a) $a^2 + 4a + 4$ b) $x^2 - 9x + 6$ c) $4x^2 - 36x + 81$ d) $y^2 + 8y - 16$
yes   no   yes   no
$(a+2)^2$ $(2x-9)^2$

Class Ex. #2
a) $x^2 + 20x + 100$ b) $x^2 - 20x + 100$ c) $25x^2 + 60x + 36$ d) $9m^2 + 24m + 16$
$(x)(10)(2)$ $(x)(-10)(2)$ $(5x)(6)(2)$ $(3m)(2)(2) = 24m$
$\qquad\qquad\qquad\qquad\qquad\qquad\qquad\qquad\qquad\qquad\qquad ? : 4 \quad 4^2 = 16$

Class Ex. #3
a) $49x^2 - 14x + 1$ b) $16 + 40x + 25x^2$ c) $\frac{1}{9}a^2 - 2ab + 9b^2$
$(7x-1)^2$ $(4+5x)^2$ $(\frac{1}{3}a - 3b)^2$

Class Ex. #4
a) $a^4 - 5a^2 - 14$ b) $x^4 + 4x^2 - 5$ c) $x^6 - 9x^3 + 14$
Let $A = a^2$ Let $A = x^2$ Let $A = x^3$
$A^2 - 5A - 14$ $A^2 + 4A - 5$ $A^2 - 9A + 14$
$= (A-7)(A+2)$ $= (A-1)(A+5)$ $= (A-2)(A-7)$
$= (a^2-7)(a^2+2)$ $= (x^2-1)(x^2+5)$ $= (x^3-2)(x^3-7)$
$\qquad\qquad\qquad\qquad = (x-1)(x+1)(x^2+5)$

Factoring Trinomials of the form $af^2 + bf + c$ where f is a monomial

Method 1

$4y^4 - 11y^2 - 3 = 4(y^2)^2 - 11(y^2) - 3$

Let $A = y^2$ $\qquad$ $4A^2 - 11A - 3$

$4A^2 - 12A + A - 3$

$= 4A(A-3) + 1(A-3) = (A-3)(4A+1) = (y^2-3)(4y^2+1)$

Method 2

$4y^4 - 11y^2 - 3 = 4y^4 - 12y^2 + 1y^2 - 3$

$= 4y^2(y^2-3) + 1(y^2-3)$

$= (y^2-3)(4y^2+1)$

Class Ex. #5
a) $4x^4 - 5x^2 - 6$ b) $y^{10} + 4y^5 - 12$
$= 4x^4 - 8x^2 + 3x^2 - 6$ $= y^{10} - 2y^5 + 6y^5 - 12$
$= 4x^2(x^2-2) + 3(x^2-2)$ $= y^5(y^5-2) + 6(y^5-2)$
$= (x^2-2)(4x^2+3)$ $= (y^5-2)(y^5+6)$

c) $2a^2b^2 - 31ab + 99$
$= 2a^2b^2 - 22ab - 9ab + 99$
$= 2ab(ab-11) - 9(ab-11)$
$= (ab-11)(2ab-9)$

Class Ex. #6   Factor completely. $8x^4 + 10x^2 - 3$.
$= 8x^4 + 12x^2 - 2x^2 - 3$
$= 4x^2(2x^2+3) - 1(2x^2+3)$
$= (2x^2+3)(4x^2-1)$
$= (2x^2+3)(2x-1)(2x+1)$

Class Ex. #7
a) $k^4 - 1$ b) $80 - 5x^4$ c) $2p^5q^4 - 162pt^4$
Let $A = k^2$ $= 5(16 - x^4)$ $= 2p(p^4q^4 - 81t^4)$
$= A^2 - 1$ $= 5(4-x^2)(4+x^2)$ $= 2p(p^2q^2 - 9t^2)(p^2q^2 + 9t^2)$
$= (A-1)(A+1)$ $= 5(2-x)(2+x)(4+x^2)$ $= 2p(pq-3t)(pq+3t)(p^2q^2+9t^2)$
$= (k^2-1)(k^2+1)$
$= (k-1)(k+1)(k^2+1)$

Assignment

1. a), c), d), f), g) are all perfect square trinomials.

2. a) 14x   b) 24x   c) 36x   d) 36   e) a   f) 120x   g) 20xy   h) 25

3. a) $(4x-1)^2$ b) $(6+5x)^2$ c) $(2a-3b)^2$

   d) $(2x-11)^2$ e) $5(x^2+2x+1)$ f) $\left(\frac{2}{3}x+\frac{1}{c}\right)^2$
   $\quad\quad\quad\quad\quad\quad = 5(x+1)^2$

4. a) x^4+9x^2+20 b) x^4-9x^2+20 c) a^4-17a^2+16
   $= (x^2+4)(x^2+5)$ $= (x^2-4)(x^2-5)$ $= (a^2-1)(a^2-16)$
   $\quad\quad\quad\quad\quad\quad = (x-2)(x+2)(x^2-5)$ $= (a-1)(a+1)(a-4)(a+4)$

   d) t^6-4t^3-21 e) $3x^4+9x^2-30$ f) $2x^5-16x^3+32x$
   $= (t^3-7)(t^3+3)$ $= 3(x^4+3x^2-10)$ $= 2x(x^4-8x^2+16)$
   $\quad\quad\quad\quad\quad\quad = 3(x^2-2)(x^2+5)$ $= 2x(x^2-4)^2$
   $\quad\quad\quad\quad\quad\quad\quad\quad\quad\quad\quad = 2x(x-2)^2(x+2)^2$

5. a) $6x^4+11x^2+5$ b) $2a^4-5a^2+2$ c) $5p^6-8p^3-4$
   $= 6x^4+6x^2+5x^2+5$ $= 2a^4-4a^2-a^2+2$ $= 5p^6-10p^3+2p^3-4$
   $= 6x^2(x^2+1)+5(x^2+1)$ $= 2a^2(a^2-2)-1(a^2-2)$ $= 5p^3(p^3-2)+2(p^3-2)$
   $= (x^2+1)(6x^2+5)$ $= (a^2-2)(2a^2-1)$ $= (p^3-2)(5p^3+2)$

   d) $16x^4+8x^2-3$ e) $4-9t^2-9t^4$ f) $4x^5-50x^3+126x$
   $= 16x^4-4x^2+12x^2-3$ $= 4+3t^2-12t^2-9t^4$ $= 2x(2x^4-25x^2+63)$
   $= 4x^2(4x^2-1)+3(4x^2-1)$ $= 1(4+3t^2)-3t^2(4+3t^2)$ $= 2x(2x^4-18x^2-7x^2+63)$
   $= (4x^2-1)(4x^2+3)$ $= (4+3t^2)(1-3t^2)$ $= 2x[2x^2(x^2-9)-7(x^2-9)]$
   $= (2x-1)(2x+1)(4x^2+3)$ $\quad\quad\quad\quad = 2x(x^2-9)(2x^2-7)$
   $\quad\quad\quad\quad\quad\quad\quad\quad\quad\quad = 2x(x-3)(x+3)(2x^2-7)$

   g) $4x^2y^2-xy-14$ h) $4\pi^2r^2-9\pi r-9$
   $= 4x^2y^2+7xy-8xy-14$ $= 4\pi^2r^2+3\pi r-12\pi r-9$
   $= xy(4xy+7)-2(4xy+7)$ $= \pi r(4\pi r+3)-3(4\pi r+3)$
   $= (4xy+7)(xy-2)$ $= (4\pi r+3)(\pi r-3)$

6. a) x^4-y^4 b) a^4-256b^4 c) $2z^4-162$
   $= (x^2-y^2)(x^2+y^2)$ $= (a^2-16b^2)(a^2+16b^2)$ $= 2(z^4-81)$
   $= (x-y)(x+y)(x^2+y^2)$ $= (a-4b)(a+4b)(a^2+16b^2)$ $= 2(z^2-9)(z^2+9)$
   $\quad\quad\quad\quad\quad\quad\quad\quad\quad\quad = 2(z-3)(z+3)(z^2+9)$

   d) $48x^4-3y^4$ e) $9a^4b^4-144c^4d^4$ f) z^8-1
   $= 3(16x^4-y^4)$ $= 9(a^4b^4-16c^4d^4)$ $= (z^4-1)(z^4+1)$
   $= 3(4x^2-y^2)(4x^2+y^2)$ $= 9(a^2b^2-4c^2d^2)(a^2b^2+4c^2d^2)$ $= (z^2-1)(z^2+1)(z^4+1)$
   $= 3(2x-y)(2x+y)(4x^2+y^2)$ $= 9(ab-2cd)(ab+2cd)(a^2b^2+4c^2d^2)$ $= (z-1)(z+1)(z^2+1)(z^4+1)$

7. $16a^8-65a^4+4.$
   $= 16a^8-64a^4-a^4+4$
   $= 16a^4(a^4-4)-1(a^4-4)$
   $= (a^4-4)(16a^4-1)$
   $= (a^2-2)(a^2+2)(4a^2-1)(4a^2+1)$
   $= (a^2-2)(a^2+2)(2a-1)(2a+1)(4a^2+1) = (2a-1)(2a+1)(a^2-2)(a^2+2)(4a^2+1)$

8. A. $x^2-14x+49$ $(x-7)^2$
   B. $144+24x+x^2$ $(12+x)^2$
   C. $4x^2-12x+36$ x
   D. $9x^4+30x^2+25$ $(3x^2+5)^2$

9. $k^4+16-17k^2$
   k^4-17k^2+16
   $= (k^2-1)(k^2-16)$
   $= (k-1)(k+1)(k-4)(k+4)$
   (D) $(k+1)(k-1)(k+4)(k-4)$

10. $(y^2-9)(y^2+9)$
    $= (y-3)(y+3)(y^2+9)$
    (B) $y+3$

11. x^4-16x^2+15
    $= (x^2-1)(x^2-15)$
    $= (x-1)(x+1)(x^2-15)$
    (A) $x+1$

12. $\left(\frac{1}{4}x+\frac{2}{3}\right)^2$ $A=\frac{1}{4}$ $AB=\frac{1}{4}\cdot\frac{2}{3}$
    $A=\frac{1}{4}$
    $B=\frac{2}{3}$ $=\frac{1}{6}=0.166...$

    0.117

13.
    $A=\frac{1}{2}bh$ $=\frac{3}{2}x^2+10x+16$
    $bh = 3x^2+20x+32$
    $bh = 3x^2+12x+8x+32$
    $bh = 3x(x+4)+8(x+4)$
    $= (x+4)(3x+8)$

    $PR = x+4 = 8$
    $PQ = 3x+8 = 20$
    $QR^2 = 8^2+20^2 = 464$
    $QR = \sqrt{464} = 21.5$

    $x+4 +12 = 3x+8$
    $8 = 2x$
    $x = 4$

21.5

Factoring Polynomial Expressions Lesson #8:
Factoring Review

Class Ex. #1

a) $9x^2 - 36$
$= 9(x^2 - 4)$
$= 9(x-2)(x+2)$

b) $x^2 - 16x - 36$
$= (x+2)(x-18)$

c) $-8x^2 + 26x + 15$
$= -8x^2 - 4x + 30x + 15$
$= -4x(2x+1) + 15(2x+1)$
$= (2x+1)(-4x+15)$
or $(1+2x)(15-4x)$

d) $24x^2 - 30x + 36x - 45$
$= 6x(4x-5) + 9(4x-5)$
$= (4x-5)(6x+9)$
$= (4x-5)(3)(2x+3)$
$= 3(4x-5)(2x+3)$

e) $3 - 3x^2 - 36x^4$
$= 3(1 - x^2 - 12x^4)$
$= 3(1 - 4x^2 + 3x^2 - 12x^4)$
$= 3[1(1-4x^2) + 3x^2(1-4x^2)]$
$= 3(1-4x^2)(1+3x^2)$
$= 3(1-2x)(1+2x)(1+3x^2)$

Assignment

Factoring Polynomial ... Lesson #8: Assignment Pages **374 to 376** Factoring Polynomial ... Lesson #8

1. a) $x^2 - 49$
$(x-7)(x+7)$

b) $x^2 - 8x + 15$
$(x-3)(x-5)$

c) $8x^2 + 32$
$8(x^2 + 4)$

d) $a^3 + a^2 + a + 1$
$= a^2(a+1) + 1(a+1)$
$= (a+1)(a^2+1)$

e) $2p^2 - 5p - 7$
$= 2p^2 + 2p - 7p - 7$
$= 2p(p+1) - 7(p+1)$
$= (p+1)(2p-7)$

f) $v^2 + 7v + 10$
$= (v+5)(v+2)$

g) $a^3 - a^2 - a + 1$
$= a^2(a-1) - 1(a-1)$
$= (a-1)(a^2-1)$
$= (a-1)(a+1)(a-1)$
$= (a+1)(a-1)^2$

h) $4 - 25t^2$
$= (2-5t)(2+5t)$

i) $x^4 - 16$
$= (x^2-4)(x^2+4)$
$= (x-2)(x+2)(x^2+4)$

2. a) $7x^2 - 19x - 6$
$= 7x^2 + 2x - 21x - 6$
$= x(7x+2) - 3(7x+2)$
$= (7x+2)(x-3)$

b) $3 + x - 2x^2$
$= 3 - 2x + 3x - 2x^2$
$= 1(3-2x) + x(3-2x)$
$= (3-2x)(1+x)$

c) $a^2 - 64b^2$
$= (a-8b)(a+8b)$

d) $108 - 3z^2$
$= 3(36 - z^2)$
$= 3(6-z)(6+z)$

e) $x^4 + 5x^2 + 4$
$= (x^2+4)(x^2+1)$

f) $8v^2 - 32v - 96$
$= 8(v^2 - 4v - 12)$
$= 8(v+2)(v-6)$

g) $625p^4 - 1$
$= (25p^2-1)(25p^2+1)$
$= (5p-1)(5p+1)(25p^2+1)$

h) $2y^4 - y^2 - 3$
$= 2y^4 + 2y^2 - 3y^2 - 3$
$= 2y^2(y^2+1) - 3(y^2+1)$
$= (y^2+1)(2y^2-3)$

i) $36 - 3x - 3x^2$
$= 3(12 - x - x^2)$
$= 3(12 - 4x + 3x - x^2)$
$= 3[4(3-x) + x(3-x)]$
$= 3(3-x)(4+x)$

---

3. Factor.

a) $b^2 - 16 - 6b + 24$
$= b^2 - 6b + 8$
$= (b-2)(b-4)$

b) $t^6 - t^3 - 6$
$= (t^3-3)(t^3+2)$

c) $36a^2 + 60a + 25$
$= (6a+5)^2$

d) $5 + 17g + 6g^2$
$= 5 + 2g + 15g + 6g^2$
$= 1(5+2g) + 3g(5+2g)$
$= (5+2g)(1+3g)$

e) $x^5 - 81x$
$= x(x^4 - 81)$
$= x(x^2-9)(x^2+9)$
$= x(x-3)(x+3)(x^2+9)$

f) $-256 + t^4$
$= t^4 - 256$
$= (t^2-16)(t^2+16)$
$= (t-4)(t+4)(t^2+16)$

g) $x^2 + y - x - xy$
$= x^2 - x - xy + y$
$= x(x-1) - y(x-1)$
$= (x-1)(x-y)$

h) $2x^4 - 15x^2 - 27$
$= 2x^4 - 18x^2 + 3x^2 - 27$
$= 2x^2(x^2-9) + 3(x^2-9)$
$= (x^2-9)(2x^2+3)$
$= (x-3)(x+3)(2x^2+3)$

i) $12a^2 + 32a - 12$
$= 4(3a^2 + 8a - 3)$
$= 4(3a^2 - a + 9a - 3)$
$= 4[a(3a-1) + 3(3a-1)]$
$= 4(3a-1)(a+3)$

4. a) $x^2 - 8xy - 33y^2$
$= (x-11y)(x+3y)$

b) $6a^2 + 19ab + 10b^2$
$= 6a^2 + 15ab + 4ab + 10b^2$
$= 3a(2a+5b) + 2b(2a+5b)$
$= (2a+5b)(3a+2b)$

c) $15t^6 + t^3p^2 - 2p^4$
$= 15t^6 + 6t^3p^2 - 5t^3p^2 - 2p^4$
$= 3t^3(5t^3+2p^2) - p^2(5t^3+2p^2)$
$= (5t^3+2p^2)(3t^3-p^2)$

5. $5(x^2 - 2x - 3) = 5(x+1)(x-3)$
C. if only 3 and 4 are correct

6. x + 4 is a factor of
(1) $3x^2 + 7x - 20$ ✓
$3x^2 + 12x - 5x - 20$
$= 3x(x+4) - 5(x+4)$
$= (x+4)(3x-5)$

(2) $48 - 3x^2$
$= 3(16 - x^2)$
$= 3(4-x)(4+x)$

(3) $3x^2 + 12x$ ✓
$= 3x(x+4)$

(4) $x^2 + 16$
no factors

B. if only 1, 2, and 3 are correct

7. $(3a+4)^2 = 9a^2 + 24a + 16$ $k = 24$

$\boxed{2\ 4}$

Factoring Polynomial Expressions Lesson #9
Enrichment Lesson - Solving Polynomial Equations

378

Class Ex. #1

$x^2 - 9x + 20 = 0$

$(x-4)(x-5) = 0$

$x - 4 = 0$ or $x - 5 = 0$

$x = \underline{4}$ or $x = \underline{5}$

The solutions are $x = \underline{4}$ and $x = \underline{5}$

Class Ex. #2

a) $x^2 - 81 = 0$
$(x-9)(x+9) = 0$
$x = 9$ or $x = -9$
$x = \pm 9$

b) $4x^2 - 9 = 0$
$(2x-3)(2x+3) = 0$
$x = \frac{3}{2}$ or $x = -\frac{3}{2}$
$x = \pm \frac{3}{2}$

c) $10x^2 - 90 = 0$
$10(x^2 - 9) = 0$
$10(x-3)(x+3) = 0$
$x = 0$ or $x = 9$
$x = 0, 9$

d) $10x^2 - 90x = 0$
$10x(x-9) = 0$
$10x(x-9) = 0$
$x = 0$ or $x = 9$
$x = \pm 3$

Class Ex. #3

a) $3x^2 - 13x - 10 = 0$
$3x^2 - 15x + 2x - 10 = 0$
$3x(x-5) + 2(x-5) = 0$
$(x-5)(3x+2) = 0$
$x = 5$ or $x = -\frac{2}{3}$
$x = -\frac{2}{3}, 5$

b) $5x^2 + 30x = -25$
$5x^2 + 30x + 25 = 0$
$5(x^2 + 6x + 5) = 0$
$5(x+5)(x+1) = 0$
$x = -5$ or $x = -1$
$x = -5, -1$

Class Ex. #4

Let length = x cm and width = $x - 5$ cm.   Area = $x(x-5)$ cm^2

$x(x-5) = 300$
$x^2 - 5x - 300 = 0$
$(x-20)(x+15) = 0$
$x = 20$ or $x = -15$
reject $x = -15$ since length cannot be negative.
$x = 20$
length = 20cm   width = 15cm
perimeter = $2(20) + 2(15)$
= 70cm

Factoring Polynomial Expressions Lesson #9: *Enrichment Lesson - Solving Polynomial Equations*   **379**

Class Ex. #5

a) Show that the area of the cross-section is $x(36-x)$ cm^2.

The two triangles are isosceles.

area of trapezoid = $\frac{1}{2}h(a+b) = \frac{1}{2}x(36-2x+36)$ $= \frac{1}{2}x(72-2x)$
$= x(36-x)$ cm^2

Factoring Polynomial Expressions Lesson #9: *Enrichment Lesson - Solving Polynomial Equations*   **379**   *(continued)*

Class Ex. #5

b) If the area of the cross-section is 260 cm^2, determine the value of x.

$x(36-x) = 260$ Since $AB = 36-2x$, x cannot $= 26$
$36x - x^2 = 260$ ($AB \neq -16$)
$0 = x^2 - 36x + 260$
$0 = (x-10)(x-26)$
$x = 10$ or $x = 26$

$\underline{x = 10 \text{ cm}}$

(Continued)

Assignment

Factoring Polynomial ... Lesson #9: Assignment Pages **379 to 382** Factoring Polynomial ... Lesson #9

1. a) $(x-2)(x+7) = 0$ b) $(3x-2)(2x+5) = 0$ c) $5x(10-x) = 0$ d) $x^2 + 2x = 0$ e) $x^2 - 121 = 0$

$x = 2, -7$ $x = \frac{2}{3}, -\frac{5}{2}$ $x = 0, 10$ $x(x+2) = 0$ $(x-11)(x+11) = 0$
$x = 0, -2$ $x = \pm 11$

f) $9x^2 - 100 = 0$ g) $36x^2 = 25$ h) $9x - 4x^2 = 0$ i) $4(49 - x^2) = 0$

$(3x-10)(3x+10) = 0$ $36x^2 - 25 = 0$ $x(9-4x) = 0$ $4(7-x)(7+x) = 0$
$x = \pm \frac{10}{3}$ $(6x-5)(6x+5) = 0$ $x = 0, \frac{9}{4}$ $x = \pm 7$
$x = \pm \frac{5}{6}$

2. a) $x^2 - 3x + 2 = 0$ b) $x^2 + 13x + 30 = 0$ c) $x^2 + 2x - 15 = 0$

$(x-1)(x-2) = 0$ $(x+10)(x+3) = 0$ $(x+5)(x-3) = 0$
$x = 1, 2$ $x = -10, -3$ $x = -5, 3$

d) $3x^2 - 10x + 3 = 0$ e) $2x^2 + 3x - 35 = 0$ f) $15 - 2x - x^2 = 0$

$3x^2 - x - 9x + 3 = 0$ $2x^2 + 10x - 7x - 35 = 0$ $15 - 5x + 3x - x^2 = 0$
$x(3x-1) - 3(3x-1) = 0$ $2x(x+5) - 7(x+5) = 0$ $5(3-x) + x(3-x) = 0$
$(3x-1)(x-3) = 0$ $(x+5)(2x-7) = 0$ $(3-x)(5+x) = 0$
$x = \frac{1}{3}, 3$ $x = -5, \frac{7}{2}$ $x = 3, -5$

3. a) $2x^2 + 5x = 7$ b) $6x^2 = 7x + 3$ c) $x(x+4) = 32$

$2x^2 + 5x - 7 = 0$ $6x^2 - 7x - 3 = 0$ $x^2 + 4x - 32 = 0$
$2x^2 + 7x - 2x - 7 = 0$ $6x^2 + 2x - 9x - 3 = 0$ $(x+8)(x-4) = 0$
$x(2x+7) - 1(2x+7) = 0$ $2x(3x+1) - 3(3x+1) = 0$ $x = -8, 4$
$(2x+7)(x-1) = 0$ $(3x+1)(2x-3) = 0$
$x = -\frac{7}{2}, 1$ $x = -\frac{1}{3}, \frac{3}{2}$

d) $(x-3)(2x+3) = 5$ e) $(2x-3)^2 = 1$ f) $(x+1)(x-1) = 5(x+1)$

$2x^2 + 3x - 6x - 9 = 5$ $4x^2 - 12x + 9 = 1$ $x^2 - 1 = 5x + 5$
$2x^2 - 3x - 14 = 0$ $4x^2 - 12x + 8 = 0$ $x^2 - 5x - 6 = 0$
$2x^2 + 4x - 7x - 14 = 0$ $4(x^2 - 3x + 2) = 0$ $(x+1)(x-6) = 0$
$2x(x+2) - 7(x+2) = 0$ $4(x-1)(x-2) = 0$ $x = -1, 6$
$(x+2)(2x-7) = 0$ $x = 1, 2$
$x = -2, \frac{7}{2}$

1. $9x^4 - 6x^3 + 3x^2$
$3x^2(3x^2 - 2x + 1)$
(D.) $3x^2 - 2x + 1$

2. $x^3y^2 - x^2y^3$
$x^2y^2(x - y)$
(C.) $x^2y^2(x - y)$

3. $3ab^2 - 6a^3b + 3ab$
$3ab(b - 2a^2 + 1)$
(D.) none of these

4.
(C.) $(x + 2)(x + 4)$

5. $a^2 - 10a - 24$
$(a + 2)(a - 12)$
D. $a - 12$

6. $12 - x - x^2$
$= 12 - 4x + 3x - x^2$
$= 4(3 - x) + x(3 - x)$
$= (3 - x)(4 + x)$
(A.) $(3 - x)(4 + x)$

7.
A	a	16	B
a	a^2	$16a$	
9	$9a$	144	
C			D

find two numbers which have $\rightarrow 9, 16$
a sum of 25 and a product of 144
perimeter $= 2(a + 16) + 2(a + 9)$
$= 2a + 32 + 2a + 18 = 4a + 50$
(C.) $4a + 50$

8. A. $b^2 + 3b$
B. $b^3 - 9b$
C. $b^2 + 2b - 15$
D. $b^2 - 6b - 27$
$b(b + 3)$
$b(b^2 - 9) = b(b - 3)(b + 3)$
$(b - 3)(b + 5)$
$(b + 3)(b - 9)$

9. $x^2 - 9x + 20 = (x - 4)(x - 5)$
A. -9 ✓
B. -12 ✓ $x^2 - 12x + 20 = (x - 2)(x - 10)$
C. 21 ✓ $x^2 + 21x + 20 = (x + 1)(x + 20)$
D. 20 ✗ $x^2 + 20x + 20$

10. $7a^2 - 28a^4$
$7a^2(1 - 4a^2)$
$= 7a^2(1 - 2a)(1 + 2a)$
(A.) $1 - 2a$

11. $6y^2 - y - 1$
find two numbers
$\dfrac{\times \quad +}{-6 \quad 1}$
$-3, 2$
$6y^2 - 3y + 2y - 1$
$= 3y(2y - 1) + 1(2y - 1)$
$= (2y - 1)(3y + 1)$
(D.) $2y - 1$

12. $2t^2 - 7t - 15$
Response 1: $2t - 3$ ✗
Response 2: $t - 5$ ✓
Response 3: $t + 5$ ✗
Response 4: $2t + 3$ ✓
$2t^2 - 10t + 3t - 15$
$= 2t(t - 5) + 3(t - 5)$
$= (t - 5)(2t + 3)$
C

13. no factors
$\dfrac{\times \quad +}{-30 \quad -7} \rightarrow -10, 3$
D

14. Response 1 $a = 1$ and $c = 36$ ✓ $x^2 - 12x + 36 = (x - 6)^2$
Response 2 $a = 36$ and $c = 1$ ✓ $36x^2 - 12x + 1 = (6x - 1)^2$
Response 3 $a = 1$ and $c = -36$ ✗ $x^2 - 12x - 36$
Response 4 $a = 36$ and $c = -1$ ✗ $36x^2 - 12x - 1$
A
In both responses 3 and 4, we require to find two numbers whose product is -36 and whose sum is -12. This cannot be done.

15. $16a^4 - 1$
$(4a^2 - 1)(4a^2 + 1)$
$= (2a - 1)(2a + 1)(4a^2 + 1)$
D. $(2a - 1)(2a + 1)(4a^2 + 1)$

---

4. a) $6a^2 - 7 - 19a = 0$
$6a^2 - 19a - 7 = 0$
$6a^2 + 2a - 21a - 7 = 0$
$2a(3a + 1) - 7(3a + 1) = 0$
$(3a + 1)(2a - 7) = 0$
$a = -\dfrac{1}{3}, \dfrac{7}{2}$

b) $21 - 8k - 2k^2 = 2k^2$
$0 = 4k^2 + 8k - 21$
$0 = 4k^2 + 14k - 6k - 21$
$0 = 2k(2k + 7) - 3(2k + 7)$
$0 = (2k + 7)(2k - 3)$
$k = -\dfrac{7}{2}, \dfrac{3}{2}$

5. a) Find the area of the piece of wood in terms of x.
area $= 10x + x(7 + x)$
$= 10x + 7x + x^2$
$= |7x + x^2|$ cm^2

b) Find the value of x if the area is 60 cm^2.
$|7x + x^2 = 60$
$x^2 + 17x - 60 = 0$
$(x + 20)(x - 3) = 0$
$x = -20, 3$ reject $x = -20$ since $x > 0$
$x = 3$

6. a) Sum $= 25(25 - 1)$
$= 600$
b) $n(n - 1) = 870$
$n^2 - n - 870 = 0$
$(n - 30)(n + 29) = 0$
$n = 30, -29$ reject $n = -29$ since $n > 0$
$n = 30$ 30 consecutive even numbers

7. a) Write a polynomial equation to model this information.
Let base $= x$ mm
height $= x + 8$ mm
area $= \dfrac{1}{2}bh = \dfrac{1}{2}x(x + 8)$ mm
$\dfrac{1}{2}x(x + 8) = 172.5$
$x(x + 8) = 345$
$x^2 + 8x - 345 = 0$

b) Determine the height of the triangle.
$x^2 + 8x - 345 = 0$
$(x - 15)(x + 23) = 0$
$x = 15, -23$
reject $x = -23$ since $x > 0$
$x = 15$ base $= 15$ mm
height $= 15 + 8 = 23$ mm

8. $x(x - 1) = 2$ is
$x^2 - x - 2 = 0$
$(x + 1)(x - 2) = 0$
$x = -1, 2$
(C.) $x = -1$ and $x = 2$

9. $24x^2 + 2x - 15 = 0$
$24x^2 + 20x - 18x - 15 = 0$
$4x(6x + 5) - 3(6x + 5) = 0$
$(6x + 5)(4x - 3) = 0$
$x = -\dfrac{5}{6}, \dfrac{3}{4}$

10. $\dfrac{1}{2}k(k + 1) = 496$
$k(k + 1) = 992$
$k^2 + k - 992 = 0$
$(k - 31)(k + 32) = 0$
$k = 31, -32$
reject $k = -32$ since $k > 0$
$k = 31$

$a = \dfrac{3}{4}$ $b = \dfrac{5}{6}$
$= 0.833...$
$\boxed{0.83}$

$\boxed{31}$

Relations and Functions Lesson #1:
Review & Preview

Class Ex. #1

a) Complete the following by writing the coordinates of the points represented by the letters on the grid.

$A(2, 4)$ $B(-3, 0)$ $C(6, -3)$
$D(0, -3)$ $O(0, 0)$

b) Write the coordinates of the point in the second quadrant.
$E(-2, 3)$

c) Write the coordinates of the point in quadrant III.
$F(-4, -3)$

d) Complete the following table using "positive" or "negative".

Quadrant	x-coordinate	y-coordinate
I	positive	positive
II	negative	positive
III	negative	negative
IV	positive	negative

---

390   Relations and Functions Lesson #1:   *Review and Preview*

Class Ex. #2

a) Draw the next two diagrams in the pattern.

b) Complete the table relating the number of toothpicks P, to the number of triangles, T.

Number of Triangles, T	1	2	3	4	5
Number of Toothpicks, P	3	5	7	9	11

c) Represent the data from the table of values on the grid.

d) Explain why it does not make sense to join the points in a straight line.
The data is discrete not continuous. Intermediate values have no meaning.

e) Describe in words the relationship between the number of toothpicks and the number of triangles.
The number of toothpicks is double the number of triangles and then add one.

f) Write an equation that can be used to determine the number of toothpicks if we know the number of triangles.
$P = 2T + 1$

g) Use the equation to determine the number of toothpicks if there are 27 triangles.
$P = 2(27) + 1 = 55$
55 toothpicks

h) Use the equation to determine the number of triangles if there are 83 toothpicks.
$83 = 2T + 1$
$82 = 2T$
$T = 41$
41 triangles

Factoring ... Lesson #10: PRACTICE TEST pages **383 to 388**   Factoring ... Lesson #10

Numerical Response

1. $25x(3 - 2x)$

$a = 25$ $b = 3$ $c = -2$
$a - b - c = 25 - 3 - (-2)$
$= 24$ ☐☐[2][4]

2. We need the two integer factors of 48 with the largest sum.

| 1 and 48 | Sum = 49 |

$x^2 - 49x + 48$ $w = 49$
$= (x - 1)(x - 48)$ ☐☐[4][9]

3. $2x(x - 5) - 3(x - 5)$
$= 2x^2 - 10x - 3x + 15$
$c = 15$ ☐☐[1][5]

4. $4a^2 + 44a + c$ $= (2a + \sqrt{c})^2$
$2(2a)(\sqrt{c}) = 44a$ $\sqrt{c} = \frac{44a}{4a} = 11$ $c = 121$
$4a\sqrt{c} = 44a$
$4a^2 + 44a + 121 = (2a + 11)^2$ ☐[1][2][1]

5. $2x^2 - 3x - 14 = (2x - 7)(x + A)$ $-7A = -14$ $A = 2$

$x^4 - 7x^2 - 18 = (x^2 + 2)(x - B)(x + B)$ $x^4 - 7x^2 - 18 = (x^2 + 2)(x^2 - 9)$
$= (x^2 + 2)(x - 3)(x + 3)$ $B = 3$

$5x^2 - 40x + 80 = C(x - D)^2$
$5x^2 - 40x + 80$
$= 5(x^2 - 8x + 16)$ $C = 5$ $D = 4$
$= 5(x - 4)^2$ ☐[2][3][5][4]

Written Response - 5 marks

Bullet 1 $x^2 + 10x + 16$ or any answer in bullet 3.

Bullet 2   Many answers are possible. e.g. $x^2 + 3x + 16$ is not able to be factored because it is not possible to find two integers which multiply to 16 and add to 3.

Bullet 3   6 polynomials are possible

$x^2 + 10x + 16$	$x^2 + 8x + 16$	$x^2 + 17x + 16$
$x^2 - 10x + 16$	$x^2 - 8x + 16$	$x^2 - 17x + 16$

Bullet 4   For example $x^2 + 10x + 9$ $x^2 + 7x + 12$

Bullet 5   If a, b, and c are all odd, then ac must be odd. To factor $ax^2 + bx + c$ using decomposition we need to find two integers which multiply to ac (which we know is odd) and add to b (which we also know is odd). It is not possible to find two numbers which multiply to an odd number and add to an odd number so a, b, and c cannot all be odd.

Class Ex. #3

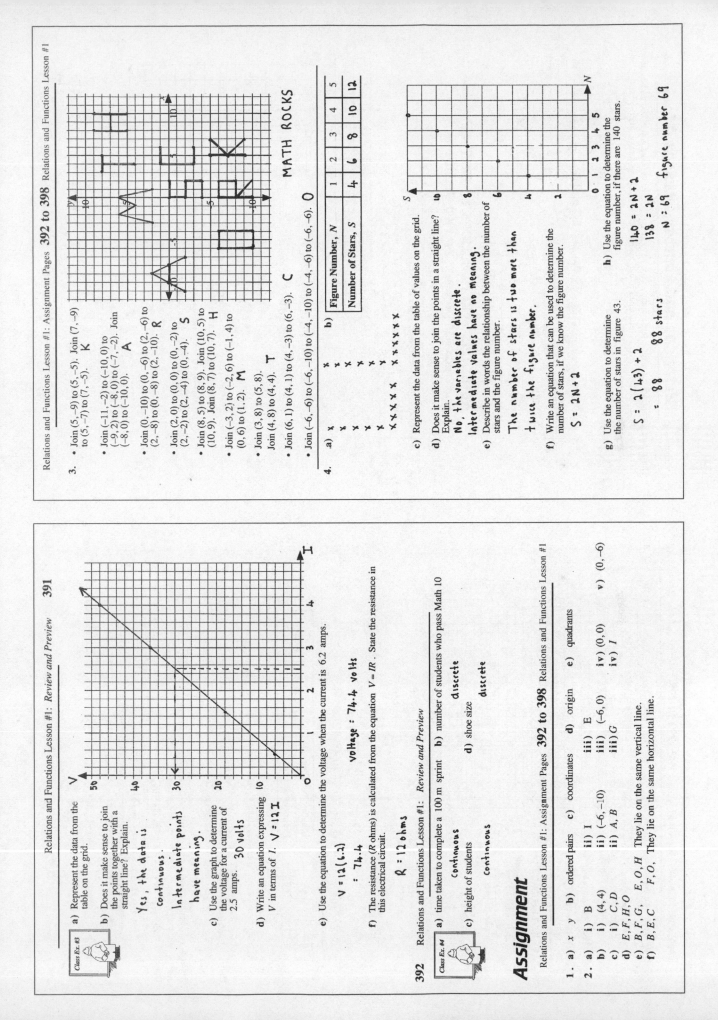

a) Represent the data from the table on the grid.

b) Does it make sense to join the points together with a straight line? Explain.

Yes, the data is continuous.

Intermediate points have meaning.

c) Use the graph to determine the voltage for a current of 2.5 amps.

30 volts

d) Write an equation expressing V in terms of I. $V = 12 I$

e) Use the equation to determine the voltage when the current is 6.2 amps.

$V = 12 (6.2)$

$= 74.4$

voltage = 74.4 volts

f) The resistance (R ohms) is calculated from the equation $V = IR$. State the resistance in this electrical circuit.

$R = 12$ ohms

---

392 Relations and Functions Lesson #1: *Review and Preview*

Assignment

1. a) x y b) ordered pairs   c) coordinates   d) origin   e) quadrants

2. a) time taken to complete a 100 m sprint   b) number of students who pass Math 10

   continuous   discrete

   c) height of students   d) shoe size

   continuous   discrete

Class Ex. #4

a) i) B   ii) I   iii) E
b) i) (4, 4)   ii) (–6, –10) iii) (–6, 0)   iv) (0, 0)   v) (0, –6)
c) i) C, D   ii) A, B   iii) G   iv) I
d) E, F, H, O
e) B, F, G, E, O, H   They lie on the same vertical line.
f) B, E, C   F, O,   They lie on the same horizontal line.

---

3. • Join (5, –9) to (5, –5). Join (7, –9) to (5, –7) to (7, –5).   **K**

   • Join (–11, –2) to (–10, 0) to (–9, 2) to (–8, 0) to (–7, –2). Join (–8, 0) to (–10, 0).   **A**

   • Join (0, –10) to (0, –6) to (2, –6) to (2, –8) to (0, –8) to (2, –10).   **R**

   • Join (2, 0) to (0, 0) to (0, –2) to (2, –2) to (2, –4) to (0, –4).   **S**

   • Join (8, 5) to (8, 9). Join (10, 5) to (10, 9). Join (8, 7) to (10, 7).   **H**

   • Join (–3, 2) to (–2, 6) to (–1, 4) to (0, 6) to (1, 2).   **M**

   • Join (3, 8) to (5, 8). Join (4, 8) to (4, 4).   **T**

   • Join (6, 1) to (4, 1) to (4, –3) to (6, –3).   **C**

   • Join (–6, –6) to (–6, –10) to (–4, –10) to (–4, –6) to (–6, –6).   **O**

   MATH ROCKS

4. a)

   x   x   x x x x x
   x   x   x
   x   x   x
   x   x   x
   x x x x   x x x x x x

   b)

Figure Number, N	1	2	3	4	5
Number of Stars, S	4	6	8	10	12

   c) Represent the data from the table of values on the grid.

   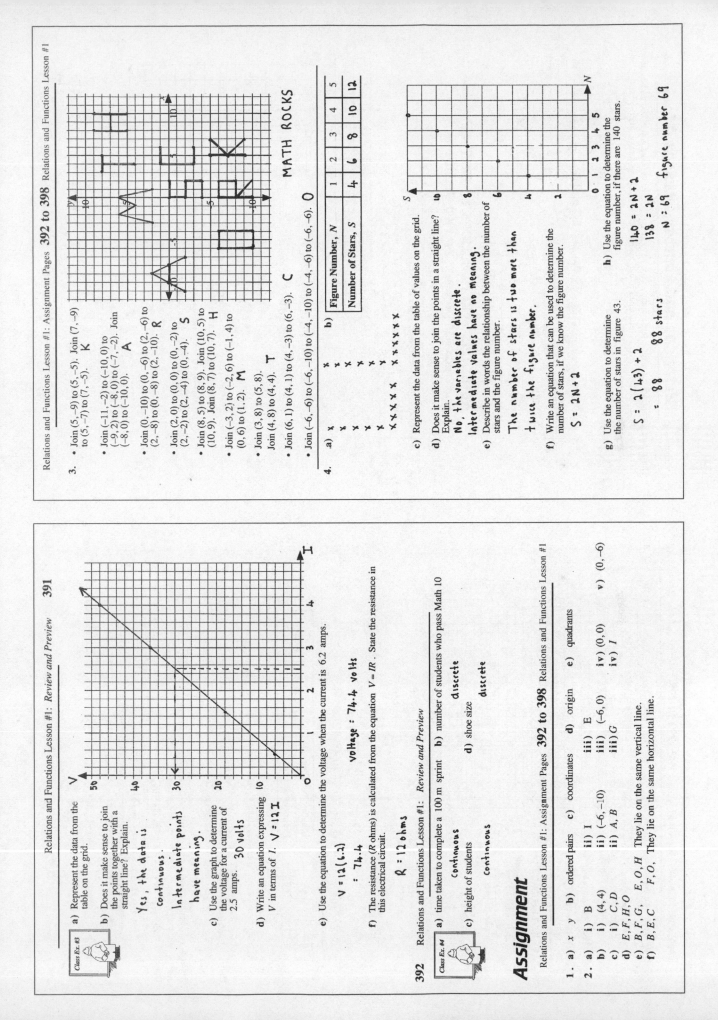

   d) Does it make sense to join the points in a straight line? Explain.

   No, the variables are discrete.

   Intermediate values have no meaning.

   e) Describe in words the relationship between the number of stars and the figure number.

   The number of stars is two more than twice the figure number.

   f) Write an equation that can be used to determine the number of stars, if we know the figure number.

   $S = 2N + 2$

   g) Use the equation to determine the number of stars in figure 43.

   $S = 2(43) + 2$

   $= 88$ 88 stars

   h) Use the equation to determine the figure number, if there are 140 stars.

   $140 = 2N + 2$

   $138 = 2N$

   $N = 69$ figure number 69

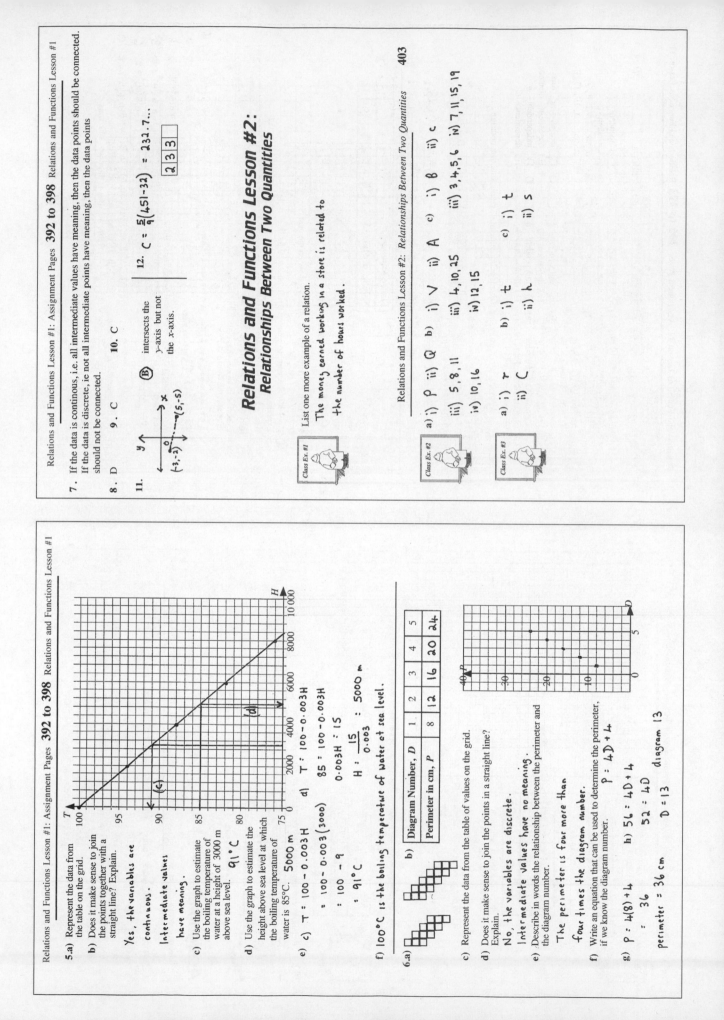

7. If the data is continous, i.e. all intermediate values have meaning, then the data points should be connected. If the data is discrete, ie not all intermediate points have meaning, then the data points should not be connected.

8. D   9. C   10. C

11. (B) intersects the y-axis but not the x-axis.

(-3,-2)   (5,-5)

12. $C = \frac{5}{9}(451-32) = 232.7... = 233$

Relations and Functions Lesson #2:
Relationships Between Two Quantities

Class Ex. #1

List one more example of a relation.
The money earned working in a store is related to the number of hours worked.

Class Ex. #2
a) i) P   ii) Q   b) i) V   ii) A   c) i) B   ii) C
   iii) 5, 8, 11   iii) 4, 10, 25   iii) 3, 4, 5, 6   iv) 7, 11, 15, 19
   iv) 10, 16   iv) 12, 15

Class Ex. #3
a) i) r   b) i) t   c) i) t
   ii) C   ii) h   ii) S

5.a) Represent the data from the table on the grid.

b) Does it make sense to join the points together with a straight line? Explain.
Yes, the variables are continuous. Intermediate values have meaning.

c) Use the graph to estimate the boiling temperature of water at a height of 3000 m above sea level.   91°C

d) Use the graph to estimate the height above sea level at which the boiling temperature of water is 85°C.   5000 m

e) c) $T = 100 - 0.003H$ d) $T = 100 - 0.003H$
   $= 100 - 0.003(3000)$ $85 = 100 - 0.003H$
   $= 100 - 9$ $0.003H = 15$
   $= 91°C$ $H = \frac{15}{0.003} = 5000\ m$

f) 100°C is the boiling temperature of water at sea level.

6.a)

b)
Diagram Number, D	1	2	3	4	5
Perimeter in cm, P	8	12	16	20	24

c) Represent the data from the table of values on the grid.

d) Does it make sense to join the points in a straight line? Explain.
No, the variables are discrete. Intermediate values have no meaning.

e) Describe in words the relationship between the perimeter and the diagram number.
The perimeter is four more than four times the diagram number.

f) Write an equation that can be used to determine the perimeter, if we know the diagram number. $P = 4D + 4$

g) $P = 4(8)+4$
   $= 36$
   perimeter = 36 cm

h) $56 = 4D + 4$
   $52 = 4D$
   $D = 13$ diagram 13

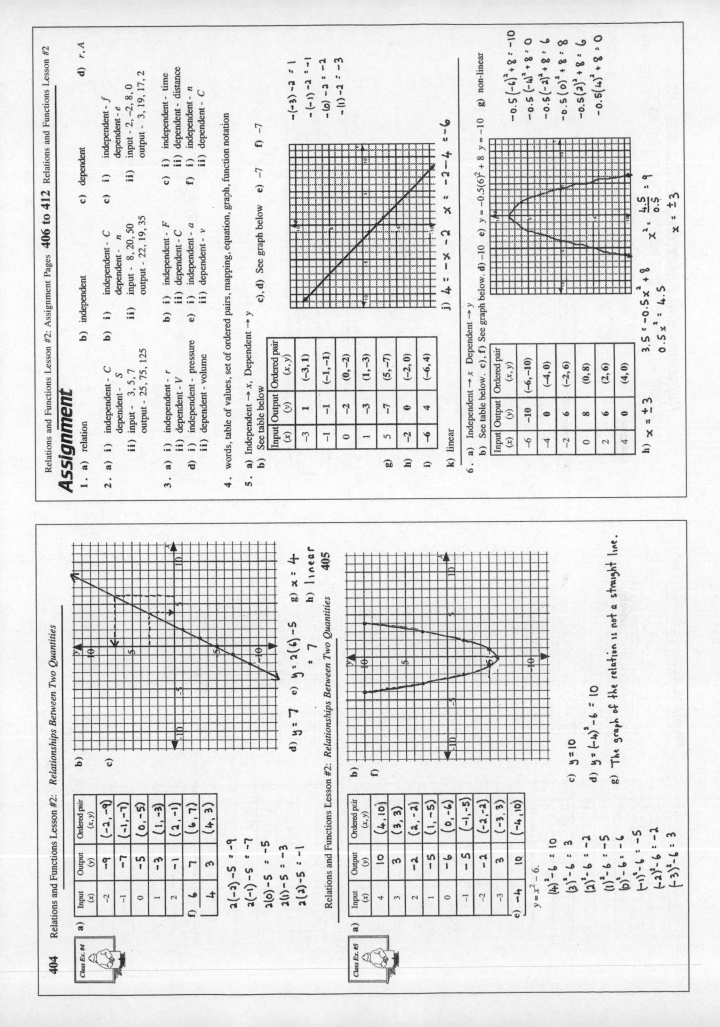

Class Ex. #4

a)

Input (x)	Output (y)	Ordered pair (x, y)
-2	-9	(-2, -9)
-1	-7	(-1, -7)
0	-5	(0, -5)
1	-3	(1, -3)
2	-1	(2, -1)
6	7	(6, 7)
4	3	(4, 3)

b)

c)
$2(-2) - 5 = -9$
$2(-1) - 5 = -7$
$2(0) - 5 = -5$
$2(1) - 5 = -3$
$2(2) - 5 = -1$

d) $y = 7$ e) $y = 2(6) - 5 = 7$ g) $x = 4$ h) linear

Class Ex. #5

a)

Input (x)	Output (y)	Ordered pair (x, y)
4	10	(4, 10)
3	3	(3, 3)
2	-2	(2, -2)
1	-5	(1, -5)
0	-6	(0, -6)
-1	-5	(-1, -5)
-2	-2	(-2, -2)
-3	3	(-3, 3)
-4	10	(-4, 10)

b)   f)

c) $y = 10$
d) $y = (-4)^2 - 6 = 10$
g) The graph of the relation is not a straight line.

e) $y = x^2 - 6$.
$(4)^2 - 6 = 10$
$(3)^2 - 6 = 3$
$(2)^2 - 6 = -2$
$(1)^2 - 6 = -5$
$(0)^2 - 6 = -6$
$(-1)^2 - 6 = -5$
$(-2)^2 - 6 = -2$
$(-3)^2 - 6 = 3$

Assignment

1. a) relation   b) independent   c) dependent   d) r, A

2. a) i) independent - C
     dependent - S
   ii) input - $3, 5, 7$
      output - $25, 75, 125$
   b) i) independent - C
     dependent - n
   ii) input - $8, 20, 50$
      output - $22, 19, 35$
   c) i) independent - f
     dependent - e
   ii) input - $2, -2, 8, 0$
      output - $3, 19, 17, 2$

3. a) i) independent - r
   ii) dependent - V
   b) i) independent - F
   ii) dependent - C
   c) i) independent - time
   ii) dependent - distance
   d) i) independent - pressure
   ii) dependent - volume
   e) i) independent - a
   ii) dependent - v
   f) i) independent - n
   ii) dependent - C

4. words, table of values, set of ordered pairs, mapping, equation, graph, function notation

5. a) Independent → x, Dependent → y
   b) See table below

Input (x)	Output (y)	Ordered pair (x, y)
-3	1	(-3, 1)
-1	-1	(-1, -1)
0	-2	(0, -2)
1	-3	(1, -3)
5	-7	(5, -7)
-2	0	(-2, 0)
-6	4	(-6, 4)

c), d) See graph below   e) -7 f) -7

$-(-3) - 2 = 1$
$-(-1) - 2 = -1$
$-(0) - 2 = -2$
$-(1) - 2 = -3$

g) linear   j) $4 = -x - 2$ $x = -2 - 4 = -6$

h) $x = \pm 3$

6. a) Independent → x   Dependent → y
   b) See table below. c), f) See graph below. d) -10 e) $y = -0.5(6)^2 + 8$ $y = -10$ g) non-linear

Input (x)	Output (y)	Ordered pair (x, y)
-6	-10	(-6, -10)
-4	0	(-4, 0)
-2	6	(-2, 6)
0	8	(0, 8)
2	6	(2, 6)
4	0	(4, 0)

$-0.5(-6)^2 + 8 = -10$
$-0.5(-4)^2 + 8 = 0$
$-0.5(-2)^2 + 8 = 6$
$-0.5(0)^2 + 8 = 8$
$-0.5(2)^2 + 8 = 6$
$-0.5(4)^2 + 8 = 0$

h) $x = \pm 3$
$3.5 = -0.5x^2 + 8$
$0.5x^2 = 4.5$
$x^2 = \dfrac{4.5}{0.5} = 9$
$x = \pm 3$

Relations and Functions Lesson #3:
x- and y-Intercepts and Interpreting Relations

Review

a) ordered pairs

b) x coordinate — independent

c) y coordinate — dependent

Exploring x- and y-intercepts

a) • Graph 1 crosses the x-axis at $(-3, 0)$.

• Graph 2 crosses the x-axis at $(-2, 0)$ and $(3, 0)$.

• Graph 3 crosses the x-axis at $(-4, 0)$ and $(4, 0)$.

b) the y-coordinate is zero

c) • Graph 1 crosses the y-axis at $(0, 5)$.

• Graph 2 crosses the y-axis at $(0, 6)$.

• Graph 3 crosses the y-axis at $(0, -4)$ and $(0, 4)$.

d) the x-coordinate is zero

414 Relations and Functions Lesson #3: *x- and y-intercepts and Interpreting Relations*

Class Ex. #1

The equation of Graph 1 on the previous page is $3y = 5x + 15$.
Algebraically determine the values of the x-intercept and the y-intercept of Graph 1.

x-intercept $\quad y=0$	y-intercept $\quad x=0$
$0 = 5x + 15$	$3y = 0 + 15$
$-15 = 5x$	$3y = 15$
$x = -3 \qquad x_{int.} : -3$	$y = 5 \qquad y_{int.} : 5$

Class Ex. #2

The equation of Graph 3 on the previous page is $x^2 + y^2 = 16$.
Calculate the x-intercept and the y-intercept of the graph of $x^2 + y^2 = 16$. Give the answer as ordered pairs.

x-intercept $\quad y=0$	y-intercept $\quad x=0$
$x^2 = 16$	$y^2 = 16$
$x = \pm 4 \qquad x_{int} : \pm 4$	$y = \pm 4 \qquad y_{int.} : \pm 4$
ordered pairs $(-4, 0)$ and $(4, 0)$	ordered pairs $(0, -4)$ and $(0, 4)$

---

7. a) i) See table below. Inputs may vary.   **ii)** See grid below.   **iii) linear**

Input (x)	Output (y)	Ordered pair (x, y)
-2	7	(-2, 7)
-1	5	(-1, 5)
0	3	(0, 3)
1	1	(1, 1)
3	-3	(3, -3)

b) i) See table below. Inputs may vary.   **ii)** See grid below.   **iii) linear**

Input (x)	Output (y)	Ordered pair (x, y)
-8	-12	(-8, -12)
-6	-11	(-6, -11)
0	-8	(0, -8)
2	-7	(2, -7)
6	-5	(6, -5)

c) i) See table below.   **ii)** See grid below.   **iii) non-linear**

Input (x)	Output (y)	Ordered pair (x, y)
4	-11	(4, -11)
3	-4	(3, -4)
2	1	(2, 1)
1	4	(1, 4)
0	5	(0, 5)
-1	4	(-1, 4)
-2	1	(-2, 1)
-3	-4	(-3, -4)
-4	-11	(-4, -11)

8. C) The outputs of a relation are shown on the horizontal axis of a Cartesian Plane.

9. $(1.5)^{4-2} = (1.5)^2 = 2.25$ $\boxed{2.25}$

Class Ex. #3

Lisa purchases a new car for $20 000. The value of the car can be represented by the formula $V = 20\,000 - 1250t$, where V is the value of the car in dollars, and t is the age of the car in years.

a) Complete the table of values and plot the ordered pairs on the grid.

Input (t)	Output (V)	Ordered pair (t, V)
0	20000	(0, 20000)
2	17500	(2, 17500)
4	15000	(4, 15000)
6	12500	(6, 12500)

Connect the points with a straight line, and extend the line.

b) What does the ordered pair (0, 20 000) represent?

The value of the new car.

c) Use the graph to estimate the t-intercept. What does the t-intercept represent?

$t_{int.} = 16$

After 16 years the car has no value.

d) Use the graph to estimate the value of the car after
i) 3 years ii) 10 years iii) 14 years.

$16250 $7500 $2500

e) Use the formula to verify d) ii).

$V = 20000 - 1250(10)$
: $7500

f) Use the graph to estimate when the car will be worth
i) $5 000   12 years   ii) half of the purchase price ($10000)   8 years

g) Use the formula to verify f) ii).

$10000 = 20000 - 1250t$
$1250t = 20000 - 10000$
$1250t = 10000$
$t = \dfrac{10000}{1250} = 8$ years

h) Complete the following statement to describe the relation:

The original value of the car is $20000. It depreciates in value by $1250 per year and has no value after __sixteen__ years.

Assignment

1. a) $y = x - 5$
$x = 0$
$y = 0 - 5$
$y_{int.} = -5$

b) $y = 3x - 15$
$x = 0$
$y = 0 - 15$
$y_{int.} = -15$

c) $2y + 3x - 12 = 0$ $x = 0$
$2y + 0 - 12 = 0$
$2y = 12$
$y = 6$ $y_{int.} = 6$

d) $0.5x - 2.4y + 0.8 = 0$
$x = 0$ $-2.4y + 0.8 = 0$
$-2.4y = -0.8$
$y = \dfrac{-0.8}{-2.4} = \dfrac{1}{3}$
$y_{int.} = \dfrac{1}{3}$

e) $2y = x^2 - 60$
$x = 0$ $2y = -60$
$y = -30$
$y_{int.} = -30$

f) $y = 0.001x^2 - 0.001x + 12.44$
$x = 0$
$y = 12.44$
$y_{int.} = 12.44$

2. a) $y = x - 2$
$y = 0$
$0 = x - 2$
$2 = x$
$x_{int.} = 2$

b) $y = 2x - 8$
$y = 0$ $0 = 2x - 8$
$8 = 2x$
$x = 4$
$x_{int.} = 4$

c) $3y + 2x - 12 = 0$
$y = 0$ $2x - 12 = 0$
$2x = 12$
$x = 6$
$x_{int.} = 6$

d) $0.6x - 2y + 0.5 = 0$
$y = 0$
$0.6x + 0.5 = 0$
$0.6x = -0.5$
$x = \dfrac{-0.5}{0.6} = -\dfrac{5}{6}$
$x_{int.} = -\dfrac{5}{6}$

e) $y = x^2 - 9$
$y = 0$ $0 = x^2 - 9$
$0 = (x - 3)(x + 3)$
$x = \pm 3$
$x_{int.} = \pm 3$

f) $y = 12 - 3x$
$y = 0$ $0 = 12 - 3x$
$3x = 12$
$x = 4$
$x_{int.} = 4$

3. a) $y = 4x + 7$
$x_{int.}$ $y = 0$
$0 = 4x + 7$
$-7 = 4x$
$x_{int.} = -\dfrac{7}{4}$ $\left(-\dfrac{7}{4}, 0\right)$
$y_{int.}$ $x = 0$
$y = 7$
$y_{int.} = 7$ (0, 7)

b) $y = 15 - 6x$
$x_{int.}$ $y = 0$
$0 = 15 - 6x$
$6x = 15$
$x = \dfrac{5}{2}$
$x_{int.} = \dfrac{5}{2}$ $\left(\dfrac{5}{2}, 0\right)$
$y_{int.}$ $x = 0$
$y = 15$
$y_{int.} = 15$ (0, 15)

c) $4x - 2y + 16 = 0$
$x_{int.}$ $y = 0$
$4x + 16 = 0$
$4x = -16$
$x_{int.} = -4$ (-4, 0)
$y_{int.}$ $x = 0$
$-2y + 16 = 0$
$16 = 2y$
$y_{int.} = 8$ (0, 8)

5. a) 45 m
b) see table and graph
c) non-linear
d) 5
e) The arrow was fired from a height of 25m above the ground
f) The number of seconds it takes to strike the ground.
g) i) approximately 44m
 ii) 43.75
h) No to the left because time cannot be negative.
No to the right because the ground stops the arrow from going further.

time (seconds)	height (metres)
0	25
1	40
2	45
3	40
4	25
5	0

6. a) see table and graph, answers may vary
b) 12 cm
c) 6 hours
d) 2 cm
e) 2.5 hours
f) Verify the answers from b) - e) using the formula.

t	0	1	3	5
h	12	10	6	2

b) $t = 0$ $h = -2(0) +12 = 12$
c) $h = 0$ $0 = -2t +12$ $2t = 12$ $t = 6$
d) $t = 5$ $h = -2(5) +12 = 2$
e) $h = 7$ $7 = -2t +12$ $2t = 5$ $t = 2.5$

7. a) approx 20 m
b) approx 4 seconds
c) approx 15 m
d) 14.7 m
e) h-int is 0.6 m. The football was punted 0.6 m above the ground.

8. $x_{int} = -8$ $y_{int} = 8$
$x_{int} = 7/2$ $y_{int} = 7/2$
$x_{int} = -2$ $y_{int} = 4/3$

B. $2x + 2y = 7$

9. x_{int} $4x^2 - 36 = 0$ y_{int} $9y^2 - 36 = 0$
$4x^2 = 36$ $9y^2 = 36$
$x^2 = 9$ $y^2 = 4$
$x = \pm 3$ $y = \pm 2$

$abcd = (-3)(3)(-2)(2)$
$= 36$ $\boxed{36}$

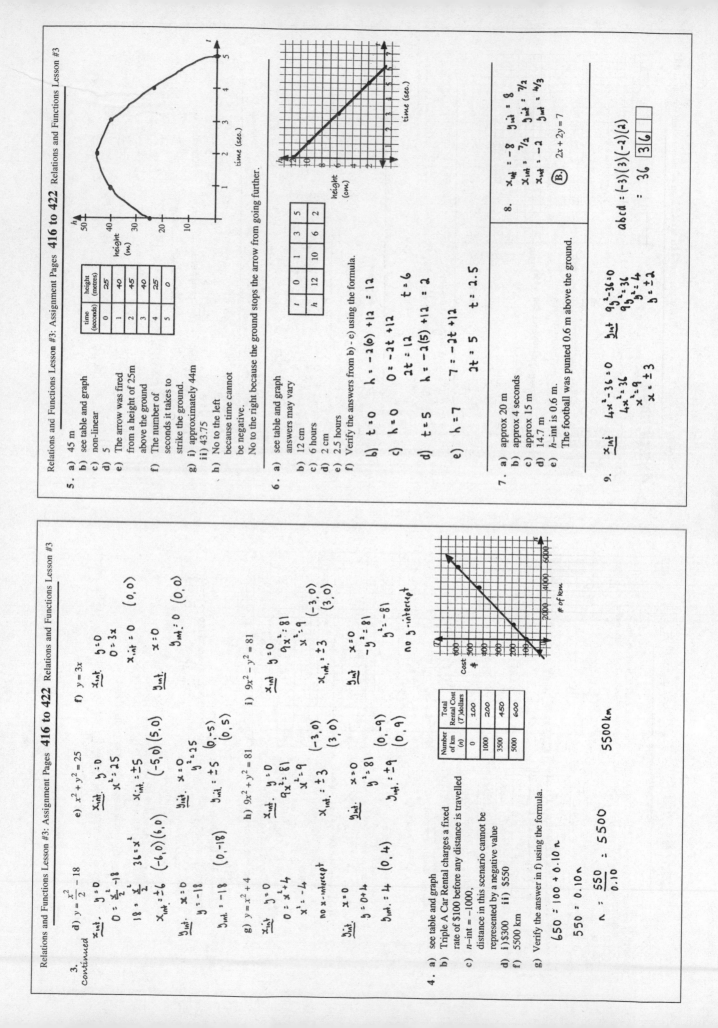

3. continued

d) $y = \dfrac{x^2}{2} - 18$
x_{int} $y=0$ $0 = \dfrac{x^2}{2} -18$ $18 = \dfrac{x^2}{2}$ $36 = x^2$ $x_{int} = \pm 6$ $(-6,0)(6,0)$
y_{int} $x=0$ $y = -18$ $y_{int} = -18$ $(0,-18)$

e) $x^2 + y^2 = 25$
x_{int} $y=0$ $x^2 = 25$ $x_{int} = \pm 5$ $(-5,0)(5,0)$
y_{int} $x=0$ $y^2 = 25$ $y_{int} = \pm 5$ $(0,-5)(0,5)$

f) $y = 3x$
x_{int} $y=0$ $0 = 3x$ $x_{int} = 0$ $(0,0)$
y_{int} $x=0$ $y_{int} = 0$ $(0,0)$

g) $y = x^2 + 4$
x_{int} $y=0$ $0 = x^2 + 4$ $x^2 = -4$ no x-intercept
y_{int} $x=0$ $y = 0+4$ $y_{int} = 4$ $(0,4)$

h) $9x^2 + y^2 = 81$
x_{int} $y=0$ $9x^2 = 81$ $x^2 = 9$ $x_{int} = \pm 3$ $(-3,0)(3,0)$
y_{int} $x=0$ $y^2 = 81$ $y_{int} = \pm 9$ $(0,-9)(0,9)$

i) $9x^2 - y^2 = 81$
x_{int} $y=0$ $9x^2 = 81$ $x^2 = 9$ $x_{int} = \pm 3$ $(-3,0)(3,0)$
y_{int} $x=0$ $-y^2 = 81$ $y^2 = -81$ no y-intercept

4. a) see table and graph
b) Triple A Car Rental charges a fixed rate of $100 before any distance is travelled
c) n-int = -1000, distance in this scenario cannot be represented by a negative value
d) i) $300   ii) $550
f) 5500 km
g) Verify the answer in f) using the formula.

$650 = 100 + 0.10\, n$
$550 = 0.10\, n$
$n = \dfrac{550}{0.10} = 5500$

5500 km

Number of km (n)	Total Rental Cost (T) dollars
0	100
1000	200
3500	450
5000	600

Class Ex. #5

a)

n	C
100	2500
200	4500
250	5500
300	6500
350	7500
400	8500
450	9500
500	10500

b) Plot the eight ordered pairs from a) on the grid.

c) If all possible ordered pairs from b) were plotted on the grid, state the domain and range of the relation, and explain why there are restrictions on both.

domain $\{n | 100 \le n \le 500, n \in N\}$

or $\{100, 101, 102 \ldots\ldots 499, 500\}$

range $\{2500, 2520, 2540 \ldots\ldots 10480, 10500\}$

There are domain restrictions because the number of people has to be a natural number.

There are range restrictions because the cost increases in steps of $20 due to the domain restrictions.

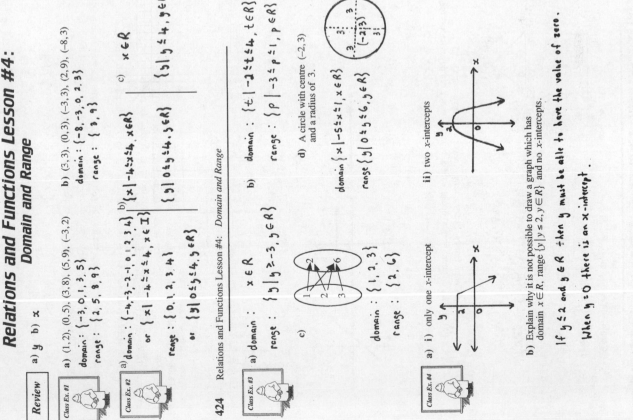

Assignment

Relations and Functions Lesson #4: Assignment Pages **426 to 432**

1. a) $D = \{2, 0, 4, -1, -3\}$ b) $D = \{-3, 0, 5, -8\}$ c) $D = \{0, 2, 4, 6\}$ d) $D = \{2, 0, -3\}$
   $R = \{3, 2, 8, 1\}$ $R = \{3, -5, -2, 1\}$ $R = \{3, 4, 5\}$ $R = \{3, 4, 5, 6\}$
   e) $D = \{1, -1, 3, 7\}$ f) $D = \{2, 3, 5, 7\}$ g) $D = \{2, 4, 6, 8\}$ h) $D = \{3, 5, 2, 4\}$
   $R = \{5\}$ $R = \{0, 1, 8, 9\}$ $R = \{1, 3, 5\}$ $R = \{0, 1, 6\}$

2. a) $D = \{-1, 0, 3, 4\}$ b) $D = \{x \in R\}$ c) $D = \{x \ge -8, x \in R\}$ d) $D = \{-5 \le x \le 5, x \in R\}$
   $R = \{5, 0, 2, 1\}$ $R = \{y \in R\}$ $R = \{y \ge 4, y \in R\}$ $R = \{-4 \le y \le 4, y \in R\}$
   e) $D = \{a \ge -10, a \in R\}$ f) $D = \{x \in R\}$ g) $D = \{x \in R\}$ h) $D = \{d < 5, d \in R\}$
   $R = \{b \in R\}$ $R = \{y \le 4, y \in R\}$ $R = \{8\}$ $R = \{t \le 4, t \in R\}$

3. In each case a relation is graphed on a grid. State the domain and range of the relation if the graph is
   a) a circle whose centre is located at $(-1, 12)$ and has a radius of 5 units.

   domain: $\{x | -6 \le x \le 4, x \in R\}$

   range: $\{y | 7 \le y \le 17, y \in R\}$

   b) a circle with centre $(-3, -5)$ and diameter 40 units.

   domain: $\{x | -23 \le x \le 17, x \in R\}$

   range: $\{y | -25 \le y \le 15, y \in R\}$

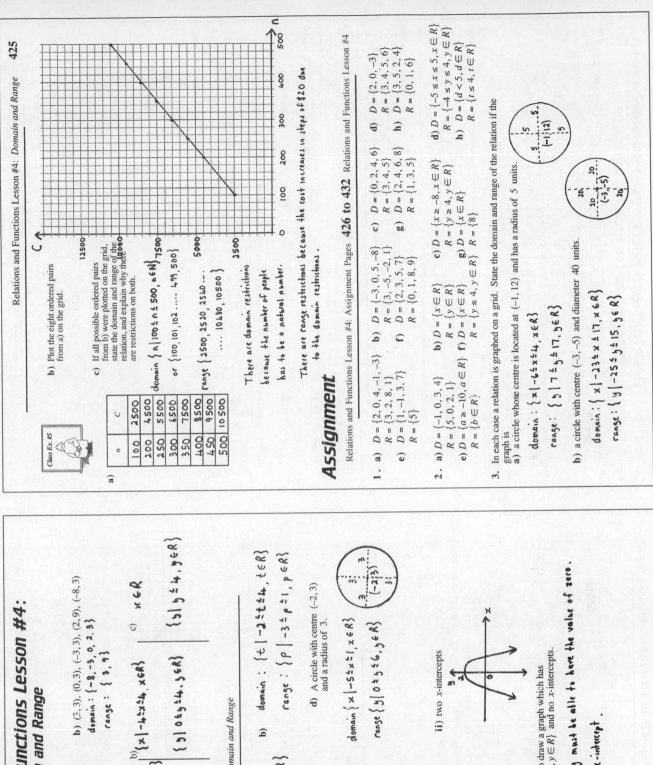

Relations and Functions Lesson #4: Domain and Range

Review   a) y   b) x

Class Ex. #1

a) $(1,2), (0,5), (3,8), (5,9), (-3,2)$
domain: $\{-3, 0, 1, 3, 5\}$
range: $\{2, 5, 8, 9\}$

b) $(3,3), (0,3), (-3,3), (2,9), (-8,3)$
domain: $\{-8, -3, 0, 2, 3\}$
range: $\{3, 9\}$

Class Ex. #2

a) domain: $\{-4, -3, -2, -1, 0, 1, 2, 3, 4\}$ b) $\{x | -4 \le x \le 4, x \in R\}$ c) $x \in R$
or $\{x | -4 \le x \le 4, x \in I\}$
range: $\{0, 1, 2, 3, 4\}$
or $\{y | 0 \le y \le 4, y \in R\}$ $\{y | 0 \le y \le 4, y \in R\}$ $\{y | y \le 4, y \in R\}$

Class Ex. #3

a) domain: $x \in R$ b) domain: $\{t | -2 \le t \le 4, t \in R\}$
   range: $\{y | y \ge -3, y \in R\}$ range: $\{p | -3 \le p \le 1, p \in R\}$

c) domain: $\{1, 2, 3\}$ range: $\{2, 6\}$

d) A circle with centre $(-2, 3)$ and a radius of 3.

domain $\{x | -5 \le x \le 1, x \in R\}$

range $\{y | 0 \le y \le 6, y \in R\}$

Class Ex. #4

a) i) only one x-intercept   ii) two x-intercepts

b) Explain why it is not possible to draw a graph which has domain $x \in R$, range $\{y | y \le 2, y \in R\}$ and no x-intercepts.

If $y \le 2$ and $y \in R$ then y must be able to have the value of zero.

When $y = 0$ there is an x-intercept.

3. Continued

c) a rectangle with vertices $A(-8,10)$, $B(-8,-2)$, $C(7,-2)$, and $D(7,10)$.

domain: $\{x \mid -8 \le x \le 7, x \in R\}$

range: $\{y \mid -2 \le y \le 10, y \in R\}$

d) a triangle with vertices $T(-50,-75)$, $U(-35,-25)$, and $V(-65,-25)$.

domain: $\{x \mid -65 \le x \le -35, x \in R\}$

range: $\{y \mid -75 \le y \le -25, y \in R\}$

4. a) $D = \{x \in R\}$ $R = \{y > 0, y \in R\}$, y-int is 400

b) $D = \{t \ge 0, t \in R\}$ different from a) because time is never a negative value.
$R = \{A \ge 400, A \in R\}$ different from a) because the amount of money can never be less than $400.

5. Answers may vary.
a) b) c)

6. Answers may vary.
a) b)

7. a) h-int = 0, d-int = 0 and 200. On the tee the ball is on the ground.
It returns to ground level 200 m from the tee.

b) max height = 25 m. The maximum height is the upper limit of the range.

c) $D = \{0 \le d \le 200, d \in R\}$ $R = \{0 \le h \le 25, h \in R\}$

d) 55 m from the tee when the ball is rising and 145m from the tee when the ball is descending.

e) 24 m

f) Starting from a height of 0 m at the tee, the golf ball increases in height to a maximum height of 25m, 100 m from the tee. Then the golf ball starts decreasing in height until it hits the ground 200 m from the tee.

8. i) A   ii) C   iii) G   iv) F   v) D   vi) F   vii) I

9. D

10. D

11.

6	0	0	0

domain $d \ge 0$
range $C \ge 60$

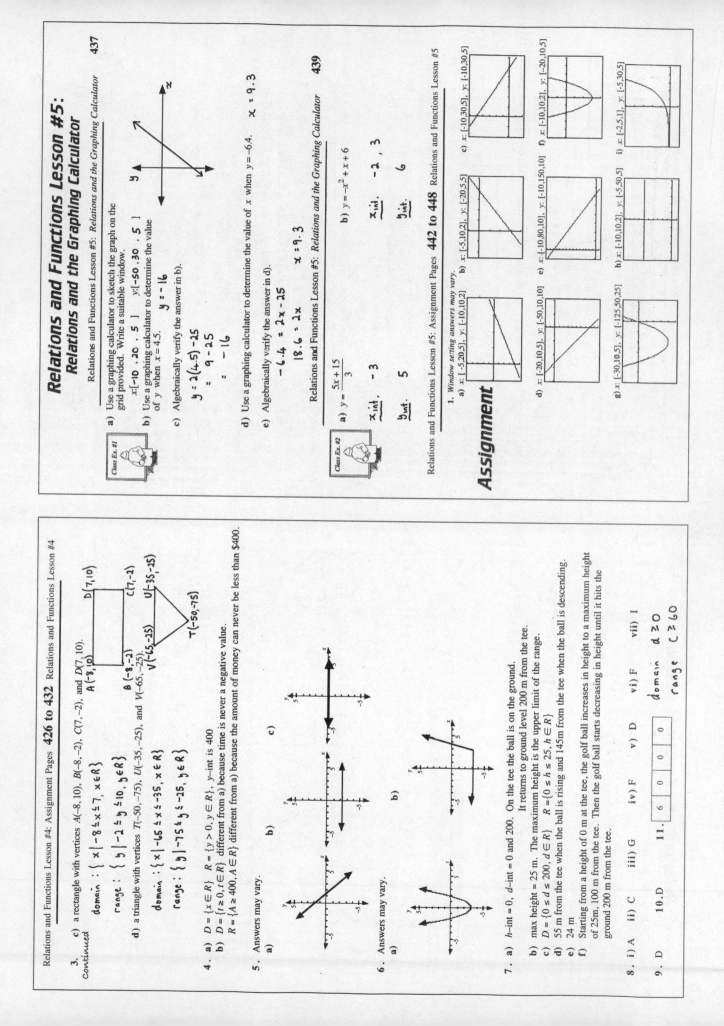

Relations and Functions Lesson #5:
Relations and the Graphing Calculator

Class Ex. #1

a) Use a graphing calculator to sketch the graph on the grid provided. Write a suitable window.

$x:[-10, 20, 5]$ $y:[-50, 30, 5]$

b) Use a graphing calculator to determine the value of y when $x=4.5$. $y = -16$

c) Algebraically verify the answer in b).
$$y = 2(4.5) - 25$$
$$= 9 - 25$$
$$= -16$$

d) Use a graphing calculator to determine the value of x when $y=-6.4$. $x = 9.3$

e) Algebraically verify the answer in d).
$$-6.4 = 2x - 25$$
$$18.6 = 2x \qquad x = 9.3$$

Class Ex. #2

a) $y = \dfrac{5x + 15}{3}$

$x_{int.}$ -3

$y_{int.}$ 5

b) $y = -x^2 + x + 6$

$x_{int.}$ -2, 3

$y_{int.}$ 6

Relations and Functions Lesson #5: Assignment Pages 442 to 448 Relations and Functions Lesson #5

Assignment

1. Window setting answers may vary.

a) $x:[-5,20,5]$, $y:[-10,10,2]$
b) $x:[-5,10,2]$, $y:[-20,5,5]$
c) $x:[-10,30,5]$, $y:[-10,30,5]$
d) $x:[-20,10,5]$, $y:[-50,10,10]$
e) $x:[-10,80,10]$, $y:[-10,150,10]$
f) $x:[-10,10,2]$, $y:[-20,10,5]$
g) $x:[-30,10,5]$, $y:[-125,50,25]$
h) $x:[-10,10,2]$, $y:[-5,50,5]$
i) $x:[-2.5,1]$, $y:[-5,30,5]$

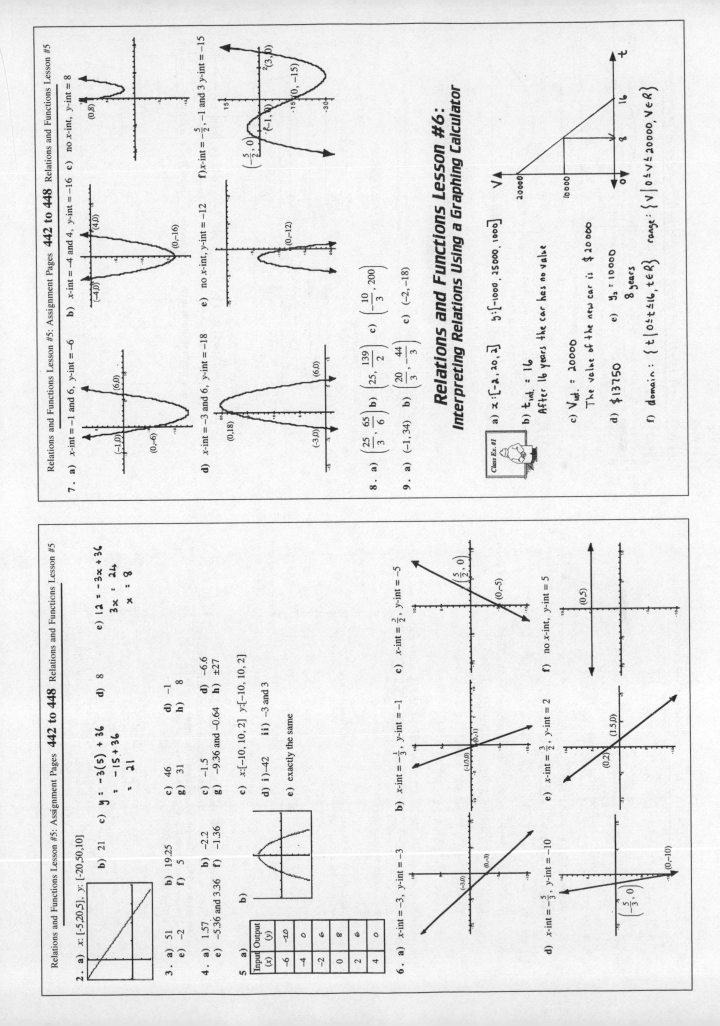

7. **a)** x-int = −1 and 6, y-int = −6   **b)** x-int = −4 and 4, y-int = −16   **c)** no x-int, y-int = 8

(6,0)   (−1,0)   (0,−6)

(−4,0)   (4,0)   (0,−16)

(0,8)

d) x-int = −3 and 6, y-int = −18   **e)** no x-int, y-int = −12   **f)** x-int = −$\frac{5}{2}$, −1 and 3, y-int = −15

(6,0)   (−3,0)   (0,18)

(0,−12)

(3,0)   (−1,0)   (0,−15) $\left(-\frac{5}{2}, 0\right)$

8. **a)** $\left(\frac{25}{3}, \frac{65}{6}\right)$ **b)** $\left(25, \frac{139}{2}\right)$ **c)** $\left(-\frac{10}{3}, 200\right)$

9. **a)** (−1, 34)   **b)** $\left(\frac{20}{3}, -\frac{44}{3}\right)$ **c)** (−2, −18)

Relations and Functions Lesson #6:
Interpreting Relations Using a Graphing Calculator

Class Ex. #1

a) $x : [-2, 20, 2]$ $y : [-1000, 35000, 1000]$

b) $t_{int.} = 16$
After 16 years the car has no value

c) $V_{int.} = 20000$
The value of the new car is $20000

d) $13750

e) $y_2 = 10000$
8 years

f) domain : $\{t \mid 0 \leq t \leq 16, t \in R\}$ range : $\{V \mid 0 \leq V \leq 20000, V \in R\}$

---

2. **a)** x: [−5,20,5], y: [−20,50,10]

b) 21   **c)** $y = -3(5) + 36$
$= -15 + 36$
$= 21$

d) 8   **e)** $12 = -3x + 36$
$3x = 24$
$x = 8$

3. **a)** 51   **b)** 19.25   **c)** 46   **d)** −1
e) −2   **f)** 5   **g)** 31   **h)** 8

4. **a)** 1.57   **b)** −2.2   **c)** −1.5   **d)** −6.6
e) −5.36 and 3.36   **f)** −1.36   **g)** −9.36 and −0.64   **h)** ±27

c) x:[−10, 10, 2] y:[−10, 10, 2]

d) **i)** −42   **ii)** −3 and 3

e) exactly the same

5. **a)**

Input (x)	Output (y)
−6	−10
−4	0
−2	6
0	8
2	6
4	0

b)

6. **a)** x-int = −3, y-int = −3   **b)** x-int = −$\frac{1}{3}$, y-int = −1   **c)** x-int = $\frac{5}{2}$, y-int = −5

(−3,0)   (0,−3)

(−1/3,0)   (0,−1)

$\left(\frac{5}{2}, 0\right)$ (0,−5)

d) x-int = −$\frac{5}{3}$, y-int = −10   **e)** x-int = $\frac{3}{2}$, y-int = 2   **f)** no x-int, y-int = 5

$\left(-\frac{5}{3}, 0\right)$ (0,−10)

(1.5,0)   (0,2)

(0,5)

Class Ex. #2

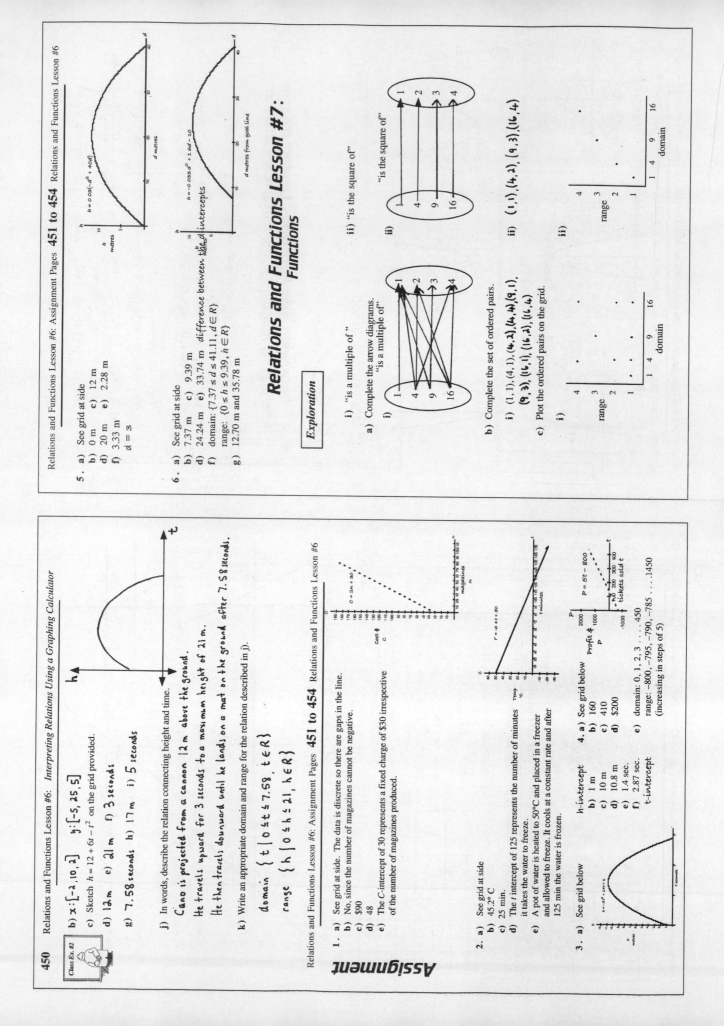

b) $x: [-2, 10, 2]$ $y: [-5, 25, 5]$

c) Sketch $h = 12 + 6t - t^2$ on the grid provided.

d) 12 m   e) 21 m   f) 3 seconds

g) 7.58 seconds   h) 17 m   i) 5 seconds

j) In words, describe the relation connecting height and time.

Cano is projected from a cannon 12 m above the ground. He travels upward for 3 seconds to a maximum height of 21 m. He then travels downward until he lands on a mat on the ground after 7.58 seconds.

k) Write an appropriate domain and range for the relation described in j).

domain $\{t \mid 0 \le t \le 7.58, t \in R\}$

range $\{h \mid 0 \le h \le 21, h \in R\}$

Relations and Functions Lesson #6: Assignment Pages **451 to 454** Relations and Functions Lesson #6

1. a) See grid at side. The data is discrete so there are gaps in the line.
   b) No, since the number of magazines cannot be negative.
   c) $90
   d) 48
   e) The C-intercept of 30 represents a fixed charge of $30 irrespective of the number of magazines produced.

2. a) See grid at side
   b) 45.2° C
   c) 25 min.
   d) The t intercept of 125 represents the number of minutes it takes the water to freeze.
   e) A pot of water is heated to 50°C and placed in a freezer and allowed to freeze. It cools at a constant rate and after 125 min the water is frozen.

3. a) See grid below

   h-intercept
   b) 1 m
   c) 10 m
   d) 10.8 m
   e) 1.4 sec.
   f) 2.87 sec.
   t-intercept

4. a) See grid below
   b) 160
   c) 410
   d) $200
   e) domain: 0, 1, 2, 3 450
      range: -800, -795, -790, -785, ...1450
      (increasing in steps of 5)

Assignment

Relations and Functions Lesson #6: Assignment Pages **451 to 454** Relations and Functions Lesson #6

5. a) See grid at side
   b) 0 m   c) 12 m
   d) 20 m   e) 2.28 m
   f) 3.33 m
   d = 3

6. a) See grid at side
   b) 7.37 m   c) 9.39 m
   d) 24.24 m   e) 33.74 m difference between the d-intercepts
   f) domain: $\{7.37 \le d \le 41.11, d \in R\}$
      range: $\{0 \le h \le 9.39, h \in R\}$
   g) 12.70 m and 35.78 m

Relations and Functions Lesson #7:
Functions

Exploration

i) "is a multiple of"   ii) "is the square of"

a) Complete the arrow diagrams.
   "is a multiple of"
   i)   ii)

b) Complete the set of ordered pairs.
   i) (1, 1), (4, 1), (4, 2), (4, 4), (9, 1), (9, 3), (16, 1), (16, 2), (16, 4)
   ii) (1, 1), (4, 2), (9, 3), (16, 4)

c) Plot the ordered pairs on the grid.
   i)   ii)

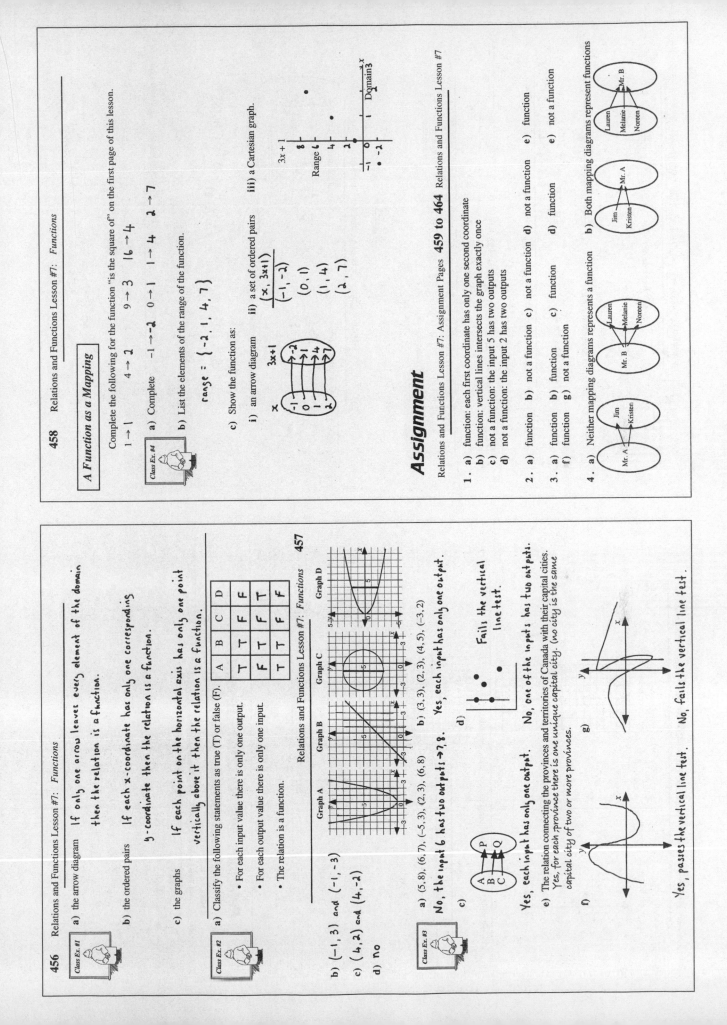

456 Relations and Functions Lesson #7: *Functions*

Class Ex. #1

a) the arrow diagram — If only one arrow leaves every element of the domain then the relation is a function.

b) the ordered pairs — If each x-coordinate has only one corresponding y-coordinate then the relation is a function.

c) the graphs — If each point on the horizontal axis has only one point vertically above it then the relation is a function.

Class Ex. #2

a) Classify the following statements as true (T) or false (F).

- For each input value there is only one output.
- For each output value there is only one input
- The relation is a function.

	A	B	C	D
	T	T	F	F
	F	T	F	T
	T	T	F	F

b) (−1, 3) and (−1, −3)

c) (4, 2) and (4, −2)

d) no

Relations and Functions Lesson #7: *Functions*   **457**

Graph A   Graph B   Graph C   Graph D

a) (5,8), (6,7), (−5,3), (2,3), (6,8)   b) (3, 3), (2,3), (4,5), (−3,2)

No, the input 6 has two outputs → 7, 8.   Yes, each input has only one output.

Class Ex. #3

c)

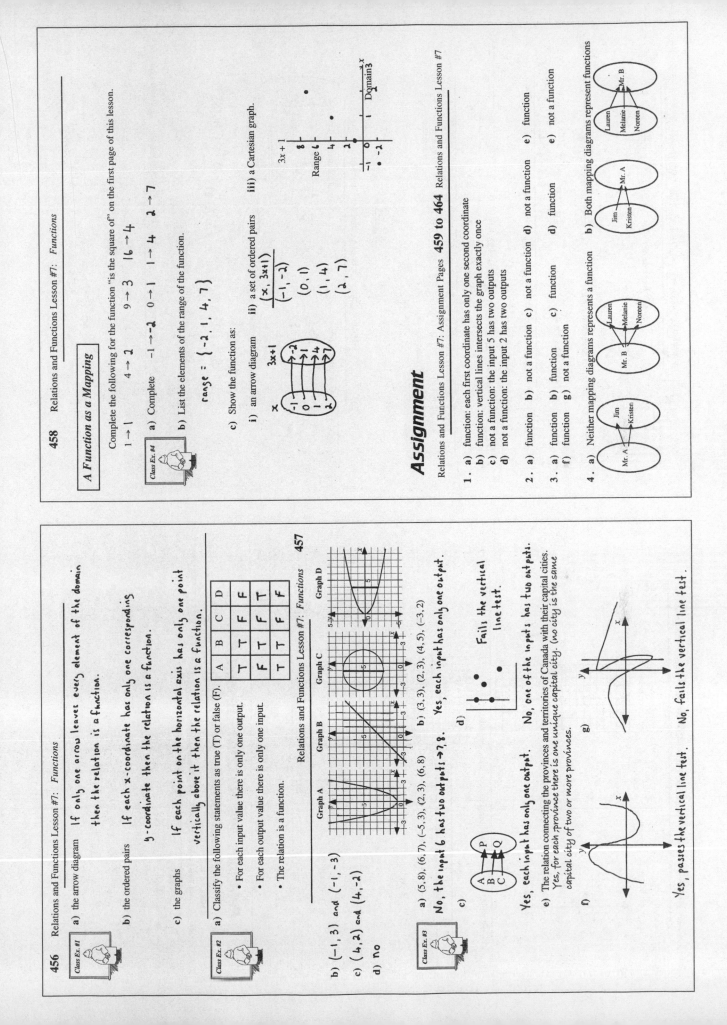

Yes, each input has only one output.   No, one of the inputs has two outputs

Fails the vertical line test.

d)

e) The relation connecting the provinces and territories of Canada with their capital cities.
Yes, for each province there is one unique capital city. (no city is the same capital city of two or more provinces.)

f)   Yes, passes the vertical line test.

g)   No, fails the vertical line test.

---

458 Relations and Functions Lesson #7: *Functions*

A Function as a Mapping

Complete the following for the function "is the square of" on the first page of this lesson.

$1 \to 1 \qquad 4 \to 2 \qquad 9 \to 3 \qquad 16 \to 4$

Class Ex. #4

a) Complete $-1 \to -2 \quad 0 \to 1 \quad 1 \to 4 \quad 2 \to 7$

b) List the elements of the range of the function.

range = $\{-2, 1, 4, 7\}$

c) Show the function as:

i) an arrow diagram $3x+1$

ii) a set of ordered pairs

$(x, 3x+1)$

$(-1, -2)$
$(0, 1)$
$(1, 4)$
$(2, 7)$

iii) a Cartesian graph.

$3x + 1$

Range   Domain

Assignment

Relations and Functions Lesson #7: Assignment Pages **459 to 464** Relations and Functions Lesson #7

1. a) function: each first coordinate has only one second coordinate
   b) function: vertical lines intersects the graph exactly once
   c) not a function: the input 5 has two outputs
   d) not a function: the input 2 has two outputs

2. a) function   b) not a function   c) not a function   d) not a function   e) function

3. a) function   b) function   c) function   d) function   e) not a function
   f) function   g) not a function

4. a) Neither mapping diagrams represents a function   b) Both mapping diagrams represent functions

5. a) {5, 7, 9, 11}
   b) see graph below

6. a) {-8, -1, 0, 1, 8}
   b) see graph below

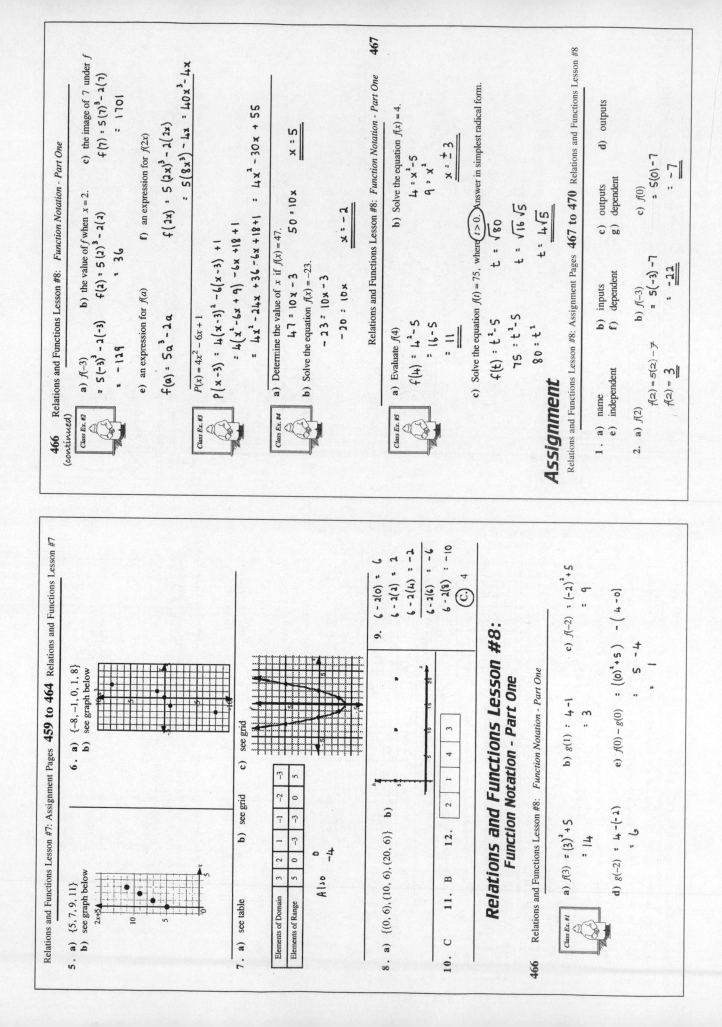

7. a) see table   b) see grid   c) see grid

Elements of Domain	3	2	1	-1	-2	-3
Elements of Range	5	0	-3	-3	0	5

Also 0
      -4

8. a) {(0, 6), (10, 6), (20, 6)}   b)

9. $6 - 2(0) = 6$
   $6 - 2(1) = 2$
   $6 - 2(4) = -2$
   $6 - 2(6) = -6$
   $6 - 2(8) = -10$
   C. 4

10. C   11. B   12. | 2 | 1 | 4 | 3 |

Relations and Functions Lesson #8:
Function Notation - Part One

466 Relations and Functions Lesson #8: *Function Notation - Part One*

Class Ex. #1
a) $f(3) = (3)^2 + 5$
   $= 14$
b) $g(1) = 4 - 1$
   $= 3$
c) $f(-2) = (-2)^2 + 5$
   $= 9$

d) $g(-2) = 4 - (-2)$
   $= 6$
e) $f(0) - g(0) = ((0)^2 + 5) - (4 - 0)$
   $= 5 - 4$
   $= 1$

---

466 Relations and Functions Lesson #8: *Function Notation - Part One*
(*continued*)

Class Ex. #2
a) $f(-3)$
   $= 5(-3)^3 - 2(-3)$
   $= -129$
b) the value of f when $x = 2$.
   $f(2) = 5(2)^3 - 2(2)$
   $= 36$
c) the image of 7 under f
   $f(7) = 5(7)^3 - 2(7)$
   $= 1701$

e) an expression for $f(a)$
   $f(a) = 5a^3 - 2a$
f) an expression for $f(2x)$
   $f(2x) = 5(2x)^3 - 2(2x)$
   $= 5(8x^3) - 4x = 40x^3 - 4x$

Class Ex. #3
$P(x) = 4x^2 - 6x + 1$
$P(x-3) = 4(x-3)^2 - 6(x-3) + 1$
$= 4(x^2 - 6x + 9) - 6x + 18 + 1$
$= 4x^2 - 24x + 36 - 6x + 18 + 1 = 4x^2 - 30x + 55$

Class Ex. #4
a) Determine the value of x if $f(x) = 47$.
   $47 = 10x - 3$
   $50 = 10x$
   $x = 5$

b) Solve the equation $f(x) = -23$.
   $-23 = 10x - 3$
   $-20 = 10x$
   $x = -2$

467 Relations and Functions Lesson #8: *Function Notation - Part One*

Class Ex. #5
a) Evaluate $f(4)$
   $f(4) = 4^2 - 5$
   $= 16 - 5$
   $= 11$

b) Solve the equation $f(x) = 4$.
   $4 = x^2 - 5$
   $9 = x^2$
   $x = \pm 3$

c) Solve the equation $f(t) = 75$, where $t > 0$. Answer in simplest radical form.
   $f(t) = t^2 - 5$
   $75 = t^2 - 5$
   $80 = t^2$
   $t = \sqrt{80}$
   $t = \sqrt{16}\sqrt{5}$
   $t = 4\sqrt{5}$

Assignment

1. a) name   b) inputs   c) outputs   d) outputs
   e) independent   f) dependent   g) dependent

2. a) $f(2)$
   $f(2) = 5(2) - 7$
   $f(2) = 3$
   b) $f(-3)$
   $= 5(-3) - 7$
   $= -22$
   c) $f(0)$
   $= 5(0) - 7$
   $= -7$

d) If $h(x) = -3x + 1$, then determine the value of x if $h(x) = 22$.

$22 = -3x + 1$
$3x = -21$
$x = -7$

e) If $P(x) = 50 - 3x^2$, then determine the values of x if $P(x) = -25$.

$-25 = 50 - 3x^2$
$3x^2 = 75$
$x^2 = 25$
$x = \pm 5$

9. a) $f(0)$
$= 6(0) - 15$
$= -15$

b) an expression for $f(2x+1)$.
$= 6(2x+1) - 15$
$= 12x + 6 - 15$
$= 12x - 9$

c) the solution to the equation $f(x) = 27$
$27 = 6x - 15$
$42 = 6x$
$x = 7$

10. a) Evaluate:

i) $C(16)$
$= \sqrt{16}$
$= 4$

ii) $C\left(\dfrac{1}{36}\right)$
$= \sqrt{\dfrac{1}{36}}$
$= \dfrac{1}{6}$

iii) $\dfrac{C(100)}{C(4)}$
$= \dfrac{\sqrt{100}}{\sqrt{4}}$
$= \dfrac{10}{2}$
$= 5$

b) If $C(x) = 9$, find x.
$\sqrt{x} = 9$
$x = 9^2 = 81$

11. a) Calculate the value of $g(4) + (-2 + 12)$.
$= (4+12) + (-2+12)$
$= 16 + 10$
$= 26$

b) If $g(a^2) = 52$, determine the values of a in simplest radical form.
$52 = a^2 + 12$
$40 = a^2$
$a = \pm\sqrt{40}$
$= \pm\sqrt{4}\sqrt{10} = \pm 2\sqrt{10}$

12. $g = 3t - 1$
$9 = 3t$
$t = 3$ (B.) 3

13. $f(20) = 8\sqrt{20} = 8\sqrt{4}\sqrt{5} = 8(2\sqrt{5}) = 16\sqrt{5}$

| 1 | 6 | |

Relations and Functions Lesson #9:
Function Notation - Part Two

Class Ex. #1   Class Ex. #2

$f(x)$

a) i) $f(x) = 7x - 23$
$y = 7x - 23$

ii) $g(t) = t^2 - 2t + 35$
$y = t^2 - 2t + 35$

b) Express the relation $y = 11x - 15$ in function notation.
$f(x) = 11x - 15$

c) $f(x) = 4 - 3x$

---

3. a) $g(4)$
$= 6 - (4)^2$
$= 6 - 16$
$= -10$

b) $g(-6)$
$= 6 - (-6)^2$
$= 6 - 36$
$= -30$

c) $g(\sqrt{3})$
$= 6 - (\sqrt{3})^2$
$= 6 - 3$
$= 3$

4. a) the image of 2 under f
$f(2) = (2)^3 + 1$
$= 8 + 1$
$= 9$

b) the value of f at -7.
$f(-7) = (-7)^3 + 1$
$= -343 + 1$
$= -342$

c) an expression for $f(a)$
$f(a) = a^3 + 1$

5. a) $f(5)$
$= (5)^3 - 2(5)^2 - 5 - 5$
$= 125 - 2(25) - 5 - 5$
$= 65$

b) $f(-3)$
$= (-3)^3 - 2(-3)^2 - (-3) - 5$
$= -27 - 2(9) + 3 - 5$
$= -47$

6. a) $f(4)$
$= 8 - 2(4)$
$= 0$

b) the value of f when $x = -4$.
$f(-4) = 8 - 2(-4)$
$= 8 + 8 = 16$

c) the image of 0.5 under f
$f(0.5) = 8 - 2(0.5)$
$= 8 - 1 = 7$

d) an expression for $f(2t)$.
$f(2t) = 8 - 2(2t)$
$= 8 - 4t$

e) an expression for $f(a + 3)$.
$f(a+3) = 8 - 2(a+3)$
$= 8 - 2a - 6$
$= 2 - 2a$

7. a) $F(-x)$
$= 3(-x)^2 - 2(-x) - 9$
$= 3x^2 + 2x - 9$

b) $F(x-5)$
$= 3(x-5)^2 - 2(x-5) - 9$
$= 3(x^2 - 10x + 25) - 2x + 10 - 9$
$= 3x^2 - 30x + 75 - 2x + 10 - 9$
$= 3x^2 - 32x + 76$

8. a) If $f(x) = 5x - 7$, then determine the value of x if $f(x) = 43$.
$43 = 5x - 7$
$50 = 5x$
$x = 10$

b) If $g(x) = 6x + 3$, then determine the value of x if $g(x) = -24$.
$-24 = 6x + 3$
$-27 = 6x$
$x = \dfrac{-27}{6} = -\dfrac{9}{2}$

c) If $g(t) = 56 - 3t$, then determine the value of t if $g(t) = 11$.
$11 = 56 - 3t$
$3t = 45$
$t = 15$

6. See table below.

    b) The horizontal line where $f(x) = 4$ has an infinite number of input values between 8 and 14.

x	$f(x)$	Ordered Pair
2	6	$(2,6)$
0	0	$(0,0)$
-6	-2	$(-6,-2)$
8	4	$(8,4)$
-8	-6	$(-8,-6)$
10	4	$(10,4)$

7. a) evaluate $f(-3)$

$f(-3) = 9 - 2(-3)$
$= 9 + 6$
$= 15$

    b) find the value of $f(t) + f(-t)$

$f(t) + f(-t) = 9 - 2t + 9 - 2(-t)$
$= 9 - 2t + 9 + 2t$
$= 18$

c) calculate the x-intercept and the y-intercept on the graph of f.

$y = 9 - 2x$

x_{int} $y=0$ $x=0$
$0 = 9 - 2x$ $y = 9 - 2(0)$
$2x = 9$ $y_{int} = 9$
$x_{int} = \frac{9}{2}$

8. a) i) The name of the function is g not f. The scale is 4 units per box, not 1 unit per box.
    ii) $g(-12) = 8$
  b) i) $x = 20$ **ii)** $x = -20, -4, 8$
  c) i) 12   **ii)** 0
  d) Domain $= \{x \mid -32 \le x \le 24, x \in R\}$, $\{g(x) \mid -16 \le g(x) \le 28\}, g(x) \in R$
  e) A horizontal line must intersect the graph at exactly two points.
    This occurs when $g(x) = 24$ and when $g(x) = 8$.
    Solution 1: $b = 24$ when $a = -28$ or 4.
    Solution 2: $b = 8$ when $a = -12$ or 12

9. a) Evaluate $f(2) - f(-1)$

$= \left(1 - (2)^2\right) - \left(1 - (-1)^4\right)$
$= (1 - 4) - (1 - 1)$
$= -3 - 0$
$= -3$

    b) Given that $f(a^{\frac{1}{4}}) = -8$, calculate the value of a.

$f(a^{\frac{1}{4}}) = 1 - (a^{\frac{1}{4}})^2 = 1 - a^{\frac{2}{4}}$
$1 - a^{\frac{4}{2}} = -8$
$-a^{\frac{4}{2}} = -8$?
$q = a^{\frac{4}{2}}$
$a = (q)^2$
$= 81$

10. $x = 0$
$f(0) = 4^0 = 1$
$(0, 1)$

B. $(0, 1)$

11. C

12. $f(x) = 0$

$0 = 5x - 11$
$11 = 5x$
$x = 2.2$
$\boxed{2.2}$

    Rose is correct and Susan is incorrect.

Class Ex. #3

The graph of a function f is shown.

a) Complete:
  i) $f(5) = -2$ **ii)** $f(-2) = 3$ **iii)** $f(4) = -1$

b) Write the ordered pairs associated with i), ii), and iii).
  i) $(5, -2)$ **ii)** $(-2, 3)$ **iii)** $(4, -1)$

c) State the value(s) of x if:
  i) $f(x) = -1$ **ii)** $f(x) = 3$ **iii)** $f(x) = 4$
    $x = 4$ $x = \pm 2$ $x = \pm 1$

d) Use the notation in a) to make a statement about the points A and B on the graph.
  $f(-5) = 1$ $f(6) = -3$

e) Write the x- and y-intercepts of the graph using function notation.
  $f(-6) = 0$ $f(0) = 5$
  $f(3) = 0$

f) Complete the following statements.
- The domain of f is $\{x \mid \underline{-6} \le x \le \underline{7}, x \in R\}$
- The range of f is $\{f(x) \mid \underline{-4} \le f(x) \le \underline{5}, f(x) \in R\}$

Assignment

1. a) $y = 10 - 3x$ **b)** $y = 12x^2 - 5$ **c)** $y = 2t + 9$

2. a) $f(x) = 17x - 9$ **b)** $f(v) = 4v + 25$ **c)** $2y = -x - 6$
    $y = -\frac{1}{2}x - 3$
    $f(x) = -\frac{1}{2}x - 3$

3. a) $f(x) = 0.5x - 0.25$ **b)** $f(t) = 4.9t^2$

4. a) i) -1 **ii)** -3 **iii)** 0
  b) i) $(3, -1)$ **ii)** $(-3, -3)$ **iii)** $(-6, 0)$
  c) i) 7   **ii)** $-4, -2, 2$ **iii)** no solution
  d) A is $f(-7) = 1$, B is $f(8) = 4$
  e) x-intercepts can be represented in function notation by; $f(-6) = 0, f(0) = 0, f(4) = 0$
    y-intercept can be represented in function notation by $f(0) = 0$
  f) $-7 \le x \le 8, \; -3 \le f(x) \le 4$

5. The function $g(x) = 3x^2 - 4$ has a domain $\{-2, -1, 0, 1, 2\}$.
  a) State the range of g.   **b)** Solve the equation $g(x) = -1$.

$g(-2) = 3(-2)^2 - 4 = 8$
$g(-1) = 3(-1)^2 - 4 = -1$
$g(0) = 3(0)^2 - 4 = -4$
$g(1) = 3(1)^2 - 4 = -1$
$g(2) = 3(2)^2 - 4 = 8$
range $= \{-4, -1, 8\}$

$g(x) = -1$
$3x^2 - 4 = -1$
$3x^2 = 3$
$x^2 = 1$
$x = \pm 1$

Relations and Functions Lesson #10:
Function Notation and Problem Solving

Class Ex. #1

A candle manufacturer found that their "Long-Last" candles melted according to the formula $h(t) = -2t + 12$, where h is the height of the candle, in cm, after t hours.

a) Use a graphing calculator to sketch the graph of the function and show the graph on the grid

b) Determine the value of $h(5)$.

$h(5) = -2(5) +12 = 2$

c) Write in words the meaning of $h(5)$.

The height of the candle after 5 hours is 2cm.

d) Evaluate the following, and explain each of their significance.

i) $h(0) = -2(0)+12 = 12$

The starting height is 12cm.

ii) $h(6) = -2(6) +12 = 0$

After 6 hours the candle has burned down too.

iii) $h(8) = -2(8) +12 = -4$

Has no meaning in the context of the question.

e) How long will it take for the candle to burn down to a height of 7 cm?

$7 = -2t + 12$
$2t = 5$
$t = 2.5$ 2.5 hours

f) Suggest an appropriate domain and range for the function.

domain: $\{t \mid 0 \le t \le 6, t \in R\}$ range $\{h(t) \mid 0 \le h(t) \le 12, h(t) \in R\}$

Assignment

1. Ivory the botanist treated a 2 cm plant with a special growth fertilizer. With this fertilizer, the plant grew at a rate modelled by the function $H(t) = \frac{5}{3}t + 2$, where $H(t)$ represents the height of the plant in cm after t days.

a) Use a graphing calculator to sketch the graph of the function and show the graph on the grid.

b) Determine the value of $H(3)$.

$H(3) = \frac{5}{3}(3) + 2 = 7$

c) Write in words the meaning of $H(3)$.

After 3 days the height is 7cm

d) Evaluate the following.

i) $H(0) = \frac{5}{3}(0) + 2 = 2$

ii) $H(6) = \frac{5}{3}(6) + 2 = 12$

iii) $H(21) = \frac{5}{3}(21) + 2 = 37$

e) How long will it take for the plant to reach a height of 21 cm?

$21 = \frac{5}{3}t + 2$
$19 = \frac{5}{3}t$
$57 = 5t$ $t = 11.4$ 11.4 days

f) It takes 27 days for the plant to mature (to reach maximum height). State the domain and range of the function $H(t)$.

$H(27) = \frac{5}{3}(27) + 2 = 47$

domain $\{t \mid 0 \le t \le 27, t \in R\}$
range $\{H(t) \mid 2 \le H(t) \le 47, H(t) \in R\}$

---

2. a) Sketch the graph of the function for a maximum of 4000 calculators.

b) Determine the value of $C(30)$.

$C(30) = 11750 + 32(30) = 12710$

c) Write in words the meaning of $C(30)$.

It costs $12710 to produce 30 calculators.

d) Evaluate $C(0)$ and explain its significance.

$C(0) = 11750$. There are fixed costs of $11750 before any calculators are produced.

e) How many calculators can be produced for $31 270?

$31270 = 11750 + 32n$
$31270 - 11750 = 32n$
$32n = 19520$ $n = 610$ 610 calculators.

f) Last month IT produced 2 600 calculators and spent $14 000 on advertising. If there are other fixed monthly costs of $24 500, and each calculator sells for $165, how much profit would be made if all the calculators are sold?

$C(2600) = 11750 + 32(2600)$
$= 94950$

Total costs = $94950 + $14000 + $24500 = $133450

Revenue = $2600 (165)$ = $429000

Profit = $429 000 - 133450 = $295 550

3. Over the last 10 years, data was recorded for the number of cups of hot chocolate sold at BGB Senior High School. It was found from the data that the warmer the weather, the less cups of hot chocolate were sold. The data can be modelled by the formula $N(t) = 150 - 10t$, where $N(t)$ is the daily number of cups of hot chocolates sold when the average daily temperature is t °C.

a) Sketch the graph of the function on the grid provided.

b) Determine the value of $N(-5)$.

$150 - 10(-5) = 200$ $N(-5) = 200$

c) Write in words the meaning of $N(-5)$.

200 cups are sold when the average temp. is -5°C.

d) What was the average temperature if 190 cups of hot chocolate were sold?

$190 = 150 - 10t$
$150 - 150 - 10t$
$10t = -40$ $t = -4$ -4°C

e) Explain how to estimate the lower limit of the domain of the relation.

Estimate the minimum average daily temperature.

f) Suggest an appropriate domain and range for the function $N(t)$ if BGB High School is located in southern Alberta.

$N(-35) = 150 - 10(-35) = 500$

domain $\{t \mid -35 \le t \le 15, t \in R\}$
range $\{N(t) \mid 0 \le N(t) \le 500, N(t) \in W\}$

Relations and Functions Lesson #11:
Interpreting Graphs of Functions

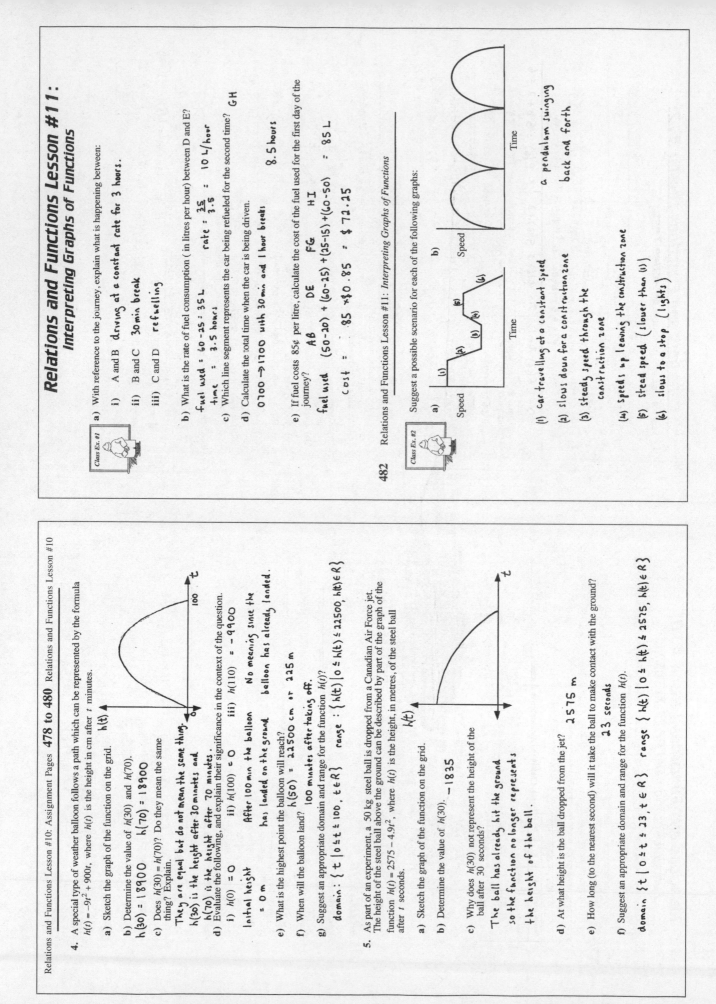

Class Ex. #1

a) With reference to the journey, explain what is happening between:

i)   A and B   driving at a constant rate for 3 hours.

ii) B and C   30 min break

iii) C and D   refuelling

b) What is the rate of fuel consumption (in litres per hour) between D and E?

fuel used = 60-25 = 35 L   rate = $\frac{35}{3.5}$ = 10 L/hour

time = 3.5 hours

c) Which line segment represents the car being refueled for the second time?   GH

d) Calculate the total time when the car is being driven.

0700 → 1700 with 30 min and 1 hour break   8.5 hours

e) If fuel costs 85¢ per litre, calculate the cost of the fuel used for the first day of the journey?   AB   DE   FG   HI

fuel used (50-20) + (60-25) + (25-15) + (60-50) = 85 L

cost = .85 ×$0.85 = $ 72.25

482   Relations and Functions Lesson #11: *Interpreting Graphs of Functions*

Class Ex. #2   Suggest a possible scenario for each of the following graphs:

a)

Speed

Time

b)

Speed

Time

a pendulum swinging
back and forth

(1) car travelling at a constant speed

(2) slows down for a construction zone

(3) steady speed through the construction zone

(4) speeds up leaving the construction zone

(5) steady speed (slower than (1))

(6) slows to a stop (lights)

---

4. A special type of weather balloon follows a path which can be represented by the formula $h(t) = -9t^2 + 900t$, where $h(t)$ is the height in cm after t minutes.

a) Sketch the graph of the function on the grid.

h(t)

100   t

b) Determine the value of $h(30)$ and $h(70)$.

h(30) = 18900   h(70) = 18900

c) Does $h(30) = h(70)$? Do they mean the same thing? Explain.

They are equal but do not mean the same thing.
h(30) is the height after 30 minutes and
h(70) is the height after 70 minutes.

d) Evaluate the following, and explain their significance in the context of the question.

i) $h(0) = 0$ ii) $h(100) = 0$ iii) $h(110) = -9900$

Initial height   After 100 min the balloon   No meaning since the
= 0 m   has landed on the ground   balloon has already landed.

e) What is the highest point the balloon will reach? $h(50) = 22500$ cm or 225 m

f) When will the balloon land?   100 minutes after taking off.

g) Suggest an appropriate domain and range for the function $h(t)$?

domain: $\{t \mid 0 \le t \le 100, t \in R\}$ range : $\{h(t) \mid 0 \le h(t) \le 22500, h(t) \in R\}$

5. As part of an experiment, a 50 kg steel ball is dropped from a Canadian Air Force jet. The height of the steel ball above the ground can be described by part of the graph of the function $h(t) = 2575 - 4.9t^2$, where $h(t)$ is the height, in metres, of the steel ball after t seconds.

a) Sketch the graph of the function on the grid.

h(t)

t

b) Determine the value of $h(30)$.   -1835

c) Why does $h(30)$ not represent the height of the ball after 30 seconds?

The ball has already hit the ground
so the function no longer represents
the height of the ball.

d) At what height is the ball dropped from the jet?   2575 m

e) How long (to the nearest second) will it take the ball to make contact with the ground?

23 seconds

f) Suggest an appropriate domain and range for the function $h(t)$.

domain $\{t \mid 0 \le t \le 23, t \in R\}$ range $\{h(t) \mid 0 \le h(t) \le 2575, h(t) \in R\}$

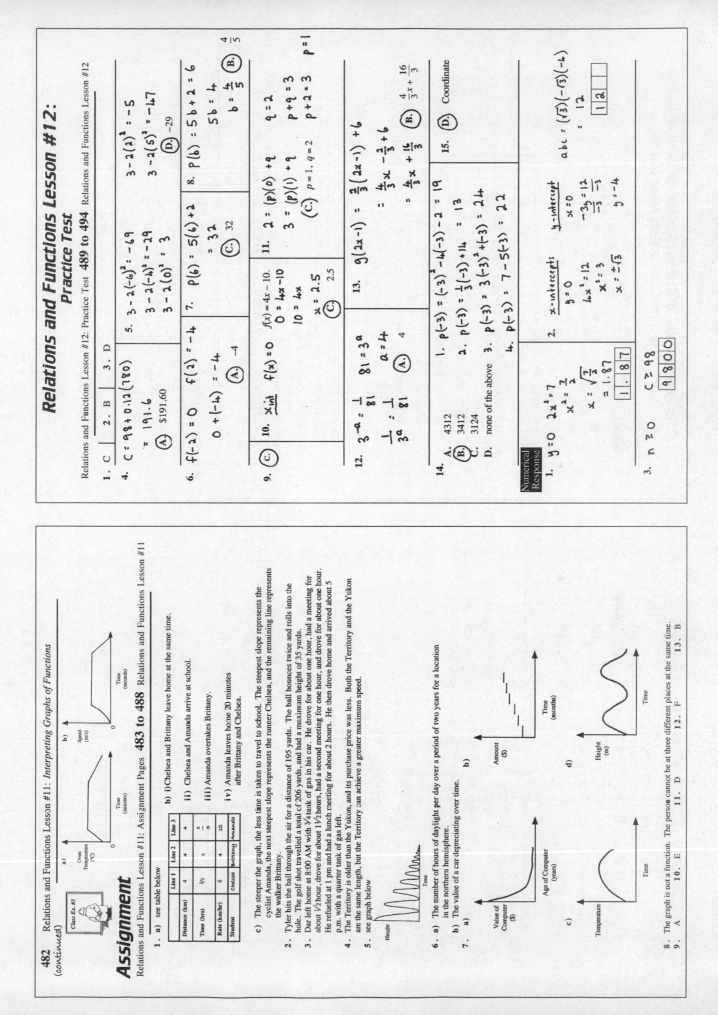

Relations and Functions Lesson #12:
Practice Test

Relations and Functions Lesson #12: Practice Test **489 to 494** Relations and Functions Lesson #12

1. C	2. B	3. D

4. $C = 98 + 0.12(780)$
$= 191.6$
(A.) $191.60

5. $3 - 2(-6)^2 = -69$
$3 - 2(-4)^2 = -29$
$3 - 2(0)^2 = 3$
(D.) -29

$3 - 2(2)^2 = -5$
$3 - 2(5)^2 = -47$

6. $f(-2) = -4$
$f(2) = -4$
$0 + (-4) = -4$
(A.) -4

7. $P(6) = 5(6) + 2$
$= 32$
(C.) 32

8. $P(b) = 5b + 2 = 6$
$5b = 4$
$b = \frac{4}{5}$
(B.) $\frac{4}{5}$

9. **(C.)**

10. x_{int} $f(x) = 0$
$f(x) = 4x - 10$.
$0 = 4x - 10$
$10 = 4x$
$x = 2.5$
(C.) 2.5

11. $2 = (P)(0) + q$ $q = 2$
$3 = (P)(1) + q$ $P + q = 3$
(C.) $p = 1, q = 2$ $P + 2 = 3$ $P = 1$

12. $3^{-a} = \frac{1}{81}$
$81 = 3^a$
$\frac{1}{3^a} = \frac{1}{81}$
$a = 4$
(A.) 4

13. $g(2x-1) = \frac{2}{3}(2x-1) + 6$
$= \frac{4}{3}x - \frac{2}{3} + 6$
$= \frac{4}{3}x + \frac{16}{3}$
(B.) $\frac{4}{3}x + \frac{16}{3}$

14.
A. 4312
(B.) 3412
C. 3124
D. none of the above

1. $P(-3) = (-3)^2 - 4(-3) - 2 = 19$
2. $P(-3) = \frac{1}{3}(-3) + 14 = 13$
3. $P(-3) = 3(-3)^2 + (-3) = 24$
4. $P(-3) = 7 - 5(-3) = 22$

15. **(D.)** Coordinate

Numerical Response

1. $y = 0$ $2x^2 = 7$
$x^2 = \frac{7}{2}$
$x = \sqrt{\frac{7}{2}}$
$= 1.87$
$\boxed{1.87}$

2.

y-intercept	x-intercept
$x = 0$	$y = 0$
$-3y = 12$	$4x^2 = 12$
$\frac{-3y}{-3} = \frac{12}{-3}$	$x^2 = 3$
$y = -4$	$x = \pm\sqrt{3}$

$abc = (\sqrt{3})(-\sqrt{3})(-4)$
$= 12$
$\boxed{12}$

3. $n \geq 0$ $C \geq 98$
$\boxed{9800}$

482
(continued)

Relations and Functions Lesson #11: *Interpreting Graphs of Functions*

Assignment

Relations and Functions Lesson #11: Assignment Pages **483 to 488** Relations and Functions Lesson #11

1. a) see table below

	Line 1	Line 2	Line 3
Distance (km)	4	4	4
Time (hrs)	2/3	1	$\frac{1}{3}$
Rate (km/hr)	6	4	12
Student	Chelsea	Brittany	Amanda

b) i) Chelsea and Brittany leave home at the same time.

   ii) Chelsea and Amanda arrive at school.

   iii) Amanda overtakes Brittany.

   iv) Amanda leaves home 20 minutes
        after Brittany and Chelsea.

c) The steeper the graph, the less time is taken to travel to school. The steepest slope represents the cyclist Amanda, the next steepest slope represents the runner Chelsea, and the remaining line represents the walker Brittany.

2. Tyler hits the ball through the air for a distance of 195 yards. The ball bounces twice and rolls into the hole. The golf shot travelled a total of 206 yards, and had a maximum height of 35 yards.

3. Dar left home at 8:00 AM with 3/4 tank of gas in his car. He drove for about one hour, had a meeting for about 1/2 hour, drove for about 1/2 hours, had a second meeting for one hour, and drove for about one hour. He refueled at 1 pm and had a lunch meeting for about 2 hours. He then drove home and arrived about 5 p.m. with a quarter tank of gas left.

4. The Territory is older than the Yukon, and its purchase price was less. Both the Territory and the Yukon are the same length, but the Territory can achieve a greater maximum speed.

5. see graph below

6. a) The number of hours of daylight per day over a period of two years for a location
      in the northern hemisphere.
   b) The value of a car depreciating over time.

7. a)
   b)
   c)
   d)

8. The graph is not a function. The person cannot be at three different places at the same time.
9. A   10. E   11. D   12. F   13. B

Characteristics of Linear Relations Lesson #1: Line Segments on a Cartesian Plane

Length of a Horizontal Line Segment

Consider the line segments shown on the grid.

a) Find the length of each line segment by counting.

- length of AB is __6__ units.
- length of CD is __10__ units.
- length of EF is __7__ units.

b) Determine the coordinates of the endpoints of each line segment.

- $AB \rightarrow$ $A(2,8)$ $B(8,8)$
- $CD \rightarrow$ $C(-3,4)$ $D(7,4)$
- $EF \rightarrow$ $E(-9,-6)$ $F(-2,-6)$

c) Complete the following.

- The difference in the x-coordinates, $x_B - x_A$, is __6__ .
- The difference in the x-coordinates, $x_D - x_C$, is __10__ .
- The difference in the x-coordinates, $x_F - x_E$, is __7__ .

d) How can the coordinates of the end points of a horizontal line segment be used to find the length of the line segment?

Subtract the x-coordinate of the left endpoint from the x-coordinate of the right endpoint.

Class Ex. #1

a) Line segment AB has endpoints $A(2,8)$ to $B(-5,8)$. Determine the length of $\overline{AB}$.

$$\text{length} = x_A - x_B = 2-(-5) = 7$$

b) Determine the length of the line segment from $P(a-2, b)$ to $Q(a+4, b)$.

$$\text{length} = x_Q - x_P = (a+4)-(a-2)$$
$$= a+4-a+2 = 6$$

Numerical Response

4. $f(x+2) = 1-2(x+2)-5(x+2)^2$

$= 1-2x-4-5(x^2+4x+4)$

$= 1-2x-4-5x^2-20x-20$

$= -5x^2-22x-23$

$a = -5$
$b = -22$
$c = -23$

$a-b-c$
$= -5-(-22)-(-23)$
$= 40$ **[4][0]**

5. $f(5) = \dfrac{5}{5+4} = \dfrac{5}{9}$ $f(5^{-1}) = \dfrac{5^{-1}}{5^{-1}+4} = \dfrac{\frac{1}{5}}{\frac{1}{5}+4} = \dfrac{1}{21}$ $\dfrac{5}{9} - \dfrac{1}{21} = \dfrac{32}{63}$

[3][2] $P = 32$

Written Response - 5 marks

1. • How high is the jet at the start of the dive?

$t=0$ $h = 81$ **81 m**

• How high is the jet above ground level at its lowest point?

Use "minimum" feature. y-coord   **60.75 m**

• When does the jet reach its lowest point in the dive?

x-coord of minimum point   After **4.5 sec**

• How high is the jet two seconds into its dive?

$x=2$ **67 m**

• After how many seconds does this height occur again within the jet's stunt dive?

graph $y_2 = 67$ "intersect"   **7 seconds**

graph $y: x^2-9x+81$

Length of a Vertical Line Segment

Consider the line segments shown on the grid.

a) Find the lengths of each line segment by counting.
- length of *GH* is __12__ units.
- length of *IJ* is __5__ units.
- length of *KL* is __6__ units.

b) Determine the coordinates of the endpoints of each line segment.
- $GH \rightarrow$ $G(-3,-8)$ $H(-3,4)$
- $IJ \rightarrow$ $I(1,2)$ $J(1,7)$
- $KL \rightarrow$ $K(6,-8)$ $L(6,-2)$

c) Complete the following.
- The difference in the y-coordinates, $y_H - y_G$, is __12__ .
- The difference in the y-coordinates, $y_J - y_I$, is __5__ .
- The difference in the y-coordinates, $y_L - y_K$, is __6__ .

d) How can the coordinates of the end points of a vertical line segment be used to find the length of the line segment?

Subtract the y-coordinate of the lower endpoint from the y-coordinate of the higher endpoint

Class Ex. #2

a) Line segment *RS* has endpoints $R(1,-4)$ to $S(1,-9)$. Determine the length of $\overline{RS}$.

length $= -4-(-9) = 5$

b) Determine the length of the line segment from $P(a,b)$ to $Q(a,b+10)$.

length $= b+10-b = 10$

Class Ex. #3

$AP = 10$ $AB^2 = 10^2 + 4^2 = 116$
$BP = 4$ $AB = \sqrt{116} = \sqrt{4} \cdot \sqrt{29}$
$\qquad\qquad = 2\sqrt{29}$
$\qquad\qquad = 10.8$

$CQ = 8$ $CD^2 = 8^2 + 4^2 = 80$
$DQ = 4$ $CD = \sqrt{80} = \sqrt{16} \cdot \sqrt{5}$
$\qquad\qquad = 4\sqrt{5}$
$\qquad\qquad = 8.9$

Assignment

Characteristics ... Lesson #1: Assignment Pages **498 to 502** Characteristics ... Lesson #1

1. a) $A(2,7)$ to $B(5,7)$ b) $C(-5,3)$ to $D(-5,12)$
   $\quad 5-2 = 3$ $\qquad 12-3 = 9$
   c) $E(2,-8)$ to $F(2,3)$ d) $G(8,-12)$ to $H(-5,-12)$
   $\quad 3-(-8) = 11$ $\qquad 8-(-5) = 13$

2. a) $I(-3,-8)$ to $J(-3,-3)$ b) $K(7,-10)$ to $L(-35,-10)$
   $\quad -3-(-8) = 5$ $\qquad 7-(-35) = 42$
   c) $M(-325,-892)$ to $N(255,-892)$ d) $P(7251,-1286)$ to $Q(7251,1289)$
   $\quad 255-(-325) = 580$ $\qquad 1289-(-1286) = 2575$

3. a) $A(p,q)$ to $B(p-4,q)$ b) $C(m-3,n+5)$ to $D(m-3,n+12)$
   $\quad$ horizontal $\qquad$ vertical
   $\quad$ length $= p-(p-4) = p-p+4 = 4$ $\quad$ length $= (n+12)-(n+5): n+12-n-5 = 7$
   c) $J(a,b)$ to $K(c,b)$ where $a > c$ d) $M(s,t)$ to $N(s,z)$, where $t > z$
   $\quad$ horizontal $\qquad$ vertical
   $\quad$ length $= a-c$ $\qquad$ length $= t-z$

4.
   base $= 13$ height $= 8$
   $A = \frac{1}{2}bh = \frac{1}{2}(13)(8)$
   $\qquad\qquad = 52$ unit^2

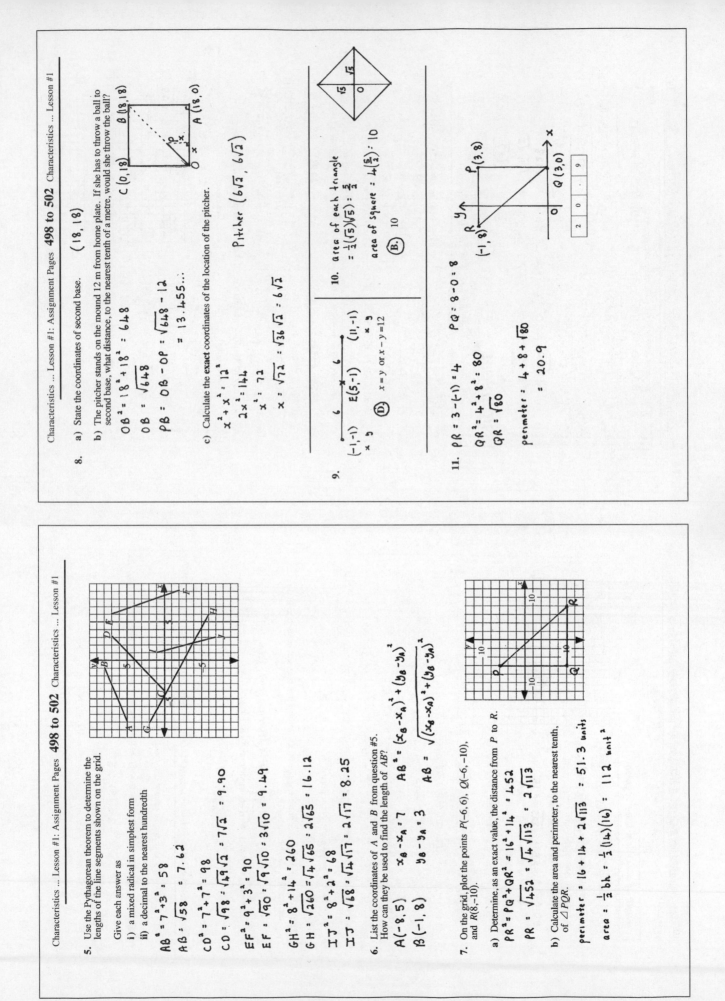

8.
a) State the coordinates of second base. $(18, 18)$

b) The pitcher stands on the mound 12 m from home plate. If she has to throw a ball to second base, what distance, to the nearest tenth of a metre, would she throw the ball?

$C(0,18)$ $B(18,18)$

$OB^2 = 18^2 + 18^2 = 648$

$OB = \sqrt{648}$

$PB = OB - OP = \sqrt{648} - 12$

$= 13.455...$

c) Calculate the **exact** coordinates of the location of the pitcher.

$x^2 + x^2 = 12^2$

$2x^2 = 144$

$x^2 = 72$

$x = \sqrt{72} = \sqrt{36}\sqrt{2} = 6\sqrt{2}$

Pitcher $(6\sqrt{2}, 6\sqrt{2})$

9.

$(-1,-1)$ 6 $(11,-1)$

$E(5,-1)$

(D) $x = y$ or $x - y = 12$

---

10. area of each triangle

$= \frac{1}{2}(\sqrt{5})(\sqrt{5}) = \frac{5}{2}$

area of square $= 4\left(\frac{5}{2}\right) = 10$

B.   10

---

11. $PR = 3 - (-1) = 4$ $PQ = 8 - 0 = 8$

$QR^2 = 4^2 + 8^2 = 80$

$QR = \sqrt{80}$

perimeter $= 4 + 8 + \sqrt{80}$

$= 20.9$

$P(3,8)$
$R(-1,8)$
$Q(3,0)$

2	0	.	9

---

5. Use the Pythagorean theorem to determine the lengths of the line segments shown on the grid.

Give each answer as
i) a mixed radical in simplest form
ii) a decimal to the nearest hundredth

$AB^2 = 7^2 + 3^2 = 58$

$AB = \sqrt{58} = 7.62$

$CD^2 = 7^2 + 7^2 = 98$

$CD = \sqrt{98} = \sqrt{49}\sqrt{2} = 7\sqrt{2} = 9.90$

$EF^2 = 9^2 + 3^2 = 90$

$EF = \sqrt{90} = \sqrt{9}\sqrt{10} = 3\sqrt{10} = 9.49$

$GH^2 = 8^2 + 14^2 = 260$

$GH = \sqrt{260} = \sqrt{4}\sqrt{65} = 2\sqrt{65} = 16.12$

$IJ^2 = 8^2 + 2^2 = 68$

$IJ = \sqrt{68} = \sqrt{4}\sqrt{17} = 2\sqrt{17} = 8.25$

6. List the coordinates of A and B from question #5. How can they be used to find the length of AB?

$A(-8,5)$ $x_B - x_A = 7$ $AB^2 = (x_B - x_A)^2 + (y_B - y_A)^2$

$B(-1,8)$ $y_B - y_A = 3$ $AB = \sqrt{(x_B - x_A)^2 + (y_B - y_A)^2}$

7. On the grid, plot the points $P(-6, 6)$, $Q(-6, -10)$, and $R(8, -10)$.

a) Determine, as an exact value, the distance from P to R.

$PR^2 = PQ^2 + QR^2 = 16^2 + 14^2 = 452$

$PR = \sqrt{452} = \sqrt{4}\sqrt{113} = 2\sqrt{113}$

b) Calculate the area and perimeter, to the nearest tenth, of $\triangle PQR$.

perimeter $= 16 + 14 + 2\sqrt{113} = 51.3$ units

area $= \frac{1}{2}bh = \frac{1}{2}(14)(16) = 112$ unit^2

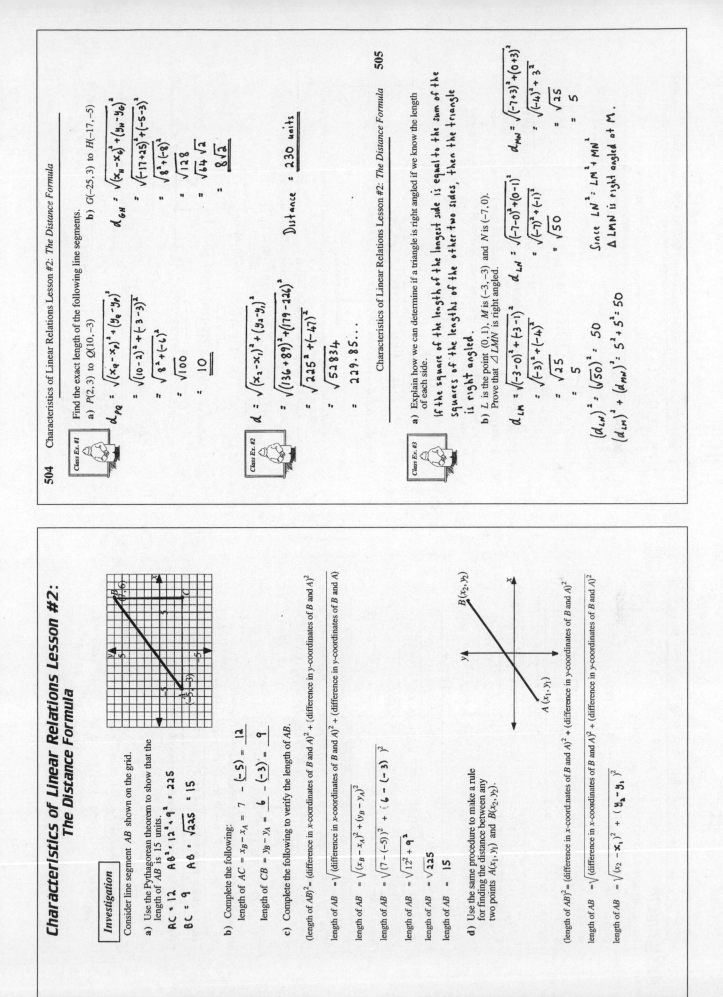

Characteristics of Linear Relations Lesson #2: The Distance Formula

Investigation

Consider line segment AB shown on the grid.

a) Use the Pythagorean theorem to show that the length of AB is 15 units.

$AC = 12$ $AB^2 = 12^2 + 9^2 = 225$
$BC = 9$ $AB = \sqrt{225} = 15$

b) Complete the following:

length of $AC = x_B - x_A = 7 - (\underline{-5}) = \underline{12}$

length of $CB = y_B - y_A = 6 - (\underline{-3}) = \underline{9}$

c) Complete the following to verify the length of AB.

(length of $AB)^2 =$ (difference in x-coordinates of B and $A)^2$ + (difference in y-coordinates of B and $A)^2$

length of $AB = \sqrt{(x_B - x_A)^2 + (y_B - y_A)^2}$

length of $AB = \sqrt{(7-(-5))^2 + (6 - (-3))^2}$

length of $AB = \sqrt{12^2 + 9^2}$

length of $AB = \sqrt{225}$

length of $AB = 15$

d) Use the same procedure to make a rule for finding the distance between any two points $A(x_1, y_1)$ and $B(x_2, y_2)$.

(length of $AB)^2 =$ (difference in x-coordinates of B and $A)^2$ + (difference in y-coordinates of B and $A)^2

length of $AB = \sqrt{(\text{difference in x-coordinates of } B \text{ and } A)^2 + (\text{difference in y-coordinates of } B \text{ and } A)^2}$

length of $AB = \sqrt{(x_2 - x_1)^2 + (y_2 - y_1)^2}$

---

504   Characteristics of Linear Relations Lesson #2: *The Distance Formula*

Class Ex. #1

Find the exact length of the following line segments.

a) $P(2,3)$ to $Q(10,-3)$

b) $G(-25,3)$ to $H(-17,-5)$

$d_{PQ} = \sqrt{(x_Q - x_P)^2 + (y_Q - y_P)^2}$
$= \sqrt{(10-2)^2 + (-3-3)^2}$
$= \sqrt{8^2 + (-6)^2}$
$= \sqrt{100}$
$= 10$

$d_{GH} = \sqrt{(x_H - x_G)^2 + (y_H - y_G)^2}$
$= \sqrt{(-17+25)^2 + (-5-3)^2}$
$= \sqrt{8^2 + (-8)^2}$
$= \sqrt{128}$
$= \sqrt{64}\sqrt{2}$
$= 8\sqrt{2}$

Class Ex. #2

$d = \sqrt{(x_2 - x_1)^2 + (y_3 - y_1)^2}$
$= \sqrt{(136+89)^2 + (179-226)^2}$
$= \sqrt{225^2 + (-47)^2}$
$= \sqrt{52834}$
$= 229.85...$

Distance $= 230$ units

Characteristics of Linear Relations Lesson #2: *The Distance Formula*   505

Class Ex. #3

a) Explain how we can determine if a triangle is right angled if we know the length of each side.

If the square of the length of the longest side is equal to the sum of the squares of the lengths of the other two sides, then the triangle is right angled.

b) L is the point $(0,1)$, M is $(-3,-3)$ and N is $(-7,0)$. Prove that $\triangle LMN$ is right angled.

$d_{LM} = \sqrt{(-3-0)^2 + (-3-1)^2}$
$= \sqrt{(-3)^2 + (-4)^2}$
$= \sqrt{25}$
$= 5$

$d_{MN} = \sqrt{(-7+3)^2 + (0+3)^2}$
$= \sqrt{(-4)^2 + 3^2}$
$= \sqrt{25}$
$= 5$

$d_{LN} = \sqrt{(-7-0)^2 + (0-1)^2}$
$= \sqrt{(-7)^2 + (-1)^2}$
$= \sqrt{50}$

$(d_{LN})^2 = (\sqrt{50})^2 = 50$
$(d_{LM})^2 + (d_{MN})^2 = 5^2 + 5^2 = 50$

Since $LN^2 = LM^2 + MN^2$
$\triangle LMN$ is right angled at M.

Assignment

1. a) $A(2, 0)$ and $B(7, 12)$

$d_{AB} = \sqrt{(7-2)^2 + (12-0)^2}$
$= \sqrt{5^2 + 12^2}$
$= \sqrt{169}$
$= 13$

b) $C(3, 7)$ and $D(6, 11)$

$d_{CD} = \sqrt{(6-3)^2 + (11-7)^2}$
$= \sqrt{3^2 + 4^2}$
$= \sqrt{25}$
$= 5$

2. a) $P(4, 0)$ and $Q(-2, -7)$

$d_{PQ} = \sqrt{(-2-4)^2 + (-7-0)^2}$
$= \sqrt{(-6)^2 + (-7)^2}$
$= \sqrt{85}$
$= 9.22$

b) $R(-2.3, 8.9)$ and $S(-3.4, -6.8)$

$d_{RS} = \sqrt{(-3.4 + 2.3)^2 + (-6.8 - 8.9)^2}$
$= \sqrt{(-1.1)^2 + (-15.7)^2}$
$= \sqrt{247.7}$
$= 15.74$

3. a) $E(6, 1)$ and $F(-2, -3)$

$d_{EF} = \sqrt{(-2-6)^2 + (-3-1)^2}$
$= \sqrt{(-8)^2 + (-4)^2}$
$= \sqrt{80} = \sqrt{16}\sqrt{5} = 4\sqrt{5}$

b) $K(-\frac{1}{2}, \frac{5}{2})$ and $L(1, 3)$

$d_{KL} = \sqrt{(1 + \frac{1}{2})^2 + (3 - \frac{5}{2})^2}$
$= \sqrt{(\frac{3}{2})^2 + (\frac{1}{2})^2}$
$= \sqrt{\frac{10}{4}} = \frac{\sqrt{10}}{\sqrt{4}} = \frac{\sqrt{10}}{2}$

4. a) Calculate the lengths of PQ, QR, and PR. What do you notice?

$d_{PQ} = \sqrt{(1+2)^2 + (6-2)^2}$
$= \sqrt{3^2 + 4^2}$
$= \sqrt{25} = 5$

$d_{QR} = \sqrt{(7-1)^2 + (14-6)^2}$
$= \sqrt{6^2 + 8^2}$
$= \sqrt{100} = 10$

$d_{PR} = \sqrt{(7+2)^2 + (14-2)^2}$
$= \sqrt{9^2 + 12^2}$
$= \sqrt{225} = 15$

$d_{PQ} + d_{QR} = d_{PR}$

b) What does this mean with regard to the points P, Q, and R?

The points P, Q, and R lie on a straight line.

5. a) Calculate the exact lengths of AB, BC, and AC in entire radical form.

$d_{AB} = \sqrt{(4-6)^2 + (4+2)^2}$
$= \sqrt{(-2)^2 + 6^2}$
$= \sqrt{40}$

$d_{BC} = \sqrt{(-3-4)^2 + (-5-4)^2}$
$= \sqrt{(-7)^2 + (-9)^2}$
$= \sqrt{130}$

$d_{AC} = \sqrt{(-3-6)^2 + (-5+2)^2}$
$= \sqrt{(-9)^2 + (-3)^2}$
$= \sqrt{90}$

b) Show how you can use the answers in a) to prove that $\angle BAC$ is a right angle.

$(d_{AB})^2 + (d_{AC})^2 : 40 + 90 = 130$
$(d_{BC})^2 : 130$

$\triangle BAC$ is right angled at A
because $BC^2 = AB^2 + AC^2$

so $\angle BAC$ is a right angle

---

6. a) $(15, 7)$ $(4, 38)$

b) Determine the length of the pass (to the nearest yard).

$d = \sqrt{(4-15)^2 + (38-7)^2}$
$= \sqrt{(-11)^2 + 31^2}$
$= \sqrt{1082}$
$= 32.89...$

length of pass = 33 yards

7. a) Taking the corner of the soccer field as the origin, list the coordinates of each home.

$J(-6, 5)$ $B(3, -4)$

b) If a block represents 135 metres, determine the direct distance, to the nearest metre, between their homes.

$d_{JB} = \sqrt{(3+6)^2 + (-4-5)^2}$
$= \sqrt{9^2 + (-9)^2}$
$= \sqrt{162}$ blocks or $\sqrt{81}\sqrt{2} = 9\sqrt{2}$ blocks

distance in metres : $135\sqrt{162}$
$= 1718$ metres

8. a) Describe the starting position relative to the family home in Grand Forks for the part of the route which is shown.

175 km north of Grand Forks.

b) Calculate the distance, to the nearest km, travelled by the van from A to E.

$d_{AB} = \sqrt{(278-0)^2 + (217-175)^2} = 281.15... $ km
$d_{BC} = \sqrt{(325-278)^2 + (89-217)^2} = 54.70...$ km
$d_{CD} = \sqrt{(436-325)^2 + (225-189)^2} = 115.74...$ km
$d_{DE} = \sqrt{(525-435)^2 + (185-225)^2} = 98.48...$ km

total $= 550.4...$
$= 550$ km

c) $\frac{550}{5} \times 95 \cancel{c} = \$104.50$

9. $d = \sqrt{(6-2)^2 + (2+1)^2}$
$= \sqrt{4^2 + 3^2}$
$= \sqrt{25}$
$= 5$ Ⓐ   5

10. $r = \sqrt{(0+6)^2 + (0+8)^2}$
$= \sqrt{6^2 + 8^2}$
$= \sqrt{100}$
$= 10$

Ⓒ   10

11. Which of the following points is equidistant from $A(-2,7)$ and $B(-6,-5)$?

A. $(0,-4)$ P
B. $(7,-10)$ Q
C. $(-1,0)$ R
D. $(4,-5)$ S

(A.) $d_{AP} = \sqrt{(0+2)^2+(-4-7)^2} = \sqrt{2^2+(-11)^2} = \sqrt{125}$
$d_{BP} = \sqrt{(0+6)^2+(-4+5)^2} = \sqrt{6^2+1^2} = \sqrt{37}$ ✗
not equidistant

(B.) $d_{AQ} = \sqrt{(7+2)^2+(-10-7)^2} = \sqrt{9^2+(-17)^2} = \sqrt{370}$
$d_{BQ} = \sqrt{(7+6)^2+(-10+5)^2} = \sqrt{13^2+(-5)^2} = \sqrt{194}$ ✗
not equidistant

(C.) $d_{AR} = \sqrt{(-1+2)^2+(0-7)^2} = \sqrt{1^2+(-7)^2} = \sqrt{50}$
$d_{BR} = \sqrt{(-1+6)^2+(0+5)^2} = \sqrt{5^2+5^2} = \sqrt{50}$ ✓
equidistant

(D.) $d_{AS} = \sqrt{(4+2)^2+(-5-7)^2} = \sqrt{6^2+(-12)^2} = \sqrt{180}$
$d_{BS} = \sqrt{(4+6)^2+(-5+5)^2} = \sqrt{10^2+0^2} = 10$ ✗
not equidistant

12. radius $= \sqrt{(4+5)^2+(-3-9)^2} = \sqrt{9^2+(-12)^2} = \sqrt{225} = 15$
diameter $= 2 \times 15 = 30$ **30.0**

Characteristics of Linear Relations Lesson #3:
The Midpoint of a Line Segment

Warm-Up #1
a)
b) A(1,3)
   B(9,3)
Determine the average (mean) of the x-coordinates.

Warm-Up #2
a)
b) C(3,6)
   D(3,-4)
Determine the average (mean) of the y-coordinates.

Warm-Up #3
a) M(-4,3)
b) Determine the average of the x-coordinates and the average of the y-coordinates.
c) $x_M = \dfrac{x_1+x_2}{2}$ $y_M = \dfrac{y_1+y_2}{2}$

Class Ex. #1 Determine the coordinates of the midpoint of the line segment with the given pair of endpoints.

a) $P(4,7)$, $Q(12,3)$ b) $E(-5,7)$, $F(-11,-2)$ c) $A(w+3, 2w)$, $C(5w-1, 7w+1)$

$M\left(\dfrac{4+12}{2}, \dfrac{7+3}{2}\right)$ $M\left(\dfrac{-5-11}{2}, \dfrac{7-2}{2}\right)$ $M\left(\dfrac{w+3+5w-1}{2}, \dfrac{2w+7w+1}{2}\right)$

$M(8,5)$ $M\left(-8, \dfrac{5}{2}\right)$ $M\left(\dfrac{6w+2}{2}, \dfrac{9w+1}{2}\right)$

$M\left(3w+1, \dfrac{9w+1}{2}\right)$

Class Ex. #2

$x_M = \dfrac{5-11}{2} = -3$

$\dfrac{y_P-10}{2} = -6 \qquad y_P-10 = -12 \qquad y_P = -2$

Assignment

1. a) $A(2,6)$, $C(4,16)$ b) $X(-3,-8)$, $Y(-11,0)$ c) $K(15,-17)$, $L(-11,3)$
$M\left(\dfrac{2+4}{2}, \dfrac{6+16}{2}\right)$ $M\left(\dfrac{-3-11}{2}, \dfrac{-8+0}{2}\right)$ $M\left(\dfrac{15-11}{2}, \dfrac{-17+3}{2}\right)$
$M(3, 11)$ $M(-7,-4)$ $M(2,-7)$

d) $A(-25,56)$, $O(0,0)$ e) $P(-2.5,5.6)$, $Q(1.5,-6.4)$ f) $E(-2,7)$, $F(6,2)$
$M\left(\dfrac{-25+0}{2}, \dfrac{56+0}{2}\right)$ $M\left(\dfrac{-2.5+1.5}{2}, \dfrac{5.6-6.4}{2}\right)$ $M\left(\dfrac{-2+6}{2}, \dfrac{7+2}{2}\right)$
$M\left(-\dfrac{25}{2}, 28\right)$ $M(-0.5, -0.4)$ $M\left(2, \dfrac{9}{2}\right)$

2. a) $C(3x,8y)$, $D(7x,-4y)$ b) $S(a+b, a+7b)$, $T(a+b, a-3b)$
$M\left(\dfrac{3x+7x}{2}, \dfrac{8y-4y}{2}\right)$ $M\left(\dfrac{a+b+a+b}{2}, \dfrac{a+7b+a-3b}{2}\right)$
$M(5x, 2y)$ $M(a+b, a+2b)$

c) $A(p+3, q-2)$, $B(p-1, q+8)$ d) $U(m-5n, m+n)$, $V(3n-m, m-m-n)$
$M\left(\dfrac{p+3+p-1}{2}, \dfrac{q-2+q+8}{2}\right)$ $M\left(\dfrac{m-5n+3n-m}{2}, \dfrac{m+n+m-n}{2}\right)$
$M(p+1, q+3)$ $M(-n, m)$

3. $A(-6,4)$ $B(12,-8)$
$\qquad\qquad P \qquad M(3,-2) \qquad Q$

$M\left(\dfrac{-6+12}{2}, \dfrac{4-8}{2}\right)$ $P\left(\dfrac{-6+3}{2}, \dfrac{4-2}{2}\right)$ $Q\left(\dfrac{3+12}{2}, \dfrac{-2-8}{2}\right)$
$M(3,-2)$ $P\left(-\dfrac{3}{2}, 1\right)$ $Q\left(\dfrac{15}{2}, -5\right)$
The points are $\left(-\dfrac{3}{2}, 1\right)$, $(3,-2)$, and $\left(\dfrac{15}{2}, -5\right)$

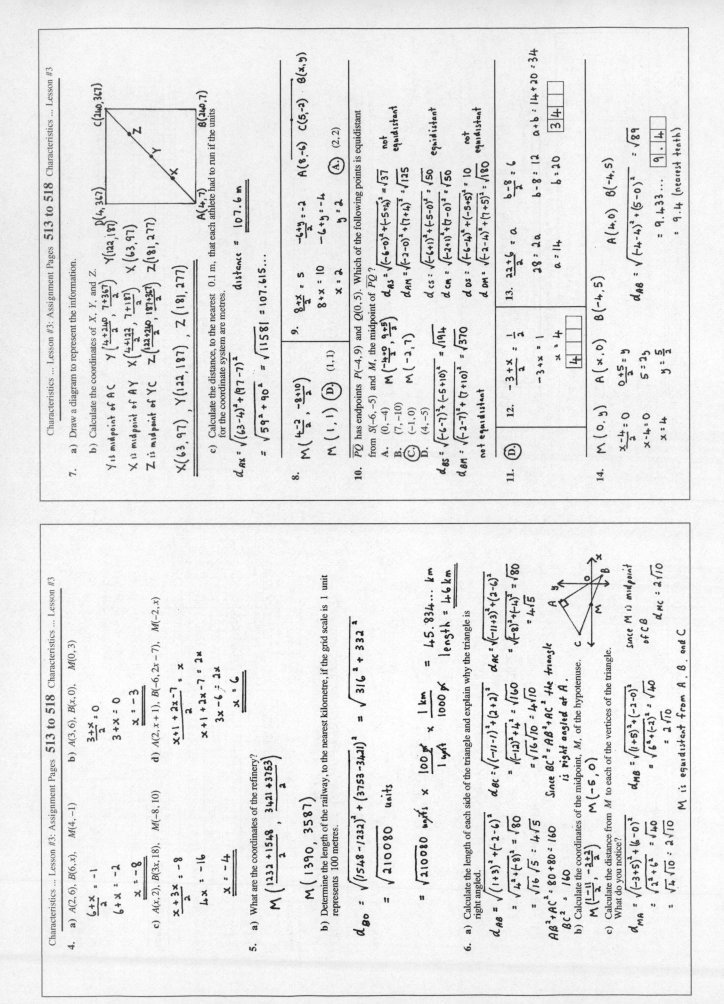

7. a) Draw a diagram to represent the information.

b) Calculate the coordinates of X, Y, and Z.

Y is midpoint of AC $Y\left(\frac{4+240}{2}, \frac{7+367}{2}\right)$ $Y(122, 187)$

X is midpoint of AY $X\left(\frac{4+122}{2}, \frac{7+187}{2}\right)$ $X(63, 97)$

Z is midpoint of YC $Z\left(\frac{122+240}{2}, \frac{187+367}{2}\right)$ $Z(181, 277)$

$X(63, 97)$, $Y(122, 187)$, $Z(181, 277)$

c) Calculate the distance, to the nearest 0.1 m, that each athlete had to run if the units for the coordinate system are metres.

distance $= 107.6$ m

$d_{AX} = \sqrt{(63-4)^2 + (97-7)^2}$

$= \sqrt{59^2 + 90^2} = \sqrt{11581} = 107.615...$

8. $M\left(\frac{4+-2}{2}, \frac{-8+10}{2}\right)$

$M(1, 1)$ (D) $(1,1)$

9. $\frac{8+x}{2} = 5$ $\frac{-6+y}{2} = -2$

$8 + x = 10$ $-6 + y = -4$

$x = 2$ $y = 2$

$A(8, -6)$ $C(5, -2)$ $B(x, y)$ (A.) $(2,2)$

10. $\overline{PQ}$ has endpoints $P(-4, 9)$ and $Q(0, 5)$. Which of the following points is equidistant from $S(-6, -5)$ and M, the midpoint of $\overline{PQ}$?

A. $(0, -4)$
B. $(7, -10)$
C. $(-1, 0)$
D. $(4, -5)$

$M\left(\frac{-4+0}{2}, \frac{9+5}{2}\right)$ $M(-2, 7)$

$d_{AS} = \sqrt{(-6-0)^2 + (-5-4)^2} = \sqrt{37}$ not equidistant

$d_{AM} = \sqrt{(-2-0)^2 + (7+4)^2} = \sqrt{125}$

$d_{CS} = \sqrt{(-6+1)^2 + (-5-0)^2} = \sqrt{50}$ equidistant

$d_{CM} = \sqrt{(-2+1)^2 + (7-0)^2} = \sqrt{50}$

$d_{DS} = \sqrt{(-6-4)^2 + (-5-5)^2} = \sqrt{10}$ not equidistant

$d_{DM} = \sqrt{(-2-4)^2 + (7+5)^2} = \sqrt{180}$

$d_{BS} = \sqrt{(-6-7)^2 + (-5+10)^2} = \sqrt{194}$

$d_{BM} = \sqrt{(-2-7)^2 + (7+10)^2} = \sqrt{370}$

not equidistant

(C.) $(-1, 0)$

11. (D.)

12. $\frac{-3+x}{2} = -\frac{1}{2}$

$-3 + x = -1$

$x = 2$

4

13. $\frac{22+6}{2} = a$ $\frac{b-8}{2} = 6$

$28 = 2a$ $b - 8 = 12$

$a = 14$ $b = 20$

$a + b = 14 + 20 = 34$

34

14. $M(0, y)$ $A(x, 0)$ $B(-4, 5)$

$\frac{x-4}{2} = 0$ $\frac{0+5}{2} = y$

$x - 4 = 0$ $5 = 2y$

$x = 4$ $y = \frac{5}{2}$

$A(4, 0)$ $B(-4, 5)$

$d_{AB} = \sqrt{(-4-4)^2 + (5-0)^2} = \sqrt{89}$

$= 9.433... = 9.4$ (nearest tenth)

9 . 4

---

4. a) $A(2, 6)$, $B(6, x)$, $M(4, -1)$ b) $A(3, 6)$, $B(x, 0)$, $M(0, 3)$

$\frac{6+x}{2} = -1$ $\frac{3+x}{2} = 0$

$6 + x = -2$ $3 + x = 0$

$x = -8$ $x = -3$

c) $A(x, 2)$, $B(3x, 18)$, $M(-8, 10)$ d) $A(2, x+1)$, $B(-6, 2x-7)$, $M(-2, x)$

$\frac{x+3x}{2} = -8$ $\frac{x+1+2x-7}{2} = x$

$4x = -16$ $x+1+2x-7 = 2x$

$x = -4$ $3x - 6 = 2x$

                     $x = 6$

5. a) What are the coordinates of the refinery?

$M\left(\frac{1232+1548}{2}, \frac{3421+3753}{2}\right)$

$M(1390, 3587)$

b) Determine the length of the railway, to the nearest kilometre, if the grid scale is 1 unit represents 100 metres.

$d_{BO} = \sqrt{(1548-1232)^2 + (3753-3421)^2} = \sqrt{316^2 + 332^2}$

$= \sqrt{210080}$ units

$= \sqrt{210080}$ units $\times \frac{100 \text{ m}}{1 \text{ unit}} \times \frac{1 \text{ km}}{1000 \text{ m}} = 45.834... \text{ km}$

$\text{length} = 46 \text{ km}$

6. a) Calculate the length of each side of the triangle and explain why the triangle is right angled.

$d_{AB} = \sqrt{(1+3)^2 + (-2-6)^2}$ $d_{BC} = \sqrt{(-11-1)^2 + (2+2)^2}$ $d_{AC} = \sqrt{(-11+3)^2 + (2-6)^2}$

$= \sqrt{4^2 + (-8)^2} = \sqrt{80}$ $= \sqrt{(-12)^2 + 4^2} = \sqrt{160}$ $= \sqrt{(-8)^2 + (-4)^2} = \sqrt{80}$

$= \sqrt{16} \sqrt{5} = 4\sqrt{5}$ $= \sqrt{16} \sqrt{10} = 4\sqrt{10}$ $= 4\sqrt{5}$

$AB^2 + AC^2 = 80 + 80 = 160$

$BC^2 = 160$

Since $BC^2 = AB^2 + AC^2$ the triangle is right angled at A.

b) Calculate the coordinates of the midpoint, M, of the hypotenuse.

$M\left(\frac{1-11}{2}, \frac{-2+2}{2}\right)$ $M(-5, 0)$

c) Calculate the distance from M to each of the vertices of the triangle. What do you notice?

$d_{MA} = \sqrt{(-5+5)^2 + (6-0)^2}$ $d_{MB} = \sqrt{(1+5)^2 + (-2-0)^2}$

$= \sqrt{2^2 + 6^2} = \sqrt{40}$ $= \sqrt{6^2 + (-2)^2} = \sqrt{40}$

$= \sqrt{4} \sqrt{10} = 2\sqrt{10}$ $= 2\sqrt{10}$

Since M is midpoint of CB

$d_{MC} = 2\sqrt{10}$

M is equidistant from A, B, and C

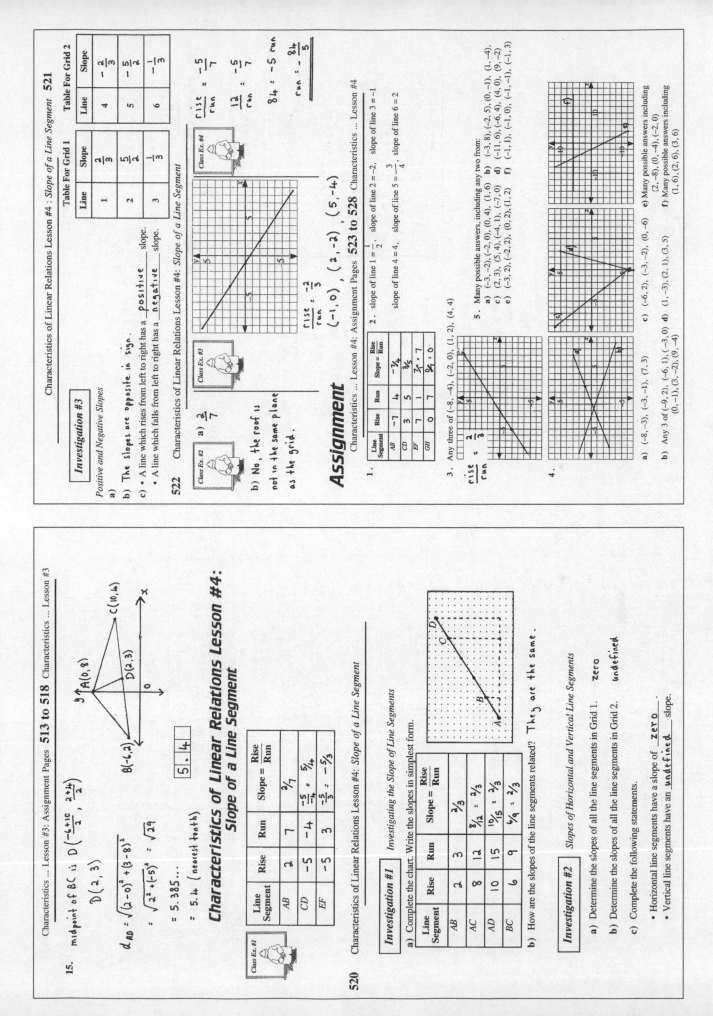

Characteristics of Linear Relations Lesson #4: *Slope of a Line Segment* 521

Table For Grid 1

Line	Slope
1	$\frac{2}{3}$
2	$\frac{5}{2}$
3	$-\frac{1}{3}$

Table For Grid 2

Line	Slope
4	$-\frac{2}{3}$
5	$-\frac{5}{2}$
6	$-\frac{1}{3}$

Investigation #3

Positive and Negative Slopes

a)

b) The slopes are opposite in sign.

c) • A line which rises from left to right has a **positive** slope.
   • A line which falls from left to right has a **negative** slope.

522   Characteristics of Linear Relations Lesson #4: *Slope of a Line Segment*

Class Ex. #2   a) $\frac{2}{7}$

Class Ex. #3   b) No, the roof is not in the same plane as the grid.

Class Ex. #4

$\frac{rise}{run} = \frac{-5}{7}$

$\frac{12}{run} = \frac{-5}{7}$

$84 = -5\,run$

$run = -\frac{84}{5}$

$\frac{rise}{run} = \frac{-2}{3}$

$(-1, 0)$, $(2, -2)$, $(5, -4)$

Assignment

Characteristics ... Lesson #4: Assignment Pages **523 to 528** Characteristics ... Lesson #4

1.

Line Segment	Rise	Run	Slope = Rise/Run
AB	-7	4	$-\frac{7}{4}$
CD	3	5	$\frac{3}{5}$
EF	7	1	$\frac{7}{1} = 7$
GH	0	7	$\frac{0}{7} = 0$

2. slope of line 1 $= \frac{1}{2}$,   slope of line 2 $= -2$,   slope of line 3 $= -1$
   slope of line 4 $= 4$,   slope of line 5 $= -\frac{3}{4}$,   slope of line 6 $= 2$

3. Any three of $(-8, -4)$, $(-2, 0)$, $(1, 2)$, $(4, 4)$

$\frac{rise}{run} = \frac{2}{3}$

4.

5. Many possible answers, including any two from:
   a) $(-3, -2), (-2, 0), (0, 4), (1, 6)$ b) $(-3, 8), (-2, 5), (0, -1), (1, -4)$.
   c) $(2, 3), (5, 4), (-4, 1), (-7, 0)$ d) $(-11, 6), (-6, 4), (4, 0), (9, -2)$
   e) $(-3, 2), (-2, 2), (0, 2), (1, 2)$ f) $(-1, 1), (-1, 0), (-1, -1), (-1, 3)$

a) $(-6, 2), (-3, -2), (0, -6)$

b) Any 3 of $(-9, 2), (-6, 1), (-3, 0)$ d) $(1, -3), (2, 1), (3, 5)$
   $(0, -1), (3, -2), (9, -4)$

e) Many possible answers including
   $(2, -8), (0, -4), (-2, 0)$
f) Many possible answers including
   $(1, 6), (2, 6), (3, 6)$

Characteristics ... Lesson #3: Assignment Pages **513 to 518** Characteristics ... Lesson #3

15. midpoint of BC is $D\left(\frac{-4+10}{2}, \frac{2+4}{2}\right)$

$D(2, 3)$

$d_{AD} = \sqrt{(2-0)^2 + (3-8)^2}$

$= \sqrt{2^2 + (-5)^2} = \sqrt{29}$

$= 5.385...$

$= 5.4$ (nearest tenth)

$\boxed{5.4}$

Class Ex. #1

Characteristics of Linear Relations Lesson #4:
Slope of a Line Segment

Line Segment	Rise	Run	Slope = Rise/Run
AB	2	7	$\frac{2}{7}$
CD	-5	-4	$\frac{-5}{-4} = \frac{5}{4}$
EF	-5	3	$\frac{-5}{3} = -\frac{5}{3}$

520   Characteristics of Linear Relations Lesson #4: *Slope of a Line Segment*

Investigation #1
Investigating the Slope of Line Segments

a) Complete the chart. Write the slopes in simplest form.

Line Segment	Rise	Run	Slope = Rise/Run
AB	2	3	$\frac{2}{3}$
AC	8	12	$\frac{8}{12} = \frac{2}{3}$
AD	10	15	$\frac{10}{15} = \frac{2}{3}$
BC	6	9	$\frac{6}{9} = \frac{2}{3}$

b) How are the slopes of the line segments related? They are the same.

Investigation #2
Slopes of Horizontal and Vertical Line Segments

a) Determine the slopes of all the line segments in Grid 1. **zero**

b) Determine the slopes of all the line segments in Grid 2. **undefined**

c) Complete the following statements.
   • Horizontal line segments have a slope of **zero**.
   • Vertical line segments have an **undefined** slope.

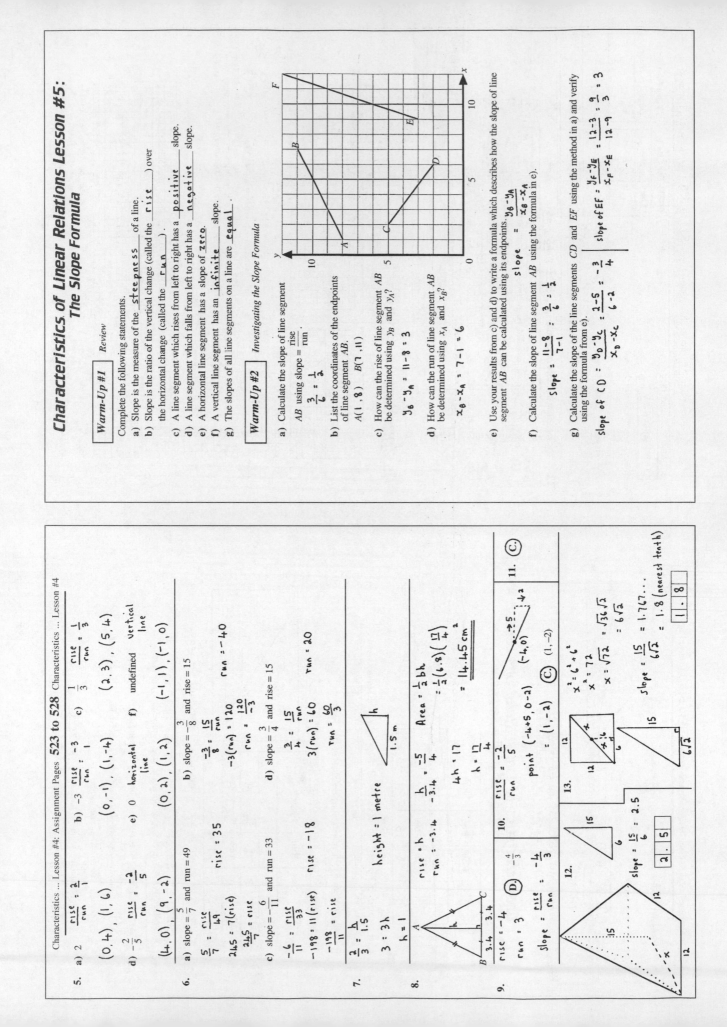

Characteristics of Linear Relations Lesson #5: The Slope Formula

Warm-Up #1   *Review*

Complete the following statements.

a) Slope is the measure of the __steepness__ of a line.

b) Slope is the ratio of the vertical change (called the __rise__) over the horizontal change (called the __run__).

c) A line segment which rises from left to right has a __positive__ slope.

d) A line segment which falls from left to right has a __negative__ slope.

e) A horizontal line segment has a slope of __zero__.

f) A vertical line segment has an __infinite__ slope.

g) The slopes of all line segments on a line are __equal__.

Warm-Up #2   *Investigating the Slope Formula*

a) Calculate the slope of line segment AB using slope = $\dfrac{\text{rise}}{\text{run}}$.

$$\dfrac{3}{6} = \dfrac{1}{2}$$

b) List the coordinates of the endpoints of line segment AB.

$A(1, 8)$ $B(7, 11)$

c) How can the rise of line segment AB be determined using y_B and y_A?

$$y_B - y_A = 11 - 8 = 3$$

d) How can the run of line segment AB be determined using x_A and x_B?

$$x_B - x_A = 7 - 1 = 6$$

e) Use your results from c) and d) to write a formula which describes how the slope of line segment AB can be calculated using its endpoints.

$$\text{slope} = \dfrac{y_B - y_A}{x_B - x_A}$$

f) Calculate the slope of line segment AB using the formula in e).

$$\text{slope} = \dfrac{11-8}{7-1} = \dfrac{3}{6} = \dfrac{1}{2}$$

g) Calculate the slope of the line segments CD and EF using the method in a) and verify using the formula from e).

$$\text{slope of } CD = \dfrac{y_D - y_C}{x_D - x_C} = \dfrac{2-5}{6-2} = \dfrac{-3}{4} \qquad \text{slope of } EF = \dfrac{y_F - y_E}{x_F - x_E} = \dfrac{12-3}{12-9} = \dfrac{9}{3} = 3$$

Characteristics ... Lesson #4: Assignment Pages **523 to 528**   Characteristics ... Lesson #4

5. a) 2 $\dfrac{\text{rise}}{\text{run}} = \dfrac{2}{1}$

$(0, 4) , (1, 6)$

b) -3 $\dfrac{\text{rise}}{\text{run}} = \dfrac{-3}{1}$

$(0, -1) , (1, -4)$

c) $\dfrac{1}{3}$ $\dfrac{\text{rise}}{\text{run}} = \dfrac{1}{3}$

$(2, 3) , (5, 4)$

d) $-\dfrac{2}{5}$ $\dfrac{\text{rise}}{\text{run}} = \dfrac{-2}{5}$

$(0, 2) , (1, 2)$

$(4, 0) , (9, -2)$

e) 0 horizontal line

$(-1, 1) , (-1, 0)$

f) undefined   vertical line

6. a) slope = $\dfrac{5}{7}$ and run = 49

$\dfrac{5}{7} = \dfrac{\text{rise}}{49}$

$\dfrac{5}{7} = 7(\text{rise})$ rise = 35

$245 = 7(\text{rise})$

$\dfrac{245}{7} = \text{rise}$

b) slope = $-\dfrac{3}{8}$ and rise = 15

$\dfrac{-3}{8} = \dfrac{15}{\text{run}}$ run = -40

$-3(\text{run}) = 120$

$\text{run} = \dfrac{120}{-3}$

c) slope = $-\dfrac{6}{11}$ and run = 33

$\dfrac{-6}{11} = \dfrac{\text{rise}}{33}$

$-198 = 11(\text{rise})$ rise = -18

$\dfrac{-198}{11} = \text{rise}$

d) slope = $\dfrac{3}{4}$ and rise = 15

$\dfrac{3}{4} = \dfrac{15}{\text{run}}$ run = 20

$3(\text{run}) = 60$

$\text{run} = \dfrac{60}{3}$

7.

$\dfrac{2}{3} = \dfrac{h}{1.5}$

$3 = 3h$

$h = 1$

height = 1 metre

height = 1 metre

8.

$\text{rise} = h$ $\dfrac{h}{-3.4} = \dfrac{-5}{4}$

$\dfrac{\text{rise}}{\text{run}} = -3.4$ $4h = 17$

$h = \dfrac{17}{4}$

Area = $\dfrac{1}{2} bh$

$= \dfrac{1}{2}(6.8)\left(\dfrac{17}{4}\right)$

$= 14.45 \text{ cm}^2$

9.

$\text{rise} = -4$

$\text{run} = 3$

$\text{slope} = \dfrac{\text{rise}}{\text{run}} = -\dfrac{4}{3}$

(D) $-\dfrac{4}{3}$

10.

$\dfrac{\text{rise}}{\text{run}} = \dfrac{-2}{5}$

point $(-4+5, 0-2)$

$= (1, -2)$

(C) $(1, -2)$

11. (C.)

12.

$\text{slope} = \dfrac{15}{6} = 2.5$

$\boxed{2.5}$

13.

$x^2 = 6^2 + 6^2$

$x^2 = 72$

$x = \sqrt{72} = \sqrt{36}\sqrt{2}$

$= 6\sqrt{2}$

$\text{slope} = \dfrac{15}{6\sqrt{2}} = \dfrac{15}{6\sqrt{2}}$

$= 1.767\ldots$

$= 1.8$ (nearest tenth)

$\boxed{1 . 8}$

Class Ex. #1

Find the slope of a line which passes through the points $G(-3, 8)$ and $H(7, -2)$.

$$m_{GH} = \frac{y_H - y_G}{x_H - x_G} = \frac{-2-8}{7+3} = \frac{-10}{10} = -1$$

Class Ex. #2

Eleanor used $\dfrac{x_F - x_E}{y_F - y_E}$ instead of $\dfrac{y_F - y_E}{x_F - x_E}$

Bonnie used $\dfrac{y_F - y_E}{x_E - x_F}$ instead of $\dfrac{y_F - y_E}{x_F - x_E}$

Carl attempted to use $\dfrac{y_E - y_F}{x_E - x_F} = \dfrac{8-6}{15-(-10)} = -3$ but replaced x_F by 10 not −10.

Correct slope $= \dfrac{6-8}{-10-15} = \dfrac{-2}{-25} = \dfrac{2}{25}$

Class Ex. #3

a) Prove that the points A, E, and C are collinear.

$$m_{AB} = \frac{y_B - y_A}{x_B - x_A} = \frac{6+3}{2-5} = \frac{9}{-3} = -3$$

$$m_{BC} = \frac{y_C - y_B}{x_C - x_B} = \frac{33-6}{-7-2} = \frac{27}{-9} = -3$$

Since $m_{AB} = m_{BC}$ the points A, B, and C are collinear.

b) Find the value of y if the point $D(-4, y)$ lies on line segment AC.

$$m_{AD} = -3$$
$$\frac{y+3}{-4-5} = -3$$
$$\frac{y+3}{-9} = -3$$
$$y+3 = 27$$
$$\underline{y = 24}$$

Assignment

1. Line 1 - positive, Line 2 - negative, Line 3 - zero, Line 4 - positive, Line 5 - undefined, Line 6 - negative

2. a) $A(12, -2)$ and $B(0, 3)$

   $m_{AB} = \dfrac{y_B - y_A}{x_B - x_A} = \dfrac{3+2}{0-12} = -\dfrac{5}{12}$

   b) $C(-2, 3)$ and $D(2, -2)$

   $m_{CD} = \dfrac{y_D - y_C}{x_D - x_C} = \dfrac{-2-3}{2+2} = -\dfrac{5}{4}$

   c) $P(-15, -2)$ and $O(0, 0)$

   $m_{PO} = \dfrac{y_O - y_P}{x_O - x_P} = \dfrac{0+2}{0+15} = \dfrac{2}{15}$

   d) $S(36, -41)$ and $T(-20, -27)$

   $m_{ST} = \dfrac{y_T - y_S}{x_T - x_S} = \dfrac{-27+41}{-20-36} = \dfrac{14}{-56} = -\dfrac{1}{4}$

   e) $U(-172, -56)$ and $V(-172, 32)$

   $m_{UV} = \dfrac{y_V - y_U}{x_V - x_U} = \dfrac{32+56}{-172+172} = \dfrac{88}{0}$

   slope is undefined

   f) $K(8, -41)$ and $L(397, -41)$

   $m_{KL} = \dfrac{y_L - y_K}{x_L - x_K} = \dfrac{-41+41}{397-8} = \dfrac{0}{389} = 0$

---

3. a) $(3, -6)$ and $(8, 4)$

   $m = \dfrac{y_2 - y_1}{x_2 - x_1} = \dfrac{4+6}{8-3} = \dfrac{10}{5} = 2$

   b) $(-12, 7)$ and $(0, -2)$

   $m = \dfrac{y_2 - y_1}{x_2 - x_1} = \dfrac{-2-7}{0+12} = \dfrac{-9}{12} = -\dfrac{3}{4}$

   c) $(-3, -8)$ and $(1, 5)$

   $m = \dfrac{y_2 - y_1}{x_2 - x_1} = \dfrac{5+8}{1+3} = \dfrac{13}{4}$

   d) $(21, 1)$ and $(-4, -9)$

   $m = \dfrac{y_2 - y_1}{x_2 - x_1} = \dfrac{-9-1}{-4-21} = \dfrac{-10}{-25} = \dfrac{2}{5}$

4. a) Calculate the slope of the hill. $m = \dfrac{47-2}{15-3} = \dfrac{45}{12} = \dfrac{15}{4}$

   b) Calculate the coordinates of the midpoint of the path up the hill.

   $M\left(\dfrac{3+15}{2}, \dfrac{2+47}{2}\right) \qquad M\left(9, \dfrac{49}{2}\right)$

   c) Calculate the length of the path to the nearest tenth of a metre.

   $d = \sqrt{(15-3)^2 + (47-2)^2}$

   $ = \sqrt{12^2 + 45^2} = \sqrt{2169} = 46.57\ldots$ length $= 46.6$ m

5. a) [graph]

   b) [graph]

   c) [graph]

   $\dfrac{k-6}{5-4} = 3$

   $\dfrac{k-6}{1} = 3 \qquad k = 9$

   $k - 6 = 3$

   $\dfrac{3-5}{k-2}, \quad \dfrac{2}{7}$

   $-2(7) = 2(k-2)$

   $-14 = 2k-4$

   $-10 = 2k$

   $k = -5$

   $\dfrac{-7+2}{3-k} = -\dfrac{1}{2}$

   $-5(2) = -1(3-k)$

   $-10 = -3 + k \qquad k = -7$

6. a) Use the slope formula to prove that the points P, Q, and R are collinear.

   $m_{PQ} = \dfrac{-7+9}{-1-4} = \dfrac{2}{-5} = -\dfrac{2}{5} \qquad m_{QR} = \dfrac{-3+7}{-11+1} = \dfrac{4}{-10} = -\dfrac{2}{5}$

   Since $m_{PQ} = m_{QR}$ the points P, Q and R are collinear.

   b) Use the distance formula to prove that the points P, Q, and R are collinear.

   $d_{PQ} = \sqrt{(-1-4)^2 + (-7+9)^2} = \sqrt{(-5)^2 + 2^2} = \sqrt{29}$

   $d_{QR} = \sqrt{(-11+1)^2 + (-3+7)^2} = \sqrt{(-10)^2 + 4^2} = \sqrt{116} = \sqrt{4}\sqrt{29} = 2\sqrt{29}$

   $d_{PR} = \sqrt{(-11-4)^2 + (-3+9)^2} = \sqrt{(-15)^2 + 6^2} = \sqrt{261} = \sqrt{9}\sqrt{29} = 3\sqrt{29}$

   Since $d_{PR} = d_{PQ} + d_{QR}$, the points P, Q and R are collinear.

   $PR = PQ + QR$

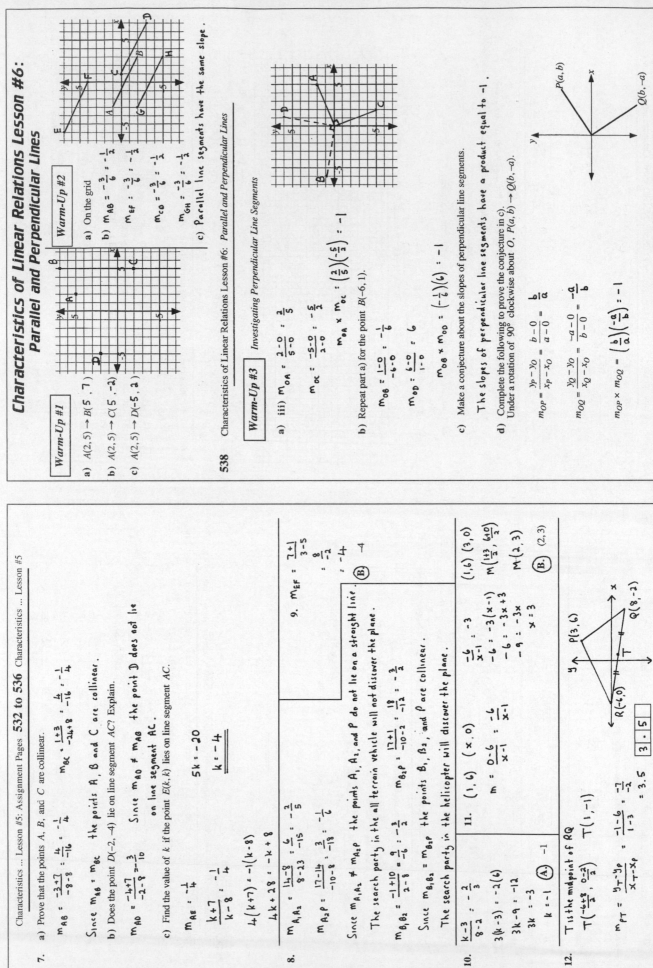

Characteristics of Linear Relations Lesson #6: Parallel and Perpendicular Lines

Warm-Up #1

a) $A(2,5) \rightarrow B(5,7)$
b) $A(2,5) \rightarrow C(5,-2)$
c) $A(2,5) \rightarrow D(-5,2)$

Warm-Up #2

a) On the grid

b) $m_{AB} = -\frac{3}{6} = -\frac{1}{2}$

$m_{EF} : -\frac{3}{6} : -\frac{1}{2}$

$m_{CD} = -\frac{3}{6} = -\frac{1}{2}$

$m_{GH} : -\frac{3}{6} = -\frac{1}{2}$

c) Parallel line segments have the same slope.

---

538 Characteristics of Linear Relations Lesson #6: Parallel and Perpendicular Lines

Warm-Up #3 Investigating Perpendicular Line Segments

a) iii) $m_{OA} = \frac{2-0}{5-0} = \frac{2}{5}$

$m_{OC} = \frac{-5-0}{2-0} = -\frac{5}{2}$

$m_{OA} \times m_{OC} = \left(\frac{2}{5}\right)\left(-\frac{5}{2}\right) = -1$

b) Repeat part a) for the point $B(-6,1)$.

$m_{OB} = \frac{1-0}{-6-0} = -\frac{1}{6}$

$m_{OD} = \frac{6-0}{1-0} = 6$

$m_{OB} \times m_{OD} = \left(-\frac{1}{6}\right)(6) = -1$

c) Make a conjecture about the slopes of perpendicular line segments.

The slopes of perpendicular line segments have a product equal to -1.

d) Complete the following to prove the conjecture in c).
Under a rotation of $90°$ clockwise about O, $P(a,b) \rightarrow Q(b,-a)$.

$m_{OP} = \frac{y_P - y_O}{x_P - x_O} = \frac{b-0}{a-0} = \frac{b}{a}$

$m_{OQ} = \frac{y_Q - y_O}{x_Q - x_O} = \frac{-a-0}{b-0} = \frac{-a}{b}$

$m_{OP} \times m_{OQ} = \left(\frac{b}{a}\right)\left(\frac{-a}{b}\right) = -1$

Characteristics ... Lesson #5: Assignment Pages 532 to 536 Characteristics ... Lesson #5

7. a) Prove that the points A, B, and C are collinear.

$m_{AB} = \frac{-3+7}{-8-8} = \frac{4}{-16} = -\frac{1}{4}$ $m_{BC} = \frac{1+3}{-24+8} = \frac{4}{-16} = -\frac{1}{4}$

Since $m_{AB} = m_{BC}$ the points A, B and C are collinear.

b) Does the point $D(-2,-4)$ lie on line segment AC? Explain.

$m_{AD} = \frac{-4+7}{-2-8} = -\frac{3}{10}$ Since $m_{AD} \neq m_{AB}$ the point D does not lie on line segment AC.

c) Find the value of k if the point $E(k,k)$ lies on line segment AC.

$m_{AE} = -\frac{1}{4}$

$\frac{k+7}{k-8} = -\frac{1}{4}$

$4(k+7) = -1(k-8)$

$4k + 28 = -k + 8$

$5k = -20$

$k = -4$

8. $m_{A_1 A_2} = \frac{14-8}{8-13} = \frac{6}{-15} = -\frac{2}{5}$

$m_{A_2 P} = \frac{17-14}{-10-8} = \frac{3}{-18} = -\frac{1}{6}$

Since $m_{A_1 A_2} \neq m_{A_2 P}$ the points A_1, A_2, and P do not lie on a straight line.

The search party in the all terrain vehicle will not discover the plane.

$m_{B_1 B_2} = \frac{-1+10}{2-8} = \frac{9}{-6} = -\frac{3}{2}$ $m_{B_2 P} = \frac{17+1}{-10-2} = \frac{18}{-12} = -\frac{3}{2}$

Since $m_{B_1 B_2} = m_{B_2 P}$ the points B_1, B_2, and P are collinear.

The search party in the helicopter will discover the plane.

9. $m_{EF} = \frac{7+1}{3-5}$

$= \frac{8}{-2}$

$= -4$

B. -4

10. (1, 6) (x, 0)

$m = \frac{0-6}{x-1} = \frac{-6}{x-1}$

$\frac{-6}{x-1} = -3$

$3(k-3) = -2(6)$

$3k - 9 = -12$

$3k = -3$

$k = -1$ **A.** -1

$-6 = -3(x-1)$

$-6 = -3x + 3$

$-9 = -3x$

$x = 3$

11. (1, 6) (x, 0)

$\frac{k-3}{8-2} = -\frac{2}{3}$

(1, 6) (3, 0)

$M\left(\frac{1+3}{2}, \frac{6+0}{2}\right)$

$M(2, 3)$

B. (2, 3)

12. T is the midpoint of RQ

$T\left(\frac{-4+8}{2}, \frac{0-2}{2}\right)$ $T(1,-1)$

$m_{PT} = \frac{y_T - y_P}{x_T - x_P} = \frac{-1-6}{1-3} = \frac{-7}{-2} = 3.5$

3.5

Class Ex. #1
a) $m_{GH} = \frac{3}{4}$
b) $m_{BF} = -\frac{4}{3}$

Class Ex. #2
a) $m_1 = \frac{1}{4}$, $m_2 = \frac{3}{12} = \frac{1}{4}$ parallel
b) $m_1 = \frac{5}{7}$, $m_2 = \frac{14}{10} = \frac{7}{5}$ neither

Class Ex. #3
$m_{PQ} = \frac{-2-7}{6-4} = -\frac{9}{2}$
a) $-\frac{9}{2}$ b) $\frac{2}{9}$

Class Ex. #4
$m_{LM} = \frac{7-2}{-2+4} = \frac{5}{2}$ $m_{LN} = \frac{0-2}{1+4} = -\frac{2}{5}$
$m_{LM} \times m_{LN} = \left(\frac{5}{2}\right)\left(-\frac{2}{5}\right) = -1$
since the product of the slopes = −1
the lines LM and LN are perpendicular.
the triangle is right-angled at L.

Class Ex. #5
a) parallel
$-\frac{3}{4} = \frac{k}{5}$
$-15 = 4k$
$k = \frac{-15}{4}$

b) perpendicular
$\left(-\frac{3}{4}\right)\left(\frac{k}{5}\right) = -1$
$-\frac{3k}{20} = -1$
$-3k = -20$
$k = \frac{20}{3}$

Assignment

1. a) slope $AB = \frac{1}{4}$ slope $CD = -\frac{1}{4}$ slope $EF = -\frac{3}{4}$ slope $GH = -\frac{3}{4}$
   b) Lines which are parallel have the same slope

2.a)

Line Segment	Slope
AB	$-\frac{2}{4} = -\frac{1}{2}$
CD	$\frac{4}{2} = 2$

Line Segment	Slope
EF	$\frac{6}{4} = \frac{3}{2}$
GH	$-\frac{2}{3}$

Line Segment	Slope
IJ	$\frac{-4}{1} = -4$
JK	$\frac{1}{4}$

b) Multiply the slopes of the pairs of perpendicular line segments.

$m_{AB} \times m_{CD}$	$m_{EF} \times m_{GH}$	$m_{IJ} \times m_{JK}$
$-\frac{1}{2} \times 2 = -1$	$\frac{3}{2} \times \left(-\frac{2}{3}\right) = -1$	$-4 \times \frac{1}{4} = -1$

c) Write a rule in reference to the slope of two lines which are perpendicular to each other.
The product of the slopes of perpendicular lines is −1.

3. a) parallel   b) perpendicular   c) parallel
   d) neither   e) perpendicular   f) perpendicular
   g) neither   h) parallel   i) neither

4. AB and GH, CD and KL, EF and IJ.
5. RS and EF, UV and PQ, ZT and KL, MN and XY.

6. $m_{AB} = -\frac{8}{6} = -\frac{4}{3}$ $m_{BC} = \frac{4}{4} = 1$
   $m_{OE} = -\frac{4}{10} = -\frac{2}{5}$ $m_{FG} = \frac{5}{2}$
   AB and BC are not perpendicular
   DE and FG are perpendicular

7. a) $m_{AB} = \frac{1-4}{-3-0} = 1$ $m = 1$
   b) perpendicular to line segment AB $m = -1$
   c) parallel to line segment BC
   $m_{BC} = \frac{-2-1}{5+3} = -\frac{3}{8}$ $m = -\frac{3}{8}$
   d) perpendicular to line segment AC
   $m_{AC} = \frac{-2-4}{5-0} = -\frac{6}{5}$ $m = \frac{5}{6}$

8. a) Explain how we can determine if $\triangle ABC$ is a right triangle.
   Determine the slope of each side of the triangle. If two of the slopes are negative reciprocals, the triangle is a right triangle.
   b) Determine if $\triangle ABC$ is a right triangle.
   $m_{AB} = \frac{-5-5}{-2-3} = \frac{-10}{-5} = 2$
   $m_{BC} = \frac{1+5}{-5+2} = \frac{6}{-3} = -2$
   $m_{AC} = \frac{1-5}{-5-3} = \frac{-4}{-8} = \frac{1}{2}$
   $m_{BC} \times m_{AC} = (-2)\left(\frac{1}{2}\right) = -1$
   $BC \perp AC$ $\angle ACB$ is a right angle
   $\triangle ABC$ is a right triangle

9. a) $\triangle PQR \rightarrow P(-3,3), Q(-1,1), R(-5,-1)$
   $m_{PQ} = \frac{1-3}{-1+3} = \frac{-2}{2} = -1$
   $m_{QR} = \frac{-1-1}{-5+1} = \frac{-2}{-4} = \frac{1}{2}$
   $m_{PR} = \frac{-1-3}{-5+3} = \frac{-4}{-2} = 2$
   no negative reciprocals
   $\triangle PQR$ is not right angled

   b) $\triangle ABC \rightarrow A(-7,9), B(3,13), C(7,3)$
   $m_{AB} = \frac{13-9}{3+7} = \frac{4}{10} = \frac{2}{5}$
   $m_{BC} = \frac{3-13}{7-3} = \frac{-10}{4} = -\frac{5}{2}$
   $m_{AC} = \frac{3-9}{7+7} = \frac{-6}{14} = -\frac{3}{7}$
   $m_{AB} \times m_{BC} = \left(\frac{2}{5}\right)\left(-\frac{5}{2}\right) = -1$
   $\triangle ABC$ is right angled at B

10. a) $4, \frac{k}{3}$ b) $-2, \frac{2}{n}$ c) $\frac{5}{6}, 3m$ d) $\frac{3}{4}, \frac{w}{6}$
    $4 = \frac{k}{3}$ $-2 = \frac{2}{n}$ $\frac{5}{6} = 3m$ $\frac{3}{4} = \frac{w}{6}$
    $k = 12$ $-2n = 2$ $\frac{5}{6} = 18m$ $18 = 4w$
    $n = -1$ $m = \frac{5}{18}$ $w = \frac{9}{2}$

11. a) $\frac{1}{3}, 3h$ b) $4, \frac{8}{p}$ c) $-5, \frac{s}{2}$ d) $-\frac{3}{4}, \frac{q}{6}$
    a) $\left(\frac{1}{3}\right)(3h) = -1$ $h = -1$
    b) $(4)\left(\frac{8}{p}\right) = -1$ $\frac{32}{p} = -1$ $32 = -p$ $p = -32$
    c) $(-5)\left(\frac{s}{2}\right) = -1$ $-\frac{5s}{2} = -1$ $-5s = -2$ $s = \frac{2}{5}$
    d) $\left(-\frac{3}{4}\right)\left(\frac{q}{6}\right) = -1$ $\frac{3q}{24} = -1$ $3q = -24$ $q = -8$

12. the diagonals of a rhombus are perpendicular.
    $m_{PR} = \frac{-3-0}{1+4} = -\frac{3}{5}$
    $m_{QS} = \frac{5}{3}$

7.
A. AB and CD have the same slope and are equal in length. ✓
B. AB and CD have the same slope and are unequal in length. ✓
C. CD has a length of 10 units and a slope of zero. ✓
D. (circled) AB and CD have the same midpoint and are equal in length.

$m_{AB} = \dfrac{-4+4}{-4+6} = 0$ horizontal line   length $= 6-(-4) = 10$

$m_{CD} = \dfrac{1+9}{1-1} = \dfrac{10}{0}$ vertical line   length $= 1-(-9) = 10$

midpoint of $AB = \left(\dfrac{6-4}{2}, \dfrac{-4-4}{2}\right) = (1,-4)$ midpoint of $CD = \left(\dfrac{1+1}{2}, \dfrac{-9+1}{2}\right) = (1,-4)$

8.
$d_{AB} = \sqrt{(3+2)^2+(-6-4)^2}$
$= \sqrt{4^2+(-10)^2}$
$= \sqrt{116}$

$d_{PQ} = \sqrt{(-3-7)^2+(-3-1)^2}$
$= \sqrt{(-10)^2+(-4)^2}$
$= \sqrt{116}$

9.
$m_{AB} = \dfrac{-6-4}{2+2} = \dfrac{-10}{4} = -\dfrac{5}{2}$ $m_{PQ} = \dfrac{-3-1}{-3-7} = \dfrac{-4}{-10} = \dfrac{2}{5}$

$\left(-\dfrac{5}{2}\right)\left(\dfrac{2}{5}\right) = -1$ $AB \perp PQ$

C. The length of line segment AB is equal to the length of line segment PQ.
(circled) D. Line segment AB is perpendicular to line segment PQ.

10.
midpoint of $AB = \left(\dfrac{-2+2}{2}, \dfrac{4-6}{2}\right) = (0,-1)$:$C(0,-1)$
midpoint of $PQ = \left(\dfrac{-3-1}{2}, \dfrac{1-3}{2}\right) = D(2,-1)$
slope of CD $= \dfrac{-1+1}{2-0} = 0$
(circled) D.

11.
$m_{KL} = \dfrac{-3-7}{-1-4} = \dfrac{-10}{-5} = 2$
$m_{\perp} = -\dfrac{1}{2}$
(circled) B. $-\dfrac{1}{2}$

12.
$m_{PQ} = \dfrac{-2+6}{-6+4} = \dfrac{4}{-2} = -2$
$d_{PQ} = \sqrt{(-6+4)^2+(-2+6)^2} = \sqrt{(-2)^2+4^2} = \sqrt{20}$
$= \sqrt{4}\sqrt{5} = 2\sqrt{5}$
(circled) A. -2 and $2\sqrt{5}$

13.
$m_{QR} = \dfrac{1+2}{0+6} = \dfrac{3}{6} = \dfrac{1}{2}$
$d_{QR} = \sqrt{(0+6)^2+(1+2)^2} = \sqrt{6^2+3^2} = \sqrt{45}$
$= \sqrt{9}\sqrt{5} = 3\sqrt{5}$
(circled) D. $\dfrac{1}{2}$ and $3\sqrt{5}$

14.
$m_{SR} = \dfrac{1+3}{0-2} = \dfrac{4}{-2} = -2$
$d_{SR} = \sqrt{(0-2)^2+(1+3)^2} = \sqrt{2^2+4^2} = \sqrt{20}$
$= 2\sqrt{5}$
(circled) D. None of the above statements is false.

15.
(circled) A. rectangle

---

13. a) $m_{JK} = \dfrac{2-6}{-2+4} = \dfrac{-4}{2} = -2$ b) $M(7,y)$ $L(1,1)$

$m_{ML} = \dfrac{1-3}{1-7} = \dfrac{-2}{-6} = \dfrac{1}{3}$ To meet at right angles m_{ML} must equal $-\dfrac{1}{2}$

Since the slopes are not negative reciprocals the lines will not meet at right angles.

$\dfrac{y-1}{7-1} = \dfrac{1}{2}$
$2(y-1) = 6$ $\dfrac{2y-2=6}{2y=8}$ $\underline{\underline{y=4}}$

14. a) the slope formula

$m_{AB} = \dfrac{6-3}{0+3} = \dfrac{3}{3} = 1$

$m_{BC} = \dfrac{1-6}{5-0} = \dfrac{-5}{5} = -1$

$m_{AB} \times m_{BC} = (1)(-1) = -1$

$AB \perp BC$

$\triangle ABC$ is right angled at B.

b) the distance formula

$d_{AB} = \sqrt{(0+3)^2+(6-3)^2} = \sqrt{18}$

$d_{BC} = \sqrt{(5-0)^2+(1-6)^2} = \sqrt{50}$

$d_{AC} = \sqrt{(5+3)^2+(1-3)^2} = \sqrt{68}$

$AC^2 = (\sqrt{68})^2 = 68$

$AB^2 + BC^2 = (\sqrt{18})^2+(\sqrt{50})^2 = 18+50 = 68$

Since $AC^2 = AB^2 + BC^2$
$\triangle ABC$ is right angled at B.

15.
$m_{AB} = \dfrac{3-2}{-2-1} = -\dfrac{1}{3}$
$m_{\perp} = 3$
(circled) C. 3

16.
$m_{UW} = \dfrac{5-p}{-6+3} = \dfrac{5-p}{-3}$ $m_{XY} = \dfrac{0-2}{9-4} = -\dfrac{2}{5}$

$m_{UW} \times m_{XY} = -1$

$\left(\dfrac{5-p}{-3}\right)\left(\dfrac{-2}{5}\right) = -1$

$\dfrac{-2(5-p)}{-15} = -1$

$-2(5-p) = 15$

$-10+2p = 15$

$2p = 25$

$p = 12.5$

$\boxed{12.5}$

Characteristics of Linear Relations Lesson #7: Practice Test

1.
$7-2 = 5$
$11-4 = 7$
$2-(-6) = 8$
$-5-(-11) = 6$
(circled) C. TV with $T(-6,1)$ and $V(2,1)$

2.
$d = \sqrt{(5-8)^2+(-2-3)^2}$
$= \sqrt{(-3)^2+(-5)^2}$
$= \sqrt{9+25}$
$= \sqrt{34}$
(circled) B. $\sqrt{34}$

3. Centre is midpoint of AB
$M\left(\dfrac{4+-2}{2}, \dfrac{2+6}{2}\right)$
$M(1,4)$
(circled) C. $(1,4)$

4. AB $m = \dfrac{6}{4} = \dfrac{3}{2}$ E

5. CD $m = \dfrac{-3}{12} = -\dfrac{1}{4}$ F

6. EF $m = \dfrac{-7}{3}$ C

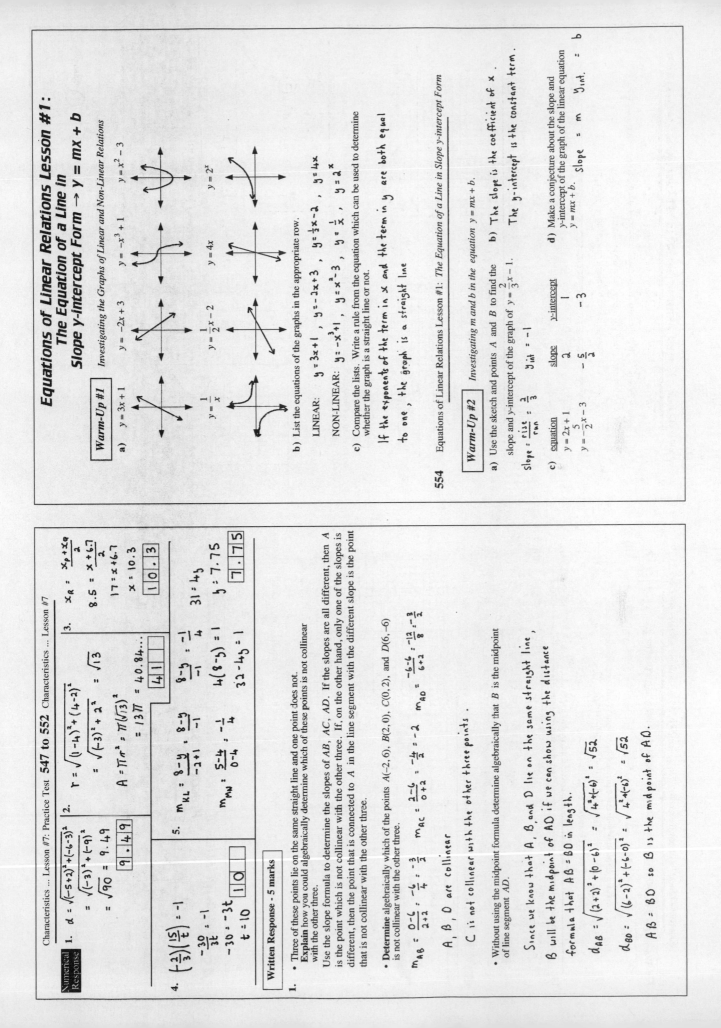

Equations of Linear Relations Lesson #1:
The Equation of a Line in Slope y-intercept Form → $y = mx + b$

Warm-Up #1
Investigating the Graphs of Linear and Non-Linear Relations

a) $y = 3x + 1$ $y = -2x + 3$ $y = -x^3 + 1$ $y = x^2 - 3$

$y = \dfrac{1}{x}$ $y = \dfrac{1}{2}x - 2$ $y = 4x$ $y = 2^x$

b) List the equations of the graphs in the appropriate row.

LINEAR: $y = 3x+1$, $y = -2x+3$, $y = \frac{1}{2}x-2$, $y = 4x$

NON-LINEAR: $y = -x^3+1$, $y = x^2-3$, $y = \frac{1}{x}$, $y = 2^x$

c) Compare the lists. Write a rule from the equation which can be used to determine whether the graph is a straight line or not.

If the exponents of the term in x and the term in y are both equal to one, the graph is a straight line.

b) The slope is the coefficient of x .

The y-intercept is the constant term.

554   Equations of Linear Relations Lesson #1: *The Equation of a Line in Slope y-intercept Form*

Warm-Up #2
Investigating m and b in the equation $y = mx + b$.

a) Use the sketch and points A and B to find the slope and y-intercept of the graph of $y = \dfrac{2}{3}x - 1$.

$\text{Slope} = \dfrac{\text{rise}}{\text{run}} = \dfrac{2}{3}$ $y_{int} = -1$

c)

equation	slope	y-intercept
$y = 2x + 1$	2	1
$y = -\frac{5}{2}x - 3$	$-\frac{5}{2}$	-3

d) Make a conjecture about the slope and y-intercept of the graph of the linear equation $y = mx + b$.   Slope $= m$ $y_{int} = b$

Characteristics ... Lesson #7: Practice Test   **547 to 552**   Characteristics ... Lesson #7

Numerical Response

1. $d = \sqrt{(-5+2)^2 + (-6-3)^2}$
$= \sqrt{(-3)^2 + (-9)^2}$
$= \sqrt{90} = 9.49$
$\boxed{9.49}$

2. $r = \sqrt{(1-4)^2 + (4+2)^2}$
$= \sqrt{(-3)^2 + 2^2} = \sqrt{13}$
$A = \pi r^2 = \pi(\sqrt{13})^2$
$= 13\pi = 40.84\ldots$
$\boxed{41}$

3. $x_R = \dfrac{x_p + x_q}{2}$
$8.5 = \dfrac{x + 6.7}{2}$
$17 = x + 6.7$
$x = 10.3$
$\boxed{10.3}$

4. $\left(-\dfrac{2}{3}\right)\left(\dfrac{15}{t}\right) = -1$
$\dfrac{-30}{3t} = -1$
$-30 = -3t$
$t = 10$
$\boxed{10}$

5. $m_{KL} = \dfrac{8-y}{-2+1} = \dfrac{8-y}{-1}$
$m_{MN} = \dfrac{5-4}{0-4} = -\dfrac{1}{4}$
$\dfrac{8-y}{-1} = -\dfrac{1}{4}$
$4(8-y) = 1$
$32 - 4y = 1$

$31 = 4y$
$y = 7.75$
$\boxed{7.75}$

Written Response - 5 marks

1. • Three of these points lie on the same straight line and one point does not.
Explain how you could algebraically determine which of these points is not collinear with the other three.

Use the slope formula to determine the slopes of AB, AC, AD. If the slopes are all different, then A is the point which is not collinear with the other three. If, on the other hand, only one of the slopes is different, then the point that is connected to A in the line segment with the different slope is the point that is not collinear with the other three.

• **Determine** algebraically which of the points $A(-2, 6)$, $B(2, 0)$, $C(0, 2)$, and $D(6, -6)$ is not collinear with the other three.

$m_{AB} = \dfrac{0-6}{2+2} = \dfrac{-6}{4} = -\dfrac{3}{2}$ $m_{AC} = \dfrac{2-6}{0+2} = \dfrac{-4}{2} = -2$ $m_{AD} = \dfrac{-6-6}{6+2} = \dfrac{-12}{8} = -\dfrac{3}{2}$

A, B, D are collinear.

C is not collinear with the other three points.

• Without using the midpoint formula determine algebraically that B is the midpoint of line segment AD.

Since we know that A, B, and D lie on the same straight line, B will be the midpoint of AD if we can show using the distance formula that $AB = BD$ in length.

$d_{AB} = \sqrt{(2+2)^2 + (0-6)^2} = \sqrt{4^2 + (-6)^2} = \sqrt{52}$

$d_{BD} = \sqrt{(6-2)^2 + (-6-0)^2} = \sqrt{4^2 + (-6)^2} = \sqrt{52}$

$AB = BD$ so B is the midpoint of AD.

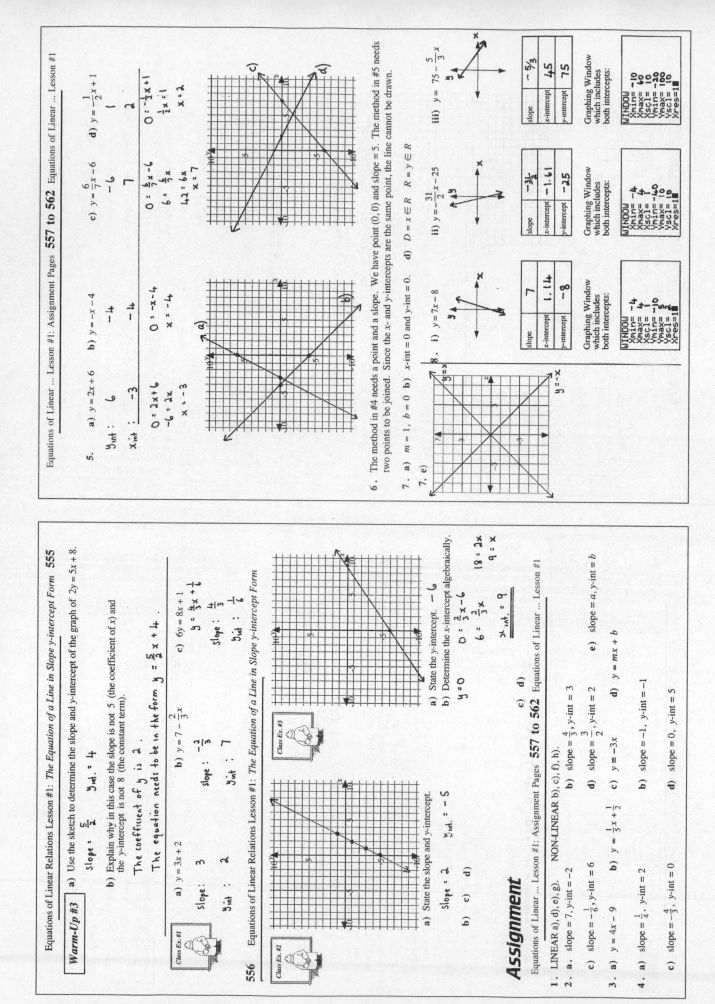

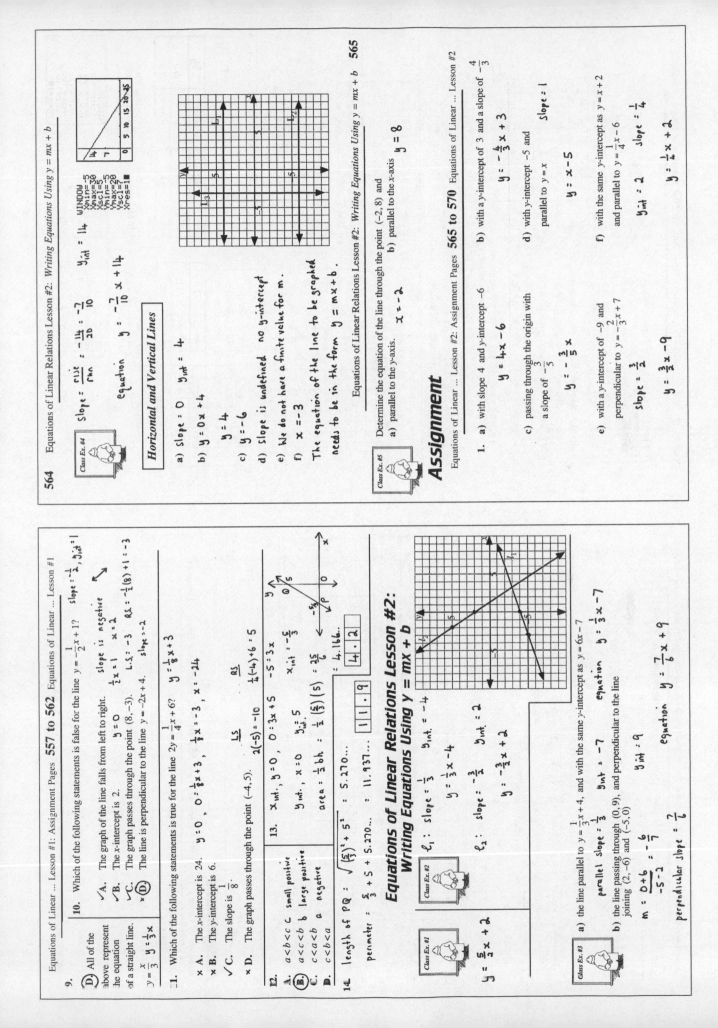

Class Ex. #4

WINDOW
Xmin=-5
Xmax=30
Xscl=5
Ymin=-5
Ymax=20
Yscl=7
Xres=1■

$slope = \dfrac{rise}{run} = \dfrac{-14}{20} = \dfrac{-7}{10}$ $y_{int} = 14$

equation $y = \dfrac{-7}{10}x + 14$

Horizontal and Vertical Lines

a) slope = 0 $y_{int} = 4$

b) $y = 0x + 4$
   $y = 4$

c) $y = -6$

d) slope is undefined   no y-intercept

e) We do not have a finite value for m.

f) $x = -3$

The equation of the line to be graphed needs to be in the form $y = mx + b$.

Class Ex. #5

Determine the equation of the line through the point $(-2, 8)$ and

a) parallel to the y-axis. $x = -2$

b) parallel to the x-axis. $y = 8$

Assignment

Equations of Linear ... Lesson #2: Assignment Pages **565 to 570**   Equations of Linear ... Lesson #2

1. a) with slope 4 and y-intercept -6
   $y = 4x - 6$

   b) with a y-intercept of 3 and a slope of $-\dfrac{4}{3}$
   $y = -\dfrac{4}{3}x + 3$

   c) passing through the origin with a slope of $-\dfrac{3}{5}$
   $y = -\dfrac{3}{5}x$

   d) with y-intercept -5 and parallel to $y = x$
   $y = x - 5$ slope = 1

   e) with a y-intercept of -9 and perpendicular to $y = -\dfrac{2}{3}x + 7$
   $slope = \dfrac{3}{2}$ $y = \dfrac{3}{2}x - 9$

   f) with the same y-intercept as $y = x + 2$ and parallel to $y = \dfrac{1}{4}x - 6$
   $y_{int} = 2$ $slope = \dfrac{1}{4}$ $y = \dfrac{1}{4}x + 2$

565

---

9. (D) All of the above represent the equation of a straight line. $y = \dfrac{x}{3}$ $y = \dfrac{1}{3}x$

10. Which of the following statements is false for the line $y = -\dfrac{1}{2}x + 1$? $slope = -\dfrac{1}{2}, \; y_{int} = 1$

   ✗ A. The graph of the line falls from left to right.   slope is negative

   ✗ B. The x-intercept is 2. $y = 0$ $\frac{1}{2}x = 1$ $x = 2$

   ✓ C. The y-intercept is 6.

   ✗ (D) The graph passes through the point $(8, -3)$.   L.S. = -3   R.S. = $-\frac{1}{2}(8) + 1 = -3$

11. Which of the following statements is true for the line $2y = \dfrac{1}{4}x + 6$? $y = \dfrac{1}{8}x + 3$

   ✗ A. The x-intercept is 24. $y = 0, \; 0 = \frac{1}{8}x + 3, \; \frac{1}{8}x = -3, \; x = -24$

   ✗ B. The y-intercept is 6.

   ✓ C. The slope is $\dfrac{1}{8}$.

   ✗ D. The graph passes through the point $(-4, 5)$. $\frac{1}{8}(-4) + 6 = 5$

12.
   A. $a < b < c$ small positive
   (B.) $a < c < b$ large positive
   C. $c < a < b$ negative
   D. $c < b < a$

13. $x_{int}, \; y = 0, \; 0 = 3x + 5$ $-5 = 3x$ $x_{int} = -\dfrac{5}{3}$

   $y_{int}, \; x = 0$ $y_{int} = 5$

   area $= \frac{1}{2}bh = \frac{1}{2}\left(\frac{5}{3}\right)(5) = \dfrac{25}{6} = 4.166...$ $\boxed{4.2}$

14. length of PQ $= \sqrt{\left(\frac{5}{3}\right)^2 + 5^2} = 5.270...$

   perimeter $= \dfrac{5}{3} + 5 + 5.270... = 11.937... = \boxed{11.9}$

565

Equations of Linear Relations Lesson #2: Writing Equations Using y = mx + b

Class Ex. #1

ℓ_1: $slope = \dfrac{1}{3}$ $y_{int} = -4$
   $y = \dfrac{1}{3}x - 4$

ℓ_2: $slope = -\dfrac{3}{2}$ $y_{int} = 2$
   $y = -\dfrac{3}{2}x + 2$

Class Ex. #2

$y = \dfrac{5}{2}x + 2$

Class Ex. #3

a) the line parallel to $y = \dfrac{1}{3}x + 4$, and with the same y-intercept as $y = 6x - 7$

   parallel slope $= \dfrac{1}{3}$ $y_{int} = -7$ equation $y = \dfrac{1}{3}x - 7$

b) the line passing through $(0, 9)$, and perpendicular to the line joining $(2, -6)$ and $(-5, 0)$

   $m = \dfrac{0 + 6}{-5 - 2} = \dfrac{6}{-2} = -\dfrac{6}{7}$

   perpendicular slope $= \dfrac{7}{6}$ $y_{int} = 9$ equation $y = \dfrac{7}{6}x + 9$

1. (continued)

g) through the point $(0, 1)$ and perpendicular to $y = 4x - 2$

perpendicular slope $= -\frac{1}{4}$

$y_{int} = 1$

$y = -\frac{1}{4}x + 1$

h) through the point $(0, 4)$ and parallel to $y = \frac{1}{10}x + 24$

parallel slope $= \frac{1}{10}$ $y_{int} = 4$

$y = \frac{1}{10}x + 4$

i) with the same y-intercept as $y = 2x - 3$ and perpendicular to $y = \frac{7}{3}x - 2$

perpendicular slope $= -\frac{3}{7}$

$y_{int} = -3$

$y = -\frac{3}{7}x - 3$

j) with the same y-intercept as $y = ax + b$ and perpendicular to $y = cx + d$

$y_{int} = b$ perpendicular slope $= -\frac{1}{c}$

$y = -\frac{1}{c}x + b$

2. ℓ_1: slope $= \frac{1}{4}$ $y_{int} = -8$

$y = \frac{1}{4}x - 8$

ℓ_2: slope $= \frac{-2}{-4} = -\frac{1}{2}$ $y_{int} = 2$

$y = -\frac{1}{2}x + 2$

ℓ_3: slope $= \frac{3}{3} = 1$ $y_{int} = 0$

$y = x$

3. a)

x-intercept	9
y-intercept	-6
slope	2/3
equation	$y = \frac{2}{3}x - 6$

b)

x-intercept	2
y-intercept	-24
slope	12
equation	$y = 12x - 24$

c)

x-intercept	-4
y-intercept	-3
slope	-3/4
equation	$y = -\frac{3}{4}x - 3$

4. $m = \frac{-6-3}{4-1} = \frac{-9}{3} = -3$

parallel slope $= -3$

$y_{int} = 16$

$y = -3x + 16$

5. $m = \frac{-3+2}{12-7} = -\frac{1}{5}$

perpendicular slope $= 5$

$y_{int} = -1$

$y = 5x - 1$

6. State the equations of the following lines:

a) through the point $(-5, 3)$ and parallel to the y-axis $x = -5$

b) through the point $(-5, 3)$ and parallel to the x-axis $y = 3$

c) through the point $(1, -1)$ and parallel to the x-axis $y = -1$

d) through the point (a, b) and parallel to the y-axis $x = a$

---

7. Consider the graph of the function with equation $y = 2$.

a) State the values of m and b.

$m = 0$ $b = 2$

b) Sketch the graph on the grid provided.

c) State the x- and y-intercepts of the graph.

no x-intercept   y-intercept $= 2$

d) Determine the domain and range of the function.

domain $x \in R$ range $y = 2$

e) On the same grid draw the line with equation $y = 2x - 4$ without using a graphing calculator.

f) State the coordinates of the point of intersection of the two lines.

$(3, 2)$

g) On the grid draw the line with equation $y = -5$.

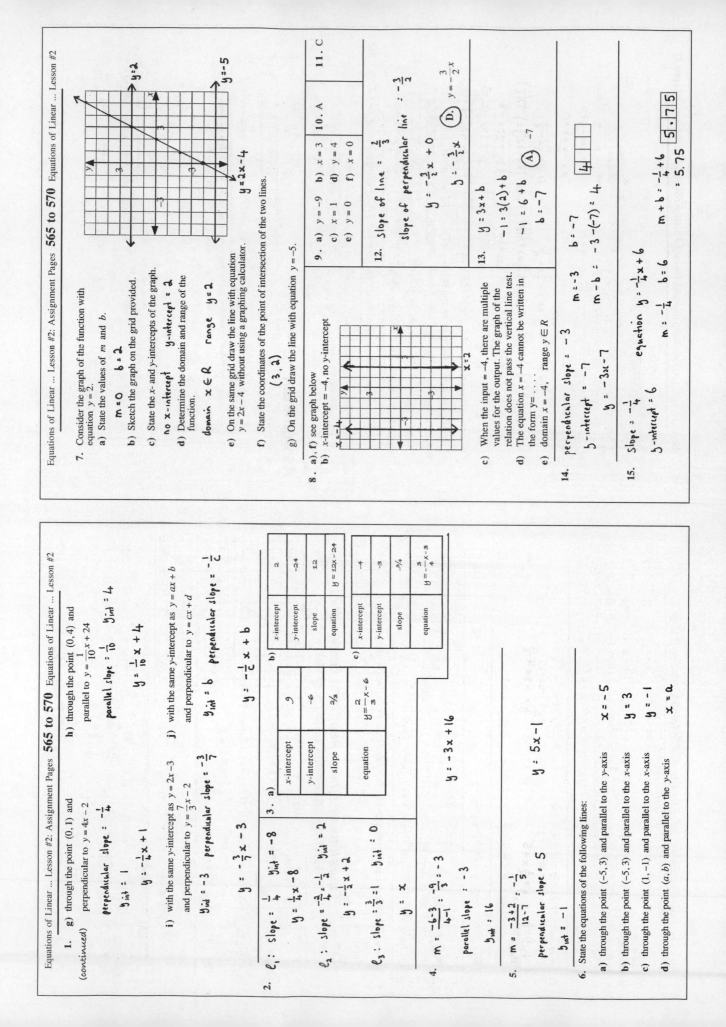

$y = 2$

$y = 2x - 4$

$y = -5$

8. a), f) see graph below

b) x-intercept $= -4$, no y-intercept

$x = -4$ $x = 2$

9. a) $y = -9$ **b)** $x = 3$
   c) $x = 1$ **d)** $y = 4$
   e) $y = 0$ **f)** $x = 0$

10. A   **11.** C

12. Slope of line $= \frac{2}{3}$

slope of perpendicular line $= -\frac{3}{2}$

$y = -\frac{3}{2}x + 0$

$y = -\frac{3}{2}x$

D. $y = -\frac{3}{2}x$

13. $y = 3x + b$

$-1 = 3(2) + b$

$-1 = 6 + b$ **A.** -7

$b = -7$

c) When the input $= -4$, there are multiple values for the output. The graph of the relation does not pass the vertical line test.

d) The equation $x = -4$ cannot be written in the form $y = \ldots$

e) domain $x = -4$,   range $y \in R$

14. perpendicular slope $= -3$ $m = -3$ $b = -7$

y-intercept $= -7$ $m - b = -3 - (-7) = 4$

$y = -3x - 7$

15. Slope $= -\frac{1}{4}$ equation $y = -\frac{1}{4}x + 6$

y-intercept $= 6$ $m = -\frac{1}{4}$ $b = 6$

$m + b = -\frac{1}{4} + 6$

$= 5.75$

4

5.75

Assignment

1. Convert the following equations from slope y-intercept form ($y = mx + b$) to general form ($Ax + By + C = 0$), where A, B, and C are integers.

a) $y = 7x - 3$
$0 = 7x - y - 3$
$7x - y - 3 = 0$

b) $y = -2x + 9$
$2x + y - 9 = 0$

c) $y = mx + b$
$0 = mx - y + b$
$mx - y + b = 0$

d) $y = -\frac{3}{4}x + 5$
$4y = 4(-\frac{3}{4}x) + 4(5)$
$4y = -3x + 20$
$3x + 4y - 20 = 0$

e) $y = \frac{2}{3}x + \frac{1}{6}$
$6y = 6(\frac{2}{3}x) + 6(\frac{1}{6})$
$6y = 4x + 1$
$0 = 4x - 6y + 1$
$4x - 6y + 1 = 0$

f) $y = \frac{5}{3}x - \frac{1}{4}$
$12y = 12(\frac{5}{3}x) - 12(\frac{1}{4})$
$12y = 20x - 3$
$0 = 20x - 12y - 3$
$20x - 12y - 3 = 0$

2. Determine the slope and y-intercept of the graph of the following lines.

a) $x + y - 11 = 0$
$y = -x + 11$
slope: -1
y-intercept: 11

b) $3x - 2y + 30 = 0$
$3x + 30 = 2y$
$y = \frac{3}{2}x + 15$
slope: $\frac{3}{2}$
y-intercept: 15

c) $8x - 3y - 3 = 0$
$8x - 3 = 3y$
$y = \frac{8}{3}x - 1$
slope: $\frac{8}{3}$
y-intercept: -1

d) $3x + 6y - 7 = 0$
$6y = -3x + 7$
$y = -\frac{1}{2}x + \frac{7}{6}$
slope: $-\frac{1}{2}$
y-intercept: $\frac{7}{6}$

e) $8y = 4x + 32$
$y = \frac{1}{2}x + 4$
slope: $\frac{1}{2}$
y-intercept: 4

f) $4x + 3y = 12$
$3y = -4x + 12$
$y = -\frac{4}{3}x + 4$
slope: $-\frac{4}{3}$
y-intercept: 4

3. Determine the slope, y-intercept, and x-intercept of the graph of the following lines.

a) $2x + y - 6 = 0$
$y = -2x + 6$
slope: -2 y_int: 6
x_int: $y = 0$ $2x - 6 = 0$
$2x = 6$
x_int: 3

b) $5x - 2y + 20 = 0$
$5x + 20 = 2y$
$y = \frac{5}{2}x + 10$
slope: $\frac{5}{2}$ y_int: 10
x_int: $y = 0$ $5x + 20 = 0$
$5x = -20$
x_int: -4

c) $4x - 5y - 3 = 0$
$4x - 3 = 5y$
$y = \frac{4}{5}x - \frac{3}{5}$
slope: $\frac{4}{5}$ y_int: $-\frac{3}{5}$
x_int: $y = 0$ $4x - 3 = 0$
$4x = 3$
x_int: $\frac{3}{4}$

Equations of Linear Relations Lesson #3:
The General Form Equation Ax + By + C = 0

Class Ex. #1

a) $y = 5x - 8$
$0 = 5x - y - 8$
$5x - y - 8 = 0$

b) $y = \frac{2}{3}x + 7$
$3y = 3(\frac{2}{3}x) + 3(7)$
$3y = 2x + 21$
$2x - 3y + 21 = 0$

c) $y = -\frac{1}{4}x + \frac{3}{5}$
$20y = 20(-\frac{1}{4}x) + 20(\frac{3}{5})$
$20y = -5x + 12$
$5x + 20y - 12 = 0$

Class Ex. #2

a) $2x - 5y + 25 = 0$
$2x + 25 = 5y$
$y = \frac{2}{5}x + 5$
slope: $\frac{2}{5}$ y_int: 5

b) $6x + 2y - 15 = 0$
$2y = -6x + 15$
$y = -3x + \frac{15}{2}$
slope: -3 y_int: $\frac{15}{2}$

Class Ex. #3

$3x + 8 = 4y$
$y = \frac{3}{4}x + 2$
y_int: 2

$5x - 6 = ky$
$y = \frac{5}{k}x - \frac{6}{k}$
y_int: $-\frac{6}{k}$

$2 = -\frac{6}{k}$
$2k = -6$
$k = -3$

572   Equations of Linear Relations Lesson #3: *The General Form Equation Ax + By + C = 0*

Class Ex. #4 Which of the following lines is/are perpendicular to the line $4x - 2y + 9 = 0$?

i) $6x + 3y - 1 = 0$
$3y = -6x + 1$
$y = -2x + \frac{1}{3}$
slope: -2

ii) $x + 2y - 12 = 0$
$2y = -x + 12$
$y = -\frac{1}{2}x + 6$
slope: $-\frac{1}{2}$

iii) $5x + 10y = 0$
$10y = -5x$
$y = -\frac{1}{2}x$
slope: $-\frac{1}{2}$

Given line: $4x + 9 = 2y$
$y = 2x + \frac{9}{2}$
slope: 2

ii) and iii) are perpendicular because $-\frac{1}{2}$ is the negative reciprocal of 2.

Class Ex. #5

$2x + 5y - 7 = 0$
$5y = -2x + 7$
$y = -\frac{2}{5}x + \frac{7}{5}$
slope: $-\frac{2}{5}$
perpendicular slope: $\frac{5}{2}$

$2x + 5y - 6 = 0$
$5y = -2x + 6$
$y = -\frac{2}{5}x + \frac{6}{5}$
y_int: 6

Equation of required line
$y = \frac{5}{2}x + 6$
$2y = 2(\frac{5}{2}x) + 2(6)$
or $2y = 5x + 12$
$5x - 2y + 12 = 0$

Class Ex. #6

$2y = 5x + 12$
$y = \frac{5}{2}x + 6$
slope: $\frac{5}{2}$, y_int: 6
Statement 1 is false.

$10x - 4y + 13 = 0$
$10x + 13 = 4y$
$y = \frac{5}{2}x + \frac{13}{4}$
slope: $\frac{5}{2}$
Statement 2 is true.

LS $= 2(1) = 2$
RS $= 5(-1) + 12 = 2$
Statement 3 is true

(C.) 2 and 3 only

9. $6x + 5y - 1 = 0$ is

$5y = -6x + 1$

$y = -\frac{6}{5}x + \frac{1}{5}$

(A.) $-\frac{6}{5}$

10.

$5y = -x - 1$, $\quad y = -\frac{1}{5}x - \frac{1}{5}$ X

$3y = -x - 3$, $\quad y = -\frac{1}{3}x - 1$ X

$x + 2 = 2y$, $\quad y = \frac{1}{2}x + \frac{1}{2}$ $y_{int} = 1$ X

(C.) $x - 2y + 2 = 0$

11.

$3y = -x - 8$

$y = -\frac{1}{3}x - \frac{8}{3}$

slope $= -\frac{1}{3}$

(D.) 3

12.

$2y = -3x - 6$

$y = -\frac{3}{2}x - 3$

$y_{int} = -3$

$P(0, -3)$

$m_{PQ} = \dfrac{y_Q - y_P}{x_Q - x_P} = \dfrac{-2+3}{6-0} = \dfrac{1}{6}$

(B.) $\frac{1}{6}$

13.

$y = \frac{4}{a}x + \frac{9}{a}$

slope $= \frac{4}{a}$

$\left(\frac{4}{a}\right)(5) = -1$

$\frac{20}{a} = -1$

$20 = -a$

$a = -20$

(D.) -20

14.

$4y = -kx + 8$

$y = -\frac{k}{4}x + 2$

$kx + 0 - 8 = 0$

$kx = 8$ $x_{int} = 8$

slope $= -\frac{k}{4}$

$y_{int} = 2$

$x_{int} = \frac{8}{k}$

(C.) 2 only

15. Line L has equation $5x - 3y + 21 = 0$. A is the point $(-6, -3)$, B is $(3, -2)$, and C is $(-3, 2)$. Which of these points lie on line L?

A.   A only

B.   A and B only

(C.)   A and C only

D.   B and C only

A: $5(-6) - 3(-3) + 21 = -30 + 9 + 21 = 0$ ✓

B: $5(3) - 3(-2) + 21 = 15 + 6 + 21 = 42$ ✗

C: $5(-3) - 3(2) + 21 = -15 - 6 + 21 = 0$ ✓

16. Given that the line joining the points $(2, 3)$ and $(8, -q)$, where $q \in W$, is perpendicular to the line $3x - 2y - 5 = 0$, then the value of q is _____.

(Record your answer in the numerical response box from left to right)

$3x - 2y - 5 = 0$

$3x - 5 = 2y$

$y = \frac{3}{2}x - \frac{5}{2}$ slope $= \frac{3}{2}$

$m = \dfrac{-q-3}{8-2} = \dfrac{-q-3}{6}$

$\left(\dfrac{-q-3}{6}\right)\left(\dfrac{3}{2}\right) = -1$

$3(-q-3) = -12$

$-3q - 9 = -12$

$3 = 3q$

$q = 1$

1

4.

$2x + 9 = 3y$ $\qquad$ $22x - 18 = 3y$

$y = \frac{2}{3}x + 3$ $\qquad$ $y = \frac{22}{3}x - 6$

slope $= \frac{2}{3}$ $\qquad$ $b_{int} = -6$

parallel slope $= \frac{2}{3}$

required equation

$y = \frac{2}{3}x - 6$

$3y = 3\left(\frac{2}{3}x\right) - 3(6)$

$3y = 2x - 18$

$2x - 3y - 18 = 0$

5.

$3x + 5 = 2y$ $\qquad$ $3x + 18 = y$

$y = \frac{3}{2}x + \frac{5}{2}$ $\qquad$ $y = 3x + 18$

slope $= \frac{3}{2}$ $\qquad$ $y_{int} = 18$

perpendicular slope $= -\frac{2}{3}$

required equation

$y = -\frac{2}{3}x + 18$

$3y = 3\left(-\frac{2}{3}x\right) + 3(18)$

$3y = -2x + 54$

$2x + 3y - 54 = 0$

6. a) Determine the value of k if the lines have the same slope.

$x + 1 = 2y$ $\qquad$ $ky = -4x + 8$

$y = \frac{1}{2}x + \frac{1}{2}$ $\qquad$ $y = -\frac{4}{k}x + \frac{8}{k}$

slope $= -\frac{4}{k}$

$\frac{1}{2} = -\frac{4}{k}$

$k = -8$

a) Determine the value of k if the lines have the same y-intercept.

$y_{int} = \frac{1}{2}$ $\qquad$ $y_{int} = \frac{8}{k}$

$\frac{1}{2} = \frac{8}{k}$

$k = 16$

7. a) Determine the value of a if the lines have the same slope.

$3x - 15 = 5y$ $\qquad$ $2y = -ax + 6$

$y = \frac{3}{5}x - 3$ $\qquad$ $y = -\frac{a}{2}x + 3$

slope $= \frac{3}{5}$ $\qquad$ slope $= -\frac{a}{2}$

$\frac{3}{5} = -\frac{a}{2}$

$6 = -5a$

$a = -\frac{6}{5}$

a) Determine the value of a if the lines have the same x-intercept.

$3x - 0 - 15 = 0$ $\qquad$ $ax + 0 - 6 = 0$

$3x = 15$ $\qquad$ $ax = 6$

$x_{int} = 5$ $\qquad$ $x_{int} = \frac{6}{a}$

$5 = \frac{6}{a}$

$a = \frac{6}{5}$

8. Equation

i) $6x - 2y + 5 = 0$ E $\qquad$ $6x + 5 = 2y$, $\quad y = 3x + \frac{5}{2}$ $\qquad$ $2(-10)$ $2(-4)$

ii) $2x - 5y = 0$ C $\qquad$ $2x = 5y$, $\quad y = \frac{2}{5}x$

iii) $x + 3y + 6 = 0$ A $\qquad$ $3y = -x - 6$, $\quad y = -\frac{1}{3}x - 2$

iv) $x - 4y + 10 = 0$ E $\qquad$ $x + 10 = 4y$, $\quad y = \frac{1}{4}x + \frac{5}{2}$

v) $2x - y - 5 = 0$ G $\qquad$ $2x - 5 = y$, $\quad y = 2x - 5$ $\qquad$ $0 = 2x - 5$, $\quad 5 = 2x$, $\quad x_{int} = \frac{5}{2}$

Equations of Linear Relations Lesson #4:
Slope-Point Form → $y - y_1 = m(x - x_1)$

Review   a) The general form of an equation of a line is $Ax + By + C = 0$.

b) The slope y-intercept form of the equation of a line is $y = mx + b$.

Investigation #1   *Slope-Point Form*

The graph of $y + 3 = 2(x-1)$ is shown on the grid.

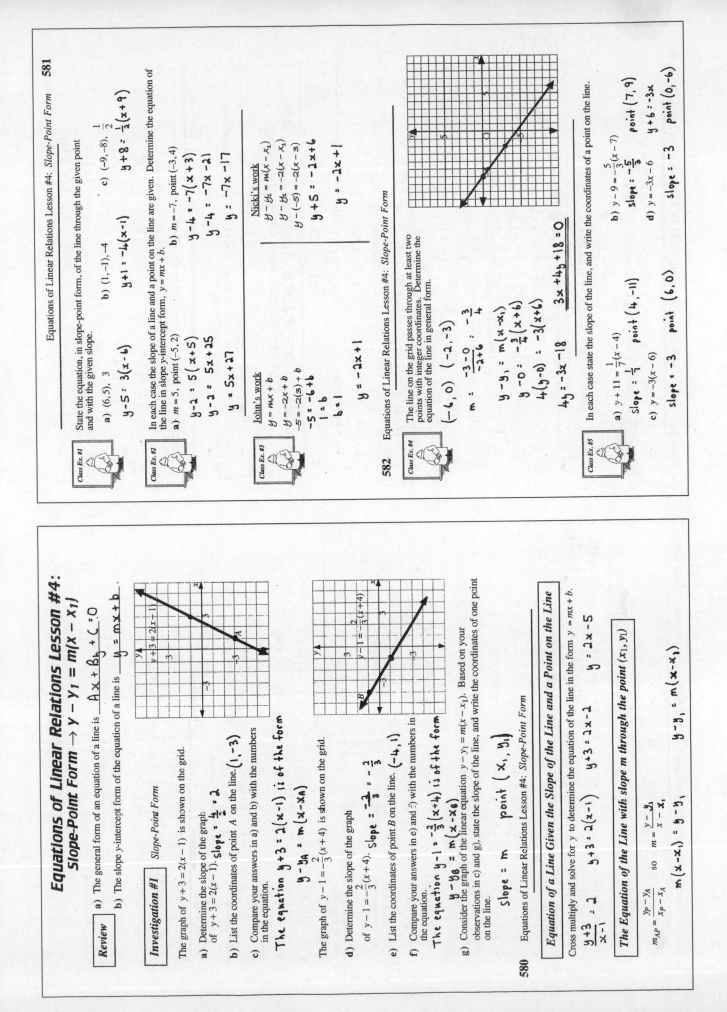

a) Determine the slope of the graph
of $y + 3 = 2(x-1)$. slope = $\frac{4}{2}$ = 2

b) List the coordinates of point A on the line. $(1, -3)$

c) Compare your answers in a) and b) with the numbers
in the equation.

The equation $y+3 = 2(x-1)$ is of the form
$y - y_A = m(x - x_A)$

The graph of $y - 1 = -\frac{2}{3}(x+4)$ is shown on the grid.

d) Determine the slope of the graph
of $y - 1 = -\frac{2}{3}(x+4)$. slope = $\frac{-2}{3}$ = $-\frac{2}{3}$

e) List the coordinates of point B on the line. $(-4, 1)$

f) Compare your answers in e) and f) with the numbers in
the equation.

The equation $y-1 = -\frac{2}{3}(x+4)$ is of the form
$y - y_B = m(x - x_B)$

g) Consider the graph of the linear equation $y - y_1 = m(x - x_1)$. Based on your
observations in c) and g), state the slope of the line, and write the coordinates of one point
on the line.

slope = m   point (x_1, y_1)

580   Equations of Linear Relations Lesson #4: *Slope-Point Form*

Equation of a Line Given the Slope of the Line and a Point on the Line

Cross multiply and solve for y to determine the equation of the line in the form $y = mx + b$.

$\frac{y+3}{x-1} = 2$ $y+3 = 2(x-1)$ $y+3 = 2x-2$ $y = 2x-5$

The Equation of the Line with slope m through the point (x_1, y_1)

$m_{AP} = \frac{y_P - y_A}{x_P - x_A}$ so $m = \frac{y - y_1}{x - x_1}$

$m(x - x_1) = y - y_1$ $y - y_1 = m(x - x_1)$

Equations of Linear Relations Lesson #4: *Slope-Form*   581

State the equation, in slope-point form, of the line through the given point
and with the given slope.

a) (6,5), 3   b) (1,-1), -4   c) (-9,-8), $\frac{1}{2}$

$y-5 = 3(x-6)$ $y+1 = -4(x-1)$ $y+8 = \frac{1}{2}(x+9)$

Class Ex. #1

In each case the slope of a line and a point on the line are given. Determine the equation of
the line in slope y-intercept form, $y = mx + b$.

a) $m = 5$, point $(-5, 2)$ b) $m = -7$, point $(-3, 4)$

Class Ex. #2

John's work
$y = mx + b$
$y = -2x + b$
$-5 = -2(3) + b$
$-5 = -6 + b$
$1 = b$
$b = 1$

$y = -2x + 1$

$y-2 = 5(x+5)$
$y-2 = 5x+25$
$y = 5x+27$

Nicki's work
$y - y_1 = m(x - x_1)$
$y - y_1 = -2(x - x_1)$
$y - (-5) = -2(x-3)$
$y+5 = -2x+6$
$y = -2x+1$

b)
$y-4 = -7(x+3)$
$y-4 = -7x-21$
$y = -7x-17$

Class Ex. #3

582   Equations of Linear Relations Lesson #4: *Slope-Point Form*

Class Ex. #4

The line on the grid passes through at least two
points with integer coordinates. Determine the
equation of the line in general form.

$(-6, 0)$ $(-2, -3)$

$m = \frac{-3 - 0}{-2 + 6} = \frac{-3}{4}$

$y - y_1 = m(x - x_1)$
$y - 0 = -\frac{3}{4}(x+6)$
$4(y-0) = -3(x+6)$
$4y = -3x - 18$
$3x + 4y + 18 = 0$

Class Ex. #5

In each case state the slope of the line, and write the coordinates of a point on the line.

a) $y + 11 = \frac{1}{7}(x-4)$ b) $y - 9 = -\frac{5}{3}(x-7)$

slope = $\frac{1}{7}$ point $(4, -11)$ slope = $-\frac{5}{3}$ point $(7, 9)$

c) $y = -3(x-6)$ d) $y = -3x-6$

slope = -3 point $(6,0)$ $y + 6 = -3x$
slope = -3 point $(0, -6)$

1.
a) $y - 3 = 4(x-9)$ b) $y + 2 = -3(x-8)$ c) $y - 7 = 1(x+5)$
d) $y - 3 = \frac{1}{2}x$ e) $y = \frac{1}{4}(x+7)$ f) $y + \frac{5}{4} = \frac{6}{5}(x+\frac{1}{2})$

2.
a) $y + 1 = 8(x-2)$
$y+1 = 8x-16$
$y = 8x-17$

b) $y - 3 = -2(x-7)$
$y-3 = -2x+14$
$y = -2x+17$

c) $y - 9 = -11(x+3)$
$y-9 = -11x-33$
$y = -11x-24$

d) $y + 3 = 7(x+12)$
$y+3 = 7x+84$
$y = 7x+81$

3. Find the equation, in slope y-intercept form, of the line through the given point and with the given slope.

a) $(2,4)$, 6
$y-4 = 6(x-2)$
$y-4 = 6x-12$
$y = 6x-8$

b) $(2,-1)$, 2
$y+1 = 2(x-2)$
$y+1 = 2x-4$
$y = 2x-5$

c) $(0,4)$, -2
$y-4 = -2(x-0)$
$y-4 = -2x$
$y = -2x+4$

d) $(-6,2)$, $\frac{1}{2}$
$y-2 = \frac{1}{2}(x+6)$
$y-2 = \frac{1}{2}x+3$
$y = \frac{1}{2}x+5$

e) $(-7,-7)$, 1
$y+7 = 1(x+7)$
$y+7 = x+7$
$y = x$

f) $(0,b)$, m
$y-b = m(x-0)$
$y-b = mx$
$y = mx+b$

4. Find the equation, in general form, of the line through the given point and with the given slope.

a) $(6,1)$, 3
$y-1 = 3(x-6)$
$y-1 = 3x-18$
$0 = 3x-y-17$
$3x-y-17 = 0$

b) $(2,-5)$, $\frac{1}{4}$
$y+5 = \frac{1}{4}(x-2)$
$4(y+5) = 1(x-2)$
$4y+20 = x-2$
$0 = x-4y-22$
$x-4y-22 = 0$

c) $(-4,2)$, $-\frac{1}{3}$
$y-2 = -\frac{1}{3}(x+4)$
$3(y-2) = -1(x+4)$
$3y-6 = -x-4$
$x+3y-2 = 0$

d) $(-9,-2)$, $\frac{2}{5}$
$y+2 = \frac{2}{5}(x+9)$
$5(y+2) = 2(x+9)$
$5y+10 = 2x+18$
$0 = 2x-5y+8$
$2x-5y+8 = 0$

e) $(0,-8)$, $-\frac{3}{4}$
$y+8 = -\frac{3}{4}(x-0)$
$4(y+8) = -3x$
$4y+32 = -3x$
$3x+4y+32 = 0$

f) $(0,0)$, $\frac{4}{3}$
$y-0 = \frac{4}{3}(x-0)$
$3y = 4x$
$0 = 4x-3y$
$4x-3y = 0$

5.
a) $y - 9 = -\frac{11}{3}(x+3)$
Slope $= -\frac{11}{3}$ point $(-3,9)$

b) $y + 3 = \frac{1}{2}x$
slope $= \frac{1}{2}$ point $(0,-3)$

c) $y - 8 = -2(x-6)$
slope $= -2$ point $(6,8)$

d) $y = 3(x+12)$

e) $y - 9 = -\frac{5}{3}x$
Slope $= -\frac{5}{3}$ point $(-12,0)$

f) $y = \frac{2}{5}x$
slope $= \frac{2}{5}$ point $(0,0)$

6. Determine the equation of each line.

ℓ_1: $(-1,1)$, $(-4,3)$ $m = \frac{3-1}{-4+1} = -\frac{2}{3}$
$y-1 = -\frac{2}{3}(x+1)$
$3(y-1) = -2(x+1)$
$3y-3 = -2x-2$
$2x+3y-1 = 0$ (A) $2x+3y-1=0$

ℓ_2: $(5,-3)$, $(3,-8)$ $m = \frac{-8+3}{3-5} = \frac{5}{2}$
$y+3 = \frac{5}{2}(x-5)$
$2(y+3) = 5(x-5)$
$2y+6 = 5x-25$
$5x-2y-31 = 0$

7.
$y-2 = -3(x-4)$
$y-2 = -3x+12$
$3x+y-14 = 0$ (A) $3x+y-14=0$

8.
$y-0 = -\frac{1}{2}(x-0)$
$y = -\frac{1}{2}x$
$2y = -x$
$x+2y = 0$ (A) $x+2y=0$

9.
$y-3 = -\frac{3}{4}(x+7)?$
$4(y-3) = -3(x+7)$
$4y-12 = -3x-21$
$3x+4y+9 = 0$ (B) $3x+4y+9=0$

10. point $(-2,0)$ $m=12$
$y-0 = 12(x+2)$
$y = 12x+24$
$0 = 12x-y+24$
$12x-y+24 = 0$

$B = -1$
$C = 24$
$B+c : -1+24 = 23$

$\boxed{23}$

Equations of Linear Relations Lesson #5:
Further Practice with Linear Equations

Class Ex. #1
$m_{PQ} = \frac{-6+1}{-2-3} = \frac{-5}{-5} = 1$

$y-y_1 = m(x-x_1)$
$y+1 = 1(x-3)$
$y+1 = x-3$
$0 = x-y-4$
$x-y-4 = 0$

Class Ex. #2
$3x+17 = 5y$
$\frac{3}{5}x + \frac{17}{5} = y$
$y = \frac{3}{5}x + \frac{17}{5}$
slope $= \frac{3}{5}$

perpendicular slope $-\frac{5}{3}$

$y-y_1 = m(x-x_1)$
$y-0 = -\frac{5}{3}(x-5)$
$3(y-0) = -5x+25$
$3y = -5x+25$
$5x+3y-25 = 0$

4. a) perpendicular to $y = x$ and with the same x-intercept as $y = 2x + 10$

$$\text{slope} = 1$$
$$\text{perpendicular slope} = -1$$
$$\text{point } (-5, 0)$$

$$y - y_1 = m(x - x_1)$$
$$y - 0 = -1(x + 5)$$
$$y = -x - 5$$
$$\underline{\underline{x + y + 5 = 0}}$$

$$0 = 2x + 10$$
$$-10 = 2x \qquad x_{int} = -5$$

b) parallel to $2x - 3y + 7 = 0$ and with the same y-intercept as $5x - 3y - 12 = 0$

$$2x + 7 = 3y$$
$$y = \tfrac{2}{3}x + \tfrac{7}{3}$$
$$\text{slope} = \tfrac{2}{3}$$
$$\text{parallel slope} = \tfrac{2}{3}$$

$$y = mx + b$$
$$y = \tfrac{2}{3}x - 4$$
$$3y = 2x - 12$$
$$\underline{\underline{2x - 3y - 12 = 0}}$$

$$5x - 12 = 3y$$
$$y = \tfrac{5}{3}x - 4$$
$$y_{int} = -4$$

5. a) perpendicular to $6x - 2y + 5 = 0$ and with the same y-intercept as $x - y + 8 = 0$

$$6x + 5 = 2y$$
$$y = 3x + \tfrac{5}{2}$$
$$\text{slope} = 3$$
$$\text{perpendicular slope} = -\tfrac{1}{3}$$

$$y = mx + b$$
$$y = -\tfrac{1}{3}x + 8$$
$$3y = -x + 24$$
$$\underline{\underline{x + 3y - 24 = 0}}$$

$$x + 8 = y$$
$$y = x + 8$$
$$y_{int} = 8$$

b) with the same x-intercept as $9x - 2y + 18 = 0$ and through the point $(4, -5)$

$$9x + 18 = 0$$
$$9x = -18$$
$$x_{int} = -2$$
$$\text{point } (-2, 0)$$

$$m = \frac{-5 - 0}{4 - (-2)} = -\tfrac{5}{6}$$

$$y - 0 = -\tfrac{5}{6}(x + 2)$$
$$6y = -5(x + 2)$$
$$6y = -5x - 10$$
$$\underline{\underline{5x + 6y + 10 = 0}}$$

6. $$m_{BC} = \frac{-1 - 5}{8 + 4} = \frac{-6}{12} = -\tfrac{1}{2}$$

$$\text{parallel slope} = -\tfrac{1}{2}$$

$$y - y_1 = m(x - x_1)$$
$$y - 9 = -\tfrac{1}{2}(x - 7)$$
$$y - 9 = -\tfrac{1}{2}x + \tfrac{7}{2}$$
$$y = -\tfrac{1}{2}x + \tfrac{25}{2}$$

7. a) If the point A has coordinates $(2, 4)$, determine the equation of AD.

$$AD \text{ is parallel to } BC \qquad m_{AD} = 3$$

$$y - 4 = 3(x - 2)$$
$$y - 4 = 3x - 6$$
$$y = 3x - 2 \quad \text{or} \quad \underline{\underline{3x - y - 2 = 0}}$$

b) Determine the equation of AB.

$$AB \perp AD \text{ so } m_{AB} = -\tfrac{1}{3}$$

$$y - 4 = -\tfrac{1}{3}(x - 2)$$
$$3(y - 4) = -1(x - 2)$$
$$3y - 12 = -x + 2$$
$$\underline{\underline{x + 3y - 14 = 0}}$$

(coordinate diagram showing line $y = 3x$ with points A, B, C, D)

Assignment

1. Find the equation, in general form, of the line through each pair of points.

a) $(7, 5)$ and $(6, 1)$

$$m = \frac{1 - 5}{6 - 7} = \frac{-4}{-1} = 4$$
$$y - 1 = 4(x - 6)$$
$$y - 1 = 4x - 24$$
$$0 = 4x - y - 23$$
$$\underline{\underline{4x - y - 23 = 0}}$$

b) $(3, -7)$ and $(-5, 9)$

$$m = \frac{9 + 7}{-5 - 3} = \frac{16}{-8} = -2$$
$$y - 9 = -2(x + 5)$$
$$y - 9 = -2x - 10$$
$$\underline{\underline{2x + y + 1 = 0}}$$

c) $(-3, 4)$ and $(11, 25)$

$$m = \frac{25 - 4}{11 + 3} = \frac{21}{14} = \frac{3}{2}$$
$$y - 4 = \tfrac{3}{2}(x + 3)$$
$$2(y - 4) = 3(x + 3)$$
$$2y - 8 = 3x + 9$$
$$\underline{\underline{3x - 2y + 17 = 0}}$$

d) $(10, -15)$ and $(-2, -12)$

$$m = \frac{-12 + 15}{-2 - 10} = \frac{3}{-12} = -\tfrac{1}{4}$$
$$y + 12 = -\tfrac{1}{4}(x + 2)$$
$$4(y + 12) = -1(x + 2)$$
$$4y + 48 = -x - 2$$
$$\underline{\underline{x + 4y + 50 = 0}}$$

e) $(4, -7)$ and $(3, -7)$

$$m = \frac{-7 + 7}{3 - 4} = 0$$
$$y + 7 = 0(x - 3)$$
$$y + 7 = 0$$
$$\underline{\underline{y}}$$

f) $(-5, -8)$ and $(-4, -10)$

$$m = \frac{-10 + 8}{-4 + 5} = \frac{-2}{1} = -2$$
$$y + 8 = -2(x + 5)$$
$$y + 8 = -2x - 10$$
$$\underline{\underline{2x + y + 18 = 0}}$$

2. i) b and f   ii) a and d

3. a) with slope $\tfrac{2}{7}$ and an x-intercept of -6

$$\text{point } (-6, 0) \qquad m = \tfrac{2}{7}$$
$$y - y_1 = m(x - x_1)$$
$$y - 0 = \tfrac{2}{7}(x + 6)$$
$$7y = 2(x + 6)$$
$$7y = 2x + 12$$
$$\underline{\underline{2x - 7y + 12 = 0}}$$

b) with a y-intercept of $-\tfrac{8}{3}$ and a slope of 7

$$\text{point } \left(0, -\tfrac{8}{3}\right) \qquad m = 7$$
$$y = mx + b$$
$$y = 7x - \tfrac{8}{3}$$
$$3y = 21x - 8$$
$$\underline{\underline{21x - 3y - 8 = 0}}$$

c) through the point $(2, 0)$ and perpendicular to $3x - 5y + 19 = 0$

$$3x + 19 = 5y$$
$$y = \tfrac{3}{5}x + \tfrac{19}{5}$$
$$\text{slope} = \tfrac{3}{5}$$
$$\text{perpendicular slope} = -\tfrac{5}{3}$$

$$y - 0 = -\tfrac{5}{3}(x - 2)$$
$$3y = -5(x - 2)$$
$$3y = -5x + 10$$
$$\underline{\underline{5x + 3y - 10 = 0}}$$

d) through the point $(3, -6)$ and parallel to $5x + 3y + 9 = 0$

$$3y = -5x - 9$$
$$y = -\tfrac{5}{3}x - 3$$
$$\text{slope} = -\tfrac{5}{3}$$
$$\text{parallel slope} = -\tfrac{5}{3}$$

$$y + 6 = -\tfrac{5}{3}(x - 3)$$
$$3(y + 6) = -5(x - 3)$$
$$3y + 18 = -5x + 15$$
$$\underline{\underline{5x + 3y + 3 = 0}}$$

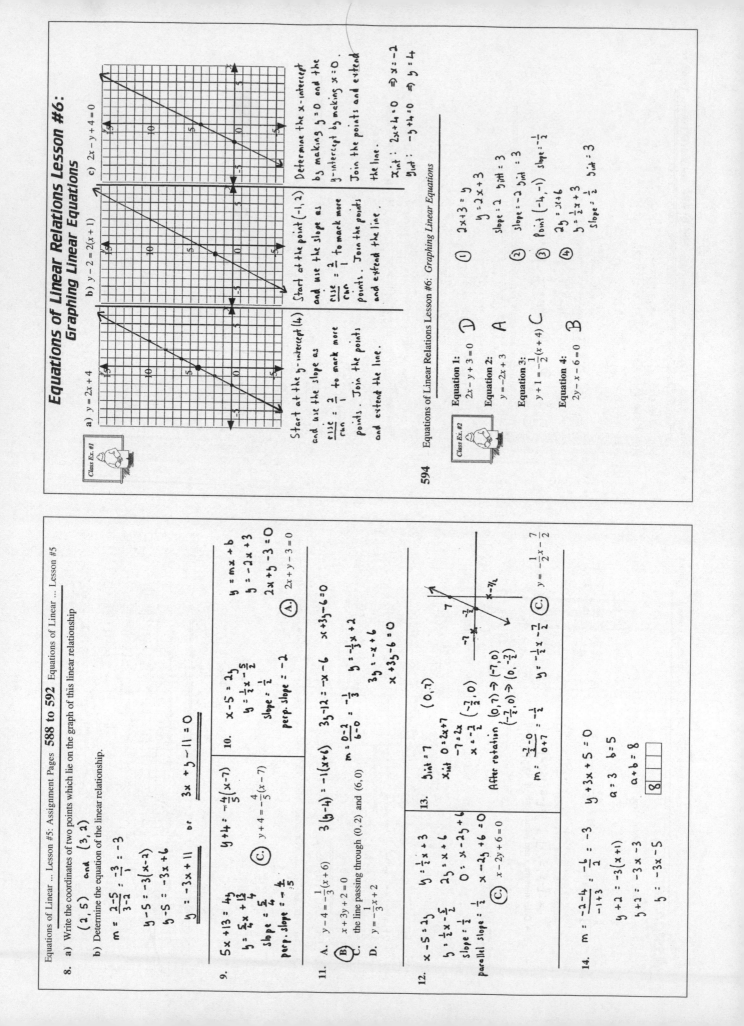

Equations of Linear Relations Lesson #6:
Graphing Linear Equations

Class Ex. #1

a) $y = 2x + 4$ b) $y - 2 = 2(x+1)$ c) $2x - y + 4 = 0$

Start at the y-intercept (4) and use the slope as $\frac{rise}{run} = \frac{2}{1}$ to mark more points. Join the points and extend the line.

Start at the point $(-1, 2)$ and use the slope as $\frac{rise}{run} = \frac{2}{1}$ to mark more points. Join the points and extend the line.

Determine the x-intercept by making $y = 0$ and the y-intercept by making $x = 0$. Join the points and extend the line.

$x_{int}: 2x+4=0 \Rightarrow x=-2$
$y_{int}: -y+4=0 \Rightarrow y=4$

594 Equations of Linear Relations Lesson #6: *Graphing Linear Equations*

Class Ex. #2

Equation 1:
$2x - y + 3 = 0$ Ⓓ

Equation 2:
$y = -2x + 3$ A

Equation 3:
$y + 1 = -\frac{1}{2}(x+4)$ C

Equation 4:
$2y - x - 6 = 0$ B

① $2x+3 = y$
   $y = 2x+3$
   slope: 2 y-int: 3

② $y = -2x + 3$
   slope: -2 y-int: 3

③ Point $(-4,-1)$ slope: $-\frac{1}{2}$
   $2y = x+6$
   $y = \frac{1}{2}x + 3$
   slope: $\frac{1}{2}$ y-int: 3

④

Equations of Linear ... Lesson #5: Assignment Pages **588 to 592** Equations of Linear ... Lesson #5

8. a) Write the coordinates of two points which lie on the graph of this linear relationship.

$(2, 5)$ and $(3, 2)$

b) Determine the equation of the linear relationship.

$m = \frac{2-5}{3-2} = \frac{-3}{1} = -3$
$y - 5 = -3(x-2)$
$y - 5 = -3x + 6$
$y = -3x + 11$ or $3x + y - 11 = 0$

9. $5x + 13 = 4y$
$y = \frac{5}{4}x + \frac{13}{4}$
slope = $\frac{5}{4}$
perp. slope = $-\frac{4}{5}$

$y + 4 = -\frac{4}{5}(x-7)$

Ⓒ $y + 4 = -\frac{4}{5}(x-7)$

10. $x - 5 = 2y$
$y = \frac{1}{2}x - \frac{5}{2}$
slope: $\frac{1}{2}$
perp. slope: -2

$y = mx + b$
$y = -2x + 3$
$2x + y - 3 = 0$

Ⓐ $2x + y - 3 = 0$

11. A. $y - 4 = -\frac{1}{3}(x+6)$
   $x + 3y + 2 = 0$
Ⓑ
   C. the line passing through $(0,2)$ and $(6,0)$
   D. $y = -\frac{1}{3}x + 2$

$3(y-4) = -1(x+6)$ $3y-12 = -x-6$ $x+3y-6=0$
$m = \frac{0-2}{6-0} = -\frac{1}{3}$ $y = -\frac{1}{3}x+2$
$3y = -x+6$
$3y = x+6$
$x + 3y - 6 = 0$

12. $x - 5 = 2y$
$y = \frac{1}{2}x - \frac{5}{2}$
slope: $\frac{1}{2}$
parallel slope: $\frac{1}{2}$
$0: x - 2y + 6$
$x - 2y + 6 = 0$

Ⓒ $x - 2y + 6 = 0$

13. $y_{int} = 7$ $(0,7)$
$x_{int}: 0 = 2x+7$
$-7 = 2x$
$x = -\frac{7}{2}$ $\left(-\frac{7}{2}, 0\right)$

After rotation $(0,7) \rightarrow (7,0)$
$\left(-\frac{7}{2}, 0\right) \rightarrow \left(0, -\frac{7}{2}\right)$

$m = \frac{-\frac{7}{2} - 0}{0+7} = -\frac{1}{2}$ $y = -\frac{1}{2}x - \frac{7}{2}$

Ⓒ $y = -\frac{1}{2}x - \frac{7}{2}$

14. $m = \frac{-2-4}{-1+3} = -\frac{6}{2} = -3$
$y + 2 = -3(x+1)$
$y + 2 = -3x - 3$
$y = -3x - 5$
$y + 3x + 5 = 0$
$a = 3$ $b = 5$
$a + b = 8$

[8]

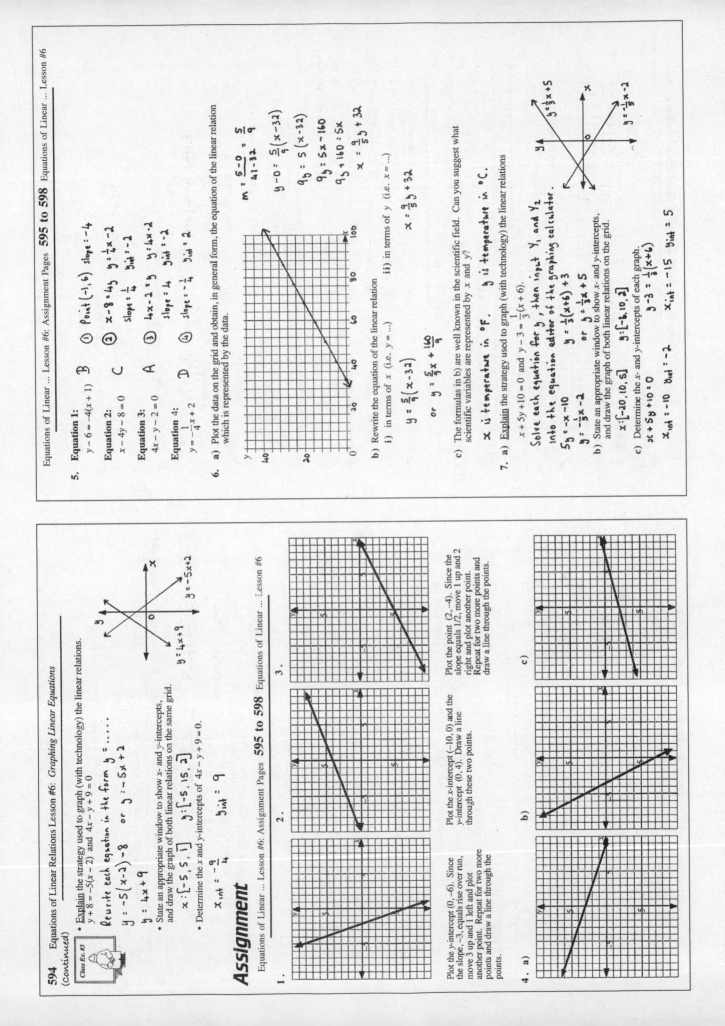

5. Equation 1:
$y - 6 = -4(x+1)$

Equation 2:
$x - 4y - 8 = 0$

Equation 3:
$4x - y - 2 = 0$

Equation 4:
$y = \frac{1}{4}x + 2$

B ① Point $(-1,6)$ slope: -4

C ② $x - 8 = 4y$ $y = \frac{1}{4}x - 2$
   slope: $\frac{1}{4}$ $y_{int}: -2$

A ③ $4x - 2 = y$ $y = 4x - 2$
   slope: 4 $y_{int}: -2$

D ④ slope: $-\frac{1}{4}$ $y_{int}: 2$

6. a) Plot the data on the grid and obtain, in general form, the equation of the linear relation which is represented by the data.

$$m = \frac{6-0}{41-32} = \frac{5}{9}$$

$$y - 0 = \frac{5}{9}(x-32)$$

$$9y = 5(x-32)$$

$$9y = 5x - 160$$

$$9y + 160 = 5x$$

$$x = \frac{9}{5}y + 32$$

b) Rewrite the equation of the linear relation

i) in terms of x (i.e. $y = ...$)

$$y = \frac{5}{9}(x-32)$$

$$\text{or } y = \frac{5}{9}x + \frac{160}{9}$$

iii) in terms of y (i.e. $x = ...$)

$$x = \frac{9}{5}y + 32$$

c) The formulas in b) are well known in the scientific field. Can you suggest what scientific variables are represented by x and y?

x is temperature in °F. y is temperature in °C.

7. a) Explain the strategy used to graph (with technology) the linear relations
$x + 5y + 10 = 0$ and $y - 3 = \frac{1}{3}(x+6)$.

Solve each equation for y, then input Y_1 and Y_2 into the equation editor of the graphing calculator.

$5y = -x - 10$ $y = \frac{1}{3}(x+6)+3$

$y = -\frac{1}{5}x - 2$ or $y = \frac{1}{3}x + 5$

b) State an appropriate window to show x- and y-intercepts, and draw the graph of both linear relations on the grid.

$x:[-20,10,5]$ $y:[-6,10,2]$

c) Determine the x- and y-intercepts of each graph.

$x + 5y + 10 = 0$ $y - 3 = \frac{1}{3}(x+6)$

$x_{int} = -10$ $y_{int} = -2$ $x_{int} = -15$ $y_{int} = 5$

($y = \frac{1}{3}x + 5$; $y = -\frac{1}{5}x - 2$)

---

594   Equations of Linear Relations Lesson #6: *Graphing Linear Equations*
(continued)

Class Ex. #3

• **Explain** the strategy used to graph (with technology) the linear relations.
$y + 8 = -5(x-2)$ and $4x - y + 9 = 0$

Rewrite each equation in the form $y = ...$

$y = -5(x-2) - 8$ or $y = -5x + 2$

$y = 4x + 9$

• State an appropriate window to show x- and y-intercepts, and draw the graph of both linear relations on the same grid.

$x:[-5,5,1]$ $y:[-5,15,2]$

($y = -5x+2$; $y = 4x+9$)

• Determine the x and y-intercepts of $4x - y + 9 = 0$.

$x_{int} = -\frac{9}{4}$ $y_{int} = 9$

Assignment

1. Plot the y-intercept $(0, -6)$. Since the slope, -3, equals rise over run, move 3 up and 1 left and plot another point. Repeat for two more points and draw a line through the points.

2. Plot the x-intercept $(-10, 0)$ and the y-intercept $(0, 4)$. Draw a line through these two points.

3. Plot the point $(2, -4)$. Since the slope equals 1/2, move 1 up and 2 right and plot another point. Repeat for two more points and draw a line through the points.

4. a)   b)   c)

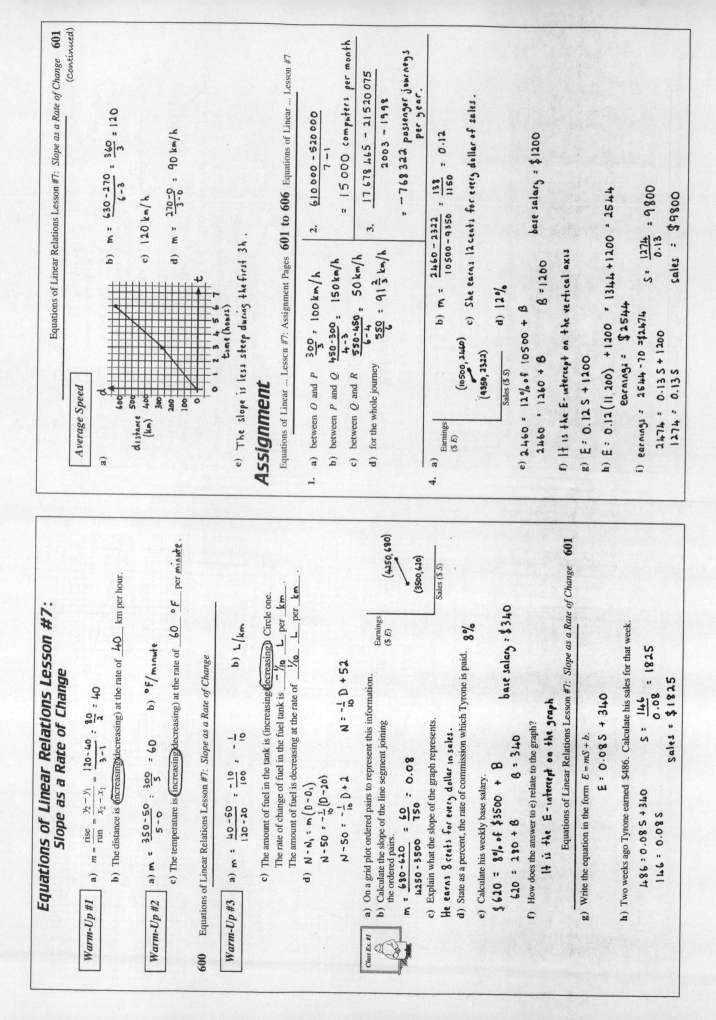

Equations of Linear Relations Lesson #7: Slope as a Rate of Change

Warm-Up #1

a) $m = \dfrac{\text{rise}}{\text{run}} = \dfrac{y_2 - y_1}{x_2 - x_1} = \dfrac{120 - 40}{3 - 1} = \dfrac{80}{2} = 40$

b) The distance is (increasing/~~decreasing~~) at the rate of __40__ km per hour.

Warm-Up #2

a) $m = \dfrac{350 - 50}{5 - 0} = \dfrac{300}{5} = 60$ b) __°F/minute__

c) The temperature is (increasing/~~decreasing~~) at the rate of __60__ °F per minute.

600   Equations of Linear Relations Lesson #7: Slope as a Rate of Change

Warm-Up #3

a) $m = \dfrac{40 - 50}{120 - 20} = \dfrac{-10}{100} = -\dfrac{1}{10}$ b) L/km

c) The amount of fuel in the tank is (increasing/~~decreasing~~) Circle one.
The rate of change of fuel in the fuel tank is __−¹⁄₁₀__ L per km.
The amount of fuel is decreasing at the rate of __¹⁄₁₀__ L per km.

d) $N - N_1 = m(D - D_1)$

$N - 50 = -\dfrac{1}{10}(D - 20)$

$N - 50 = -\dfrac{1}{10}D + 2$ $N = -\dfrac{1}{10}D + 52$

Class Ex. #1

a) On a grid plot ordered pairs to represent this information.

b) Calculate the slope of the line segment joining the ordered pairs.

$m = \dfrac{680 - 620}{4250 - 3500} = \dfrac{60}{750} = 0.08$

Earnings (E)

(4450, 680)

(3500, 620)

Sales (S)

c) Explain what the slope of the graph represents.
He earns 8 cents for every dollar in sales.

d) State as a percent, the rate of commission which Tyrone is paid. __8%__

e) Calculate his weekly base salary.
$620 = 8\%$ of $3500 + B$ base salary: $340
$620 = 280 + B$ $B = 340$

f) How does the answer to e) relate to the graph?
It is the E-intercept on the graph

g) Write the equation in the form $E = mS + b$.
$E = 0.08S + 340$

h) Two weeks ago Tyrone earned $486. Calculate his sales for that week.
$486 = 0.08S + 340$ $S = \dfrac{146}{0.08} = 1825$
$146 = 0.08S$ sales = $1825

Equations of Linear Relations Lesson #7: Slope as a Rate of Change   601

Equations of Linear Relations Lesson #7: Slope as a Rate of Change   601
(Continued)

Average Speed

a)

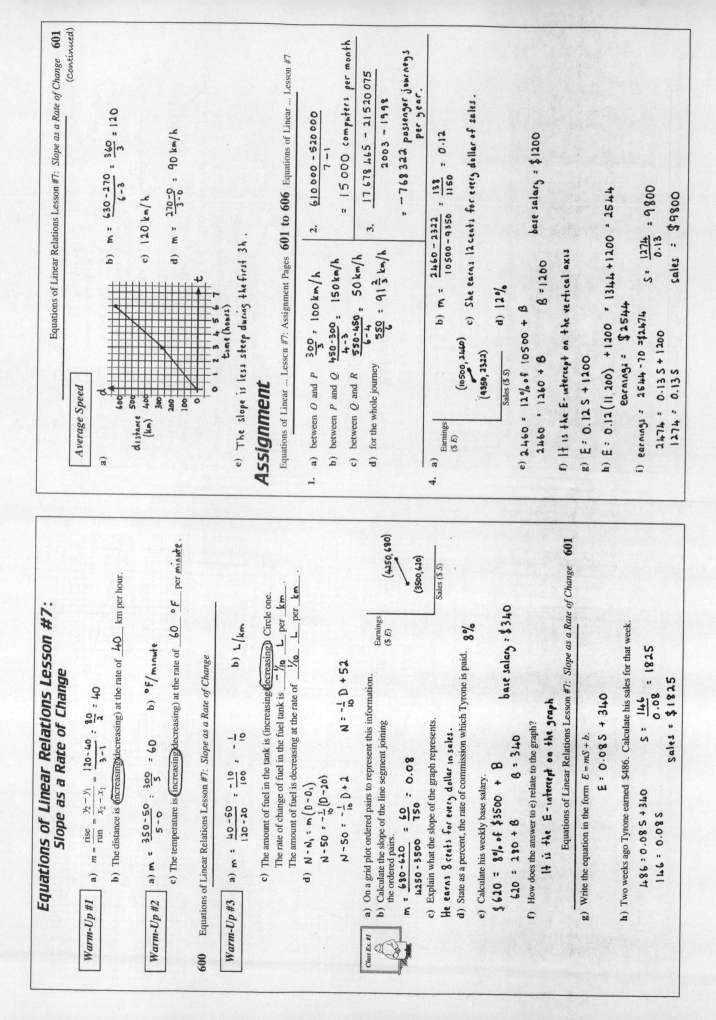

b) $m = \dfrac{630 - 270}{6 - 3} = \dfrac{360}{3} = 120$

c) 120 km/h

d) $m = \dfrac{270 - 0}{3 - 0} = 90$ km/h

e) The slope is less steep during the first 3h.

Assignment

Equations of Linear ... Lesson #7: Assignment Pages **601 to 606**   Equations of Linear ... Lesson #7

1. a) between O and P $\dfrac{300}{3} = 100$ km/h

b) between P and Q $\dfrac{450 - 300}{4 - 3} = \dfrac{150}{1} = 150$ km/h

c) between Q and R $\dfrac{550 - 450}{6 - 4} = \dfrac{550}{6} = 91\frac{2}{3}$ km/h

d) for the whole journey $\dfrac{550}{6} = 91\frac{2}{3}$ km/h

2. $\dfrac{610000 - 520000}{7 - 1}$

$= 15\,000$ computers per month

3. $\dfrac{17\,678\,465 - 21\,520\,075}{2003 - 1998}$

$= -768\,322$ passenger journeys per year.

4. a)

Earnings (E)

(10500, 2460)

(9350, 2322)

Sales (S)

b) $m = \dfrac{2460 - 2322}{10500 - 9350} = \dfrac{138}{1150} = 0.12$

c) She earns 12 cents for every dollar of sales.

d) 12%

e) $2460 = 12\%$ of $10500 + B$
$2460 = 1260 + B$ $B = 1200$ base salary: $1200

f) It is the E-intercept on the vertical axis

g) $E = 0.12S + 1200$

h) $E = 0.12(11200) + 1200 = 2544$
earnings: $2544

i) earnings: $2644 - 70 = \$2474$ $S = \dfrac{1274}{0.13} = 9800$
$2474 = 0.13S + 1200$ sales = $9800
$1274 = 0.13S$

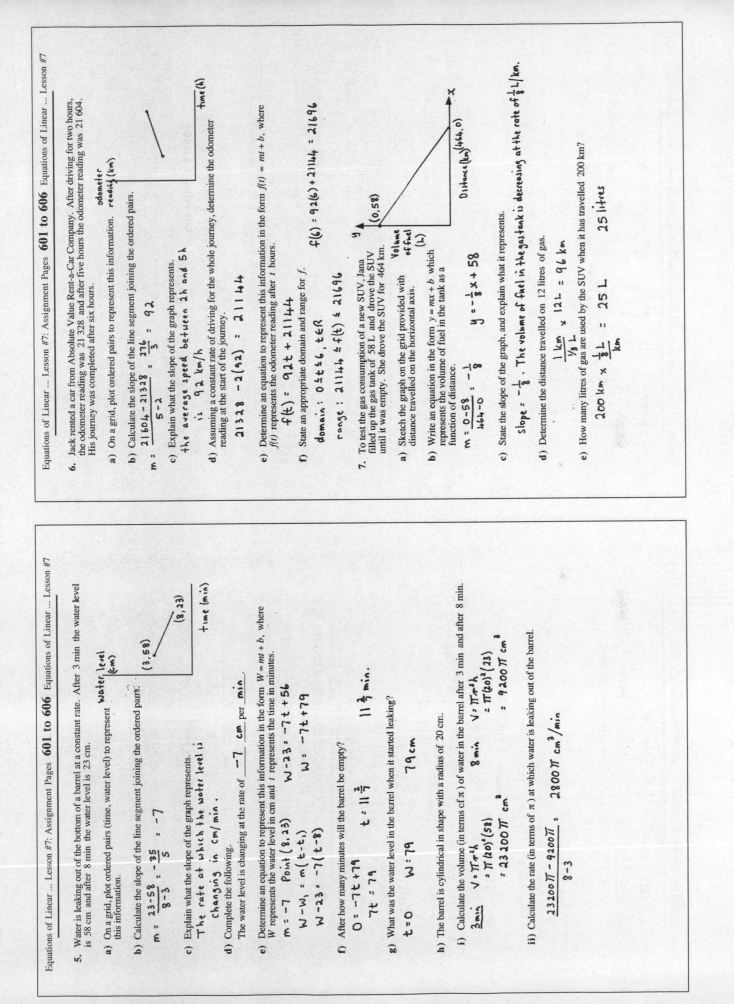

5. Water is leaking out of the bottom of a barrel at a constant rate. After 3 min the water level is 58 cm and after 8 min the water level is 23 cm.

a) On a grid, plot ordered pairs (time, water level) to represent this information.

water level (cm)

(3, 58)

(8, 23)

time (min)

b) Calculate the slope of the line segment joining the ordered pairs.

$m = \dfrac{23-58}{8-3} = \dfrac{-35}{5} = -7$

c) Explain what the slope of the graph represents.

The rate at which the water level is changing in cm/min.

d) Complete the following.
The water level is changing at the rate of __−7__ cm per min.

e) Determine an equation to represent this information in the form $W = mt + b$, where W represents the water level in cm and t represents the time in minutes.

$m = -7 \quad$ Point $(8, 23)$

$W - W_1 = m(t - t_1)$

$W - 23 = -7(t - 8)$

$W - 23 = -7t + 56$

$W = -7t + 79$

f) After how many minutes will the barrel be empty?

$0 = -7t + 79$

$7t = 79$

$t = 11\frac{2}{7} \qquad 11\frac{2}{7}$ min.

g) What was the water level in the barrel when it started leaking?

$t = 0 \qquad W = 79 \qquad 79\,cm$

h) The barrel is cylindrical in shape with a radius of 20 cm.

i) Calculate the volume (in terms of π) of water in the barrel after 3 min and after 8 min.

3min $\quad V = \pi r^2 h \qquad$ 8 min $\quad V = \pi r^2 h$

$= \pi (20)^2 (58) \qquad\qquad = \pi (20)^2 (23)$

$= 23\,200\,\pi \; cm^3 \qquad\qquad = 9\,200\,\pi \; cm^3$

ii) Calculate the rate (in terms of π) at which water is leaking out of the barrel.

$\dfrac{23\,200\,\pi - 9\,200\,\pi}{8-3} = 2800\,\pi \; cm^3/min$

---

6. Jack rented a car from Absolute Value Rent-a-Car Company. After driving for two hours, the odometer reading was 21 328 and after five hours the odometer reading was 21 604. His journey was completed after six hours.

a) On a grid, plot ordered pairs to represent this information.

odometer reading (km)

time (h)

b) Calculate the slope of the line segment joining the ordered pairs.

$m = \dfrac{21\,604 - 21\,328}{5-2} = \dfrac{276}{3} = 92$

c) Explain what the slope of the graph represents.

the average speed between 2h and 5h is 92 km/h

d) Assuming a constant rate of driving for the whole journey, determine the odometer reading at the start of the journey.

$21\,328 - 2(92) = 21\,144$

e) Determine an equation to represent this information in the form $f(t) = mt + b$, where $f(t)$ represents the odometer reading after t hours.

$f(t) = 92t + 21\,144$

f) State an appropriate domain and range for f.

$f(6) = 92(6) + 21\,144 = 21\,696$

domain: $0 \le t \le 6, \; t \in R$

range: $21\,144 \le f(t) \le 21\,696$

7. To test the gas consumption of a new SUV, Jana filled up the gas tank of 58 L and drove the SUV until it was empty. She drove the SUV for 464 km.

a) Sketch the graph on the grid provided with distance travelled on the horizontal axis.

y

(0, 58)

Volume of fuel (L)

(464, 0)

Distance (km)

x

b) Write an equation in the form $y = mx + b$ which represents the volume of fuel in the tank as a function of distance.

$m = \dfrac{0 - 58}{464 - 0} = -\dfrac{1}{8} \qquad y = -\dfrac{1}{8}x + 58$

c) State the slope of the graph, and explain what it represents.

slope $= -\dfrac{1}{8}$. The volume of fuel in the gas tank is decreasing at the rate of $\frac{1}{8}$ L/km.

d) Determine the distance travelled on 12 litres of gas.

$\dfrac{1\,km}{\frac{1}{8}\,L} \times 12\,L = 96\,km$

e) How many litres of gas are used by the SUV when it has travelled 200 km?

$200\,km \times \dfrac{\frac{1}{8}\,L}{km} = 25\,L \qquad 25\ litres$

8.

$by = -ax - c$
$y = -\frac{a}{b}x - \frac{c}{b}$

$ey = -dx - f$
$y = -\frac{d}{e}x - \frac{f}{e}$

$-ae = -bd$
$-\frac{a}{b} = -\frac{d}{e}$

$ae = bd$
$0 = ae - bd$
$ce - bd = 0$

(A.) $ce - bd = 0$

9. 1) $7x = y$ → $y = 7x$ $m = 7$
2) $y = -7x + 6$ $m = -7$
3) $x + 4 = 7y$ $y = \frac{1}{7}x + \frac{4}{7}$ $m = \frac{1}{7}$
4) $7y = -x - 2$ $y = -\frac{1}{7}x - \frac{2}{7}$ $m = -\frac{1}{7}$

(C.) both 1) and 4)   and   2) and 3)

10. $m = \frac{-1+2}{-2+5} = \frac{1}{3}$

$y + 1 = \frac{1}{3}(x+2)$
$3(y+1) = x + 2$
$3y + 3 = x + 2$
$0 = x - 3y - 1$

(D.) $x - 3y - 1 = 0$

11. $m_{\ell_1} = \frac{rise}{run} = \frac{6}{3} = 2$ $m_\perp = -\frac{1}{2}$

x_{int} of $\ell_2 = 2$

$m = -\frac{1}{2}$ point $(2, 0)$

$y - 0 = -\frac{1}{2}(x - 2)$
$2y = -(x - 2)$
$2y = -x + 2$
$x + 2y - 2 = 0$

(A.) $x + 2y - 2 = 0$

12. $x + 4 = 2y$
$y = \frac{1}{2}x + 2$
$m_{AB} = \frac{1}{2}$ $m_{CD} = -2$
$C(0, 2)$
$y - 2 = -2(x - 0)$
$y - 2 = -2x$
$2x + y - 2 = 0$

(B.) $2x + y - 2 = 0$

13. $m_{SR} = -3$
$y - 7 = -3(x + 4)$
$y - 7 = -3x - 12$
$3x + y + 5 = 0$
$3x + y = -5$

(C.) $3x + y = -5$

14. Which of the following lines is/are perpendicular to the line $9x + y + 2 = 0$? $y = -9x - 2$ $m = -9$

i) $9y + x = 2$ ii) $9y - x = 2$ iii) $y = 9x + 2$ iv) $9y = x + 2$

i) $y = -\frac{1}{9}x + \frac{2}{9}$ ii) $9y = x + 2$ iii) $y = 9x + 2$ iv) $9y = x + 2$
$y = -\frac{1}{9}x + \frac{2}{9}$ $y = \frac{1}{9}x + \frac{2}{9}$ $y = \frac{1}{9}x + \frac{2}{9}$
$m = -\frac{1}{9}$

ii) and iv) are perpendicular

A.   i) and ii) only
B.   ii) only
C.   iv) only
D.   some other combination of i), ii), iii), and iv)

(D.)

15. $m = \frac{-1-5}{-2+3} = \frac{-6}{1} = -6$

i) $LS = -37$ $RS = -6(-4) - 13 = -37$
$y + 1 = -6(x+2)$
$y + 1 = -6x - 12$
$y = -6x - 13$

ii) $0 = -6x - 13$ $6x = -13$ $x = -\frac{13}{6}$

iii) $m_{\ell_1} = -6$

A.   i) and ii) only
B.   i) and iii) only
C.   ii) and iii) only
D.   i), ii), and iii)

(D.)

---

8. a) $(0, 2.85)$ $(4, 2.25)$

$m = \frac{2.25 - 2.85}{4 - 0}$
$= \frac{-0.6}{4} = -0.15$
$= -0.15$

$h(t) = -0.15t + 2.85$

b) slope $= -0.15$. It represents the rate at which the water level is changing.

c) Determine an appropriate domain and range for h.

$h = 0$ when the height of the river returns to regular level.

$0 = -0.15t + 2.85$
$0.15t = 2.85$
$t = \frac{2.85}{0.15} = 19$

domain $0 \le t \le 19$, $t \in R$.
range $0 \le h(t) \le 2.85$, $h(t) \in R$.

9. $(3, 155)$, $(4.5, 215)$

$m = \frac{215 - 155}{4.5 - 3} = 40$

$y - 155 = 40(x - 3)$
$y - 155 = 40x - 120$
$y = 40x + 35$

when $x = 7$
$y = 40(7) + 35$
$= 315$

(C.) $35 and $315

10. $(0, 18)$ $(250, 18.8)$

$m = \frac{18.8 - 18}{250}$
$= 0.0032$

$= 0.0032°C$ per m
$= 3.2°C$ per km

$\boxed{3.2}$

Equations of Linear Relations Lesson #8: Practice Test

1. $3y = 2x - 12$
$y = \frac{2}{3}x - 4$
(B.) $\frac{2}{3}$

2. $y = 5x - 10$
$y_{int} = -10$
(D.) -10

3. $y = 3x - 4$
(C.) $y = 3x - 4$

4. $5y + x + 6 = 0$
$5y = -x - 6$
$y = -\frac{1}{5}x - \frac{6}{5}$
slope $-\frac{1}{5}$
perpendicular slope: 5
(A.) $y = 5x$

5. i) $3(8) - 5(4) - 4 = 0$ ✓   iii) $3(-3) - 5(1) - 4 = -18$ ✗
ii) $3(0) - 5(-0.8) - 4 = 0$ ✓   iv) $3(-1) - 5(2) - 4 = -20$ ✗
(B.) i) and iii) only

6. $x = 0$
$-3y + 9 = 0$
$9 = 3y$
$y = 3$
$(0, 3)$
(B.) $(0, 3)$

7. The equation of the line PQ is $P(-8, 0)$ $Q(0, 6)$

$m_{PQ} = \frac{6 - 0}{0 + 8} = \frac{6}{8} = \frac{3}{4}$

$y = mx + b$
$y = \frac{3}{4}x + 6$
$4y = 3x + 24$
$0 = 3x - 4y + 24$
$3x - 4y + 24 = 0$

A. $3x + 4y + 24 = 0$
B. $3x + 4y + 32 = 0$
C. $3x - 4y + 24 = 0$
D. $3x - 4y + 32 = 0$

(C.)

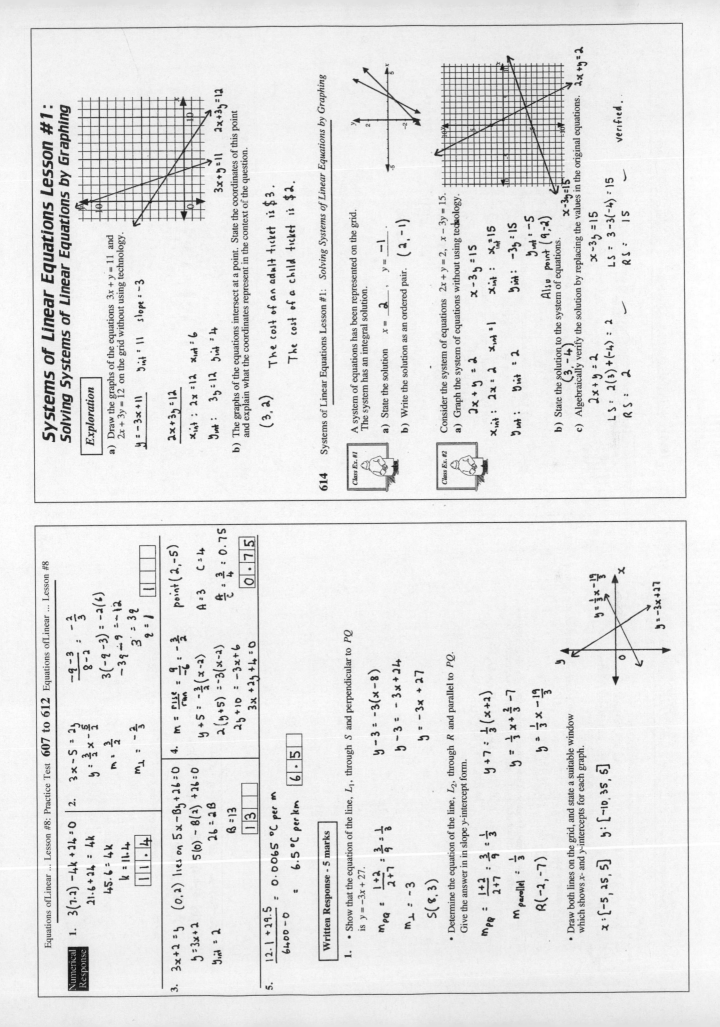

Systems of Linear Equations Lesson #1:
Solving Systems of Linear Equations by Graphing

Exploration

a) Draw the graphs of the equations $3x + y = 11$ and $2x + 3y = 12$ on the grid without using technology.

$y = -3x + 11$ $y\text{-int}: 11$ $slope: -3$

$2x + 3y = 12$
$x\text{-int}: 2x = 12$ $x\text{-int} = 6$
$y\text{-int}: 3y = 12$ $y\text{-int} = 4$

$3x + y = 11$

b) The graphs of the equations intersect at a point. State the coordinates of this point and explain what the coordinates represent in the context of the question.

$(3, 2)$ The cost of an adult ticket is $3.
The cost of a child ticket is $2.

---

614   Systems of Linear Equations Lesson #1: *Solving Systems of Linear Equations by Graphing*

Class Ex. #1 A system of equations has been represented on the grid. The system has an integral solution.

a) State the solution $x = 2$, $y = -1$.
b) Write the solution as an ordered pair. $(2, -1)$

Class Ex. #2 Consider the system of equations $2x + y = 2$, $x - 3y = 15$.

a) Graph the system of equations without using technology.

$2x + y = 2$ $x - 3y = 15$
$x\text{-int}: 2x = 2$ $x\text{-int} = 1$ $x\text{-int}: x = 15$
$y\text{-int}: y = 2$ $y\text{-int}: -3y = 15$ $y\text{-int} = -5$
Also point $(9, 2)$

b) State the solution to the system of equations. $(3, -4)$

c) Algebraically verify the solution by replacing the values in the original equations.

$2x + y = 2$ $x - 3y = 15$
LS: $2(3) + (-4) = 2$ LS: $3 - 3(-4) = 15$
RS: 2 RS: 15 verified.

Equations of Linear ... Lesson #8: Practice Test   607 to 612   Equations of Linear ... Lesson #8

1. $3(7.2) - 4k + 24 = 0$
$21.6 + 24 = 4k$
$45.6 = 4k$
$k = 11.4$ [1][1].[4]

2. $3x - 5 = 2y$ $\dfrac{-9-3}{8-2} ; -\dfrac{2}{3}$
$y = \dfrac{3}{2}x - \dfrac{5}{2}$ $3(-9-3) = -2(6)$
$m = \dfrac{3}{2}$ $-3y - 9 = -12$
$m_\perp = -\dfrac{2}{3}$ $-3y = 3y$
   $y = 1$

point $(2, -5)$
$A = 3$ $C = 4$
$\dfrac{A}{C} = \dfrac{3}{4} : 0.75$ [0].[7][5]

3. $3x + 2 = y$ $(0,2)$ lies on $5x - 8y + 26 = 0$
$y = 3x + 2$ $5(0) - 8(2) + 26 = 0$
$y\text{-int} = 2$ $26 = 2B$
   $B = 13$ [1][3]

4. $m = \dfrac{rise}{run} = \dfrac{9}{-6} : -\dfrac{3}{2}$
$y + 5 = -\dfrac{3}{2}(x - 2)$
$2(y + 5) = -3(x - 2)$
$2y + 10 = -3x + 6$
$3x + 2y + 4 = 0$

5. $\dfrac{12.1 + 29.5}{6400 - 0} = 0.0065$ °C per m
$= 6.5$ °C per km   [6].[5]

Written Response - 5 marks

1. • Show that the equation of the line, L_1, through S and perpendicular to PQ is $y = -3x + 27$.

$m_{PQ} = \dfrac{1+2}{2+7} = \dfrac{3}{9} = \dfrac{1}{3}$
$m_\perp = -3$
$S(8, 3)$

$y - 3 = -3(x - 8)$
$y - 3 = -3x + 24$
$y = -3x + 27$

• Determine the equation of the line, L_2, through R and parallel to PQ. Give the answer in slope-intercept form.

$m_{PQ} = \dfrac{1+2}{2+7} = \dfrac{3}{9} = \dfrac{1}{3}$
$m_{parallel} = \dfrac{1}{3}$
$R(-2, -7)$

$y + 7 = \dfrac{1}{3}(x + 2)$
$y = \dfrac{1}{3}x + \dfrac{2}{3} - 7$
$y = \dfrac{1}{3}x - \dfrac{19}{3}$

• Draw both lines on the grid, and state a suitable window which shows x- and y-intercepts for each graph.

$x:[-5, 25, 5]$ $y:[-10, 35, 5]$

$y = \dfrac{1}{3}x - \dfrac{19}{3}$
$y = -3x + 27$

Class Ex. #3

a) Rewrite each equation in slope y-intercept form.

$y = -3x + 11$ $3y = -2x + 12$

$y = -\frac{2}{3}x + 4$

b) Use a graphing calculator to graph each equation.

c) State a suitable window which shows both sets of x- and y-intercepts and the point of intersection.

$x: [-5, 10,]$ $y: [-10, 15, 2]$

d) Solve the system of equations using the features of the graphing calculator. Confirm the amount of the entry fees established in the exploration.

$(3, 2)$ confirms the amount of the entry fees in the exploration.

Class Ex. #4

a) Solve the following system of equations using a graphing calculator.

$$6a + 7b = 5$$
$$3a = 14b$$

$7b = -6a + 5$ $14b = 3a$ graph $y_1 = -\frac{6}{7}x + \frac{5}{7}$

$b = -\frac{6}{7}a + \frac{5}{7}$ $b = \frac{3}{14}a$ $y_2 = \frac{3}{14}x$

b) List the answers as exact values using the technique above.

$a = \frac{2}{3}$ $b = \frac{1}{7}$

c) Algebraically verify the solution.

$\underline{6a + 7b = 5}$

$LS = 6\left(\frac{2}{3}\right) + 7\left(\frac{1}{7}\right) = 4 + 1 = 5$

$RS = 5$

$LS = RS$

$\underline{3a = 14b}$

$LS = 3\left(\frac{2}{3}\right) = 2$

$RS = 14\left(\frac{1}{7}\right) = 2$

$LS = RS$

verified

1. Consider the system of equations $x - 2y = 3$, $x + y = 0$.

   a) Write each equation in slope y-intercept form.

   $x - 3 = 2y$ $\qquad$ $y = -x$

   $y = \frac{1}{2}x - \frac{3}{2}$

   b) Complete the table of values for each equation.

   $x - 2y = 3$

x	y
-3	-3
-1	-2
1	-1
3	0
5	1

   $x + y = 0$

x	y
-4	4
-2	2
0	0
2	-2
4	-4

   c) Draw the lines on the grid and state the solution to the system.

   Solution: $x = 1$, $y = -1$

   d) Verify the solution.

   $x - 2y = 3$ $\qquad$ $x + y = 0$

   $LS: 1 - 2(-1) = 3$ $\qquad$ $LS: 1 + (-1) = 0$

   $RS: 3$ $\qquad\qquad$ $RS: 0$

   $LS = RS$ $\qquad\qquad$ $LS = RS$

2. The following system of equations is given: $x - y = 7$, $x + 5y = -5$.

   a) Without using technology, graph each equation and hence solve the system.

   $x - y = 7$ $\qquad$ $x + 5y = -5$

   $x_{int} = 7$ $\qquad$ $x_{int}: -5$

   $y_{int} = -7$ $\qquad$ $y_{int}: -1$

   Solution: $x = 5$, $y = -2$

   b) Verify the solution.

   $x - y = 7$ $\qquad$ $x + 5y = -5$

   $LS = 5 - (-2) = 7$ $\qquad$ $LS = 5 + 5(-2) = -5$

   $RS: 7$ $\qquad\qquad$ $RS: -5$

   $LS = RS$ $\qquad\qquad$ $LS = RS$ $\qquad$ verified

---

3. a) $y = 3x - 7$ $\qquad$ b) $y = -x$ $\qquad$ $x = -4.5$ $\qquad$ c) $y = x - 2$ $\qquad$ $x = -8$

   $\qquad\qquad x = 4$ $\qquad\qquad y = -x + 9$ $\qquad y = 4.5$ $\qquad\qquad y = -\frac{3}{4}x - 4$ $\qquad y = -10$

   $\qquad\qquad y = 5$

   $y = 3x - 7$ $\qquad\qquad\qquad y = -x$ $\qquad\qquad\qquad\qquad y = x - 2$

   $LS: 5$ $\qquad\qquad\qquad LS: 4.5$ $\qquad\qquad\qquad\qquad LS: -10$

   $RS: 3(4) - 7 = 5$ $\quad LS = RS$ $\quad RS: -(-4.5) = 4.5$ $\quad LS = RS$ $\quad RS: -8 - 2 = -10$ $\quad LS = RS$

   $y = -x + 9$ $\qquad\qquad\qquad y = -\frac{1}{3}x + 3$ $\qquad\qquad\qquad y = -\frac{3}{4}x - 4$

   $LS: 5$ $\qquad\qquad\qquad LS: 4.5$ $\qquad\qquad\qquad\qquad LS: -10$

   $RS: -4 + 9 = 5$ $\quad LS = RS$ $\quad RS: -\frac{1}{3}(-4.5) + 3 = 4.5$ $\quad LS = RS$ $\quad RS: \frac{3}{4}(-8) - 4 = -10$ $\quad LS = RS$

   d) $3x + 2y = 5$ $\qquad x = 1.4$ $\qquad$ e) $4a - b = 6$ $\qquad a = 1$ $\qquad$ f) $0.6p - 0.8q = 2.6$ $\qquad p: 3$

   $\qquad x - y = 1$ $\qquad\quad y = 0.4$ $\qquad\qquad 3a + b = 1$ $\qquad b = -2$ $\qquad\qquad 5p + 6q = 9$ $\qquad q = -1$

   $3x + 2y = 5$ $\qquad\qquad\qquad 4a - b = 6$ $\qquad\qquad\qquad\qquad 0.6p - 0.8q = 2.6$

   $LS: 3(1.4) + 2(0.4) = 5$ $\qquad LS: 4(1) - (-2) = 6$ $\qquad\qquad LS: 0.6(3) - 0.8(-1) = 2.6$

   $RS: 5$ $\qquad LS = RS$ $\qquad\qquad RS: 6$ $\qquad LS = RS$ $\qquad\qquad RS: 2.6$ $\qquad LS = RS$

   $x - y = 1$ $\qquad\qquad\qquad 3a + b = 1$ $\qquad\qquad\qquad\qquad 5p + 6q = 9$

   $LS: 1.4 - 0.4 = 1$ $\qquad\qquad LS: 3(1) + (-2) = 1$ $\qquad\qquad LS: 5(3) + 6(-1) = 9$

   $RS: 1$ $\qquad LS = RS$ $\qquad\qquad RS: 1$ $\qquad LS = RS$ $\qquad\qquad RS: 9$ $\qquad LS = RS$

4. a) $4x - y + 6 = 0$, $y = x + 2$ $\qquad$ b) $y = 0.3x - 5.9$, $y = 2.4x + 6.9$

   $y = 4x + 6$

   $x = -\frac{4}{3}$, $y = \frac{2}{3}$

   c) $8x - 3y = 5$, $5x + 3y = 2$ $\qquad$ d) $8a - 7b + 80 = 0$, $7a + 14b - 177 = 0$

   $8x - 3y = 3y$ $\qquad$ $3y = -5x + 2$ $\qquad\qquad$ $8a + 80 = 7b$ $\qquad$ $14b = 7a + 177$

   $8x - 5 = 3y$ $\qquad y = -\frac{5}{3}x + \frac{2}{3}$ $\qquad\quad b = \frac{8}{7}a + \frac{80}{7}$ $\qquad b = -\frac{1}{2}a + \frac{177}{14}$

   $y = \frac{8}{3}x - \frac{5}{3}$

   $x = \frac{7}{13}$, $y = -\frac{3}{13}$ $\qquad\qquad\qquad x = \frac{-128}{21}$, $y = \frac{-544}{70}$ $\qquad\qquad a = \frac{17}{23}$, $b = \frac{1976}{161}$

5. $x - 6 = 2y$ $\qquad$ $6y = -x + 12$ $\qquad$ 6. $7x - 19 = 5y$ $\qquad$ $3y = -2x + 17$

   $y = \frac{1}{2}x - 3$ $\qquad y = -\frac{1}{6}x + \frac{11}{3}$ $\qquad\qquad y = \frac{7}{5}x - \frac{19}{5}$ $\qquad y = -\frac{2}{3}x + \frac{17}{3}$

   graph: intersect at $x = 10$, $y = 2$ $\qquad$ graph: intersect at $x = 4.58...$

   $\boxed{\text{D.}}$ (10, 2) $\qquad\qquad\qquad\qquad\qquad\qquad\qquad \boxed{4 \cdot 6}$

7. graph: $y_1 = 2x - 24$ $\quad x = 36$ $\quad y = 48$

   $y_2 = \frac{4}{3}x$

   pear costs 48 cents $\qquad \boxed{4\,8}$

Systems of Linear Equations Lesson #2:
Determining the Number of Solutions to a System of Linear Equations

Exploration

a) Let x dollars be the cost of a burger and y dollars be the cost of a salad. Write a system of equations for each scenario.

Burger Shack
$$4x + 2y = 28$$
$$6x + y = 34$$

Big's Burgers
$$x + 3y = 18$$
$$3x + 9y = 54$$

The Burger Haven
$$2x + 4y = 32$$
$$3x + 6y = 42$$

b) Consider the equations for the Burger Shack. Write each equation in terms of y and use a graphing calculator to determine the cost of a burger and the cost of a salad.

$$2y = -4x + 28 \qquad y = -2x + 14$$
$$y = -6x + 34$$

burger $5
salad $4

c) Repeat part b) for Big's Burgers. Can you determine the cost of a burger and the cost of a salad? Explain.

$$3y = -x + 18 \qquad y = -\tfrac{1}{3}x + 6$$
$$9y = -3x + 54 \qquad y = -\tfrac{1}{3}x + 6$$

No, both equations are the same.

d) Repeat part b) for The Burger Haven. Can you determine the cost of a burger and the cost of a salad? Explain how you can tell that the student must have made an error in at least one of the calculations.

$$4y = -2x + 32 \qquad y = -\tfrac{1}{2}x + 8$$
$$6y = -3x + 42 \qquad y = -\tfrac{1}{2}x + 7$$

The lines are parallel.
(1 burger and 2 salads cannot cost $16 and $14).

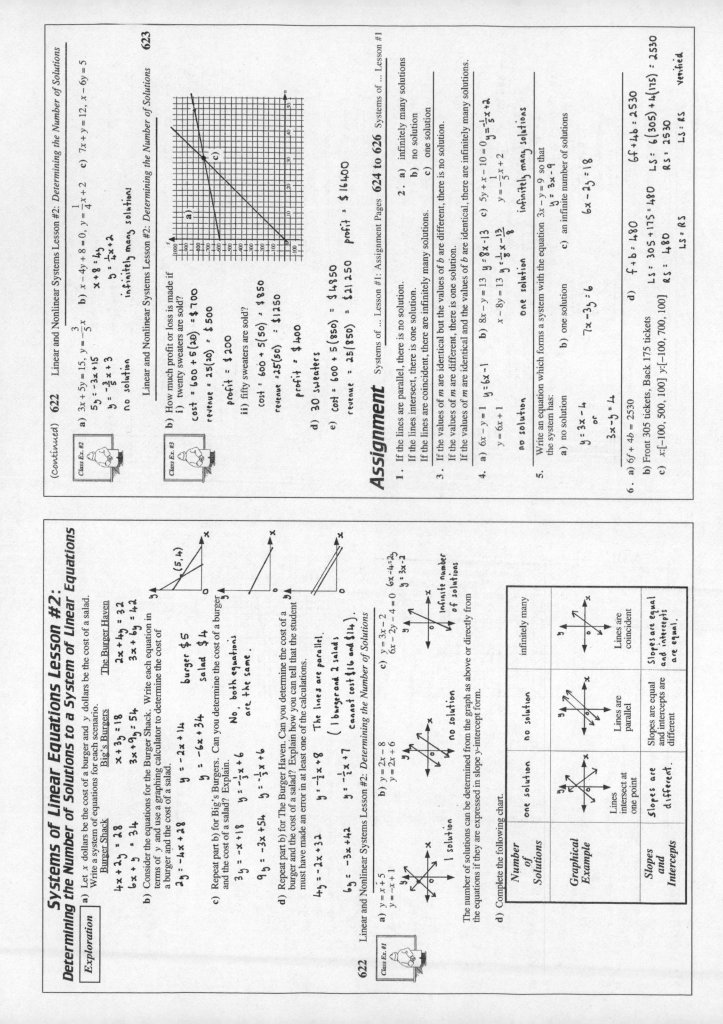

(5, 4)

622 Linear and Nonlinear Systems Lesson #2: Determining the Number of Solutions

Class Ex. #1

a) $y = x + 5$
   $y = -x + 1$

1 solution

b) $y = 2x - 8$
   $y = 2x + 6$

no solution

c) $y = 3x - 2$
   $6x - 2y - 4 = 0$
   $6x - 4 = 2y$
   $y = 3x - 2$

Infinite number of solutions

The number of solutions can be determined from the graph as above or directly from the equations if they are expressed in slope y-intercept form.

d) Complete the following chart.

Number of Solutions	one solution	no solution	infinitely many
Graphical Example	Lines intersect at one point	Lines are parallel	Lines are coincident
Slopes and Intercepts	Slopes are different.	Slopes are equal and intercepts are different	Slopes are equal and intercepts are equal.

(continued) 622 Linear and Nonlinear Systems Lesson #2: Determining the Number of Solutions

Class Ex. #2

a) $3x + 5y = 15$, $y = -\tfrac{3}{5}x$
   $5y = -3x + 15$
   $y = -\tfrac{3}{5}x + 3$
   no solution

b) $x - 4y + 8 = 0$, $y = \tfrac{1}{4}x + 2$
   $x + 8 = 4y$
   $y = \tfrac{1}{4}x + 2$
   infinitely many solutions

c) $7x + y = 12$, $x - 6y = 5$

Linear and Nonlinear Systems Lesson #2: Determining the Number of Solutions 623

Class Ex. #3

b) How much profit or loss is made if
   i) twenty sweaters are sold?

   cost = $600 + 5(20) = $700
   revenue = $25(20) = $500

   profit = $200

   ii) fifty sweaters are sold?

   cost = $600 + 5(50) = $850
   revenue = $25(50) = $1250

   profit = $400

d) 30 sweaters

e) cost = $600 + 5(850) = $4850
   revenue = $25(850) = $21 250
   profit = $16 400

Assignment

Systems of ... Lesson #1: Assignment Pages **624 to 626** Systems of ... Lesson #1

1. If the lines are parallel, there is no solution.
   If the lines intersect, there is one solution.
   If the lines are coincident, there are infinitely many solutions.

2. a) infinitely many solutions
   b) no solution
   c) one solution

3. If the values of m are identical but the values of b are different, there is no solution.
   If the values of m are different, there is one solution.
   If the values of m are identical and the values of b are identical, there are infinitely many solutions.

4. a) $6x - y = 1$ $y = 6x - 1$
      $y = 6x + 1$
   no solution

   b) $8x - y = 13$ $y = 8x - 13$
      $x - 8y = 13$ $y = \tfrac{1}{8}x - \tfrac{13}{8}$
   one solution

   c) $5y + x - 10 = 0$ $y = -\tfrac{1}{5}x + 2$
      $y = -\tfrac{1}{5}x + 2$
   infinitely many solutions

5. Write an equation which forms a system with the equation $3x - y = 9$ so that the system has:
   a) no solution
      $y = 3x - 4$
      or
      $3x - y = 4$

   b) one solution
      $7x - 3y = 6$

   c) an infinite number of solutions
      $6x - 2y = 18$

6. a) $6f + 4b = 2530$
   b) Front 305 tickets, Back 175 tickets
   c) $x:[-100, 500, 100]$ $y:[-100, 700, 100]$

   $f + b = 480$
   $7x - 3y = 6$
   $6f + 4b = 2530$

   $305 + 175 = 480$
   LS : $6(305) + 4(175) = 2530$
   LS = RS   RS : 2530   LS : $6(305) + 4(175) = 2530$
                            LS = RS   verified

7. Let \$x be the cost of a pencil and \$y be the cost of a crayon. Form two equations from the given information. These are $6x + 4y = 3.4$ $3x + 10y = 4.9$ Write each equation in slope y-intercept form. Graph the system of equations and determine the coordinates (x, y) of the intersection point. The answer is $8x + 12y = 8(0.3) + 12(0.4) = 7.2$ Answer = \$7.20

8. $4x - 3y = 9$ $y = \frac{4}{3}x - 3$
    $8x - 6y = 81$ $y = \frac{4}{3}x - \frac{27}{2}$
    (A) no solution

9. graph $y_1 = -\frac{3}{2}x + 24$ Intersection point $(24, -12)$
           $y_2 = -\frac{2}{3}x + 4$
           $x - 2y = 24 - 2(-12) = 48$
           $\boxed{4\,8\,.\,0}$

10. $ky = -10x - 8$ $-15x - 12 = 6y$
     $y = -\frac{10}{k}x - \frac{8}{k}$ $y = -\frac{15}{6}x - 2$
     $-\frac{8}{k} = -2$
     $-8 = -2k$ $k = 4$ $\boxed{4}$

11. $5y = -ax + 10$ $2y = -6x + 7$
     $y = -\frac{a}{5}x + 2$ $y = -3x + \frac{7}{2}$
     $-\frac{a}{5} = -3$
     $-a = -15$ $a = 15$ $\boxed{1\,5}$ $a = 15$

Systems of Linear Equations Lesson #3:
Solving Systems of Linear Equations by Substitution

Class Ex. #1

a) Solve the system using the method of substitution by rewriting the first equation in the form $x = \ldots\ldots$

$x = -4y + 17$

$x + 4y = 17$

$2(-4y + 17) - y = 7$
$-8y + 34 - y = 7$
$-9y = -27$
$y = 3$

$x = -4y + 17$
$x + 4(3) = 17$
$x + 12 = 17$
$x = 5$

$\underline{x = 5}$
$\underline{y = 3}$

b) Solve the system using the method of substitution by rewriting the first equation in the form $y = \ldots\ldots$

$4y = -x + 17$
$y = -\frac{1}{4}x + \frac{17}{4}$

$2x - \left(-\frac{1}{4}x + \frac{17}{4}\right) = 7$
$2x + \frac{1}{4}x - \frac{17}{4} = 7$
$8x + 1x - 17 = 28$
$9x = 45$
$x = 5$

$y = -\frac{1}{4}(5) + \frac{17}{4}$
$y = -\frac{5}{4} + \frac{17}{4} = 3$

$\underline{x = 5}$
$\underline{y = 3}$

c) Verify that the solution satisfies both equations.

$x + 4y = 17$ $2x - y = 7$
$LS = 5 + 4(3) = 17$ $LS = 2(5) - 3 = 7$
$RS = 17$ $RS = 7$
$LS = RS$ $LS = RS$ verified

d) Check the solution using a graphing calculator. $x = 5 , y = 3$

Class Ex. #2

Consider the following system of equations: $4x + 3y = 0$, $8x - 9y = 5$.

a) Solve and verify the system using the method of substitution.

$3y = -4x$ $8x - 9\left(-\frac{4}{3}x\right) = 5$ $x = -\frac{1}{4}$ $y = -\frac{1}{3}$
$y = -\frac{4}{3}x$ $8x + 12x = 5$
                 $20x = 5$
                 $x = \frac{1}{4}$

verify: $4x + 3y = 0$
$LS = 4\left(\frac{1}{4}\right) + 3\left(-\frac{1}{3}\right) = 0$
$RS = 0$ $LS = RS$

$y = -\frac{4}{3}x$ ... $y = -\frac{4}{3}\left(\frac{1}{4}\right) = -\frac{1}{3}$

b) Check the solution using a graphing calculator.

$8x - 9y = 5$
$LS = 8\left(\frac{1}{4}\right) - 9\left(-\frac{1}{3}\right) = 5$
$RS = 5$ $LS = RS$
verified

Class Ex. #3

Consider the following system of equations: $5(2a - 3) + b = 5$, $6a - 2(b - 4) = 20$.

a) Solve the system using the method of substitution.

$10a - 15 + b = 5$ $6a - 2(b - 4) = 20$
$10a + b = 20$ $6a - 2(-10a + 20 - 4) = 20$
$b = -10a + 20$ $6a + 20a - 40 + 8 = 20$
                        $26a = 52$
                        $a = 2$

$b = -10(2) + 20$
$b = 0$

$\underline{a = 2}$
$\underline{b = 0}$

b) Verify algebraically that the solution satisfies both equations.

$5(2a - 3) + b = 5$ $6a - 2(b - 4) = 20$
$LS = 5(2(2) - 3) + 0 = 5$ $LS = 6(2) - 2(0 - 4) = 12 + 8 = 20$
$RS = 5$ $RS = 20$
$LS = RS$ $LS = RS$ verified

Enrichment

Solve the following system using substitution.

$4x - 3y - 5z = 6$
$z = 2x$
$-2x + 5y - 14 = 0$

$4x - 3y - 5z = 6$ $-2x + 5y - 14 = 0$
$4x - 3y - 5(2x) = 6$ $-2(-2) + 5y - 14 = 0$
$4x - 3y - 10x = 6$ $4 + 5y - 14 = 0$
$-6x - 3y = 6$ $5y = 10$
$-2x - y = 2$ $y = 2$

$z = 2x = 2(-2) = -4$

$\underline{x = -2 \quad y = 2 \quad z = -4}$

1.

a) $y = x+2$, $3x+4y=1$

$3x+4y=1$
$3x+4(x+2)=1$
$3x+4x+8=1$
$7x=-7$
$x=-1$
$y=x+2=(-1)+2=1$
$y=1$

$\underline{x=-1,\ y=1}$

$y=x+2$
LS$=1$
RS$=-1+2=1$
LS = RS
verified

b) $x-2y=10$, $x+5y+4=0$

$x=2y+10$
$2y+10+5y+4=0$
$7y=-14$
$y=-2$
$x-2(-2)=10$
$x+4=10$
$x=6$

$\underline{x=6,\ y=-2}$

$x-2y=10$ $x+5y+4=0$
LS$=6-2(-2)=10$ LS$=6+5(-2)+4=0$
AS$=10$ RS$=0$
LS = RS   LS = RS
verified

c) $4p+q=0$, $7p+4q=3$

$q=-4p$
$7p+4(-4p)=3$
$7p-16p=3$
$-9p=3$
$p=-\frac{1}{3}$
$q=-4\left(-\frac{1}{3}\right)=\frac{4}{3}$
$q=\frac{4}{3}$

$\underline{p=-\frac{1}{3},\ q=\frac{4}{3}}$

$4p+q=0$ $7p+4q=3$
LS$=4\left(-\frac{1}{3}\right)+\frac{4}{3}=0$ LS$=7\left(-\frac{1}{3}\right)+4\left(\frac{4}{3}\right)=3$
RS$=0$ RS$=3$
LS = RS   LS = RS
verified

d) $6u-3v+4=0$, $3u=3v-5$

$6\left(v-\frac{5}{3}\right)-3v+4=0$
$6v-10-3v+4=0$
$3v=6$
$v=2$
$u=2-\frac{5}{3}=\frac{1}{3}$

$\underline{u=\frac{1}{3},\ v=2}$

$6u-3v+4=0$ $3u=3v-5$
LS$=6\left(\frac{1}{3}\right)-3(2)+4=0$ LS$=3\left(\frac{1}{3}\right)=1$
RS$=0$ RS$=3(2)-5=1$
LS = RS   LS = RS
verified

2. Solve each of the following systems by substitution. Check each solution.

a) $2x-5y=-7$ $\frac{1}{2}x-y=3$

$y=\frac{1}{2}x-3$
$2x-5\left(\frac{1}{2}x-3\right)=-7$
$2x-\frac{5}{2}x+15=-7$
$-\frac{1}{2}x=-22$ $x=44$
$y=\frac{1}{2}x-3=\frac{1}{2}(44)-3=19$

$\underline{x=44,\ y=19}$

$2x-5y=-7$ $\frac{1}{2}x-y=3$
LS$=2(44)-5(19)=-7$ LS$=\frac{1}{2}(44)-19=3$
RS$=-7$ RS$=3$
LS = RS   LS = RS
verified

b) $2(x+2)+y=8$

$7x-2(y-3)+24=0$

$2x+4+y=8$ $y=-2x+4$
$7x-2(-2x+4-3)+24=0$
$7x-2(-2x+1)+24=0$
$7x+4x-8+6+24=0$
$11x=-22$
$x=-2$
$y=-2(-2)+4=8$

$\underline{x=-2,\ y=8}$

$2(x+2)+y=8$ $7x-2(y-3)+24=0$
LS$=2(-2+2)+8=8$ LS$=7(-2)-2(8-3)+24=0$
RS$=8$ RS$=0$
LS = RS   LS = RS
verified

c) $4(x-5)+2(y+7)=5$
$6x-4(y+1)=16$

$4x-20+2y+14=5$
$4x+2y=11$
$2y=-4x+11$
$y=-2x+\frac{11}{2}$
$6x-4\left(-2x+\frac{11}{2}+1\right)=16$
$6x+8x-22-4=16$
$14x=42$ $x=3$
$y=-2(3)+\frac{11}{2}=-\frac{1}{2}$

$\underline{x=3,\ y=-\frac{1}{2}}$

$4(x-5)+2(y+7)=5$ $6x-4(y+1)=16$
LS$=4(3-5)+2\left(-\frac{1}{2}+7\right)=5$ LS$=6(3)-4\left(-\frac{1}{2}+1\right)=16$
RS$=5$ RS$=16$
LS = RS   LS = RS
verified

d) $4(2x+3)-(y-7)=-5$
$5(1-4x)-4(4-2y)=49$

$8x+12-y+7=-5$
$8x+24=y$ $y=8x+24$
$5(1-4x)-4(4-2(8x+24))=49$
$5-20x-4(4-16x-48)=49$
$5-20x-16+64x+192=49$
$44x=-132$
$x=-3$
$y=8(-3)+24=0$

$\underline{x=-3,\ y=0}$

$4(2x+3)-(y-7)=-5$ $5(1-4x)-4(4-2y)=49$
LS$=4(2(-3)+3)-(0-7)=-5$ LS$=5(1-4(-3))-4(4-2(0))=49$
RS$=-5$ RS$=49$
LS = RS   LS = RS
verified

3. The straight line $px + qy + 14 = 0$ passes through the points $(-3, 1)$ and $(-4, 6)$.

a) Substitute the x and y-coordinates of the two points into the equation of the line to form two equations in p and q.

$$-3p + q + 14 = 0$$
$$-4p + 6q + 14 = 0$$

b) Solve this system of equations by substitution to determine the values of p and q and write the equation of the line.

$q = 3p - 14$
$-4p + 6(3p - 14) + 14 = 0$
$-4p + 18p - 84 + 14 = 0$
$14p = 70 \quad p = 5$
$q = 3(5) - 14 = 1$

$p = 5 \quad q = 1$

$$\underline{5x + y + 14 = 0}$$

c) Verify the equation in b) using the slope formula and the point-slope equation of a line formula.

$m = \dfrac{6-1}{-4+3} = \dfrac{5}{-1} = -5$

$y - y_1 = m(x - x_1)$
$y - 1 = -5(x + 3)$
$y - 1 = -5x - 15$
$$\underline{5x + y + 14 = 0}$$

4. Solve the following systems by substitution. Explain the results.

a) $y = 3x - 7$
   $6x - 2y = 14$

$6x - 2(3x - 7) = 14$
$6x - 6x + 14 = 14$
$0 = 0$

The two equations are identical.
There are an infinite number of solutions.

b) $x = 3y + 2$
   $2x - 6y = 5$

$2(3y + 2) - 6y = 5$
$6y + 4 - 6y = 5$
$4 = 5$

The two lines are parallel.
There are no solutions.

5. $x = 10 - 2y \qquad 10 - 2y - 2y = 2 \qquad x = 10 - 2(2)$
   $8 = 4y \qquad x = 6$
   $y = 2 \qquad x + y : 6 + 2 = 8$

   (A) 8

6. $6\left(\dfrac{x}{2}\right) - 6\left(\dfrac{y}{3}\right) = 6(1)$ $\qquad 3x - 6 = 2y$

   $3x - 2y = 6$ $\qquad$ or $\qquad y = \dfrac{1}{2}(3x - 6)$
   $3x = 2y + 6$ $\qquad\qquad\qquad y = \dfrac{1}{2}(3x - 6)$
   $x = \dfrac{1}{3}(2y + 6)$

   (D) $y = \dfrac{1}{2}(3x - 6)$

7. If $s - 8t + 20 = 5s - 7t + 1 = 0$, then the value of $s + t$, to the nearest tenth, is ____.

$s = 8t - 20$
$5(8t - 20) - 7t + 1 = 0 \qquad s = 8(3) - 20$
$40t - 100 - 7t + 1 = 0 \qquad s = 4$
$33t = 99$
$t = 3 \qquad s + t : 3 + 4 = 7$

(Record your answer in the numerical response box from left to right)

7	.	0

---

8. a) $y = 3x$
      $2x - y = -4$
      $x - 5z = 4$

   $2x - 3x = -4$
   $-x = -4 \quad x = 4$
   $y = 3(4) \quad y = 12$
   $4 - 5z = 4$
   $0 = 5z \quad z = 0$

   $$\underline{x = 4, \quad y = 12, \quad z = 0}$$

   b) $x = 2y + 1$
      $y + 3z + 5 = 0$
      $x - 3z = 0$

   $x = 3z$
   $3z = 2y + 1 \qquad z = \dfrac{2}{3}y + \dfrac{1}{3}$
   $y + 3\left(\dfrac{2}{3}y + \dfrac{1}{3}\right) + 5 = 0$
   $y + 2y + 1 + 5 = 0$
   $3y = -6 \quad y = -2$
   $z = \dfrac{1}{3}(-1) + \dfrac{1}{3} = -\dfrac{2}{3} + \dfrac{1}{3} = -1$
   $x = 3(-1) = -3$

   $$\underline{x = -3, \quad y = -2, \quad z = -1}$$

Systems of Linear Equations Lesson #4:
Solving Systems of Linear Equations by Elimination

Class Ex. #1

Consider the system of equations:
$2x + 7y = 13$
$3x - 7y = 2$

a) Add the two equations. This will eliminate the variable y.

$5x = 15$
$x = 3$

b) Use the equation in a) to determine the value of x and hence solve the system.

$2x + 7y = 13$
$2(3) + 7y = 13$
$6 + 7y = 13$
$7y = 7$
$y = 1$

$$\underline{x = 3, \quad y = 1}$$

c) Verify the solution satisfies both equations.

LS	RS
$2x + 7y = 13$	13
$2(3) + 7(1) = 13$	
$= 13$	

LS	RS
$3x - 7y = 2$	2
$3(3) - 7(1) = 2$	
$= 2$	

Class Ex. #2

Consider the system of equations:
$2x + 6y = 6$
$2x + 3y = 4.5$

a) Subtract the two equations. This will eliminate the variable x.

$3y = 1.5$
$y = 0.5$

b) Use the equation in a) to determine the value of y and hence solve the system.

$2x + 6y = 6$
$2x + 6(0.5) = 6$
$2x + 3 = 6$
$2x = 3$
$x = 1.5$

$$\underline{x = 1.5 \left(\tfrac{3}{2}\right) \quad y = 0.5 \left(\tfrac{1}{2}\right)}$$

c) Verify the solution satisfies both equations.

LS	RS
$2x + 6y = 6$	6
$2(1.5) + 6(0.5)$	
$= 6$	

LS	RS
$2x + 3y = 4.5$	4.5
$2(1.5) + 3(0.5)$	
$= 4.5$	

634

Systems of Linear Equations Lesson #4:   *Solving Linear Systems by Elimination*

Class Ex. #3

Consider the system of equations: $2x + 3y = 4$
$4x - y = 22$

a) Does adding or subtracting the equations eliminate either of the variables?   **no**

b) Multiply the second equation by 3 and then add the two equations.
$2x + 3y = 4$
$12x - 3y = 66$ **Add** $14x = 70$

c) Solve and verify the system.
$x = 5$ $\underline{x = 5, \; y = -2}$
$2x + 3y = 4$
$2(5) + 3y = 4$
$10 + 3y = 4$
$3y = -6$
$y = -2$

LS: $2(5)+3(-2) = 4$
$4x - y = 22$
$4(5)-(-2)$
$= 4 = RS$
$= 22 = RS$ verified

d) Consider the original system. Multiply the first equation by an appropriate number which will eliminate x by addition or subtraction. Solve the system.
$4x + 6y = 8$ $2x + 3y = 4$
$4x - y = 22$ $2x + 3(-2) = 4$
Subtract $7y = -14$ $2x - 6 = 4$ $2x = 10$ $x = 5$
$y = -2$

$\underline{x = 5, \; y = -2}$

Class Ex. #4

Consider the system of equations: $5a + 3b = 3$
$3a - 7b = 81$

a) Choose appropriate whole numbers to multiply each equation so that the system can be solved by eliminating b.   equation 1 (×7)   equation 2 (×3)

b) Solve and verify the system by eliminating b. $\underline{a = 6, \; b = -9}$
$35a + 21b = 21$ $5a + 3b = 3$ $5a+3b=3$
$9a - 21b = 243$ $5(6)+3b = 3$ LS: $5(6)+3(-9)$ $3a-7b=81$
Add $44a = 264$ $30+3b = 3$ $= 3 = RS$ LS: $3(6)-7(-9)$
$a = 6$ $3b = -27$ $= 81 = RS$ verified
                      $b = -9$

c) Choose appropriate whole numbers to multiply each equation so that the system can be solved by eliminating a.   equation 1 × 3   equation 2 × 5

d) Solve the system by eliminating a. $\underline{a = 6, \; b = -9}$
$15a + 9b = 9$ $5a + 3b = 3$
$15a - 35b = 405$ $5a + 3(-9) = 3$
Subtract $44b = -396$ $5a - 27 = 3$ $5a = 30$ $a = 6$
$b = -9$

Systems of Linear Equations Lesson #4:   *Solving Linear Systems by Elimination*

Class Ex. #5

Solve the following system using elimination. $4x + 2y - 13 = 0$, $3x = 5y + 26$
$4x + 2y = 13$ (×5)
$3x - 5y = 26$ (×2)
$20x + 10y = 65$
$6x - 10y = 52$
Add $26x = 117$ $x = \dfrac{9}{2}$

$4x + 2y = 13$
$4\left(\dfrac{9}{2}\right) + 2y = 13$
$18 + 2y = 13$
$2y = -5$
$y = -\dfrac{5}{2}$

$\underline{x = \dfrac{9}{2}, \; y = -\dfrac{5}{2}}$

Class Ex. #6

Solve the following system using elimination.
$\dfrac{x-2}{3} - \dfrac{y+2}{5} = 2$, (×15) $\dfrac{3}{5}(x+1) - \dfrac{4}{5}(y-3) = \dfrac{21}{2}$ (×10)

$15\left(\dfrac{x-2}{3}\right) - 15\left(\dfrac{y+2}{5}\right) = 15(2)$
$5(x-2) - 3(y+2) = 30$
$5x - 10 - 3y - 6 = 30$
$5x - 3y = 46$

$10\left(\dfrac{3}{5}(x+1)\right) - 10\left(\dfrac{4}{5}(y-3)\right) = 10\left(\dfrac{21}{2}\right)$
$6(x+1) - 8(y-3) = 105$
$6x + 6 - 8y + 24 = 105$
$6x - 8y = 75$

$5x - 3y = 46$ (×8)
$6x - 8y = 75$ (×3)
$40x - 24y = 368$
$-18x + 24y = -225$
Add $22x = 143$ $x = \dfrac{13}{2}$

$6x - 8y = 75$
$6\left(\dfrac{13}{2}\right) - 8y = 75$
$39 - 8y = 75$
$-8y = 36$
$y = -\dfrac{9}{2}$

$\underline{x = \dfrac{13}{2}, \; y = -\dfrac{9}{2}}$

Assignment

Systems of ... Lesson #4: Assignment Pages **635 to 640**   Systems of ... Lesson #4

1. In each of the following systems:
   • solve the system using the method of elimination by adding the equations.
   • verify the solution satisfies both equations.

a) $8x - y = 10$
$4x + y = 14$
$12x = 24$, $x = 2$
$4(2) + y = 14$
$8 + y = 14$ $y = 6$
$\underline{x = 2, \; y = 6}$

$8x-y=10$ $4x+y=14$
$8(2)-6=10$ $4(2)+6=14$
$= 10 = RS$ $= 14 = RS$
verified

b) $x + 3y = 10$
$5x - 3y = 14$
$6x = 24$, $x = 4$
$4 + 3y = 10$
$3y = 6$ $y = 2$
$\underline{x = 4, \; y = 2}$

$x+3y=10$ $5x-3y=14$
$4+3(2)=10$ $5(4)-3(2)=14$
$= 10 = RS$ $= 14 = RS$
verified

c) $x + 2y = 3$
$-x + 3y = 2$
$5y = 5$, $y = 1$
$x + 2(1) = 3$
$x + 2 = 3$ $x = 1$
$\underline{x = 1, \; y = 1}$

$x+2y=3$ $-x+3y=2$
$1+2(1)=3$ $-1+3(1)=2$
$= 3 = RS$ $= 2 = RS$
verified

d) $4a - 3b = 2$
$-4a - b = 6$
$-4b = 8$ $b = -2$
$4a-3(-2)=2$, $4a+6=2$, $4a=-4$ $a=-1$
$\underline{a = -1, \; b = -2}$

$4a-3b=2$ $-4a-b=6$
$4(-1)-3(-2)$ $-4(-1)-(-2)=6$
$= 2 = RS$ $= 6 = RS$
verified

2. In each of the following systems:
 • solve the system using the method of elimination by subtracting the equations.
 • verify the solution satisfies both equations.

a) $7x + y = 15$
$3x + y = 3$

$4x = 12 \quad x = 3$
$3(3) + y = 3$
$9 + y = 3 \quad y = -6$
$x = 3, \ y = -6$

$7x + y = 15 \quad | \quad 3x + y = 3$
$LS = 7(3) + (-6) \quad LS = 3(3) + (-6)$
$= 15 = RS \qquad = 3 = RS$
verified

b) $5m + 3n = 10$
$5m - 2n = -15$

$5n = 25 \quad n = 5$
$5m + 3(5) = 10$
$5m + 15 = 10 \quad 5m = -5$
$m = -1$

$m = -1, \ n = 5$
$5m + 3n = 10 \quad | \quad 5m - 2n = -15$
$LS = 5(-1) + 3(5) \quad LS = 5(-1) - 2(5)$
$= 10 = RS \qquad = -15 = RS$
verified

c) $-x - 10y = 6$
$-x + y = 0$

$-11y = 6 \quad y = -\frac{6}{11}$
$-x + (-\frac{6}{11}) = 0$
$-\frac{6}{11} = x \quad x = -\frac{6}{11}$

$x = -\frac{6}{11}, \ y = -\frac{6}{11}$
$-x - 10y = 6 \quad | \quad -x + y = 0$
$LS = -(-\frac{6}{11}) - 10(-\frac{6}{11}) \quad LS = -(-\frac{6}{11}) + (-\frac{6}{11})$
$= 6 = RS \qquad = 0 = RS$
verified

d) $4a - 3b = -18$
$-2a - 3b = -9$

$6a = -9 \quad a = -\frac{3}{2}$
$4(-\frac{3}{2}) - 3b = -18$
$-6 - 3b = -18 \quad 12 = 3b \quad b = 4$
$a = -\frac{3}{2}, \ b = 4$

$4a - 3b = -18 \quad | \quad -2a - 3b = -9$
$LS = 4(-\frac{3}{2}) - 3(4) \quad LS = -2(-\frac{3}{2}) - 3(4)$
$= -18 = RS \qquad = -9 = RS$
verified

3. Solve and verify each of the following systems using the method of elimination.

a) $-10p + 10q = 3$
$10p + 5q = 6$

$15q = 9 \quad q = \frac{3}{5}$
$10p + 5(\frac{3}{5}) = 6 \quad 10p + 3 = 6$
$10p = 3 \quad p = \frac{3}{10}$
$p = \frac{3}{10}, \ q = \frac{3}{5}$

$-10p + 10q = 3 \quad | \quad 10p + 5q = 6$
$LS = -10(\frac{3}{10}) + 10(\frac{3}{5}) \quad LS = 10(\frac{3}{10}) + 5(\frac{3}{5})$
$= 3 = RS \qquad = 6 = RS$
verified

b) $x + 4y = -0.5$
$5x + 4y = 2.3$

$-4x = -2.8 \quad x = 0.7$
$0.7 + 4y = -0.5$
$4y = -1.2 \quad y = -0.3$
$x = 0.7, \ y = -0.3$

$x + 4y = -0.5 \quad | \quad 5x + 4y = 2.3$
$LS = 0.7 + 4(-0.3) \quad LS = 5(0.7) + 4(-0.3)$
$= -0.5 = RS \qquad = 2.3 = RS$
verified

c) $4x + 2y - 31 = 0$
$-4x + 6y - 13 = 0$

$8y - 44 = 0 \quad 8y = 44 \quad y = \frac{11}{2}$
$4x + 2(\frac{11}{2}) - 31 = 0 \quad 4x + 11 - 31 = 0$
$4x = 20 \quad x = 5$
$x = 5, \ y = \frac{11}{2}$

$4x + 2y - 31 = 0 \quad | \quad -4x + 6y - 13 = 0$
$LS = 4(5) + 2(\frac{11}{2}) - 31 \quad LS = -4(5) + 6(\frac{11}{2}) - 13$
$= 0 = RS \qquad = 0 = RS$
verified

4. Solve each of the following systems by elimination. Check each solution.

a) $2a + 5b = 16$
$a - b = 1 \quad (\times 2)$

$2a + 5b = 16$
$2a - 2b = 2$
Subtract $\quad 7b = 14 \quad b = 2$
$a - 2 = 1 \quad a = 3$
$a = 3, \ b = 2$

$2a + 5b = 16 \quad | \quad a - b = 1$
$LS = 2(3) + 5(2) \quad LS = 3 - 2$
$= 16 = RS \qquad = 1 = RS$
verified

b) $4x - 3y = 9$
$2x - 5y = 1 \quad (\times 2)$

$4x - 3y = 9$
$4x - 10y = 2$
Subtract $\quad 7y = 7 \quad y = 1$
$2x - 5(1) = 1 \quad 2x - 5 = 1$
$2x = 6 \quad x = 3$
$x = 3, \ y = 1$

$4x - 3y = 9 \quad | \quad 2x - 5y = 1$
$LS = 4(3) - 3(1) \quad LS = 2(3) - 5(1)$
$= 9 = RS \qquad = 1 = RS$
verified

c) $5x - 2y = 0.6$
$2x + y = 1.5 \quad (\times 2)$

$5x - 2y = 0.6$
$4x + 2y = 3$
add $\quad 9x = 3.6 \quad x = 0.4$
$2(0.4) + y = 1.5$
$0.8 + y = 1.5 \quad y = 0.7$
$x = 0.4, \ y = 0.7$

$5x - 2y = 0.6 \quad | \quad 2x + y = 1.5$
$LS = 5(0.4) - 2(0.7) \quad LS = 2(0.4) + 0.7$
$= 0.6 = RS \qquad = 1.5 = RS$
verified

---

5. Solve each of the following systems by elimination. Check each solution.

a) $2x + 4y = 7$, $4x - 3y = 3$
$\quad (\times 2)$

$4x + 8y = 14 \quad$ Subtract $\quad 11y = 11$
$4x - 3y = 3 \quad\quad\quad\quad y = 1$
$2x + 4(1) = 7 \quad 2x + 4 = 7$
$2x = 3 \quad x = \frac{3}{2}$
$x = \frac{3}{2}, \ y = 1$

$2x + 4y = 7 \quad | \quad 4x - 3y = 3$
$LS = 2(\frac{3}{2}) + 4(1) \quad LS = 4(\frac{3}{2}) - 3(1)$
$= 7 = RS \qquad = 3 = RS$

b) $5x = 8y$, $4x - 3y + 17 = 0$

$5x - 8y = 0 \quad (\times 4)$
$4x - 3y = -17 \quad (\times 5)$
$20x - 32y = 0$
$20x - 15y = -85$
Subtract $\quad -17y = 85 \quad y = -5$
$5x = 8(-5) \quad 5x = -40 \quad x = -8$
$x = -8, \ y = -5$

$5x = 8y \quad | \quad 4x - 3y + 17 = 0$
$LS = 5(-8) \quad LS = 4(-8) - 3(-5) + 17$
$RS = 8(-5) = -40 \quad = 0 = RS$
$= -40$

c) $7e + 4f - 1 = 0$, $5e + 3f + 1 = 0$

$7e + 4f = 1 \quad (\times 3)$
$5e + 3f = -1 \quad (\times 4)$
$21e + 12f = 3$
$20e + 12f = -4$
Subtract $\quad e = 7$
$7(7) + 4f = 1 \quad 49 + 4f = 1$
$4f = -48 \quad f = -12$
$e = 7, \ f = -12$

$7e + 4f - 1 = 0 \quad | \quad 5e + 3f + 1 = 0$
$LS = 7(7) + 4(-12) - 1 \quad LS = 5(7) + 3(-12) + 1$
$= 0 = RS \qquad = 0 = RS$

d) $3x + 2y - 6 = 0$, $9x = 5y + 18$

$3x + 2y = 6 \quad (\times 3)$
$9x - 5y = 18$
$9x + 6y = 18$
$9x - 5y = 18$
Subtract $\quad 11y = 0 \quad y = 0$
$3x + 2(0) = 6 \quad 3x = 6 \quad x = 2$
$x = 2, \ y = 0$

$3x + 2y - 6 = 0 \quad | \quad 9x = 5y + 18$
$LS = 3(2) + 2(0) - 6 \quad LS = 9(2) = 18$
$= 0 = RS \qquad RS = 5(0) + 18 = 18$
$\quad LS = RS$

6. Consider the system of equations $x - 2y + 1 = 0$, $2x + 3y = 12$. Solve the system by:

a) elimination
$x - 2y = -1 \quad (\times 2)$
$2x + 3y = 12$
$2x - 4y = -2$
$2x + 3y = 12$
Subtract $\quad -7y = -14 \quad y = 2$
$2x + 3(2) = 12$
$2x + 6 = 12 \quad 2x = 6 \quad x = 3$
$x = 3, \ y = 2$

b) substitution.
$x = 2y - 1$
$2(2y - 1) + 3y = 12$
$4y - 2 + 3y = 12$
$7y = 14 \quad y = 2$
$x = 2y - 1 = 2(2) - 1 = 3$
$x = 3, \ y = 2$

Which method do you prefer?

7. Consider the system of equations: $11x + 3y + 2 = 0$, $11x - 5y - 62 = 0$.

Solve the system by:
a) elimination   b) substitution.

$11x + 3y = -2$
$11x - 5y = 62$
Subtract: $8y = -64$ $y = -8$

$11x + 3(-8) = -2$
$11x - 24 = -2$
$11x = 22$ $x = 2$

$$x = 2,\ y = -8$$

b) substitution:

$3y = -11x - 2$ $y = -\frac{11}{3}x - \frac{2}{3}$
$11x - 5\left(-\frac{11}{3}x - \frac{2}{3}\right) - 62 = 0$
$11x + \frac{55}{3}x + \frac{10}{3} = 62$
$\frac{88}{3}x = \frac{176}{3}$
$x = 2$
$y = -\frac{11}{3}(2) - \frac{2}{3} = -8$

$$x = 2,\ y = -8$$

Which method do you prefer? personal choice

8. Solve each of the following systems by elimination. Explain the results.

a) $-2x + 6y - 1 = 0$, $5x - 15y + 2.5 = 0$

$-2x + 6y = 1$ (×5)
$5x - 15y = -2.5$ (×2)

$-10x + 30y = 5$
$10x - 30y = -5$
Add: $0 = 0$

$-2x + 6y = 1$
$6y = 2x + 1$ $y = \frac{1}{6}(2x+1)$

There are an infinite number
of solutions of the form
$x = a$ $y = \frac{1}{6}(2a+1)$.

The graphs of the equations are identical.

b) $2x - 4y = 7$, $-7x + 14y = -21$

$2x - 4y = 7$ (×7)
$-7x + 14y = -21$ (×2)

$14x - 28y = 49$
$-14x + 28y = -42$
Add: $0 = 7$

There are no solutions
Since the graphs of the equations
are parallel lines

---

9. Solve each of the following systems by elimination.

a) $3x - \frac{1}{2}y = 5$ (×2)
   $\frac{1}{3}x + \frac{1}{4}y = 3$ (×4)

$6x - y = 10$
$\frac{4}{3}x + y = 12$
Add $\frac{22}{3}x = 22$ $x = 3$

$\frac{22}{3}x = 22$ $x = 3$

$6(3) - y = 10$
$18 - y = 10$
$8 = y$ $y = 8$

$$x = 3,\ y = 8$$

check in original equations.

b) $\frac{m}{2} - \frac{n-4}{4} = 2$ (×8)
   $\frac{3m}{4} - \frac{n}{5} = 5$ (×20)

$8\left(\frac{m}{2}\right) - 8\left(\frac{n-4}{4}\right) = 8(2)$
$20\left(\frac{3m}{4}\right) - 20\left(\frac{n}{5}\right) = 20(5)$
$4m - 2(n-4) = 16$
$15m - 4n = 100$
$4m - 2n = 8$ (×-2)
$15m - 4n = 100$

$-8m + 4n = -16$
$15m - 4n = 100$
add $7m = 84$ $m = 12$
$4(12) - 2n = 8$
$48 - 2n = 8$
$40 = 2n$ $n = 20$

$$m = 12,\ n = 20$$

check in original equations

c) $\frac{1}{2}(2x - y) + \frac{3}{4}x = 6$ (×4)
   $\frac{1}{2}x - \frac{2}{3}y = 2$ (×6)

$2(2x-y) + 3x = 24$
$3x - 2y = 4$
$4x - 2y + 3x = 24$
$3x - 2y = 4$
$7x - 2y = 24$
$3x - 2y = 4$
Subtract $4x = 20$ $x = 5$
$3(5) - 2y = 4$
$15 - 2y = 4$
$11 = 2y$ $y = \frac{11}{2}$

$$x = 5,\ y = \frac{11}{2}$$

check in original
equations.

10. $2x + b = 8$ (×2)
$5x + 2b = 2$
$4x + 2b = 16$
$5x + 2b = 2$
Subtract $-x = 14$
$x = -14$

$\boxed{C.}$ $x = -14$

11. $x + y = 0$, $\frac{1}{2}x + \frac{2}{3}y = 1$ is (×6)
$x + y = 0$ (×2)

check in original equations

$2x + 2y = 0$
$3x + 2y = 6$
Subtract $-x = -6$ $x = 6$
$y = -6$

$\boxed{A.}$ $x = 6, y = -6$

12. $\frac{1}{3}x + 5 = \frac{2}{3}y$ (×3)
$\frac{1}{2}x + \frac{1}{3}y - \frac{1}{3}$ (×6)

$x + 15 = 2y$ $x = 2y - 15$
$3x + 2y = 2$
$3(2y-15) + 2y = 2$
$6y - 45 + 2y = 2$
$8y = 47$
$y = \frac{47}{8}$

$x = 2\left(\frac{47}{8}\right) - 15$
$x = \frac{47}{4} - 15$
$x = -\frac{13}{4}$

$y - \frac{1}{2}x = \frac{47}{8} - \frac{1}{2}\left(\frac{-13}{4}\right)$
$= \frac{47}{8} + \frac{13}{8} = \frac{60}{8}$
$= \frac{15}{2} = 7.5$

$\boxed{7 \cdot 15}$

Systems Of Linear Equations Lesson #5:
Applications of Systems of Linear Equations - Part One

Class Ex. #1

Let x be the larger number and y be the smaller number.

$x - y = 9$ 　　 $x = 2y + 3$

$2y + 3 - y = 9$ 　 $y = 6$

$2x + 2y = 40$ 　 $2x + 2(x-4) = 40$ 　 $x = 15$ 　 $y = 6$

The numbers are 15 and 6

check

$x - y = 9$	LS	RS
	$15-6$	9
	$= 9$	

$x = 2y+3$	LS	RS
	15	$2(6)+3$
		$= 15$

Class Ex. #2

[rectangle: y m by x m]

$2x + 2y = 40$ 　 $y = x - 4$

$2x + 2(x-4) = 40$

$2x + 2x - 8 = 40$

$4x = 48$ 　 $x = 12$

$y = x - 4 = 12 - 4 = 8$

$x = 12,\ y = 8$

check

$2x+2y=40$	LS	RS
$2(12)+2(8)$	40	
$=40$		

$y = x-4$	LS	RS
	8	$12-4$
		$= 8$

The length is 12 m.
The width is 8 m.

Class Ex. #3

Let x be the number of five-dollar bills and y be the number of ten-dollar bills.

$5x + 10y = 260$

$x + y = 33$ 　 (×5)

$5x + 10y = 260$

$5x + 5y = 165$

subtract: $5y = 95$

$y = 19$

$x + 19 = 33$

$x = 14$

$x = 14,\ y = 19$

check:

$5x+10y=260$	LS	RS
$5(14)+10(19)$	260	
$= 260$		

$x + y = 33$	LS	RS
$14+19$	33	
$=33$		

There are 14 five-dollar bills and 19 ten-dollar bills.

Class Ex. #4

Let x be invested in the first fund and y be invested in the second fund.

$x + y = 48000$

$0.105x + 0.12y = 5520$ 　 × 100

$12x + 12y = 576000$

$10.5x + 12y = 552000$

subtract $1.5x = 24000$

$x = 16000$

$16000 + y = 48000$

$y = 32000$

$x = 16000,\ y = 32000$

$16000 is invested in the first fund
and $32000 is invested in the second fund.

check: $x + y = 48000$

$16000 + 32000$

$= 48000 = RS$

check: $0.105x + 0.12y = 5520$

LS: $0.105(16000) + 0.12(32000) = 5520 = RS$

Assignment

1. [rectangle: y cm by x cm]

$2x + 2y = 64$ 　 $2(y+14)+2y=64$ 　 $x = y+14$

$x = y+14$ 　 $2y+28+2y=64$ 　 $x = 23,\ y = 9$

　　　　 $4y=36,\ y=9$

check:

$2x+2y=64$	LS	RS
$2(23)+2(9)$	64	
$= 64$		

$x = y+14$	LS	RS
	23	$9+14$
		$= 23$

The length is 23 cm and the width is 9 cm

2. Let the larger number be x and the smaller number be y.

$x + y = 3$ 　 $y = 3-x$

$2x = 3y + 36$

$2x = 3(3-x) + 36$

$2x = 9 - 3x + 36$

$5x = 45$

$x = 9$

$y = 3 - 9 = -6$

The numbers are 9 and −6

check:

$x+y=3$	LS	RS
$9+(-6)$	3	
$= 3$		

$2x=3y+36$	LS	RS
$2(9)$	$3(-6)+36$	
$=18$	$=18$	

3. Let x be the cost of a pencil and y be the cost of a pen.

$5x + 4y = 6.15$ 　 (×2)

$3x + 8y = 9.85$

$10x + 8y = 12.30$

$3x + 8y = 9.85$

subtract: $7x = 2.45$

$x = 0.35$

$5(0.35) + 4y = 6.15$

$1.75 + 4y = 6.15$

$4y = 4.40$ 　 $y = 1.10$

pencil costs 35 cents

pen costs $1.10

check.

$5x+4y=6.15$ 　 　 $3x+8y=9.85$

LS $= 5(0.35)+4(1.10)$ 　 LS: $3(0.35)+8(1.10)$

$= 6.15 = RS$ 　 　 $= 9.85 = RS$

$8(0.35) + 7(1.10) = 10.50$

Eight pencils and seven pens costs $10.50.

4. The perimeter of a rectangle is 40 cm. If the length were doubled and the width halved, the perimeter would be increased by 16 cm. Find the dimensions of the original rectangle.

[rectangle: y cm by x cm]

$2x + 2y = 40$

$2(2x) + 2\left(\frac{1}{2}y\right) = 40+16$

$x = 12,\ y = 8$

$2x + 2y = 40$

$2x + 2(56-4x) = 40$

$2x + 112 - 8x = 40$

$-6x = -72,\ x = 12$

$y = 56 - 4x$

$y = 56 - 4(12) = 8$

check:

$2x+2y=40$	LS	RS
$2(12)+2(8)$	40	
$=40$		

$4x+y=56$	LS	RS
$4(12)+8$	56	
$= 56$		

The length is 12 cm and the width is 8 cm.

9.

Let x = amount invested in the Balanced Fund
and y = amount invested in the Emerging Markets Fund

$\frac{3}{4}(56000) = 42000$

$x + y = 42000$ $y = 42000 - x$ $x = 30000$ $y = 12000$
$0.065x - 0.03y = 1590$
$0.065x - 0.03(42000 - x) = 1590$
$0.065x - 1260 + 0.03x = 1590$
$0.095x = 2850$ $x = 30000$
$y = 42000 - 30000 = 12000$

check: $x + y = 42000$

LS	RS
$30000 + 12000$	42000
$= 42000$	

LS	RS
$0.065(30000)$	1590
$-0.03(12000)$	
$= 1590$	

$\$30000$ in Balanced Fund

$\$12000$ in Emerging Markets Fund

10.

Let x = amount at 9% and y = amount at 6%.

$x + y = 7000$ $y = 7000 - x$ $x = 4000$, $y = 3000$
$0.06y = \frac{1}{2}(0.09x)$
$0.06(7000 - x) = \frac{1}{2}(0.09x)$
$0.06(7000 - x) = 0.045x$
$420 - 0.06x = 0.045x$
$420 = 0.105x$ $x = 4000$
$y = 7000 - x = 7000 - 4000 = 3000$

check: $x + y = 7000$

LS	RS
$4000 + 3000$	7000
$= 7000$	

LS	RS
$0.06(3000)$	$\frac{1}{2}(0.09(4000))$
$= 180$	180

Shoji invested $4000 at 9% and $3000 at 6%.

11.

a) Without a calculator determine the next two terms in the sequence.

1.1, 1.4, 1.9, 2.6, ...

$2.6 + 0.9 = 3.5$ $3.5 + 1.1 = 4.6$

Centre

$+0.3$ $+0.5$ $+0.7$ $+0.9$ $+1.1$

1.1 1.4 1.9 2.6

$n=1$ $n=2$

b) The height, h metres, of the nth rod is given by the formula $h = a + bn^2$. Using the terms of the sequence given to form a system of equations, determine the values of a and b and state the formula.

$1.1 = a + b(1)^2$
$1.4 = a + b(2)^2$
$a + b = 1.1$
$a + 4b = 1.4$
subtract: $-3b = -0.3$ $b = 0.1$
$a + 0.1 = 1.1$ $a = 1$

$h = 1 + 0.1n^2$

c) Use this formula to verify the answers in a)

$n = 5$ $h = 1 + 0.1(5)^2 = 3.5$
$n = 6$ $h = 1 + 0.1(6)^2 = 4.6$

5.

Let x = # hours old machine was in operation.
and y = # hours new machine was in operation.

$x + y = 15$, $y = 15 - x$
$30x + 40y = 545$
$30x + 40(15 - x) = 545$
$30x + 600 - 40x = 545$
$-10x = -55$
$x = 5.5$
$y = 15 - x = 15 - 5.5 = 9.5$

check: $x + y = 15$

LS	RS
$5.5 + 9.5$	15
$= 15$	

LS	RS
$30(5.5) + 40(9.5)$	545
$= 545$	

The old machine operated for $5\frac{1}{2}$ hours and the new machine operated for $9\frac{1}{2}$ hours

6.

Let x be the cost of a rink level seat and y be the cost of an upper level seat

$x = 3y$
$5x = 8y + 112$
$5(3y) = 8y + 112$
$15y - 8y = 112$
$7y = 112$ $y = 16$
$x = 3(16) = 48$

check: $x = 3y$

LS	RS
48	$3(16)$
	$= 48$

$5x = 8y + 112$

LS	RS
$5(48)$	$8(16) + 112$
$= 240$	$= 240$

A seat at rink level costs $48

7.

Let x = # quarters and y = # dimes.

$x + y = 103$ $y = 103 - x$
$0.25x + 0.1y = 21.4$
$25x + 10y = 2140$
$25x + 10(103 - x) = 2140$
$25x + 1030 - 10x = 2140$
$15x = 1110$, $x = 74$
$y = 103 - x = 103 - 74 = 29$

$x = 74$, $y = 29$

check: $x + y = 103$

LS	RS
$74 + 29$	103
$= 103$	

$0.25x + 0.1y = 21.4$

LS	RS
$0.25(74) + 0.1(29)$	21.4
$= 21.4$	

She saved 74 quarters and 29 dimes.

8.

Let x = income in year 1 and y = expenditure in year 1.

$x - y = 5000$ $x = y + 5000$ $x = 40000$ $y = 35000$
$1.1x - 0.84y = 14600$
$1.1(y + 5000) - 0.84y = 14600$
$1.1y + 5500 - 0.84y = 14600$
$0.26y = 9100$ $y = 35000$
$x = 35000 + 5000 = 40000$

check: $x - y = 5000$

LS	RS
$40000 - 35000$	5000
$= 5000$	

$1.1x - 0.84y = 14600$

LS	RS
$1.1(40000) - 0.84(35000)$	14600
$= 14600$	

$40000 + 10\% = 44000$

Income in year 2 = $44000

12.

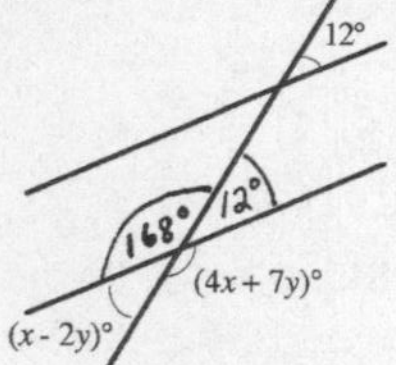

$x - 2y = 12 \quad (\times 4) \qquad 4x - 8y = 48$

$4x + 7y = 168 \qquad 4x + 7y = 168$

subtract: $-15y = -120$

$y = 8$

$x - 2(8) = 12$

$x - 16 = 12 \qquad x = 28$

$x + y = 28 + 8 = 36$

3	6	

13. Let x = units digit and y = tens digit

$y\,x$ = original number

$x + y = 11$

$x\,y$ = new number

original number $= 10y + x$

new number $= 10x + y$

$10x + y = 10y + x + 27$

$9x - 9y = 27 \qquad 9x - 9y = 27$

$x + y = 11 \quad (\times 9) \qquad 9x + 9y = 99$

Add. $18x = 126 \qquad x = 7 \qquad y = 4$

4	7	

Systems of Linear Equations Lesson #6:
Applications of Systems of Linear Equations - Part Two

Class Ex. #1

Let x = # kg of cashew nuts and y = # kg of Brazil nuts.

$x + y = 50 \qquad y = 50 - x$

$22x + 16y = 18(50)$

$22x + 16(50 - x) = 900$

$22x + 800 - 16x = 900$

$6x = 100 \qquad x = \frac{50}{3} = 16\frac{2}{3}$

$y = 50 - x = 50 - 16\frac{2}{3} = 33\frac{1}{3}$

check: $x + y = 50$

LS	RS
$16\frac{2}{3} + 33\frac{1}{3} = 50$	50

$22x + 16y = 900$

LS	RS
$22(16\frac{2}{3}) + 16(33\frac{1}{3}) = 900$	900

The mixture had $16\frac{2}{3}$ kg of Cashew nuts and $33\frac{1}{3}$ kg of Brazil nuts.

Class Ex. #2

Let x = # mL of 45% HCl and y = # mL of 70% HCl.

$x + y = 180 \qquad y = 180 - x$

$0.45x + 0.70y = 0.60(180)$

$0.45x + 0.7(180 - x) = 108$

$0.45x + 126 - 0.7x = 108$

$-0.25x = -18$

$x = 72$

$y = 180 - 72 = 108$

check: $x + y = 180$

LS	RS
$72 + 108 = 180$	180

$0.45x + 0.7y = 108$

LS	RS
$0.45(72) + 0.7(108) = 108$	108

72 mL of 45% HCl solution and 108 mL of 70% HCl solution are mixed.

Class Ex. #3

driving time $= 16\frac{1}{2} - 1 - \frac{1}{2} = 15$ hours

	Distance (km)	Speed (km/h)	Time (h)
Highway	$100x$	100	x
Mountainous Roads	$75y$	75	y

$x = 4.8 \qquad y = 10.2$

$x + y = 15 \qquad y = 15 - x$

$100x + 75y = 1245$

$100x + 75(15 - x) = 1245$

$100x + 1125 - 75x = 1245$

$25x = 120 \qquad x = 4.8$

$y = 15 - 4.8 = 10.2$

check: $x + y = 15$

LS	RS
$4.8 + 10.2 = 15$	15

$100x + 75y = 1245$

LS	RS
$100(4.8) + 75(10.2) = 1245$	1245

She spent 4.8 hours on the divided highways

Class Ex. #4

Let x km/h be the speed of the boat in still water and y km/h be the speed of the current.

	Distance (km)	Speed (km/h)	Time (h)
Downstream	$3(x+y)$	$x + y$	3
Upstream	$4(x-y)$	$x - y$	4

$3(x+y) = 36 \qquad 3x + 3y = 36 \quad (\times 4)$

$4(x-y) = 36 \qquad 4x - 4y = 36 \quad (\times 3)$

$12x + 12y = 144$

$12x - 12y = 108$

Add: $24x = 252 \qquad x = 10.5$

$3x + 3y = 36$

$3(10.5) + 3y = 36 \qquad 31.5 + 3y = 36$

$3y = 4.5 \qquad y = 1.5$

$x = 10.5, \; y = 1.5$

check: $3(x+y) = 36$

LS	RS
$3(10.5 + 1.5) = 36$	36

$4(x-y) = 36$

LS	RS
$4(10.5 - 1.5) = 36$	36

Still water speed = 10.5 km/h

Current speed = 1.5 km/h

Assignment

1. Let x = # kg at \$6 per kg and y = # kg at \$4.50 per kg.

$x + y = 112 \qquad y = 112 - x$

$6x + 4.5y = 612$

$6x + 4.5(112 - x) = 612$

$6x + 504 - 4.5x = 612$

$1.5x = 108$

$x = 72$

$y = 112 - 72$

$y = 40$

$x = 72, \; y = 40$

check: $x + y = 112$

LS	RS
$72 + 40 = 112$	112

$6x + 4.5y = 612$

LS	RS
$6(72) + 4.5(40)$	612

72 kg of \$6 per kg candy and 40 kg of \$4.50 per kg candy.

2. Let x = percentage of raisins in Type A and y = percentage of raisins in Type B.

$300x + 500y = 8800$

$x = 2y$

$300(2y)+500y = 8800$
$600y+500y = 8800$
$1100y = 8800$
$y = 8$
$x = 2(8) = 16$

check: $300x+500y = 8800$
$300(16)+500(8)$
$= 8800$

	LS	RS
$300x+500y$	$300(16)+500(8)$	8800
	$= 8800$	
$x = 2y$	16	$2(8) = 16$

Type A has 16% raisins and Type B has 8% raisins.

3. a) How many ml of each solution are mixed to make the 61% sulfuric acid solution?

Let x = #ml of 40% sulfuric acid and y = #ml of 75% sulfuric acid.

$x+y = 800 \qquad y = 800-x$
$0.4x+0.75y = 0.61(800)$
$0.4x+0.75y = 480$
$0.4x+0.75(800-x) = 488$
$0.4x+600-0.75x = 488$
$-0.35x = -112$
$x = 320$
$y = 800-320 = 480$

check: $x+y = 800$
$x = 320, y = 480$

	LS	RS
$x+y$	$320+480$	800
	$= 800$	
$0.4x+0.75y$	$0.4(320)+0.75(480)$	488
	$= 488$	

320 ml of 40% sulfuric acid and 480ml of 75% sulfuric acid.

b) What is the maximum volume, rounded down to the nearest ml, of 61% sulfuric acid solution which the scientist could mix with the original bottles of sulfuric acid?

use 1 litre of 75% sulfuric acid

$\dfrac{x}{320} = \dfrac{1000}{480}$
$480x = 320000$
$x = 666.6...$

1000 ml of 75% sulfuric acid
666 ml of 40% sulfuric acid
maximum volume = 1666 ml

4. a) $\dfrac{21}{24} = 87.5\%$ gold

b) How many grams of 12 carat gold and of 21 carat gold are needed to produce the mixture?

Let x = #grams of 12 carat gold and y = #grams of 21 carat gold.

$x+y = 90 \qquad y = 90-x$
$0.5x+0.875y = 0.75(90)$
$0.5x+0.875y = 67.5$
$0.5x+0.875(90-x) = 67.5$
$0.5x+78.75-0.875x = 67.5$
$-0.375x = -11.25$
$x = 30$
$y = 90-x = 90-30 = 60$

check: $x+y = 90$
$x = 30, y = 60$

	LS	RS
$x+y$	$30+60$	90
	$= 90$	
$0.5x+0.875y$	$0.5(30)+0.875(60)$	67.5
	$= 67.5$	

30g of 12 carat gold and 60g of 21 carat gold.

---

5. A train travels 315 km in the same time that a car travels 265 km. If the train travels on average 20 km/h faster than the car, find the average speed of the car and the time taken to travel 265 km.

	Distance(km)	Speed(km/h)	Time(h)
Train	315	x	$\dfrac{315}{x}$
Car	265	y	$\dfrac{265}{y}$

$\dfrac{315}{x} = \dfrac{265}{y}$

$315y = 265x$

$x = y+20$
$315y = 265(y+20)$
$315y = 265y + 5300$
$50y = 5300 \quad y = 106$
$x = 106+20 = 126$

check: $\dfrac{315}{x} = \dfrac{265}{y}$

	LS	RS
	$\dfrac{315}{126} = 2.5$	$\dfrac{265}{106} = 2.5$
$x = y+20$	126	$106+20 = 126$

Average speed of car = 106 km/h
Time taken = $2\tfrac{1}{2}$ hours

6. A small plane flying into a wind takes 3h to travel the 780 km journey from Lethbridge to Fort McMurray and reaches Lethbridge in $2\tfrac{1}{2}$h. At the same time, a similar plane leaves Fort McMurray and reaches Fort McMurray... If the planes have the same cruising speed in windless conditions, determine the speed of the wind.

Let x km/h = plane speed and y km/h = wind speed.

	Distance(km)	Speed(km/h)	Time(h)
L→FM	$3(x-y)$	$x-y$	3
FM→L	$2.5(x+y)$	$x+y$	2.5

$3(x-y) = 780$
$2.5(x+y) = 780$

$3x-3y = 780 \quad (\div 5)$
$2.5x+2.5y = 780 \quad (\div 6)$

$15x-15y = 3900$
$15x+15y = 4680$
$30x = 8580$
$x = 286$
$3(286)-3y = 780$
$-3y = -78, \; y = 26$

check: $3x-3y = 780$

	LS	RS
	$3(286)-3(26)$	780
	$= 780$	
$2.5x+2.5y = 780$	$2.5(286)+2.5(26)$	780
	$= 780$	

Wind speed is 26 km/h.

7. A cyclist leaves home at 7:30 am to cycle to school 7 km away. He cycles at 10 km/h until he has a puncture; then he has to push his bicycle the rest of the way at 3 km/h. He arrives at school at 8:40 am. How far did he have to push his bicycle?

	Distance(km)	Speed(km/h)	Time(h)
Cycle	x	10	$\dfrac{x}{10}$
Push	y	3	$\dfrac{y}{3}$

7:30am → 8:40am = 1h 10min = $\dfrac{7}{6}$ h

$x+y = 7 \qquad y = 7-x$
$\dfrac{x}{10}+\dfrac{y}{3} = \dfrac{7}{6} \quad (\times 30)$
$3x+10y = 35$

$3x+10(7-x) = 35$
$3x+70-10x = 35$
$-7x = -35$
$x = 5$
$y = 7-5 = 2$

check: $x+y = 7$
$x = 5, \; y = 2$

	LS	RS
$x+y = 7$	$5+2$	7
	$= 7$	
$\dfrac{x}{10}+\dfrac{y}{3} = \dfrac{7}{6}$	$\dfrac{5}{10}+\dfrac{2}{3}$	$\dfrac{7}{6}$
	$= \dfrac{7}{6}$	

He had to push his bicycle 2 km.

4.
A. $b = 0.25$ and $c = -2$
B. (B) $b = 0.25$ and $c = 2$
C. $b = 0$ and $c = 0$
D. $b = 4$ and $c = -8$

$by = x - c$

$y = \frac{1}{b}x - \frac{c}{b}$

For an infinite number of solutions the equations must be identical.

$\frac{1}{b} = 4$ $\quad c = 8b$

$b = \frac{1}{4} = 0.25$ $\quad = 8(\frac{1}{4}) = 2$

5. (A.)

6.
A. $x - 2y = 3,$ $x + 5y = -11$
B. $3x - 3y = -9,$ $x - 4y = -6$
C. $2x - 10y = 6,$ $x + 5y = -3$
D. $x + y = -3,$ $-2x + 5y = -1$

replace $x = -2$ $y = -1$ in the left side of each equation to see which equation is satisfied by the point.

A. $(-2) - 2(-1) = 0$ ✗
B. $3(-2) - 3(-1) = -3$ ✗
C. $2(-2) - 10(-1) = 6$ $(-2) + 5(-1) = -7$ ✗
D. $(-2) + (-1) = -3$ $-2(-2) + 5(-1) = -1$ ✓   (D.)

7.
$\frac{3}{12}(\frac{x}{4}) - \frac{4}{12}(\frac{y}{3}) = 12(2)$

$3x - 4y = 24$

$3x = 4y + 24$

$x = \frac{1}{3}(4y + 24)$ (B.)

8.
$3a - 2b = 14$ $\quad 3a - 2b = 14$
$2a + b = 7 \times 2$ $\quad 4a + 2b = 14$
add $7a = 28$ (D.)

9.
$x + y = 12$
$x - y = 2$
add $2x = 14$
$x = 7$
$x + 2y$
$7 + 2(5) = 17$
$7 + y = 12$
$y = 5$ (B.)

10.
$3x - 6 + y = 7$
$3x + y = 13$

$\frac{4x - 3y + 3 = 16}{4x - 3y = 13}$

$3x + y = 13 \times 4$
$4x - 3y = 13 \times 3$

$3x + y = 13 \times 4$
$4x - 3y = 13 \times 3$

$12x + 4y = 52$
$12x - 9y = 39$
Subtract $\frac{}{13y = 13}$
$y = 1$ (C.) 1

11.
$\frac{4}{12}(\frac{2p}{3}) - \frac{3}{12}(\frac{3q}{4}) = 12(\frac{11}{2})$

$8p - 9q = 66$

$8p - 9q = 66$
$10p + 3q = 54 \times 3$

$8p - 9q = 66$
$30p + 9q = 162$
add $\frac{}{38p = 228}$
$p = \frac{228}{38} = 6$ (A.) 6

12.
$\frac{2x + y}{3} = 5$
$2x + y = 15$

$\frac{3x - y}{5} = 5$
$3x - y = 15$

$2x + y = 15$
$3x - y = 15$
add $5x = 20$
$x = 4$

$2x + y = 15$
$2(4) + y = 15$
$8 + y = 15$
$y = 7$ (B.) 7

8.
(A.) 25
B. $33\frac{1}{3}$
C. 50
D. 75

Let $x = \#$ kgs of first type and $y = \#$ kgs of second type.

$x + y = 100$ $\quad y = 100 - x$

$8x + 12y = 11(100)$

$8x + 12(100 - x) = 1100$

$8x + 1200 - 12x = 1100$

$-4x = -100$

$x = 25$ $\quad$ 25 kgs of first type.

9.
1 pm → 9 pm = 8h

driving time $= 8h - 1h - \frac{1}{2}h = 6\frac{1}{2}h$.

	Distance (km)	Speed (km/h)	Time (h)
First Part	$110x$	110	x
Second Part	$90y$	90	y

$110x + 90y = 675$

$x + y = 6.5 \times (90)$

$110x + 90y = 675$
$90x + 90y = 585$
Subtract: $20x = 90$ $x = 4.5$ $y = 2$

$4.5h = 4(60) + 30$ min
$= 270$ min

$\boxed{270}$

Systems of Linear Equations Lesson #7:
Practice Test

1.
$x - 3y = 8$ $\quad x - 3(-3) = 8$
$x + 4y = -13$ $\quad x + 9 = 8$
Subtract $\frac{-7y = 21}{-7 \quad -7}$ $x = -1$
$y = -3$ $(-1, -3)$ (C.) $(-1, -3)$

2.
$6x - 24 = 2y$
$y = 3x - 12$
parallel lines

$5y = 15x - 64$
$y = 3x - \frac{64}{5}$ (A.) zero

3. Consider the following two systems of equations.

a) $y = \frac{2}{3}x + 1,$ $\quad y = \frac{1}{2}x - 2$

b) $4x + 5y = 18,$ $\quad 2x + 3y = 1$

Solve the above systems of equations using a graphing calculator and determine which one of the following statements is true.

A. In system a), $x + y = 29.$ ✗
B. In system b), $x + y = 40.5.$ ✗
C. (C.) One of the values of x is 42.5 more than the other.
D. One of the values of y is 42.5 more than the other.

$y = -4x + 18$ $\quad 3y = -2x + 1$
$5y = -4x + 18$ $\quad 3y = -2x + 1$
$y = -\frac{4}{5}x + \frac{18}{5}$ $\quad y = -\frac{2}{3}x + \frac{1}{3}$

a) $x = -18, y = -11$ b) $x = 24.5$ $y = -16$

4. $x = -1$ $\\ y = 1$ $a(-1) + 1 = b$ $-a - b = -1$ $-\frac{3}{4} - b = -1$

$x = -5$ $\\ y = 4$ $a(-5) + 4 = b$ $-5a - b = -4$ $\frac{1}{4} = b$

subtract $4a = 3$ $b = \frac{1}{4}$

$a = \frac{3}{4}$ $ab = \left(\frac{3}{4}\right)\left(\frac{1}{4}\right) = \frac{3}{16}$

$= 0.1875$ $\boxed{0 \cdot 1 \,9}$

5. $x + y = 100$ $y = 100 - x$

$\frac{x}{12} + \frac{y}{28} = 5$ $84\left(\frac{x}{12}\right) + 84\left(\frac{y}{28}\right) = 84(5)$

$7x + 3y = 420$

$7x + 3(100 - x) = 420$

$7x + 300 - 3x = 420$

$4x = 120$

$x = 30$ $\boxed{3\,0}$

---

1. • What factor would determine which plan is most economical?

The expected number of hours of internet use per month.

• Let y = total cost per month in dollars and x = number of hours of use per month. Write a linear equation for each of the three plans.

Plan 1 : $y = 20 + 0.4x$ Plan 2 : $y = 15 + 0.8x$ Plan 3 : $y = 60$

• Use a graphical method to determine when plans 1 and 2 are equally economical to use. State the graphing window used.

12.5 hours. $x : [0, 50, 10]$ $y : [0, 50, 10]$

• Verify the solution in the bullet above algebraically.

$y = 20 + 0.4x$ $20 + 0.4x = 15 + 0.8x$

$20 - 15 = 0.8x - 0.4x$

$\frac{5}{0.4} = \frac{0.4x}{0.4}$

$x = 12.5$ **12.5 hours**

• For each of plans 1 and 2 determine the number of hours of use which could be obtained for $60.

Plan 1 : $60 = 20 + 0.4x$ Plan 2 : $60 = 15 + 0.8x$

$\frac{40}{0.4} = \frac{0.4x}{0.4}$ $\frac{45}{0.8} = \frac{0.8x}{0.8}$

$x = 100$ $x = 56.25$ or $56\frac{1}{4}$

100 hours $\underline{56\frac{1}{4}\ \text{hours}}$

• Devise a simple rule which would determine which plan is most economical depending on the expected number of hours of internet use per month.

Plan 2 for up to 12.5 h , Plan 1 for between 12.5 h and 100 h, Plan 3 for more than 100 h.

---

13. $\text{time} = \frac{\text{distance}}{\text{speed}}$

distance : $x + y = 100$

time : $\frac{x}{12} + \frac{y}{28} = 5$

B. $x + y = 100$, $\frac{x}{12} + \frac{y}{28} = 5$

14. $2a + 3b = 2 \quad 2\left(\frac{1}{2}\right) + 3b = 2$

$8a - 9b = 1 \quad \times 3 \quad 1 + 3b = 2$

$3b = 1$

$6a + 9b = 6$ $b = \frac{1}{3} \Rightarrow y = 3$

$8a - 9b = 1$

add $14a = 7$ $xy = (2)(3) = 6$

$a = \frac{7}{14} = \frac{1}{2}$

$a = \frac{1}{2} \Rightarrow x = 2$ **A.** 6

15. **A.** 3 km

B. 4 km

C. 5 km

D. 6 km

House → Library	D	S	T
walk	x	8	$x/8$
run	y	12	$y/12$

Library → House	D	S	T
walk	$x - y$	8	$\frac{x-y}{8}$
run	$2y$	12	$\frac{2y}{12}$

Let x = distance walked (in km)

y = distance run (in km)

$\frac{x}{8} + \frac{y}{12} = \frac{20}{60}$

$\frac{x-y}{8} + \frac{y}{6} = \frac{17\frac{1}{2}}{60}$

$120\left(\frac{x}{8}\right) + 120\left(\frac{y}{12}\right) = 120\left(\frac{20}{60}\right)$

$120\left[\frac{x-y}{8}\right] + 120\left(\frac{y}{6}\right) = 120\left(17\frac{1}{2}\right)\frac{1}{60}$

$15x + 10y = 40$

$15(x - y) + 20y = 35$

$15x - 15y + 20y = 35$

$15x + 5y = 35$

$3x + 2y = 8$

$3x + y = 7$

$3x + 2y = 8$

$3x + y = 7$

subtract

$y = 1$

$3x + 1 = 7$

$3x = 6$ $x = 2$

$x + y = 2 + 1 = 3$

1. $(3, 4)$ graph $y_1 = x + 4$ $y = 2.666...$ $x + 2b = 4$ $y = -\frac{1}{2}x + 4$

$3 + 4 = 7$ $y_2 = -\frac{1}{2}x + 2$ $2y = -x + 4$ $y = -\frac{1}{2}x + 2$

$\boxed{7}$ $\boxed{2 \cdot 6\,7}$

3. $m - 2n - 30 = 0$ $2m - n - 39 = 0$

$m - 2n = 30$ $2m - n = 39$

$m - 2n = 30 \quad \times 2$ $2m - 4n = 60$

$2m - n = 39$ $2m - n = 39$

subtract $-3n = 21$

$n = -7$

$m - 2n = 30$

$m - 2(-7) = 30$

$m + 14 = 30$

$m = 16$

$m - n = 16 - (-7)$

$= 23$ $\boxed{2\,3}$